I0123965

THE FIRST 100 DAYS

45TH PRESIDENT OF THE UNITED STATES OF AMERCIA DONALD TRUMP

PART 1

Chronicled *by*
D Francis
and
Daniel Francis

Copyright © D Francis, © Daniel Francis 2017.

The right of D Francis and Daniel Francis to be identified as the authors of this work has been asserted by them in accordance with the copyright, designs and patents act 1988. Without trying to limit the rights under copyright reserved above, no part of this publication may be reproduced, stored in or introduced into retrieval system, or transmitted, in any form or by any means (electronic, mechanical, photocopying, recording or otherwise), without the prior written permission, of the copyright owners.

ISBN-13:978-0992854836
ISBN-10:0992854830

DF Books Limited
www.13june2005.com

Front Cover Picture Credit: The White House
Source of contents and Credit: The White House and The US State Department website (to the extent that any copyright is retained by The White House and The US State Department, fair use is sought.)

To the extent that third party sources have been used, fair use is sought.

This book has been produced for educational purposes.

Purpose

The purpose of this book is to document the historic speeches of the 45th President of the United States of America, Donald Trump.

A selection of the Official Speeches and Remarks of President Trump, Vice President Pence and The First Lady are presented in two books.

Limited to the first one-hundred days of the Trump Presidency; from Inauguration Day on 20 January 2017 to 29 April 2017.

Chapters 1- 85 are housed in this book, and in the second book, Part 2 - chapters 86 -170.

Due to print restrictions the entire selection of speeches and remarks could not be housed in one single book.

Disclaimer:
The transcripts might not be verbatim.

Some of these speeches, remarks or information have been sourced directly from the White House or US Government websites; and thus represent their transcription of the speeches and remarks made, or represent the speeches as written for delivery or their understanding.

The transcriptions might not be perfect and are subject to human error.

Some key words and phrases have been highlighted.

English-American spelling, direct from White House press releases, errors included.

The version presented might not be the latest version or update, as posted on third party websites.

A few speeches and remarks are no longer visible on the White House website. No explanation has been provided as to why a particular post has been removed.

Other speeches and remarks have been transcribed direct from internet footage, such as YouTube etc.

The compilers are not professional transcribers. Some allowance should be given for transcription difficulties due to the audio quality of the video posts, presentation by the speaker, inaudibility of the speaker, venue, human error, and mishearing.

There is no intention to misrepresent a speaker, and any and all suggestions otherwise will be denied and defended.

President Donald J. Trump

Donald J. Trump is the 45th President of the United States. He believes the United States has incredible potential and will go on to exceed anything that it has achieved in the past. His campaign slogan was Make America Great Again, and that is exactly what he intends to do.

Donald J. Trump is the very definition of the American success story. Throughout his life he has continually set the standards of business and entrepreneurial excellence, especially with his interests in real estate, sports, and entertainment. Likewise, his entry into politics and public service resulted in the Presidential victory in, miraculously, his first ever run for office.

After graduating from the Wharton School of Finance, Mr. Trump followed in his father's footsteps as a real estate developer, and he entered the world of real estate development in New York. The Trump signature soon became synonymous with the most prestigious of addresses in Manhattan and subsequently throughout the world. An accomplished author, Mr. Trump has authored over fourteen bestsellers and his first book, *The Art of the Deal*, in addition to being the #1 book of the year, is considered a business classic.

Mr. Trump announced his candidacy on June 16, 2015, and after seventeen Republican contenders suspended their campaigns, he accepted the Republican nomination for President of the United States in July of 2016. Mr. Trump won the election on November 8 of 2016 in the largest electoral college landslide for a Republican in 28 years. He won over 2,600 counties nationwide, the most since President Reagan in 1984. Additionally, he won over 62 million votes in the popular vote, the highest all-time for a Republican nominee. He also won 306 electoral votes, the most for a Republican since George H.W. Bush in 1988. Millions of Americans rallied behind his message of rebuilding our country and disrupting the status quo—this was a truly national victory and a historic movement.

Donald J. Trump campaigned in places he knew Republicans have had difficulty winning—Flint, Michigan, charter schools in inner-city Cleveland, and Hispanic churches in Florida—because he wanted to bring his message of economic empowerment to all Americans. Millions of new Republicans trusted Mr. Trump with their vote because of his focus on delivering prosperity through better trade deals, and as a result there were healthy margins of victory in newly red areas. It is clear that President Trump's win is one that brought Americans of all backgrounds together, and he is ready to deliver results for the nation on day one and every day of his tenure.

President Trump has been married to his wife, Melania, for twelve years and they are parents to their son, Barron. Additionally, Mr. Trump has four adult children, Don Jr., Ivanka, Eric and Tiffany, and eight grandchildren.

Follow President Trump on Twitter at @POTUS.

Source Credit:
The White House

Vice President Mike Pence

Michael R. Pence is the 48th and current Vice President of the United States.

Michael R. Pence was born in Columbus, Indiana, on June 7, 1959, one of six children born to Edward and Nancy Pence. As a young boy he had a front row seat to the American Dream. After his grandfather immigrated to the United States when he was 17, his family settled in the Midwest. The future Vice President watched his Mom and Dad build everything that matters – a family, a business, and a good name. Sitting at the feet of his mother and his father, who started a successful convenience store business in their small Indiana town, he was raised to believe in the importance of hard work, faith, and family.

Vice President Pence set off for Hanover College, earning his bachelor's degree in history in 1981. While there, he renewed his Christian faith which remains the driving force in his life. He later attended Indiana University School of Law and met the love of his life, Second Lady Karen Pence.

After graduating, Vice President Pence practiced law, led the Indiana Policy Review Foundation, and began hosting The Mike Pence Show, a syndicated talk radio show and a weekly television public affairs program in Indiana. Along the way he became the proud father to three children, Michael, Charlotte, and Audrey.

Growing up in Indiana, surrounded by good, hardworking Hoosiers, Vice President Pence always knew that he needed to give back to the state and the country that had given him so much. In 2000, he launched a successful bid for his local congressional seat, entering the United States House of Representatives at the age of 40.

The people of East-Central Indiana elected Vice President Pence six times to represent them in Congress. On Capitol Hill he established himself as a champion of limited government, fiscal responsibility, economic development, educational opportunity, and the U.S. Constitution. His colleagues quickly recognized his leadership ability and unanimously elected him to serve as Chairman of the House Republican Study Committee and House Republican Conference Chairman. In this role, the Vice President helped make government smaller and more effective, reduce spending, and return power to state and local governments.

In 2013, Vice President Pence left the nation's capital when Hoosiers elected him the 50th Governor of Indiana. He brought the same limited government and low tax philosophy to the Indiana Statehouse. As Governor, he enacted the largest income tax cut in Indiana history, lowering individual income tax rates, the business personal property tax, and the corporate income tax in order to strengthen the State's competitive edge and attract new investment and good-paying jobs. Due to his relentless focus on jobs, the state's unemployment rate fell by half during his four years in office, and at the end of his term, more Hoosiers were working than at any point in the state's 200-year history.

As Governor of Indiana, Vice President Pence increased school funding, expanded school choice, and created the first state-funded Pre-K plan in Indiana history. He made career and technical education a priority in every high school. Under Vice President Pence's leadership, Indiana, known as "The Crossroads of America," invested more than $800 million in new money for roads and bridges across the state. Despite the record tax cuts and new investments in roads and schools, the state remained fiscally responsible, as the Vice President worked with members of the Indiana General Assembly to pass two honestly balanced budgets that left the state with strong reserves and AAA credit ratings that were the envy of the nation.

It was Indiana's success story, Vice President Pence's record of legislative and executive experience, and his strong family values that prompted President Donald Trump to select Mike Pence as his running mate in July 2016. The American people elected President Donald Trump and Vice President Pence on November 8, 2016. President Donald Trump and Vice President Pence entered office on January 20, 2017.

Vice President Mike Pence remains grateful for the grace of God, the love and support of his family, and the blessings of liberty that are every American's birthright. He looks forward to working with the American people as together they seek to Make America Great Again.

Follow the Office of the Vice President on Twitter at @VP.

Source Credit:
The White House

First Lady Melania Trump

First Lady of the United States Melania Trump is the wife of President Donald J. Trump, and was born on April 26, 1970 in Slovenia.

Melania Knavs began her modeling career at the age of sixteen. She would pursue a degree at the University of Ljubljana in Slovenia, but paused her studies to advance her modeling career in Milan and Paris before moving to New York in 1996.

As a model, Melania has appeared in high profile ad campaigns and worked with some of the top photographers in the fashion industry, including Patrick Demarchelier, Helmut Newton, Arthur Elgort, Ellen Von Unwerth, Peter Arnell, Antoine Verglas and Mario Testino. She has graced the covers of Vogue, Harper's Bazaar, British GQ, Ocean Drive, Avenue, In Style, and New York Magazine. Her major layouts include the Sports Illustrated Swimsuit Issue, Allure, Vogue, Self, Glamour, Vanity Fair, and Elle. In addition, Melania has appeared in numerous television commercials and television programs, including co-hosting The View with Barbara Walters.

With a penchant and passion for the arts, architecture, design, fashion and beauty, Melania has thrived on the cultural diversification of New York City.

This passion can only be surpassed by her dedication to helping others, and her generosity has been noted. She was Honorary Chairwoman for Martha Graham Dance Company in April 2005, is an active member of the Police Athletic League which honored her with Woman of The Year 2006, has been an Honorary Chairwoman for The

Boy's Club of New York for five consecutive years, and in 2005 The American Red Cross awarded her with Goodwill Ambassador which she has proudly served for four years. In April of 2008, she was asked by Love Our Children USA and NASDAQ to participate in the Fifth Annual National Love Our Children Day and the beginning of National Child Abuse Prevention month by ringing the closing bell at NASDAQ. In 2010, Melania was the Chairwoman for The American Heart Association which raised $1.7 Million for research. Melania's philanthropic interests represent her humanitarian side, and she remains an indefatigable and dedicated New Yorker.

Melania married Donald Trump in January 2005. In March of 2006 they welcomed their first child, Barron William Trump.

Melania is also a successful entrepreneur. In April 2010, Melania Trump launched her own jewelry collection.

In 2006, Melania Trump proudly became a citizen of the United States of America. She is only the second First Lady born outside of the United States. The first was Louisa Adams, wife to John Quincy Adams, the nation's sixth president.

Mrs. Trump cares deeply about issues impacting women and children, and she has focused her platform as First Lady on the problem of cyber bullying among our youth.

Source Credit:
The White house

TABLE OF CONTENTS

Chapter 1

The Inaugural Address
REMARKS OF PRESIDENT DONALD J. TRUMP
AS PREPARED FOR DELIVERY
INAUGURAL ADDRESS
FRIDAY, JANUARY 20, 2017
WASHINGTON, D.C.

20 January 2017

As Prepared for Delivery –

Chief Justice Roberts, President Carter, President Clinton, President Bush, President Obama, fellow Americans, and people of the world: Thank you.

We, the citizens of America, are now joined in a great national effort to rebuild our country and to restore its **promise** for all of our people.

Together, we will determine the course of America and the world for years to come.

We will face challenges. We will confront hardships. But we will get the job done.

Every four years, we gather on these steps to carry out the orderly and peaceful transfer of power, and we are grateful to President Obama and First Lady Michelle Obama for their gracious aid throughout this transition. They have been magnificent.

Today's ceremony, however, has very special meaning.

Because today we are not merely transferring power from one Administration to another, or from one party to another – but we are transferring power from Washington, D.C. and giving it back to you, the **American People**.

For too long, a small group in our nation's Capital has reaped the rewards of government while the people have borne the cost.

Washington flourished – but the people did not share in its wealth.

Politicians prospered – but the jobs left, and the factories closed.

The establishment protected itself, but not the citizens of our country.

Their victories have not been your victories; their triumphs have not been your triumphs; and while they celebrated in our nation's Capital, there was little to celebrate for struggling families all across our land.

That all changes – starting right here, and right now, because this moment is your moment: it belongs to you. It belongs to everyone gathered here today and everyone watching all across America.

This is your day. This is your celebration.

And this, the United States of America, is your country. What truly matters is not which party controls our government, but whether our government is controlled by the people.

January 20th 2017, will be remembered as the day the people became the rulers of this nation **Again**.

The forgotten men and women of our country will be forgotten no longer.

Everyone is listening to you now.

You came by the tens of millions to become part of a historic MOVEMENT the likes of which the world has never seen before.

At the center of this MOVEMENT is a crucial conviction: that a nation exists to serve its citizens.

Americans want great schools for their children, safe neighborhoods for their families, and good jobs for themselves.

These are the just and reasonable demands of a righteous public.

But for too many of our citizens, a different reality exists: Mothers and children trapped in poverty in our inner cities; rusted-out factories scattered like tombstones across the landscape of our nation; an education system, flush with cash, but which leaves our young and beautiful students deprived of knowledge; and the crime and gangs and drugs that have stolen too many lives and robbed our country of so much unrealized potential.

This American carnage stops right here and stops right now.

We are one nation – and their pain is our pain. Their

dreams are our **dreams**; and their success will be our success. We share one heart, one home, and one glorious destiny.

The oath of office I take today is an oath of allegiance to all Americans.

For many decades, we've enriched foreign industry at the expense of American industry.

Subsidized the armies of other countries while allowing for the very sad depletion of our military.

We've defended other nation's borders while refusing to defend our own.

And spent trillions of dollars overseas while America's infrastructure has fallen into disrepair and decay.

We've made other countries rich while the wealth, strength, and confidence of our country has disappeared over the horizon.

One by one, the factories shuttered and left our shores, with not even a thought about the millions upon millions of American workers left behind.

The wealth of our middle class has been ripped from their homes and then redistributed across the entire world. But that is the past. And now we are looking only to the future.

We assembled here today are issuing a new decree to be heard in every city, in every foreign capital, and in every hall of power.

From this day forward, **a new vision** will govern our land. From this moment on, it's going to be **America First**.

Every decision on trade, on taxes, on immigration, on foreign affairs, will be made to benefit American workers and American families.

We must protect our borders from the ravages of other countries making our products, stealing our companies, and destroying our jobs. Protection will lead to great prosperity and strength.

I will fight for you with every breath in my body – and I will never, ever let you down.

America will start winning **Again**, winning like never before. We will bring back our jobs. We will bring back our borders. We will bring back our wealth. And we will bring back our **dreams**.

We will build new roads, and highways, and bridges, and airports, and tunnels, and railways all across our wonderful nation.

We will get our people off of welfare and back to work – rebuilding our country with American hands and American labor.

We will follow two simple rules: **Buy American and Hire American**.

We will seek friendship and goodwill with the nations of the world – but we do so with the understanding that it is the right of all nations to put their own interests **First**.

We do not seek to impose our way of life on anyone, but rather to let it shine as an example for everyone to follow.

We will reinforce old alliances and form new ones – and unite the civilized world against Radical Islamic Terrorism, which we will eradicate completely from the face of the Earth.

At the bedrock of our politics will be a total allegiance to the United States of America, and through our loyalty to our country, we will rediscover our loyalty to each other. When you open your heart to patriotism, there is no room for prejudice.

The Bible tells us, "how good and pleasant it is when God's people live together in unity."

We must speak our minds openly, debate our disagreements honestly, but always pursue solidarity.

When America is united, America is totally unstoppable. There should be no fear – we are protected, and we will always be protected.

We will be protected by the great men and women of our military and law enforcement and, most importantly, we are protected by God.

Finally, **we must think BIG and dream even BIGGER**.

In America, we understand that a nation is only living as long as it is striving.

We will no longer accept politicians who are all talk and no action – constantly complaining but never doing anything about it.

The time for empty talk is over.

Now arrives the hour of action.

Do not let anyone tell you it cannot be done. No challenge can match the heart and fight and **Spirit** of America.

We will not fail. Our country will thrive and **Prosper Again**. We stand at the BIRTH OF A NEW MILLENNIUM, ready to unlock the mysteries of space, to free the Earth from the miseries of disease, and to harness the energies, industries and technologies of tomorrow.

A new national **pride** will stir our souls, lift our sights, and heal our divisions.

It is time to remember that old wisdom our soldiers will never forget: that whether we are black or brown or white, we all bleed the same red blood of patriots, we all enjoy the same glorious freedoms, and we all salute the same great American Flag.

And whether a child is born in the urban sprawl of Detroit or the windswept plains of Nebraska, they look up at the same night sky, they fill their heart with the same **dreams**, and they are infused with the breath of life by the same Almighty Creator.

So to All Americans, in every city near and far, small and large, from mountain to mountain, and from ocean to ocean, hear these words:

You will never be ignored **Again**.

Your voice, your hopes, and your **dreams**, will define our **American destiny**.

And your courage and goodness and love will

forever guide us along the way.

Together, We Will **Make America Strong Again**.

We Will **Make America Wealthy Again**.

We Will **Make America Proud Again**.

We Will **Make America Safe Again**.

And, Yes, Together, **We Will Make America Great Again**.

Thank you. God Bless You. And God Bless America.

[Photo: Screengrab.]

Chapter 2

20 January 2017

UNKNOWN ORATOR: Ladies and gentlemen, please direct your attention to the stage for the arrival of the President and the First Lady.

Ladies and gentlemen, it is our honor to present to you the 45th President of the United States, Donald Trump and the First Lady of the United States, Melania Trump.

PRESIDENT TRUMP: That is what I call great talent. Thank you very much. Great Talent.

Well we did it. (Applause.)

We began this journey and they said WE, WE and ME, we didn't have a chance but we knew we were going to win, and we won. And today we had a great day. People that were not so nice to me, were saying we did a really good job today. (Applause.)

They hated to do it, but they did it. And I respect that. I respect that.

But I have to say that crowd was unbelievable today. You know, I looked at the rain which just never came [*].

You know, we finished the speech, went inside and it poured.

Then we came outside. The helicopter scene was an incredible scene, an incredible scene, so beautiful. Like from a movie set, so beautiful.

And then, and then amazingly it rained. And then we went out -- It's like god was looking down on us. I will tell you.

I want to thank all of our supporters. My number one supporter Melania, what she puts up with oh. (Cheering.)

Thank you honey.

Now, we really did something that is so special. And this evening is so special. And this evening is so special. And this whole day and yesterday, so incredible. So many people made such a difference.

Vice President, Mike Pence. No more elect. (Cheering.)

Was incredible. And all of the people.

You are going to see things happening over the next few weeks, oh you're going to be so happy. You're gonna be.

Because you know there are very elegant people tonight, but they are very political people. We want to see great things happen for our country. We want to **Make America Great Again** and we will and we will.

So now it's a tremendous honor to have my first dance with Melania.

We be joined by our Vice President. We will be joined by some very wonderful, wonderful children as we go along.

They happen to be my children, not Mike's children.

And I just want to again; I want to thank everybody. We always felt we were going to do it. It's a MOVEMENT like they have never seen anywhere time anywhere in the world, this was a MOVEMENT. And now the work begins. Now the work begins. There's no games right. There's no games. Right. We are not playing games. The work begins. I want to thank everybody.

We love you.

We will be working for you. And we are going to be producing results.

Thank you everybody.

Have a great night. Thank you. Thank you.

UNKNOWN ORATOR: Now that President and the First Lady of the United States will take their first dance.

Ladies and gentlemen, the First Couple - Donald and Melania Trump.

[Music and singing – *I Did It My Way.*]

Donald Trump mouths *I Did It My Way.*

[Vice President Mike Pence and the Second Lady, Mrs Pence joined them half-way through the song, then within minutes Donald Trump's adult children, their spouses and partner joined them.]

[*NOTE: From the video footage, it was clear that it rained during the Oath.]

*"But I have to say that crowd was unbelievable today.
You know, I looked at the rain which just never came."*

[Photo: Screengrabs.]

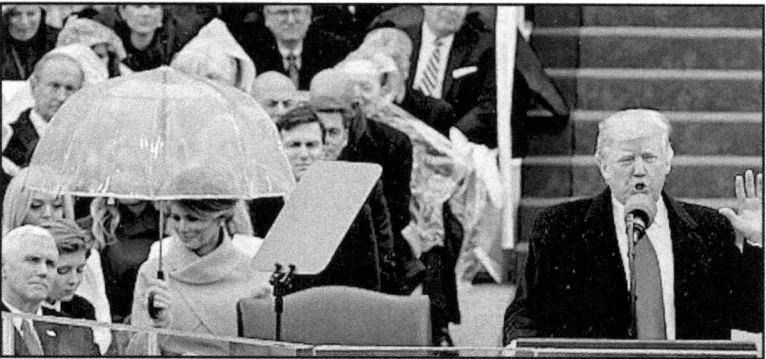

Chapter 3

REMARKS BY PRESIDENT TRUMP AT THE FREEDOM INAUGURAL BALL

WALTER E WASHINGTON CONVENTION CENTER

20 January 2017

UNKNOWN ORATOR: Ladies and gentlemen, it is our honor to present to you - The 45th President of the United States, Donald J Trump and The First Lady of the United States, Melania Trump.

[Short Musical Introduction and Applause.]

UNKNOWN ORATOR: Ladies and gentlemen, it is our honor to present to you - The 45th President of the United States, Donald J Trump and the First Lady of the United States, Melania Trump.

[Longer Musical Introduction and Applause.]

[Donald Trump and Melania Trump Enter.]

PRESIDENT TRUMP: Thank you. Thank you very much. Hello folks.

Our First Lady.

Well we just want to thank everybody.

This has been an amazing journey for all of us, not just ME

and not just Melania. It's been an amazing. It's been an amazing journey.

And now the work begins. We have to get it done and we will get it done. There is so much **Spirit** in our country. This is such a great country and we are going to do things. We will not be taking advantage of anymore, Okay.

We will not.

We are gong to have those companies come pouring back in. So seen what been happening over the last three-weeks. And we are going to have a lot of things happen and you are going to read about them and I don't know.

Let me ask you. Should I keep the twitter going or not? Keep it Going? I think so, I think so.

You know, the enemies keep saying oh it's terrible but you know it's a way of bypassing dishonest media, right?

You go wah, wah. [President Trump made a circular move-ment with his arm.]

So, but I just want to thank you.

We started out and we weren't given a great chance. But WE knew we were going to win.

It took two weeks before we went number one. Not a long time.

The first week was composed in terms of the phoney polls, was composed of two days. So were at number one and we stayed there the enter route during the primaries. And then boy did I work those last four-weeks. I worked.

That was some job, we did a good job together. And I will tell you what, many people in this room went to all the rallies with us. Right. They went to those rallies.

I saw one person on television tonight, incredible family, her and her husband.

She said, 'We've gone to forty-two Trump rallies'. I said, forty-two, forty-two. But we did, we had a lot of people who went to a lot of the rallies. And it showed up.

And, when we went in, I really felt, that last week in particular, I said how are we going to lose, how can we lose. It's too much.

There has never been a MOVEMENT like this, anywhere in the world, there has never been anything like this. So, I am so looking forward. I already just, I have just left actually, the Oval Office, because ... because.

Our great General 'Mad Dog' Mattis was approved, was approved tonight. The Senate approved he was first. And I went to sign. And Mike Pence who is coming out in a second signed, you saw what happened. Right, he just swore him in.

And General Kelly. The border, the border, oh that border we are going to have a border **Again**. And he was approved tonight by the Senate, so we are starting to work, and we are going to do a great job.

We are not going to let you down. Remember the theme. **Make America Great Again, AND Make America Great**

Again, I will tell you why, I have had it since I tried to get to know so many people in this country, GREATER THAN EVER BEFORE.

It will happen. So, I want to thank everybody for being with us. For sticking with us. It has been an amazing experience. And now the fun begins. It's okay, so now the fun begins.

We are going to do a really good job. And I will be fight every single ... of the day for you.

Thank you, thank you everybody, thank you and have a great time. Thank you.

[Cheering.]

UNKNOWN ORATOR: And now the President and First Lady of the United States will take their first dance.

Ladies and Gentlemen the First Couple, Donald and Melania Trump.

[Instrumental Introduction Music – *I Did It My Way.*]

[Donald Trump and Melania started dancing.]

[Vocals.]

[Vice President Pence and the Second Lady, Mrs Pence entered the stage, and started dancing.]

[Donald Trump's adult children, spouses and partner entered the stage and started dancing.]

[Audience cheered and shouted 'USA'.]

"Let me ask you.
Should I keep the twitter going or not?

Keep it Going?
I think so, I think so."

"You know,
the enemies keep saying oh it's terrible but
you know
it's a way of bypassing dishonest media,
right? "

[Photo: Screengrab.]

Chapter 4

20 January 2017

PRESIDENT TRUMP: Well, Thank you very much. What a great honor. These events are going on all over the city. We are having a lot of fun tonight. And I want to tell you, what a day it's been.

Our First Lady has been working, very, very hard. Very, very hard. (Cheering.)

But I just want to thank you on behalf of Melania and myself and the family and really millions and millions of people all over the world. The job you have done is absolutely incredible. (Cheering.)

Absolutely incredible. Because this our military, this is our law enforcement, this is our first responders. You are amazing people. You are amazing people. And I like you for a lot of reasons.

Also I like the fact that you all voted for me. You all voted for me.

I just, I just met your joint chiefs of staff and they are incredible.

And I'll tell you what, they know what to do and they know what to do and they know what to do fast.

And we are going to see what happens, but we have a great country and we want to do what's appropriate.

We have been pushed around by a lot of different people lots of bad things are happening, but I think you're going to see a big improvement, really. And I just want to tell you that General Mattis was just approved by the Senate. (Cheering.)

First one.

General Kelly was just approved by the Senate, and isn't it something?

Two generals were the first ones with all the people and all the politicians, the generals get approved first.

Maybe that's the way it's supposed to be. Maybe that's the way.

Now, we have some folks right now in Afghanistan right? And think they hear me.

There's about a six-second delay, but think they hear me. Do you guys hear me; I think maybe? Let's see how good we are doing.

Yes, they hear me. They hear me.

How is it over there? How is it going? Good. Go ahead.

What questions do you have? Don't be like these people.

Don't be too tough on me. Go ahead.

UNKNOWN FEMALE: Hi Sir, I'm … First Calvary Division, United States Army. On behalf of everybody here in Afghanistan, I would just like to say congratulations to your new position.

PRESIDENT TRUMP: That's very nice.

[AUDIENCE: We love you, we love you.]

PRESIDENT TRUMP: Thank you.

PRESIDENT TRUMP: Thank you very much. That's so nice. Thank you. Thank you. That's very nice. Thank you. We couldn't hear too clearly but I believe she just congratulated US… not me … US on this victory. And I want to thank you.

UNKNOWN MALE: On behalf of … Air Base, we would like to congratulate you on being elected as the new President of the United States.

PRESIDENT TRUMP: Thank you very much. So nice. Thank you.

By the way, I have to tell you, it's a ten-second delay but I like them much better than I like the media right?

These are much finer people, nicer people. That's great.

Thank you very much. Go ahead.

Thank you.

PHILIP CAMPBELL, SERGEANT FIRST CLASS, US ARMY:
My name is Sergeant, First Class Philip Campbell. I'm with
the Army, Illinois Army National Guard out of (inaudible).
Congratulations on becoming the President of the United
States Sir.

PRESIDENT TRUMP: Thank you so very, That's really, really
nice. Thank you. I will tell you I'm with you all the way. You
have somebody that's going to be right alongside of you.
We are going to do it together. We are going to do it together. And honestly, not only the support you have given
me, the courage that you show is incredible. And it's going
to be appreciated. It's appreciate now but it's going to be
appreciated more than ever before. You're going to see.
OK. Thank you very much.

Go ahead. Go ahead. Take one more.

I love these ten-second delays. It gives you plenty of time
to think about an answer. But go ahead.

MARINE CORPS GUNNERY, ROBERT GALA: Good Evening
Mr President. I am Sergeant Robert Gala, with the (inaudiable) liaison team, advising and assisting our coalition
partners here in Afghanistan. On behalf of all the Marines
here in Afghanistan we'd just like to say congratulations
and good luck to you on your term.

PRESIDENT TRUMP: Thank you very much. Really nice. And
we are going to have some people going over and seeing
you soon and you are doing an amazing job over there.
How about taking one more over there. One more. Go
ahead. I think he hears us right. Got it? Want to do one
more? So far I love these questions, so far, each one – 'I
want to congratulate you', these are the nicest questions.

Go ahead.

UNKNOWN MALE: (Inaudiable.) Yes Sir, I am in the United States Army, I am a 25 Sierra Satellite Communications Operator Maintainer, and I would like to congulate you on your Inauguration, Sir.

PRESIDENT TRUMP: You are the nicest people. (Cheering.)

But they are only nice right now to me. But they are probably, definitely not so nice in otherways.

I want to thank you; you are amazing people. We are with you one-thousand-percent, a-thousand-percent.

And you are doing just and incredible job. Thank you all very much and we will see you, and keep fighting, we are going to win, we are going to win. We are going to win. Keep fighting. Thank you, thank you all.

[Audience chanted "USA".]

PRESIDENT TRUMP: Why can't all people be like that.

Six questions* and six congratualations. This is very special.

So we have done two of these, and we had big crowds, ten thousand.

And I guess there are two more I am supposed to go to. At some point I am going to say, but first of all - I am going to say – speech today.

And actually event the media said that the crowd was massive. So finally that was it went all the way down to the

Washington Monument. There was supposed to be rain.

It was beautiful.

The theme was **MAKE AMERICA GREAT AGAIN**.

We had tremendous victories. I want to thank you all.

FIRST LADY: We will fight, we will win and we will **Make America Great Again**.

AUDIENCE: A good looking couple.

[Vocals – *I will Always Love You.*]

[The First Couple danced.]

[The Vice President Mike Pence and the Second Lady entered and started dancing.]

[Members of the forces entered and danced with the President, First Lady, Vice President and Second Lady. **]

[Donald Trump's children, their spouses and partner entered and started dancing.]

[Photo: Screengrab]

[*NOTE: Heard five questions / congratulatory comments from the service men and women.]

[**NOTE: Part of an article posted on the Department od Defense's website:

"As is tradition at the Inaugural Ball honoring the military, the new Commander in Chief and the First Lady each shared a dance with a military member, as did Vice President Michael R. Pence and his wife, Karen.

"The president danced with Navy Petty Officer 2nd Class Catherine Cartmell, a Newport, Rhode Island, native who is a religious program specialist in the Office of the Chief of Navy Chaplains. Mrs. Trump danced with Army Staff Sgt. Jose A. Medina from Ponce, Puerto Rico, a human resource specialist who is assigned to Headquarters and Headquarters Company, 4th Battalion, 3rd U.S. Infantry Regiment (The Old Guard) and served in Iraq and Afghanistan.

"The Vice President danced with Air Force Master Sgt. Tiffany Bradbury, who was born in Pusan, South Korea, and serves at Headquarters U.S. Air Force as recruiter superintendent of enlisted accessions policy. She served in Operation Southern Watch in Saudi Arabia. Mrs. Pence danced with Marine Corps Sgt. Angel Rodriguez from Camden, New Jersey, who is assigned to Marine Barracks Washington as a post supply warehouse chief and has served in Operation Enduring Freedom in Afghanistan."]

[US Department of Defense, website.]

Chapter 5

21 January 2017

3:21 P.M. EST

VICE PRESIDENT PENCE: Thank you to the Acting Director Meroe Park. Thank you for 27 years serving the United States of America here at CIA. (Applause.)

It's a great privilege for me to be with you today and to have the opportunity to introduce at his first event, on his first full day, the new President of the United States, Donald Trump. (Applause.)

As you can imagine, it's deeply humbling for my family and I to find ourselves in this role. I'm grateful to our new President for the opportunity he's given me and the opportunity the American people have given us to serve. But it's especially humbling for me to be before all of you today -- men and women of character, who have sacrificed greatly -- and to stand before this hallowed wall, this memorial wall, where we remember 117 who paid the ultimate sacrifice for our freedom.

I can assure you this new President and our entire team recognizes and appreciates the sacrifices of all of the men and women of the intelligence community of the United States of America. (Applause.)

I've gotten to know our new President. We traveled a lot together. When the cameras are off and the -- lights are off, I'll tell you two things I know for sure. Number one, I've never met anyone more dedicated to the safety and security of the people of the United States of America, or anyone who is a greater strategic thinker about how we accomplish that for this nation. In fact, to understand the life of our new President is -- his whole life was strategy. He built an extraordinary success in the private sector, and I know he's going to **Make America Safe Again**. (Applause.)

And lastly, I can honestly tell you, for all my years serving in the Congress, serving as governor of my home state, traveling cross-country and seeing the connection that he's made to men and women who serve and protect in every capacity in this country, I've never met anyone with a greater heart for those who every day, in diverse ways, protect the people of this nation through their character and their service and their sacrifice.

And so let me say, it is my high honor and distinct privilege to introduce all of you the President of the United States. (Applause.)

PRESIDENT TRUMP: Well, I want to thank everybody. Very, very special people. And it is true, this is my first stop, officially. We're not talking about the balls, or we're not talking about even the speeches -- although they did treat me nicely on that speech yesterday. (Laughter.)

I always call them the dishonest media, but they treated me nicely. (Laughter.)

But I want to say that there is nobody that feels stronger about the intelligence community and the CIA than Donald

Trump. There's nobody. (Applause.)

The wall behind me is very, very special. We've been touring for quite a while, and I'll tell you what -- 29? I can't believe it.

AUDIENCE MEMBER: Twenty-eight.

PRESIDENT TRUMP: Oh, 28. We got to reduce it. That's amazing. And we really appreciate what you've done in terms of showing us something very special. And your whole group, these are really special, amazing people. Very, very few people could do the job you people do.

And I want to just let you know, I am so behind you. And I know maybe sometimes you haven't gotten the backing that you've wanted, and you're going to get so much backing. Maybe you're going to say, please don't give us so much backing. (Laughter.)

Mr. President, please, we don't need that much backing. (Laughter.)

But you're going to have that. And I think everybody in this room knows it.

You know, the military and the law enforcement, generally speaking, but all of it -- but the military gave us tremendous percentages of votes. We were unbelievably successful in the election with getting the vote of the military. And probably almost everybody in this room voted for me, but I will not ask you to raise your hands if you did. (Laughter.)

But I would guarantee a big portion, because we're all on the same wavelength, folks. (Applause.)

We're all on the same wavelength, right? He knows. It took Brian about 30-seconds to figure that one out, right, because we know we're on the same wavelength.

But we're going to do great things. We're going to do great things. We've been fighting these wars for longer than any wars we've ever fought. We have not used the real abilities that we have. We've been restrained. We have to get rid of ISIS. Have to get rid of ISIS. We have no choice. (Applause.)

Radical Islamic terrorism. And I said it yesterday -- it has to be eradicated just off the face of the Earth. This is evil. This is evil. And you know, I can understand the other side. We can all understand the other side. There can be wars between countries, there can be wars. You can understand what happened. This is something nobody can even understand. This is a level of evil that we haven't seen. And you're going to go to it, and you're going to do a phenomenal job. But we're going to end it. It's time. It's time right now to end it.

You have somebody coming on who is extraordinary. For the different positions of "Secretary of This" and "Secretary of That" and all of these great positions, I'd see five, six, seven, eight people. And we had a great transition. We had an amazing team of talent. And, by the way, General Flynn is right over here. Put up your hand. What a good guy. (Applause.)

And Reince and my whole group. Reince -- you know -- they don't care about Reince. He's like this political guy that turned out to be a superstar, right? We don't have to talk about Reince.

But we did -- we had such a tremendous, tremendous success. So when I'm interviewing all of these candidates that Reince and his whole group is putting in front, it went very, very quickly, and, in this case, went so quickly -- because I would see six or seven or eight for Secretary of Agriculture, who we just named the other day, Sonny Perdue, former governor of Georgia. Fantastic guy. But I'd see six, seven, eight people for a certain position. Everybody wanted it. But I met Mike Pompeo, and it was the only guy I met. I didn't want to meet anybody else. I said, cancel everybody else. Cancel. Now, he was approved, essentially, but they're doing little political games with me. He was one of the three. Now, last night, as you know, General Mattis, fantastic guy, and General Kelly got approved. (Applause.)

And Mike Pompeo was supposed to be in that group. It was going to be the three of them. Can you imagine all of these guys? People respect -- you know; they respect that military sense. All my political people, they're not doing so well. The political people aren't doing so well but you. We're going to get them all through, but some will take a little bit longer than others.

But Mike was literally -- I had a group of -- what, we had nine different people? Now, I must say, I didn't mind cancelling eight appointments. That wasn't the worst thing in the world. But I met him and I said, he is so good. Number one in his class at West Point.

Now, I know a lot about West Point. I'm a person that very strongly believes in academics. In fact, every time I say I had an uncle who was a great professor at MIT for 35 years who did a fantastic job in so many different ways, academically -- was an academic genius -- and then they say, is Donald Trump an intellectual? Trust me, I'm like a smart persona. (Laughter.)

And I recognized immediately. So he was number one at West Point, and he was also essentially number one at Harvard Law School. And then he decided to go into the military. And he ran for Congress. And everything he's done has been a homerun. People like him, but much more importantly to me, everybody respects him. And when I told Paul Ryan that I wanted to do this, I would say he may be the only person that was not totally thrilled -- right, Mike? Because he said, I don't want to lose this guy. But you will be getting a total star. You're going to be getting a total gem. He's a gem. (Applause.)

You'll see. You'll see. And many of you know him anyway. But you're going to see. And again, we have some great people going in. But this one is something -- is going to be very special, because this is one, if I had to name the most important, this would certainly be perhaps -- you know, in certain ways, you could say my most important. You do the job like everybody in this room is capable of doing. And the generals are wonderful, and the fighting is wonderful. But if you give them the right direction, boy, does the fighting become easier. And, boy, do we lose so fewer lives, and win so quickly. And that's what we have to do. We have to start winning **Again**.

You know, when I was young and when I was -- of course, I feel young. I feel like I'm 30, 35, 39. (Laughter.)

Somebody said, are you young? I said, I think I'm young. You know, I was stopping -- when we were in the final month of that campaign, four stops, five stops, seven stops. Speeches, speeches, in front of 25,000, 30,000 people, 15,000, 19,000 from stop to stop. I feel young.

When I was young -- and I think we're all sort of young.

When I was young, we were always winning things in this country. We'd win with trade. We'd win with wars. At a certain age, I remember hearing from one of my instructors, 'The United States has never lost a war.'

And then, after that, it's like we haven't won anything.

We don't win anymore. The old expression, 'to the victor belong the spoils' -- you remember.

I always used to say, keep the oil. I wasn't a fan of Iraq. I didn't want to go into Iraq. But I will tell you, when we were in, we got out wrong.

And I always said, in addition to that, keep the oil. Now, I said it for economic reasons.

But if you think about it, Mike, if we kept the oil you probably wouldn't have ISIS because that's where they made their money in the first place. So we should have kept the oil.

But okay. (Laughter.)

Maybe you'll have another chance. But the fact is, should have kept the oil.

I believe that this group is going to be one of the most important groups in this country toward making us **safe**, toward making us winners **Again**, toward ending all of the problems. We have so many problems that are interrelated that we don't even think of, but interrelated to the kind of havoc and fear that this sick group of people has caused.

So I can only say that I am with you 1,000 percent.

And the reason you're my first stop is that, as you know, I have a running war with the media. They are among the most dishonest human beings on Earth. (Laughter and applause.)

And they sort of made it sound like I had a feud with the intelligence community. And I just want to let you know, the reason you're the number-one stop is exactly the opposite -- exactly. And they understand that, too.

And I was explaining about the numbers. We did a thing yesterday at the speech. Did everybody like the speech? (Applause.)

I've been given good reviews. But we had a massive field of people. You saw them. Packed. I get up this morning, I turn on one of the networks, and they show an empty field.

I say, wait a minute, I made a speech.

I looked out, the field was -- it looked like a million, million and a half people.

They showed a field where there were practically nobody standing there. And they said, Donald Trump did not draw well.

I said, it was almost raining, the rain should have scared them away, but God looked down and he said, we're not going to let it rain on your speech.

In fact, when I first started, I said, oh, no.

The first line, I got hit by a couple of drops. And I said, oh, this is too bad, but we'll go right through it. But the truth is that it stopped immediately. It was amazing. And then it became really sunny.

And then I walked off and it poured right after I left. It poured. But, you know, we have something that's amazing because we had -- it looked -- honestly, it looked like a million and a half people. Whatever it was, it was. But it went all the way back to the Washington Monument.

And I turn on -- and by mistake I get this network, and it showed an empty field. And it said we drew 250,000 people. Now, that's not bad, but it's a lie. We had 250,000 people literally around -- you know, in the little bowl that we constructed. That was 250,000 people. The rest of the 20-block area, all the way back to the Washington Monument, was packed.

So we caught them, and we caught them in a beauty. And I think they're going to pay a big price.

We had another one yesterday, which was interesting. In the Oval Office there's a beautiful statue of Dr. Martin Luther King [Jr.].

And I also happen to like Churchill, Winston Churchill. I think most of us like Churchill. He doesn't come from our country, but had a lot to do with it. Helped us; real ally.

And, as you know, the Churchill statue was taken out -- the bust. And as you also probably have read, the Prime Minister is coming over to our country very shortly. And they wanted to know whether or not I'd like it back. I say, absolutely, but in the meantime we have a bust of Churchill.

So a reporter for *Time* magazine -- and I have been on there [sic] cover, like, 14 or 15 times*. I think we have the all-time record in the history of *Time* magazine.

Like, if Tom Brady is on the cover, it's one time, because he won the Super Bowl or something, right? (Laughter.)

I've been on it for 15 times this year. I don't think that's a record, Mike, that can ever be broken. Do you agree with that? What do you think?

But I will say that they said -- it was very interesting -- that Donald Trump took down the bust, the statue, of Dr. Martin Luther King [Jr.]. And it was right there.

But there was a cameraman that was in front of it. (Laughter.)

So Zeke -- Zeke from Time magazine writes a story about I took down. I would never do that because I have great respect for Dr. Martin Luther King [Jr.]. But this is how dishonest the media is.

Now, the big story -- the retraction was, like, where?

Was it a line? Or do they even bother putting it in?

So I only like to say that because I love honesty.

I like honest reporting.

I will tell you, final time -- although I will say it, when you let in your thousands of other people that have been trying to come in -- because I am coming back -- we're going to have to get you a larger room. (Applause.)

34   Chapter 5

We may have to get you a larger room. You know?

And maybe, maybe, it will be built by somebody that knows how to build, and we won't have columns. (Laughter.)

You understand that? (Applause.)

We get rid of the columns.

No, I just wanted to really say that I love you, I respect you. There's nobody I respect more. You're going to do a fantastic job. And we're going to start winning **Again**, and you're going to be leading the charge.

So thank you all very much. (Applause.)

Thank you -- you're beautiful. Thank you all very much. Have a good time. I'll be back. I'll be back. Thank you.

END
3:40 P.M. EST

[*NOTE: An *abc2news* article, posted on their website, on 30 June 2017 at 9.44 reported that President Trump had been on the *Time* magazine cover, fourteen times.

However, President Trump didn't hold the *all-time* record. The article presented the following information:

> Nixon had forty-three covers
> Reagan had thirty-nine covers
> Clinton had thirty-five covers and
> Obama had twenty-three covers.]

Chapter 6

26 January 2017

SEN. JAMES LANKFORD (R-OKLAHOMA): Father you have called us all and you have given us a task and a responsibility. Pray, that you would make us equal to the task. That you will give us the wisdom that we need, that you would give us the patience and the grace and the joy, in the task that we need.

Father we join millions of Americans, in praying for the President and the Vice President, that you will give them the wisdom to make wise choices and to have confidence to know what to do, and the boldness to do it.

Pray, that you given them unique discernment in the task. Give them the ability to make right-choices, whether it be people and staff, whether it be direction and executive actions they take.

Father, I pray for their staff. There are thousands of people right now getting organized around this new presidency. Equip them, make them ready for the task.

Father, you have called us all, to speak for those who cannot speak for themselves. To stand up for justice and to speak out in the defense of the poor and the needy.

God, I pray that you will help us to do that in the days ahead.

Bless our President and our Vice President. Use this time, to prepare us and to draw us together as a nation.
In the name of Jesus, I pray. Amen. (Audience: Amen.)

UNKNOWN ORATOR: Please welcome, the Speaker of the House of Representatives – Paul Ryan (Applause and cheering.)

UNKNOWN ORATOR: Please welcome, the Vice President of the United States – Mike Pence. (Applause and cheering.)

UNKNOWN ORATOR: Please welcome, to introduce our special guest, the Majority Leader of the Senate, Mitch McConnell. (Applause and cheering.)

MITCH MCCONNELL (R-KY): Not many Americans know this, but at the beginning of our country, the Presidents were all part of the establishment. (Laughter.)

For forty-years from Washington down to John Quincy Adams and then Andrew Jackson came along. He was the voice of the people. And regular people sent this new President to the Oval Office, to the Whitehouse, and he made history by serving two terms and changing America.

My first visit to our new President at the Oral Office the other day, I looked up behind his desk and there was a sculpture of Andrew Johnson [*]. How appropriate.

Join me in welcoming the next President who is going to make history and turn America around – Donald Trump.

(Applause and cheering.)

PRESIDENT DONALD TRUMP: Thank you very much, Mitch. So nice, thank you. Thank you very much. Thank you.

Thank you.

So nice. Nice to WIN, do we agree?

It's been a while. Been a while since we had this position.

Nice to win. And I want to thank everybody in the room. So many friends. Thank you very much. Sit down everybody. Let's enjoy ourselves.

It's great to be in Philadelphia. I went to school in Philadelphia. This is a very special place in our nation's history. It's the place where we launched our American Independence. The State of Pennsylvania is very special to me for lots of reasons. Especially from a couple of months ago. Remember? (Applause.)

Pennsylvania cannot be WON. Remember?

Pennsylvania cannot be WON.

Right, Congressman?

There is NO path to victory for Trump in Pennsylvania.

Except we won. Now it has been a long time, since you guys did this, but uh, it was just a great victory. It was a great evening. It was a great evening; I will tell you. But it sort-of started in Pennsylvania.

They all said that Pennsylvania was the bride that got away. That it was the state that everybody from the Republican Party that ran in Pennsylvania for thirty-eight years thought they won, except they never won.

And I thought I won, too, but I was afraid to say it Mitch, because it just seemed that it wasn't working out. So I just said, 'You know what? I think we did great, let's see what happens.' But good things happened. So we love this state, and we will see it many times again.

Now is the DAWN OF A NEW ERA of American Independence. A rededication to the idea that the PEOPLE are in charge of their own destiny. I want to thank Majority Leader McConnell, great guy. And Speaker Paul Ryan, very very special. And he is writing his heart out. Right? And we're actually gonna sign the stuff that you're writing. You're not wasting your time. (Applause.)

He would write and he'd send it up, but nothin' would happen, but now it's gonna happen. For their leadership, and for inviting me here today, thank you very much.

And thank you, leader McCarthy, Senator Cornyn, Congressman Scalise, Congresswoman Cathy McMorris Rodgers, and Congressman Messer for your leadership as well. It's been terrific.

This Congress is going to be the busiest Congress we've had in decades, maybe ever. Maybe ever, think about that. And think of everything we can achieve, and remember who we must achieve it for. We're here now because tens of millions of Americans have placed their hopes in us, to transfer power from Washington DC and give it back to the people. (Applause.)

So important. Now we have to deliver. Enough all-talk, no-action. We have to deliver. This is our chance to achieve great and lasting change for our beloved nation. Since taking office, I have taken major contractual steps to restore the rule of law and return POWER to everyday Americans. (Applause.)

And even though it's only been a few days, we've done it in record numbers. We've issued executive orders to build the Keystone and Dakota Pipelines. (Applause.)

And issued a new requirement for American pipelines to be made with American steel, and fabricated in the United States. (Applause.)

And I was sitting at my desk, and I'm getting ready to sign Keystone and Dakota, I say 'Where's the pipe coming from?' And I won't tell you where, but you wouldn't be happy.

I say, 'Why is it we build pipelines, and we're not using pipes that are made in our country?' I say, 'Let's put that little clause in.' Like it's a one sentence clause. But that clause is gonna attract a lot of people. And we're gonna make that pipe right here in America, okay? (Applause.)

If people want to build pipelines on our land, we want the pipe to be manufactured, and not only that, manufactured here, but you will see a level of quality that you're not going to see when they bring pipe from far distances, have to bring it in small chunks and then fabricate it on the land. Give me a break. We can do much better than that. And we're going to do it much better, and it's going to end up costing less money, believe me.

We've reinstated the Mexico City policy. A long standing policy. (Applause.)

Isn't that nice. (Applause.)

And by the way, on Friday, lot of people are going to be showing up to Washington. Right, Mike? A lot of people. You know, the press never gives them the credit that they deserve. They'll have three hundred, four hundred, five hundred, six hundred thousand people. You won't even read about it.

When other people show up, you read big time about it. Right? So it's not fair, but nothing fair about the media. (Laughter.)

Nothing.

A long standing policy to insure taxpayer dollars do not fund abortion services overseas. (Applause.)

We've issued executive orders to remove wasteful regulations that slow down commerce and delay infrastructure which we desperately need. The very beginning of a massive effort to reduce the crushing regulations on our economy, and we are going to reduce regulations big time. (Applause.)

We've also withdrawn from the Trans Pacific Partnership, paving the way for new one-on-one trade deals that protect and defend the American worker and believe me, we're gonna have a lot of trade deals ... Mitch, don't worry about it. (Laughter.)

Just give me a little time. But they'll be one-on-one. They

won't be a whole big mash pot. They'll be one-on-one deals, and if that particular country doesn't treat us fairly we send 'em a thirty-day termination. Notice of termination. And then they'll come and say, 'No, please don't do that.' And we'll negotiate a better deal during that thirty-day period. The other way, you can't get out of it. It's like a quicksand. Plus, we're going to have very, very strong controls over monetary manipulation and devaluation, which they didn't have in TPP. So this is going to be so much better, and we're already on it.

I would like to have my Commerce Secretary Wilbur approved; because I hear he did fantastically well, but they're not quick with the pen on signing these people, because we'd like to have him approved as soon as possible. So, I know, and Mitch said it will be done, and it will be. They could move faster on the other side; I will say that. Could move faster. (Laughter and applause.)

I mean, I'm meeting with the Prime Minister tomorrow, as you know - Great Britain. So I'm meeting with her tomorrow, I don't have my Commerce Secretary, they want to talk trade. So I'll have to handle it myself. (Laughter.)

Which is okay.

We've put in place the first steps in our immigration plan, ordering the IMMEDIATE construction of the border wall. Putting an end to catch-and-release. Expediting the removal of criminal al[iens], this is so important to me. From day-one I've said it. And I mean the IMMEDIATE removal of criminal ALIENS, they're gonna be gone fast. (Applause.)

And finally, at long last, cracking down on Sanctuary Cities. (Applause.)

It's time to restore the civil rights of Americans. To protect their jobs, their hopes and their dreams for a MUCH better future.

Congress passed these laws to serve our citizens, and it's about time those laws were properly enforced. They're not enforced. (Applause.)

The hour of justice for the American worker has arrived. Border security is a serious, serious, national issue and problem.

A lack of security poses a substantial threat to the sovereignty and safety of the United States of America and its citizens. Most of illegal immigration is coming from our southern border. I've said many times that the American people will NOT pay for the wall, and I've made that clear to the government of Mexico.

NAFTA has been a terrible deal. A total disaster from its inception costing us as much as sixty-billion-dollars a year with Mexico alone in trade deficits. You say who, who negotiates these deals?

Not to mention millions of jobs, and thousands and thousands of factories and plants closing down all over our country. On top of that, are the trillions of dollars the US taxpayers have spent to pay the cost of illegal immigration. Much of it is then is sent back, and much of it goes back to other countries. And oftentimes, because they don't respect us, the other countries will not accept the criminals that we send back to them that are illegally in our country. I promise you they will start accepting them again, quickly. (Applause.)

We're not gonna have 'em any longer.

I will not allow the taxpayers or the citizens of the United States to pay the cost of this defective transaction, NAFTA. One that should have been renegotiated many years ago, except that the politicians were too preoccupied to do so. Now these people are not in that category, you understand that. This is a different group. I think, right?

To that end, the President of Mexico and myself have agreed to cancel our planned meeting scheduled for next week.

Unless Mexico is going to treat the United States fairly, with respect, such a meeting will be fruitless, and I want to go a different route. We have no choice.

Paul Ryan and other leaders in Congress and I, and Mike Pence who, by the way, how good a choice was Vice President Mike Pence? Stand up. (Applause.)

Everybody loves him. (Cheering.)

Fact, anytime I got myself into a jam early, you know I haven't been doing this stuff too long. But any time I got myself into a jam, oftentimes they'd say on television, 'Yeah. But look. He picked Mike Pence. So he's gotta have something going, right?' So Mike really helped me a lot. (Laughter.)

Well, we're working on a tax reform bill that will reduce our trade deficits, increase American exports, and will generate revenue from Mexico that will pay for the wall if we decide to go that route.

It is time that the American people had a President fighting as hard for its citizens as other countries do for theirs. And that is exactly what I am going to do for you, believe me. (Applause.)

Thank you. Thank you.

It's time that somebody fought for our country and didn't let anyone take advantage of us anymore. The world has taken advantage of us for many years. Not gonna happen anymore.

We will have an ambitious legislative agenda as well. Our legislative work starts with repealing and replacing Obamacare. (Applause.)

And saving families from the catastrophic rise in premiums and debilitating loss of choice and and just about everything else. And remember this for this room in particular. Obamacare is a disaster. The Democrats are up and they're saying, oh, and they're putting up signs like it's wonderful. It's a disaster.

I actually talked with Paul and the group about just doing nothing for two-years, and the Dems would come begging to do something. Because '17 is going to be catastrophic price increases. Your deductibles are through the roof; you can't use it. You can't use it. And they would come to us. Except we have one problem. We have to take care of the American people immediately. So we can't wait. (Applause.)

But every time they tell you about Obamacare, we're taking them out of a big jam. Big jam. We're putting ourselves at risk, to a certain extent, because we're taking it off their platter. But I think, Congressman, I think we have no choice. I think we have no choice. We have to get it going. If we, I'm serious, if we waited two-years, it's gonna explode like you've never seen an explosion. Nobody's going to be able to afford it. It's a disaster.

And that's politically what we should do, but we don't want to do that. We want to get something done, and get it done right. And by the way, Tom Price is gonna do a phenomenal job. I don't know if he's here, but he's gonna do a phenomenal job. (Applause.)

On my first day in office, I signed an Executive Order to roll back the burdens of Obamacare and pave the way for real reform. Like health savings accounts that empower individuals to choose the customized plan that is truly right for them, and have so many choices. Tom Price will soon be leading Health and Human Services. He is a true advocate for patients. He's going to do a phenomenal job; we have no doubt about that.

He joins an all-star roster that includes many of your colleagues. Ryan Zinke, Mick Mulvaney, these guys have had a pretty tough time in Congress, too, but they, uh, in the Senate, but actually came out very well. Mike Pompeo, is Mike here? Mike? Mike Pompeo, phenomenal guy, and Jeff Sessions. Jeff is a fine person. Jeff was one of my earliest endorsers.

Never endorsed a presidential candidate before and he was one of my earliest endorsers, respected by everybody. And did unbelievably in front of committee. Unbelievable. In addition to fixing our health care, we're going to pursue new trade deals that create higher wages and more opportunities for American workers, bringing back those magnificent words '**Made in the USA**.'

We used to have that. We don't have it anymore. (Applause.)

It's going to be **AMERICA FIRST AGAIN**. We will create millions of new, good-paying jobs by removing the economic burdens that cripple our ability to compete. At the canter of that agenda is bold tax reform that massively lowers taxes for our middle class and for all American businesses.

We will also pursue financial reform that will help striving Americans get the credit they need to realize their **dreams**. Republicans have always been the party of American industry and the American worker. We must embrace that heritage rebuilding this country with American goods and American labor. And we've started, believe me. Over the last couple of months, I don't know, I'd like to say I did about as much as anybody or more in terms of getting industry to start coming back to our before I took office. But we have a lot of great news with Ford, and General Motors, and Fiat Chrysler, and so many others. We have a lot of great news. Lockheed is adding a lot of different people, a lot of additional people. Boeing, we have a lot of positive things happening, and it's really gonna start bursting out. You're going to be seeing it very soon.

We want to get our people off of welfare and back to work. (Applause.)

So important. It's out of control. It's out of control.

And we believe that the world's best country ought to have the world's best infrastructure. It's what our people de-

serve, and it's what we will insure they get.
Our infrastructure's in serious trouble.

We will build new roads and highways and tunnels and airports and railways across the nation. We will fix our existing product before we build anything brand new, however.
We have to fix what we have. It's a mess. So we're gonna
fix it first. The thing I do best in life is build. We will fix it
first; cos we have a lot of things that are in bad shape.
And we will rebuild our military and take care of our great
veterans. (Applause.)

We're working hard with the veterans. Thank you.

We're going to do something very special with the veterans. It's time.

At the same time, we will unleash the full power of American energy, ending the job killing restrictions on shale, oil,
natural gas, and clean, beautiful coal. And we're going to
put our coal miners back to work. (Applause.)

Thank you.

And we will protect our farmers, our ranchers, our hunters,
our anglers, and all who enjoy the outdoors.

But to be a rich country, we must also be a **safe** country.
Right now too many families don't feel secure. Just look at
the thirty largest cities. In the last year alone, the murder
rate has increased by an estimated fourteen percent.
Here in Philadelphia, the murder rate has been steady. I
mean just terribly increasing.

And then you look at Chicago. WHAT'S GOING ON IN

CHICAGO? I said the other day, 'What the hell is going on?'

UNKNOWN AUDIENCE MEMBER: DEMOCRATS. (Laughter.)

PRESIDENT TRUMP: Lot of truth to it. (Laughter.)

That is why we will continue to stand with the incredible men and women of law enforcement. (Applause.)

Yesterday, I had the honor of swearing in General John Kelly as our Secretary of Homeland Security. He's gonna be amazing. (Applause.)

Tomorrow, I will swear in General James Mattis as our new Secretary of Defense. (Applause.)

These men have devoted their lives to defending America, and now I look forward to working with THEM, along with our great new head of the C.S.A., you know we have, we have so many different people that we are putting in office. I think it's the group of all-stars like nobody has seen before, right?

Where is, where is Pompeo? Where the hell is he? Did he ever come here? Oh, he's working? He is, he is so ... he is going to be another one of the big stars. I have to mention him every single time. One of YOU. (Applause.)

And with you in Congress to keep our country safe from the many threats we face today. That includes protecting Americans from radical Islamic terrorism. (Applause.)

We also need to keep the ballot box **safe** from illegal voting.

And believe me, you take a look at what's registering, folks. They like to say, "Oh, Trump, Trump Trump." Take a look at what's registering.

We are going to protect the integrity of the ballot box, and we are going to defend the votes of the American citizens, so important. All of us here today, for the same reason, to serve the citizens of our country.

We are not here for ourselves, we are here for them. We are here for the PEOPLE. We are blessed by divinity, and honored by history with the task of preserving this great republic, and expanding its blessings to every single American. (Applause.)

Thank you. Thank you.

All of us are joined in this effort. All of us are bound by duty, and bound by God to give our full devotion to this country and its people.

That obligation forms the moral foundation of our agenda. That agenda includes a lean, efficient government, appointing Supreme Court Justices, so important. (Applause.)

Who will uphold and defend our constitution.

Reducing taxation and regulation. Fair trade that creates a level playing field, as opposed to what we have right now. And fostering respect for our country and its flag.

We are now only at the beginning of this incredible journey together.

I am honored to be your partner in this amazing quest.

I am privileged to stand with you, shoulder to shoulder, as we work every single day to **MAKE AMERICA GREAT AGAIN**.

Thank you. God bless you, and God bless America.

It's a great honor to be here. Thank you very much.

Thank you.

[*NOTE: Mitch McConnell probably meant to say Andrew Jackson but said Andrew Johnson. Andrew Jackson was the seventh President of the United States, following: George Washington (1), John Adams (2), Thomas Jefferson (3), James Madison (4), James Monroe (5) and John Quincy Adams (6). George Washington took office on 30 April 1789 and Andrew Jackson took office forty-years later in 1829. Andrew Johnson was the seventeenth President of the United States and took office seventy-six years from the date Washington was sworn in. Johnson took office in 1865. Andrew Jackson's portrait hangs in the Oval Office, above the sculpture of The Bronco Buster, circa January 2017.]

"Now is the dawn
of a new era of
American Independence."

Chapter 7

MARCH FOR LIFE REMARKS OF VICE PRESIDENT PENCE
AS PREPARED FOR DELIVERY
MARCH FOR LIFE
FRIDAY, JANUARY 27, 2017
WASHINGTON, D.C.

27 January 2017

As Prepared for Delivery –

On behalf of President Donald Trump, my wife Karen, and our daughter Charlotte, I'd like to welcome you all to Washington, D.C. for the 44th annual *March for Life*.

And I am deeply humbled to be the first Vice President of the United States to ever have the privilege to attend this historic gathering.

More than two-hundred and forty years ago, our Founders wrote words that have echoed through the ages.

They declared "these truths to be self-evident." That we are, all of us, "endowed by our Creator with certain unalienable rights," and "that among these are LIFE, LIBERTY, and the PURSUIT of HAPPINESS."

Forty-four years ago, our Supreme Court turned away from the first of these timeless ideals.

But today, three generations hence, because of all of you, and the many more who stand with us in marches just like this across this nation, life is winning in America **Again**.

That is evident in the election of pro-life majorities in the Congress of the United States.

But it is no more evident than in the historic election of a president who stands for a stronger America, a more prosperous America, and a president who I proudly say stands for the right to life – President Donald Trump.

President Trump actually asked me to be here today to thank all of you for your support and for your stand for life and for your compassion for the women and children of this nation.

One week ago today, on the steps of the Capitol, we saw the inauguration of the 45th President of the United States. Our President is a man with broad shoulders and a big heart. His vision, his energy, and his optimism are boundless, and I know he will **Make America Great Again**.

From his first day in office, he has been keeping his promises to the American people.

And at 1600 Pennsylvania Avenue, we're in the promise-keeping business.

That's why, on Monday President Trump reinstated the Mexico City policy to prevent foreign aid from funding organizations that promote or perform abortions.

That's why this administration will work with Congress to end taxpayer funding for abortion and abortion providers, and we will devote those resources to health-care services for women across America.

And that's why, next week, President Donald Trump will

announce a Supreme Court nominee who will uphold the God-given liberties enshrined in our Constitution in the tradition of the late and great Justice Antonin Scalia.

Life is winning in America. And today is a celebration of the progress that we have made in the cause.

You know, I have long believed that a society can be judged by how we care for our most vulnerable – the aged, the infirm, the disabled, and the unborn.

We've come to a historic moment in the cause of life, and we must meet this moment with respect and compassion for every American.

Life is winning in America for many reasons.

Life is winning through the steady advance of science that illuminates when life begins.

Life is winning through the generosity of millions of adoptive families, who open their hearts and homes to children in need.

Life is winning through the compassion of caregivers and volunteers at crisis pregnancy centres and faith-based organizations who minister to women, in cities and towns across this country.

And life is winning through the quiet counsels between mothers and daughters, grandmothers and granddaughters, between friends across kitchen tables, and over coffee on college campuses the truth is being told and compassion is overcoming convenience, hope is defeating despair.

In a word, life is winning in America because of all of you. So I urge you to press on.

But as it is written, "let your gentleness be evident to all." Let this movement be known for love, not anger – for compassion, not confrontation. When it comes to matters of the heart, there's nothing stronger than gentleness.

I believe we will continue to win the hearts and the minds of the rising generation if our hearts first break for young mothers and their unborn children and we do all we can to meet them where they are, with generosity, not judgment.

To heal our land and restore a culture of life we must continue to be a movement that embraces all and cares for all out of respect for the dignity and worth of every person. Enshrined on the walls of the Jefferson Memorial are the words of our third president, who admonished us to remember that "God who gave us life gave us liberty."

On behalf of the President of the United States, and my little family, we thank you for your stand for life, for your compassion, for your love for the women and children of this nation.

Be assured, we will not grow weary. We will not rest until we restore a culture of life for ourselves and our posterity. God Bless you, and God Bless the United States of America.

"...I have long believed that a society can be judged by how we care for our most vulnerable..."

Chapter 8

27 January 2017

PRESIDENT DONALD J. TRUMP: Thank you very much. I am honored to have Prime Minister Theresa May here for our first official visit from a foreign leader. This is our first visit, so -- great honor.

The special relationship between our two countries has been one of the great forces in history for justice and for peace. And, by the way, my mother was born in Scotland -- Stornoway -- which is serious Scotland.

Today, the United States renews our deep bond with Britain -- military, financial, cultural, and political. We have one of the great bonds. We pledge our lasting support to this most special relationship. Together, America and the United Kingdom are a beacon for prosperity and the rule of law. That is why the United States respects the sovereignty of the British people and their right of self-determination. A free and independent Britain is a blessing to the world, and our relationship has never been stronger.

Both America and Britain understand that governments must be responsive to everyday working people, that governments must represent their own citizens.

Madam Prime Minister, we look forward to working closely with you as we strengthen our mutual ties in commerce, business and foreign affairs. Great days lie ahead for our two peoples and our two countries.

On behalf of our nation, I thank you for joining us here today. It's a really great honor. Thank you very much.

PRIME MINISTER THERESA MAY: Well, thank you very much, Mr. President. And can I start by saying that I'm so pleased that I've been able to be here today. And thank you for inviting me so soon after your inauguration. And I'm delighted to be able to congratulate you on what was a stunning election victory.

And, as you say, the invitation is an indication of the strength and importance of the special relationship that exists between our two countries -- a relationship based on the bonds of history, of family, kinship and common interest. And in a further sign of the importance of that relationship, I have today been able to convey Her Majesty The Queen's hope that President Trump and the First Lady would pay a state visit to the United Kingdom later this year. And I'm delighted that the President has accepted that invitation.

Now, today, we're discussing a number of topics, and there's much on which we agree. The President has mentioned foreign policy. We're discussing how we can work even more closely together in order to take on and defeat Daesh and the ideology of Islamist extremism wherever it's found.

Our two nations are already leading efforts to face up to this challenge, and we're making progress with Daesh losing territory and fighters, but we need to redouble our efforts. And today, we are discussing how we can do this by deepening intelligence and security cooperation and, critically, by stepping up our efforts to counter Daesh in cyberspace. Because we know we will not eradicate this threat until we defeat the idea -- the ideology that lies behind it.

Our talks will be continuing later. I'm sure we'll discuss other topics -- Syria and Russia.

On defense and security cooperation, we are united in our recognition of NATO as the bulwark of our collective defense. And today, we've reaffirmed our unshakeable commitment to this alliance.

Mr. President, I think you said -- you confirmed that you're 100 percent behind NATO. But we're also discussing the importance of NATO continuing to ensure it is as equipped to fight terrorism and cyber warfare as it is to fight more conventional forms of war.

And I've agreed to continue my efforts to encourage my fellow European leaders to deliver on their commitments to spend 2 percent of their GDP on defense so that the burden is more fairly shared. It's only by investing properly in our defense that we can ensure we're properly equipped to face our shared challenges together.

And finally, the President and I have mentioned future economic cooperation and trade. Trade between our two countries is already worth over $150 billion pounds a year. The U.S. is the single-biggest source of inward investment to the UK, and together we've around $1 trillion invested in each other's economies.

And the UK-U.S. defense relationship is the broadest, deepest, and most advanced of any two countries sharing military hardware and expertise. And I think the President and I are ambitious to build on this relationship in order to grow our respective economies, provide the high-skilled, high-paid jobs of the future for working people across America and across the UK.

And so we are discussing how we can establish a trade negotiation agreement, take forward immediate, high-level talks, lay the groundwork for a UK-U.S. trade agreement, and identify the practical steps we can take now in order to enable companies in both countries to trade and do business with one another more easily.

And I'm convinced that a trade deal between the U.S. and the UK is in the national interest of both countries and will cement the crucial relationship that exists between us, particularly as the UK leaves the European Union and reaches out to the world.

Today's talks I think are a significant moment for President Trump and I to build our relationship. And I look forward to continuing to work with you as we deliver on the promises of freedom and prosperity for all the people of our respective countries.

Chapter 9

PRESIDENT TRUMP'S FIRST WEEKLY ADDRESS
THE PRESIDENT'S WEEKLY ADDRESS AIRED
SATURDAY, JANUARY 28, 2017 ON
FACEBOOK LIVE AT 12:45 PM EST.
VISIT: HTTPS://WWW.FACEBOOK.COM/POTUS

28 January 2017

Transcript:

My fellow Americans,
One week ago, our administration assumed the enormous responsibilities that you, the American People, have placed in us.

There is much work to do in the days ahead, but I wanted to give you an update on what we have accomplished already.

In my first few days as your President, I've met with the leaders of some of our nation's top manufacturing companies and labor unions.

My message was clear: we want to make things in America, and we want to use American workers.

Since my election, many companies have announced they are no longer moving jobs out of our country but are instead keeping and creating jobs right here in America.

Every day, we are fulfilling the promise we made to the American People. Here are just a few of the executive actions that I have taken in the last few days –

-- An order to prepare for repealing and replacing Obamacare, it's about time.

-- The withdrawal from the Trans-Pacific Partnership so that we can negotiate one-on-one deals that protect American workers. That would have been a disastrous deal for our workers.

-- An order to begin construction of the Keystone and Dakota Access pipelines, following a renegotiation of terms, with a requirement that pipelines installed in America be built with American steel and manufactured here.

-- A directive to expedite permits for new infrastructure and new manufacturing plants.

-- An order to immediately begin the border wall and to crack down on sanctuary cities. They are not safe; we have to take care of that horrible situation.

This administration has hit the ground running at a record pace, everybody is talking about it.

We are doing it with speed and we are doing it with intelligence and we will never, ever stop fighting on behalf of the American People.

God bless you, and God Bless America.

Chapter 10

31 January 2017

As Delivered –

Well, good afternoon, everyone. Thank you for being here.
On behalf of the President of the United States, it is my
great privilege to welcome America's new Secretary of the
Department of Transportation, Elaine Chao. (Applause.)

It's also an honor to be joined today by her husband, Senate Majority Leader Mitch McConnell, as well as her father,
Dr. James Chao, and by such an impressive and successful
family. We're honored that so many of you could be with
us today to share this moment with this family and with
this country.

Elaine, this day is a familiar one for you. You've already
served your country in many capacities, most notably as
Secretary of Labor for eight years under President George
W. Bush. And your tenure at the department was widely
lauded and continues to be celebrated as among the most
significant in the history of that department.

Prior to that you were actually Deputy Secretary of the
Department of Transportation and Chairman of the Federal
Maritime Commission.

And you bring a wealth of experience now to leading this department in the Trump administration.

Your significant experience in the private sector, ranging from business to non-profits; your history of service and your accomplishments are lengthy.

And I know the President is grateful for your willingness to step forward and bring your extraordinary talents to bear serving the country once again.

President Trump and I are appreciative that once again you have answered the call to serve America and advance the interests of the people of this country.

Your leadership and your experience will serve well as the Secretary of Transportation, overseeing what we anticipate will be historic investments in our nation's roads, bridges, airports, and above all, in our future.

The President and I are confident that you will do more than your share as our new Secretary of the Department of Transportation to **Make America Great Again**.

And we thank you. (Applause.)

(The Oath is administered.) (Applause.)

Chapter 11

01 February 2017

THE PRESIDENT: Hello, everybody. These are a lot of my friends, but you have been so helpful. And we did well. The election, it came out really well. Next time we'll triple it up or quadruple it, right? We want to get over 51, right? At least 51.

Well, this is Black History Month, so this is our little breakfast, our little get-together. Hi, Lynne, how are you?

MS. PATTON: Hi, how are you?

THE PRESIDENT: Nice to see you. And just a few notes. During this month, we honor the tremendous history of the African Americans throughout our country -- throughout the world, if you really think about it, right? And their story is one of unimaginable sacrifice, hard work and faith in America.

I've gotten a real glimpse -- during the campaign, I'd go around with Ben to a lot of different places that I wasn't so familiar with. They're incredible people. And I want to thank Ben Carson, who's going to be heading up HUD. It's a big job, and it's a job that's not only housing, it's mind and spirit, right, Ben? And you understand that. Nobody is going to be better than Ben.

Last month, we celebrated the life of the Reverend Martin Luther King, Jr., whose incredible example is unique in American history. You read all about Dr. Martin Luther King [Jr.] a week ago when somebody said I took the statue out of my office, and it turned out that that was fake news. (Laughter.)

It was fake news. The statue is cherished. It's one of the favorite things in the -- and we have some good ones. We have Lincoln and we have Jefferson and we have Dr. Martin Luther King [Jr.], and we have -- but they said the statue, the bust of Dr. Martin Luther King [Jr.] was taken out of the office. And it was never even touched.

So I think it was a disgrace, but that's the way the press is. Very unfortunate.

I am very proud now that we have a museum on the National Mall where people can learn about Reverend King [Jr.], so many other things.

Frederick Douglass is an example of somebody who's done an amazing job and is being recognized more and more, I notice -- Harriet Tubman, Rosa Parks, and millions more black Americans who made America what it is today. Big impact.

I am proud to honor this heritage, and we'll be honoring it more and more. The folks at the table in almost all cases have been great friends and supporters. And Darrell -- I met Darrell when he was defending me on television. (Laughter.)

And the people that were on the other side of the argument didn't have a chance, right? And Paris has done an amazing job in a very hostile CNN community. (Laughter.)

He's all by himself -- seven people and Paris. So I'll take Paris over the seven. (Laughter.)

But I don't watch CNN so I don't get to see you as much as I want to. (Laughter.)

I don't like watching fake news.

PARTICIPANT: None of us watch it either anymore.

THE PRESIDENT: But Fox has treated me very nice -- wherever Fox is, thank you.

We're going to need better schools, and we need them soon. We need more jobs; we need better wages -- a lot better wages. We're going to work very hard on the inner city. Ben is going to be doing that big league. It's one of his big things that we're going to be looking at.

We need safer communities, and we're going to do that with law enforcement. We're going to make it **safe**. We're going to make it much better than it is right now. Right now it's terrible, and I saw you talking about it the other night, Paris, on something else that was really -- you did a fantastic job the other night on a very unrelated show. I'm ready to do my part -- it's the only time I can see him. I'm ready to do my part, and I will say this: We're going to work together.

This is a great group. This is a group that's been so special to me. You really helped me a lot. If you remember, I wasn't going to do well with the African American community, and after they heard me speaking and talking about the inner city and lots of other things, we ended up getting -- I won't go into details, but we ended up getting substantially more than other candidates who had run in the past years. And now, we're going to take that to new levels. I want to thank my television star over here. (Laughter.)

Omarosa is actually a very nice person. Nobody knows that, but -- (laughter) -- I don't want to destroy her reputation. She is a very good person and she's been helpful right from the beginning of the campaign. And I appreciate it. I really do. Very special.

And so I want to thank everybody for being here. Could we maybe just go around the room and we'll introduce ourselves. And the press can stay for that, and I'm sure they have no questions about last night because it was such a good launch. We have a fantastic, hopefully, new justice of the Supreme Court. And hopefully, that will be -- he'll be approved very, very quickly. He's outstanding in every way -- academically. He's done almost as well as you did, Darrell, in college. (Laughter.)

Not quite, right? But he's a great man and I think he'll be a great, great justice. And he's being very well-received. It was a big evening. Very big evening.

So, Paris, why don't we start with you? Go ahead.

MR. DENNARD: Pleasure to be here, Mr. President. Honor to be here. Paris Dennard. Thurgood Marshall College Fund represents the 47 publically supported historically black colleges and universities, which I know you are very much in support of. So it's a pleasure to be here, sir.

THE PRESIDENT: Well, I'm glad you're in support of me

because I'd be all -- I'd be in the wilderness without you guys. You are so effective. I appreciate it.

MR. DENNARD: Thank you.

THE PRESIDENT: Thank you.

MR. CLEVELAND: Bill Cleveland. I'm a retired Capitol police officer, former vice mayor of the city of Alexandria, and substitute teacher in the Alexandria school system. Glad to be here.

THE PRESIDENT: Thank you. Thank you.

MR. MATTHEWS: Bill is also a Vietnam veteran, sir.

THE PRESIDENT: Oh, good.

MR. MATTHEWS: I'm Earl Matthews, sir. I work for you at the Department of Defense. I was sworn in an hour after you were. Also a veteran and a long-time supporter of yours. I've worked for you since late summer. I'm happy to be here.

THE PRESIDENT: Lieutenant Colonel -- good job.

MS. SCOTT: I'm Belinda Scott, Darrell's wife. New Spirit Revival Center from Cleveland, Ohio. Pastor of New Spirit. Great amount of support in the African American community where we are. We love the Lord, we love our new President, and we are praying for our President on a regular basis.

THE PRESIDENT: You know, the one thing I didn't understand about Belinda -- I thought they were married maybe five or six years, because look how they look so young. (Laughter.)

Should you say how many years you've been married?

MS. SCOTT: Thirty-five.

PASTOR SCOTT: We've been together for 38.

MS. SCOTT: Been together for -- but in the Lord – (laughter) -- 35, yes.

PASTOR SCOTT: Two years under – (inaudible) (Laughter.)

THE PRESIDENT: That's actually amazing. I wouldn't have known.

MS. SCOTT: But can I say this -- I am so grateful that our President gives us that ear to listen to the community -- to listen. And people like us are just here to constantly put that message out into the community. And we love you for that. We love you for listening and we thank you for that.

THE PRESIDENT: Thank you. Thank you very much.

PASTOR SCOTT: Darrell Scott, pastor at New Spirit Revival Center and black Trump supporter. (Laughter and applause.)

But speaking of the community, let me just say this real-quick. Omarosa, I told you I'm going to try to throw it in. I was recently contacted by some of the top gang thugs initiative Chicago for a sit-down. They reached out to me because they associated me with you. They respect you, they believe in what you're doing, and they want to have a sit-down about lowering that body count. So in a couple of weeks, I'm going into Chicago.

THE PRESIDENT: That's a great idea because Chicago is totally out of control.

PASTOR SCOTT: Well, I let him know -- I said, we've got to lower that body count. We don't want to talk about anything else -- get that body count down. And they agreed. But the principle is they can do it. These are guys straight from the streets -- no politicians -- straight street guys. But they're going to commit that if they lower that body count, we'll come in and we'll do some social programs. So they're in agreement.

THE PRESIDENT: If they're not going to solve the problem -- and what you're doing is the right thing -- then we're going to solve the problem for them because we're going to have to do something about Chicago. Because what's happening in Chicago should not be happening in this country.

PASTOR SCOTT: But they want to work with this administration.

THE PRESIDENT: Good.

PASTOR SCOTT: They want to. They reached out -- I didn't reach out to them. They reached out to me.

THE PRESIDENT: I understand.

PASTOR SCOTT: They want to work with this administration. They believe in this administration. They didn't believe in the prior administration. They told me this out of their mouth. But they see hope with you.

PRESIDENT TRUMP: I love it.

MR. WILLIAMS: Mr. President, I'm a member of what we call the media, but we try to be fair and objective. (Laughter.)

Not all media seems to be the opposition party. There are those that see the good that you're doing. We report it. I'm just honored to have a seat at the table today.

THE PRESIDENT: Thank you. And it is -- I mean, a lot of the media is actually the opposition party. They're so biased and really is a disgrace. Some of you are fantastic and fair, but so much of the media is opposition party and knowingly saying incorrect things. So it's a very sad situation. But we seem to be doing well. It's almost like, in the meantime, we won. So maybe they don't have the influence they think, but they really are -- they really have to straighten out their act. They're very dishonest people. James.

PASTOR DAVIS: Pastor James Davis. We've been -- Mr. President, we've been a supporter of yours from the beginning alongside Mr. Michael Cohen and Dr. Darrell Scott with the National Diversity Coalition. It helped to bring out a huge number in the black community with respect to the vote. And we're still happy to be in support as we go forward.

THE PRESIDENT: Thank you. You've been great. Thank you, James.

And, Lynne.

MS. PATTON: Hi, Mr. President. Yes, I am, as you know,

the former vice president of the wonderful charity that your son founded -- *Trump Foundation*. I've been with your family for about eight years now, right, Jared? And I was an RNC speaker and I will be landing with Dr. Carson at HUD as one of his senior advisors --

THE PRESIDENT: Oh, that's great. You've got a good person.

MS. PATTON: -- and Director of the Office of Public Liaison.

THE PRESIDENT: That's great. You did a fantastic job.

MS. PATTON: Thank you.

MR. ROBINSON: Mr. President, my name is Gerard Robinson. I'm a resident fellow at the American Enterprise Institute, and I was proud to be the leader of the education policy team for the Trump transition.

THE PRESIDENT: Thank you.

MR. BELL: Mr. President, good to be with you. I'm Ashley Bell, Gainesville. Chairman Priebus called me out (inaudible) African American outreach for your campaign. I'm glad you support Omarosa, glad to be here, and I'll be wanting to help you out at the State Department.

THE PRESIDENT: Fantastic. Thank you. Thank you very much.

MS. MANIGAULT: Tucker was a star at the Inauguration.

MR. DAVIS: I'm Tucker Davis. I ran your campaign in West Virginia, working for you in the --

THE PRESIDENT: We did well in West Virginia. (Laughter.)

MR. DAVIS: Coal miners love you.

THE PRESIDENT: And we love the coal miners. We're going to put them back to work.

MR. DAVIS: Absolutely.

MS. LEVELL: Leah LeVell. I was at the RNC and also at PIC. And I helped launch the video series every week -- the midweek message that reached out to millennials and college students and helped launch the college Republican chapter at Howard University.

MS. MANIGAULT: That's Chris LeVell's daughter. We snagged her. (Laughter.)

THE PRESIDENT: Oh, really? Great job.

MS. ALEXANDER: Mr. President, Monica Alexander, executive administrative assistant in the office of public liaison, supporting Omarosa.

PRESIDENT TRUMP: Okay, well, that's nice.

MR. SMITH: Mr. President, Ja'Ron Smith. I'm with the Domestic Policy Council, Andy Bremberg's team, and I'll be focusing on urban affairs and revitalization.

THE PRESIDENT: Fantastic.

MS. MANIGAULT: And Howard graduate. (Laughter.)

THE PRESIDENT: Howard graduate. That's good

stuff. Thank you, everybody. Thank you.

END
10:04 A.M. EST

"You read all about
Dr. Martin Luther King [Jr.]

a week ago
when somebody said
I took the statue out of my office,

and it turned out that that was
fake news."

Chapter 12

REMARKS BY PRESIDENT TRUMP IN MEETING WITH SCOTUS GROUPS ROOSEVELT ROOM

01 February 2017

11:44 A.M. EST

THE PRESIDENT: One person that likes me at this table, I can tell you that. (Laughter.)

MR. COLLAMORE: More than one.

THE PRESIDENT: I have a lot of them. I have a lot. You've been great friends and supporters and appreciated for, number one, the election. And I appreciate all of the help in deciding who to pick for the United States Supreme Court. And, Leonard, you were fantastic. All of you were. And Jim DeMint -- I don't know if Jim is here or not but they were great, Heritage. You really did. You really helped. And the rollout has been fantastic. I don't know how anybody can oppose him, frankly. I don't know how anybody can oppose him at all, but it really has been a beautiful thing to see.

So we had a very successful event. He's a terrific person, by the way. I got to know him reasonably well before we did the announcement, and he is just a spectacular man. I think he will be a spectacular -- you know, you tell me, how would they go about -- Leonard, how would they go about opposing him? He's perfect in almost every way. But they'll look for the "almost," right? They'll say, what's the "almost?"

MR. LEO: He's got an impeccable record.

THE PRESIDENT: Well, Federalist really -- they really did a great job. So we're going to be talking about working with the judge and maybe making this a fast process. And nominating a justice of the Supreme Court is one of the most important things that I can do as President.

I've always said this -- as I watched Presidents -- I'd say the most important thing. And I think I want to refine that a little bit. I think probably defense of our country might be now -- you know, it's -- otherwise we don't need the Supreme Court so badly, right? We're doing well in that regard, very well. I think we have problems that are a lot bigger than people understood. I think I was left something isn't -- had a lot of problems, but I think we'll straighten out those problems. I think we'll straight them out very strongly.

Judge Gorsuch is an exceptionally qualified person from the standpoint of experience and education. Columbia with honors, Harvard Law School with honors, Oxford at the highest level. Great, great student, great intellect. Supreme Court Justices White and Kennedy he clerked. And so I just think it's really great that we're having this meeting, because we want to have him go through an elegant process as opposed to a demeaning process. Because they're very demeaning on the other side and they want to make you look as bad as possible. And, of course, the press can be very demeaning too, but I'm sure the press will be very dignified in this case.

But I really want -- that's the word -- I really think he's a very dignified man. I'd like to see him go through a dignified process. I think he deserves that. And hopefully it will go quickly and we'll see what happens.

So what we might do is -- just before they leave -- we might ask for the folks in the room just to give yourself a quick -- your name and a little introduction. And, Wayne, I would say they know you. Perhaps they know you better than they know me. (Laughter.)

MR. LAPIERRE: I doubt that. Wayne LaPierre, National Rifle Association.

MS. NANCE: I'm Penny Nance. I'm the CEO and president of Concerned Women for America.

MS. YOEST: I'm Charmaine Yoest. I'm with American Values and thank you, Mr. President, for this nomination.

THE PRESIDENT: Thank you very much.

MS. DUGGAN: I'm Juanita Duggan with the National Independent Business Association, NFIB. Thank you.

MR. COLLAMORE: Tom Collamore with the U.S. Chamber of Commerce. Mr. President, congratulations on the fantastic nomination.

THE PRESIDENT: Thank you. Thank you.

MR. NORQUIST: Grover Norquist, Americans for Tax Reform. And thank you for winning the election.

THE PRESIDENT: Thank you.

MR. LEO: Leonard Leo, the Federalist Society.

MS. DANNENFELSER: Margorie Dannenfelser, the Susan B. Anthony List.

MR. BLACKWELL: Morton Blackwell, the Leadership Institute.

MR. O'STEEN: David O'Steen, National Right to Life. Thank you for such a quick, expert nomination.

THE PRESIDENT: Thank you. Thank you very much.

MS. WHITE: Paula White, Chairman of the Evangelical Advisory Council.

THE PRESIDENT: Thank you, Paula. Thank you for the help during the campaign.

So, with that, I'll ask you to all hit the road. (Laughter.)

Q   Mr. President, as you pointed out last night, the judge was confirmed on a unanimous voice. Well, he's -- can I ask a question, Mr. President? You all right? Thank you. As you pointed out last night, Judge Gorsuch was confirmed on a unanimous voice vote in 2006. Now, a number of Democrats say they are going to oppose him. What would you say to those Democrats? And would you encourage Senator McConnell to invoke the nuclear option if he feels he can't get 60 votes?

THE PRESIDENT: I think there's a certain dishonesty if they go against their vote from not very long ago. And he did get a unanimous endorsement, and he's somebody that should get it. I mean, you can't do better from an educational, from an experience, from any standpoint. A great judge; he'll be a great justice.

So, no, I feel that it's very dishonest if they go about doing that. And, yes, if we end up with the same gridlock that they've had in Washington for the last -- longer than eight years, in all fairness to President Obama, a lot longer than eight years -- but if we end up with that gridlock, I would say, if you can, Mitch, go nuclear. Because that would be an absolute shame if a man of this quality was caught up in the web. So I would say it's up to Mitch, but I would say go for it.

END
11:50 A.M. EST

"I would say,
if you can, Mitch,
go nuclear.
Because that would be
an absolute shame
if a man of this quality
was caught up in the web.
So I would say it's up to Mitch,
but I would say go for it."

Chapter 13

01 February 2017

7:12 P.M. EST

THE VICE PRESIDENT: Welcome to the White House. Ladies and gentlemen, the President of the United States.

THE PRESIDENT: Thank you very much, Mike. Just returned from an amazing visit with a great, great family at Dover, and it was something -- very sad, very beautiful. Ryan, a great man.

Secretary Tillerson, I first want to congratulate you, Renda, and your entire family on this incredible honor -- and it is that, an incredible honor. You bring the unique skills and deep, deep insights -- and I've gotten to see it first-hand -- into foreign diplomacy our nation needs to foster stability and security in a world too often trapped -- and right now it's trapped -- in violence and in war.

You understand that the job of our diplomats and the mission of the State Department is to serve the interests of the United States of America to make our nation safer, our country more prosperous, and our people much more secure. In that mission, you also understand the importance of strengthening our alliances and forming new alliances to enhance our strategic interests and the safety of our people.

Your whole life has prepared you for this moment, and you really have had a tremendous life -- heading up one of the great companies of the world and doing it magnificently, absolutely magnificently. And I can say this is a man that's respected all over the world, before he even begins.

But as Renda said, now he's beginning his big, big, and most important journey. This is where you were meant to be, right here, today, at this crossroads in history. It's time to bring a clear-eyed focus to foreign affairs, to take a fresh look at the world around us, and to seek new solutions grounded in very ancient truths. These truths include the fact that nations have a right to protect to their interests, that all people have a right to freely pursue their own destiny, and that all of us are better off when we act in concert and not in conflict. And there's rarely been conflict like we have in the world today -- very sad.

I am excited for you. I am excited for your family. And perhaps most importantly, I am excited for our great country. Though you inherit enormous challenges in the Middle East and around the world, I do believe we can achieve peace and stability in these very, very troubled times.

May God bless you in this journey. And may God bless our very, very special and great country. Thank you very much. Mike, you can do the honors. Thank you.

(The Secretary is sworn in.)

SECRETARY TILLERSON: Well, first, I want to express my profound thanks to President Trump for giving me this extraordinary opportunity to serve my country. I also want to thank Vice President Pence for giving me the honor of swearing me into this office today.

I have a few folks in the room that are with me that have helped me over the last month to get to this point of confirmation. They represent a much larger cadre of people who have worked enormously long hours, tirelessly, helping me and guiding me through the confirmation process. And to them, I will always be eternally grateful for the sacrifice they've made of their time and effort these past weeks.

I've also received over the last month so many messages, letters, phone calls of best wishes, encouragement, prayers from family, friends and colleagues who know me well. But I've also received an enormous outpouring of wonderful messages from people all over the country whom I do not know -- words of encouragement and their prayers. And it's their messages that are going to really stand in steadfast reminder to me as I enter the responsibilities of Secretary of State, that as I serve this President, I serve their interest and will always represent the interest of all of the American people at all times.

And again, Mr. President, thank you for this extraordinary opportunity. (Applause.)

THE PRESIDENT: He left a very good job for this, I want to tell you. (Laughter and applause.)

END
7:19 P.M. EST

Chapter 14

**REMARKS BY PRESIDENT TRUMP AT
NATIONAL PRAYER BREAKFAST
WASHINGTON HILTON**

02 February 2017

9:11 A.M. EST

THE PRESIDENT: Thank you, Mark. So nice. (Applause.)

Thank you very much. Thank you. Thank you very much. It's a great honor to be here this morning. And so many faith leaders -- very, very important people to me -- from across our magnificent nation, and so many leaders from all across the globe.

Today we continue a tradition begun by President Eisenhower some 64 years ago. This gathering is a testament to the power of faith, and is one of the great customs of our nation, and I hope to be here seven more times with you. (Laughter and applause.)

I want very much to thank our co-chairs, Senator Bowzman and Senator Coons, and all of the congressional leadership -- they're all over the place. We have a lot of very distinguished guests.

And we have one guest who was just sworn in last night -- Rex Tillerson, Secretary of State. (Applause.)

Going to do a great job. Some people didn't like Rex because he actually got along with leaders of the world. I said, no, you have to understand, that's a good thing. (Laughter.)

That's a good thing, not a bad thing. He's respected all over the world, and I think he's going to go down as one of our great, great secretaries. We appreciate it. Thank you, thank you, Rex. (Applause.)

Thank you as well to Senate Chaplain Barry Black for his moving words. And I don't know, Chaplain, whether or not that's an appointed position. Is that an appointed position? I don't even know if you're a Democrat or if you're a Republican, but I'm appointing you for another year -- the hell with it. (Laughter and applause.)

And I think it's not even my appointment, it's the Senate's appointment, but we'll talk to them. Your son is here. Your job is very, very secure, okay? (Laughter.)

Thank you, Barry. Appreciate it very much.

I also want to thank my great friends, though, Roma. Where's Roma? Beautiful Roma Downey. The voice of an angel. She's got the voice -- every time I hear it, that voice is so beautiful. Everything is so beautiful about Roma, including her husband because he's a special, special friend, Mark Burnett -- for the wonderful introduction. So true. So true. I said to the agent, I'm sorry. The only thing more -- I actually got on the phone and fired him myself because he said, you don't want to do it, it'll never work, it'll never, ever work. You don't want to do it. I said, listen -- but I really fired him after it became the number-one show. It became so successful, and he wanted a commission, and he didn't want to do it. That's what I really said. (Laughter.)

But we had tremendous success on "The Apprentice." And when I ran for President, I had to leave the show. That's when I knew for sure I was doing it.

And they hired a big, big movie star -- Arnold Schwarzenegger -- to take my place. And we know how that turned out. (Laughter.)

The ratings went right down the tubes. It's been a total disaster. And Mark will never, ever bet against Trump again. And I want to just pray for Arnold, if we can, for those ratings, okay? (Laughter.)

But we've had an amazing life together, the last 14, 15 years. And an outstanding man, and thank you very much for introducing me. Appreciate it. It's a great honor. (Applause.)

I also want to thank my dear friend, Vice President Mike Pence, who has been incredible. (Applause.)

And incredible wife, Karen. And every time I was in a little trouble with something, where they were questioning me, they'd say, but he picked Mike Pence -- (laughter) -- so he has to know what he's doing. And it's true, he's been -- you know, on the scale of 0 to 10, I rate him a 12, okay? So I want to thank you. Thank you very much. Apprentice [sic] it. (Applause.)

But most importantly today, I want to thank the American people. Your faith and prayers have sustained me and inspired me through some very, very tough times. All around America, I have met amazing people whose words of worship and encouragement have been a constant source of strength. What I hear most often as I travel the country are five words that never, ever fail to touch my heart. That's: "I am praying for you." I hear it so often -- "I am praying for you, Mr. President." (Applause.)

No one has inspired me more in my travels than the families of the United States military, men and women who have put their lives on the line every day for their country and their countrymen. I just came back yesterday from Dover Air Force Base to join the family of Chief William "Ryan" Owens, as America's fallen hero was returned home. Very, very sad, but very, very beautiful. Very, very beautiful. His family was there. Incredible family, loved him so much. So devastated -- he was so devastated. But the ceremony was amazing.

He died in defense of our nation. He gave his life in defense of our people. Our debt to him and our debt to his family is eternal and everlasting.

"Greater love hath no man than this: that a man lay down his life for his friends." We will never forget the men and women who wear the uniform, believe me. (Applause.)

Thank you.

From generation to generation, their vigilance has kept our liberty alive. Our freedom is won by their sacrifice, and our security has been earned with their sweat and blood and tears. God has blessed this land to give us such incredible heroes and patriots. They are very, very special, and we are going to take care of them. (Applause.)

Our soldiers understand that what matters is not party or ideology or creed, but the bonds of loyalty that link us all together as one. America is a nation of believers. In towns all across our land, it's plain to see what we easily forget -- so easily we forget this -- that the quality of our lives is not defined by our material success, but by our spiritual success. I will tell you that. And I tell you that from somebody that has had material success and knows tremendous numbers of people with great material success -- the most material success.

Many of those people are very, very miserable, unhappy people. And I know a lot of people without that, but they have great families, they have great faith. They don't have money -- at least not nearly to the extent -- and they're happy. Those to me are the successful people, I have to tell you. (Applause.)

I was blessed to be raised in a churched home. My mother and father taught me that to whom much is given much is expected. I was sworn in on the very bible from which my mother would teach us as young children. And that faith lives on in my heart every single day.

The people in this room come from many, many backgrounds. You represent so many religions and so many views. But we are all united by our faith in our Creator and our firm knowledge that we are all equal in His eyes. We are not just flesh and bone and blood. We are human beings, with souls. Our Republic was formed on the basis that freedom is not a gift from government, but that freedom is a gift from God. (Applause.)

It was the great Thomas Jefferson who said, "The God who gave us life, gave us liberty." Jefferson asked, "Can the liberties of a nation be secure when we have removed a conviction that these liberties are the gift of God?"

Among those freedoms is the right to worship according to our own beliefs. That is why I will get rid of, and totally destroy, the Johnson Amendment and allow our representatives of faith to speak freely and without fear of retribution. I will do that -- remember. (Applause.)

Freedom of religion is a sacred right, but it is also a right under threat all around us, and the world is under serious, serious threat in so many different ways. And I've never seen it so much and so openly as since I took the position of President. The world is in trouble, but we're going to straighten it out. Okay? That's what I do. I fix things. We're going to straighten it out. (Applause.)

Believe me. When you hear about the tough phone calls I'm having, don't worry about it. Just don't worry about it. (Laughter.)

They're tough. We have to be tough. It's time we're going to be a little tough, folks. We're taken advantage of by every nation in the world, virtually. It's not going to happen anymore. It's not going to happen anymore.
We have seen unimaginable violence carried out in the name of religion. Acts of wanton slaughter against religious minorities. Horrors on a scale that defy description. Terrorism is a fundamental threat to religious freedom. It must be stopped, and it will be stopped. It may not be pretty for a little while. It will be stopped. (Applause.)

We have seen -- and, by the way, General, as you know, James "Mad Dog" -- I shouldn't say it in this room -- Mattis. Now, there's a reason they call him "Mad Dog Mattis" -- he never lost a battle. Always wins them and always wins them fast. He's our new Secretary of Defense who will be working with Rex. He's right now in South Korea, going to Japan, going to some other spots. And I'll tell you what, I've gotten to know him really well. He's the real deal. We have somebody who's the real deal working for us, and that's what we need. So, you watch. You just watch. (Applause.)

Things will be different.

We have seen peace-loving Muslims brutalized, victimized, murdered and oppressed by ISIS killers. We have seen threats of extermination against the Jewish people. We have seen a campaign of ISIS and genocide against Christians, where they cut off heads. Not since the Middle Ages have we seen that. We haven't seen that, the cutting off of heads. Now they cut off their heads, they drown people in steel cages. Haven't seen this -- I haven't seen this. Nobody has seen this for many, many years.

All nations have a moral obligation to speak out against such violence. All nations have a duty to work together to confront it and to confront it viciously, if we have to. So I want to express clearly today to the American people that my administration will do everything in its power to defend and protect religious liberty in our land. America must forever remain a tolerant society where all faiths are respected, and where all of our citizens can feel safe and secure. We have to feel **safe** and secure.

In recent days, we have begun to take necessary action to achieve that goal. Our nation has the most generous immigration system in the world. But these are those and there are those that would exploit that generosity to undermine the values that we hold so dear. We need security. There are those who would seek to enter our country for the purpose of spreading violence or oppressing other people based upon their faith or their lifestyle. Not right. We will not allow a beachhead of intolerance to spread in our nation. You look all over the world and you see what's happening.

So in the coming days, we will develop a system to help ensure that those admitted into our country fully embrace our values of religious and personal liberty, and that they reject any form of oppression and discrimination. We want people to come into our nation, but we want people to love us and to love our values -- not to hate us and to hate our values. We will be a safe country. We will be a free country. And we will be a country where all citizens can practice their beliefs without fear of hostility or fear of violence. America will flourish as long as our liberty and, in particular, our religious liberty is allowed to flourish. (Applause.)

America will succeed as long as our most vulnerable citizens -- and we have some that are so vulnerable -- have a path to success. And America will thrive as long as we continue to have faith in each other and faith in God. (Applause.)

That faith in God has inspired men and women to sacrifice for the needy, to deploy to wars overseas, and to lock arms at home, to ensure equal rights for every man, woman and child in our land. It's that faith that sent the pilgrims across the oceans, the pioneers across the plains, and the young people all across America to chase their **dreams**. They are chasing their **dreams**. We are going to bring those **dreams** back. As long as we have God, we are never, ever alone. Whether it's the soldier on the night watch or the single parent on the night shift, God will always give us solace and strength and comfort.

We need to carry on and to keep carrying on. For us here in Washington, we must never, ever stop asking God for the wisdom to serve the public according to his will. That's why -- (applause) -- thank you. That's why President Eisenhower and Senator Carlson had the wisdom to gather together 64 years ago to begin this truly great tradition. But that's not all they did together. Let me tell you the rest of the story. Just one year later, Senator Carlson was among the members of Congress to send to the President's desk a joint resolution that added "under God" to our Pledge of Allegiance. That's a great thing. (Applause.) Because that's what we are and that is what we will always be, and that is what our people want: one beautiful nation, under God.

Thank you. God bless you. And God bless America. Thank you very much. Thank you. Thank you. (Applause.)

END
9:30 A.M. EST

"And I want
to just pray for Arnold,
if we can,
for those ratings,
okay?"

Chapter 15

02 February 2017

1:11 P.M. EST

THE PRESIDENT: So it's great to have
Harley-Davidson. What a great, great group of people and
what a fantastic job you do. And thank you for all of the
votes you gave me in Wisconsin. Some people thought
that was an upset; I thought we were going to win it. From
the beginning, we thought we were going to win it.

Harley-Davidson is a true American icon, one of the
greats. Your motorcycles have carried American service
members in the war -- in the wars. They take care of
our police officers. And I see it so often -- whenever I go
-- whenever there's a motorcycle group, oftentimes it's a
Harley. And the sound of that Harley is a little different, I
have to tell you. It's really good.

So thank you, Harley-Davidson, for building things in America. And I think you're going to even expand -- I know your
business is now doing very well and there's a lot of spirit
right now in the country that you weren't having so much
in the last number of months that you have right now. You
see what's happening.

I'm especially honored to welcome the steelworkers and

the machinists to the White House.

Who is a steelworker here? Well, you're all steelworkers, essentially, right?

But you folks have been terrific to me. Sometimes your top people didn't support me but the steelworkers supported me, right? A lot of your top people are going to be losing their jobs pretty soon I guess but they're all coming around -- we're getting them. But the workers supported us big league. We want to make it easier for businesses to create more jobs and more factories in the United States, and you're a great example of it. That means we have to make America the best country on Earth to do business, and that's what we're in the process of doing -- we're redoing NAFTA, redoing a lot of our trade deals, and we're negotiating properly with countries -- even countries that are allies -- a lot of people taking advantage of us, a lot of countries taking advantage of us, really terribly taking advantage of us.

We had one instance in Australia -- I have a lot of respect for Australia, I love Australia as a country -- but we had a problem where, for whatever reason, President Obama said that they were going to take probably well over a thousand illegal immigrants who were in prisons and they were going to bring them and take them into this country. And I just said why? I just wanted to ask a question -- I could ask that question of you -- why? One thousand-two-hundred-fifty -- it could be 2,000, it could be more than that, and I said, why? Why are we doing this? What's the purpose? So we'll see what happens. But a previous administration does something, you have to respect that, but you can also say, why are we doing this? That's why we're in the jams that we're in.

And you guys especially, the steelworkers, understand what I'm saying, right? So I just -- we have some wonderful allies and we're going to keep it that way, but we have to be treated fairly also. We have to be treated fairly. In this administration, our allegiance will be to the American workers and to American businesses, like Harley-Davidson, that were very strong in the 1980s and I remember this -- you were victims of trading abuse -- big trading abuse, where they were dumping all sorts of competitors all over the place. And Ronald Reagan stepped in and he put on large tariffs and you wouldn't be talking about Harley-Davidson probably right now if he didn't do that.

But we're going to help you, too, and we're going to make it really great for business -- not just you, but for everybody. We're going to be competitive with anybody in the world. We're going to be doing taxing policies very soon it's going to be coming out. And I know health care is a big problem for every country -- every company as you know has suffered from Obamacare because of the tremendous cost and that's one of the things that we're working on hardest -- that and tax policy, and tariffs and trade.

So I think you will be very happy. It's an honor to have you at lunch. I really appreciate your support. You've given me tremendous support, your workers in particular have given tremendous support. I want to thank the people of Wisconsin in particular. It's been amazing what happened up there. It was a big shocker that evening when they showed -- wow -- I'll never forget, wow, Wisconsin just went for Trump. Then all of these people, especially that guy right there -- (laughter) -- not but then they said, what's going on? Wisconsin just went for Trump. And then Michigan went for Trump and Pennsylvania. So they were great.

You're just great people. These are amazing people and they get it. So, again, to all of you at the table today, thank you very much. We appreciate it. We really appreciate it greatly.

Q   Mr. President, is military action off the table in Iran?

THE PRESIDENT: Nothing is off the table.

Q   Mr. President, the Russians are thanking you for easing sanctions.

THE PRESIDENT: I haven't eased anything.

Q   That's what they said.

THE PRESIDENT: Well, I haven't eased anything.

END
1:16 P.M. EST

So thank you,
Harley-Davidson,
for building things in
America.

Chapter 16

**Remarks by President Trump in Strategy and Policy Forum
State Dining Room**

03 February 2017

10:16 A.M. EST

THE PRESIDENT: Well, thank you, everybody, for being here this morning. This is a really world-class group and I want to thank and congratulate Steve. You have done, as usual, an amazing job. Steve called me up the day after the election -- it might have even been the same night, Jamie, to be honest with you. You know Steve -- (inaudible) -- in fact, I think maybe one minute. And he said, I'd like to put together a group of world-class leaders and that's what he's done. So good job, Steve.

A couple of things happened this morning -- 227,000 jobs, great spirit in the country right now. So we're very happy about that. I think that it's going to continue big league. We're bringing back jobs, we're bringing down your taxes. We're getting rid of your regulations. And I think it's going to be some really very exciting times ahead. We're going to be doing -- we're doing it, we're going to be coming up with a tax bill soon, a health care bill even sooner. And it's really working out.

Toby from the Cleveland Clinic has been helping us a lot with the veterans, and we appreciate that, Toby. You've been amazing. And I and all of our friends, we really appreciate it.

One of the things that I heard this morning in watching the news was that, amazingly, it's never happened before, that politics has become a much bigger subject than the Super Bowl -- this is usually Super Bowl territory. And I have to say that politics is more interesting to people. So that's good.

I see we have Larry here -- where is Larry Fink? Larry did a great job for me. He managed a lot of my money, and, I have to tell you, he got me great returns last year. (Laughter.)

And then they go crazy -- they'll meet very smart people that made money, why don't you let other people to run the economy? I said, no, we have to get the right people. And the people that voted for me understand that, and that's what they want.

So when I campaigned for office, I promised the American people that I'd ask for our country's best and brightest, and we have that. Wilbur is representing us as secretary. I tell you, you're going to be so great -- Secretary of Commerce, Wilbur Ross. In fact, Carl Icahn got called up, and he goes, I hear you got Wilbur. Everybody calls him Wilbur. I've never heard him called -- what, we just know him as Wilbur, right? We've got the great Jack Welch, the legendary Jack Welch. We appreciate him.

We're looking forward in a little while, and we have coming in a few moments, to discuss all of the things that you think we can do to bring back our jobs, to get taxes even lower than what they'll be cutting them. We have a great plan, but I want to have your input on the plan in particular and to do what we have to do in terms of regulation. We have some of the bankers here. There's nobody better to tell me about Dodd-Frank than Jamie, so you're going to tell me about it. But we expect to be cutting a lot out of Dodd-Frank, because, frankly, I have so many people, friends of mine that have nice businesses that can't borrow money, they just can't get any money because the banks just won't let them borrow because of the rules and regulations in Dodd-Frank. So we'll be talking about that, Jamie, in terms of the banking industry.

And with that, I just want to introduce somebody I've known for a long time. He's done a fantastic job, and we're thinking of have these meetings -- I think we'll start maybe on a monthly basis. It will go to a quarterly basis, because all of a sudden monthly basis sounds like a lot.

But we really want your input. We have the biggest, the brightest in the world. They're in this country, in this case. We also have a manufacturing group which is worldwide, where we have, as you know, great companies representing. But these are the biggest and the best minds in this country, and I really appreciate you being here. And I want to thank Steve. And Steve is going to say a few words.

MR. SCHWARZMAN: Sure. Well, I'd like to just start out and thank everybody for being here. The purpose of this group isn't for general discussion, which is okay. But the real purpose is to get things done, to advise the government as to areas where we can do things a lot better as a country, for all Americans, and de-bottleneck some things. We have a full agenda, unlike a lot of other meetings that happen of this general type. We're going to cover some of the immigration things. We're going to cover regulatory, I believe. We're going to cover tax and trade, women in the workplace, infrastructure and education. And in each of those areas we'll get suggestions, ways to make things happen, happen faster to improve the country.

And anybody can say anything else they want. But it's really important that we mobilize the non-governmental sector, and also, importantly, that we do it on a bipartisan basis. Apparently, a first in Washington for a (inaudible) Washington. And everybody on the group was selected because they're terrific, because they have domain expertise, because they want the country to do better. And we had no criteria -- we have all kinds of different people from different backgrounds and different political persuasions. And if we can make things work right, that's the way the country is supposed to work.

And so it's a big sacrifice for the people who are here to spend the time. Everybody is busy. That's America. So to puts those things aside to focus on this, not just for me, but there's prep work that goes into any successful meeting -- means these people who attended have taken the time to care about their country.

And so that's the spirit in which we're approaching things. I want to thank everybody on the committee here. You're terrific.

THE PRESIDENT: Thank you very much. We're going to go around the room, but before we do that I just want to say that so many people I call friends of mine in big business, and they wanted to be in the committee. And I call Steve and I say, Steve, can we get so-and-so? No. (Laughter.) I said, what do you mean no? (Laughter.)

It's a big business, massive business -- you know, public companies. And every once in a while I'd call him -- Steve, how about this one? I don't -- he's a corporate raider, these people don't want to be sitting with corporate raiders. (Laughter.)

Five raiders that wanted to come. But he's been very, very selective. And we'll be putting a couple of more (inaudible). He's been very selective.

I thought we might go around the room -- Mary and I met last week, we had a fantastic meeting on the auto industry. We had Ford there, we had a lot of companies. We had some great companies -- Fiat-Chrysler, Sergio. And I will tell you, I learned a lot about the automobile business. I thought I knew a lot, but they are being so stymied, so restricted with regulation and so many other reasons, and they're pouring back into the country already.

If you look at Mark, who was telling us what they're doing with Ford, and Bill Ford, too. A lot of jobs are going to be coming back into Ohio and Michigan and Pennsylvania, and all of the places that really have been hurt so badly. So maybe we can start with Mary. We'll just go around the room real fast so that everybody -- pretty much everybody knows each other, but it would be nice to see.

MS. BARRA: Mary Barra, Chairman and CEO of General Motors.

MR. MCMILLON: Doug McMillon, Walmart.

MR. FINK: Larry Fink, BlackRock.

MR. LESSER: Rich Lesser, Boston Consulting Group.

MR. MCNERNEY: Jim McNerney, the old Boeing

guy. (Laughter.)

MR. ATKINS: Paul Atkins, Patomak Global Partners.

MR. WARSH: Kevin Warsh, Stanford University.

MR. MUSK: Elon Musk, Tesla and SpaceX.

MR. COSGROVE: Toby Cosgrove, Cleveland Clinic.

MR. DIMON: Jamie Dimon, JPMorgan Chase.

MR. YERGIN: Dan Yergin, IHS Markit.

MR. WELCH: Jack Welch, retired. (Laughter.)

MR. WEINBERGER: Mark Weinberger -- someday, maybe, I hope — (Laughter.)

-- but EY.

MR. OGUNLESI: Adebayo Ogunlesi, Global Infrastructure Partners.

MS. ROMETTY: Ginni Rometty, IBM.

MS. NOOYI: Indra Nooyi, PepsiCo.

MS. SCHWARZMAN: Steve Schwarzman from Blackstone.

THE PRESIDENT: Okay. Thank you very much. Thank you, folks. Thank you, press.

END
10:24 A.M. EST

Chapter 17

03 February 2017

1:18 P.M. EST

THE PRESIDENT: Today we're signing core principles for regulating the United States financial system. It doesn't get much better than that, right?

THE PRESIDENT: Would you like to --

MS. WAGNER: It's my baby. (Laughter.)

THE PRESIDENT: Why don't you explain this.

MS. WAGNER: What we're doing is we are returning to the American people, low- and middle- income investors, and retirees, their control of their own retirement savings. This is about Main Street, and it's been a labor of love for me for over four years as chairman. And I have had -- this is a big day, a big moment for Americans. (Inaudible.)

THE PRESIDENT: And she means that so much.

(Executive Order is signed.)

THE PRESIDENT: Chairman, I think we should hand the pen to this very special person.

PARTICIPANT: Absolutely, Mr. President. She earned it. She earned it.

THE PRESIDENT: Thank you.

MS. WAGNER: Thank you. I'm grateful.

Q   Mr. President, do you have anything to say about the decision to make the Iran -- should they be expecting more?

THE PRESIDENT: They're not behaving.

END
1:20 P.M. EST

Chapter 18

03 February 2017

Transcript:

My fellow Americans,
This week I nominated Neil Gorsuch for the United States Supreme Court.

Judge Gorsuch is one of the most qualified people ever to be nominated for this post. He is a graduate of Columbia, Harvard and Oxford. He is a man of principle. He has an impeccable resume. He is widely respected by everyone. And, Judge Gorsuch's proven track record upholding the Constitution makes him the ideal person to fill the vacancy left by the late, great Antonin Scalia, a truly fabulous justice.

Ten years ago, the Senate unanimously approved Judge Gorsuch's nomination to serve on the Tenth Circuit Court of Appeals. I urge members of both parties to support Judge Gorsuch and, in so doing, to protect our laws and our freedoms.

This week we also took significant action to roll back the massive regulation that is devastating our economy and crippling American companies and jobs.

That's why I have issued a new executive order to create

a permanent structure of regulatory reduction. This order requires that for every 1 new regulation, 2 old regulations must—and I mean must—be eliminated. It's out of control. The January employment report shows that the private sector added 237,000 jobs last month. A lot of that has to do with the spirit our country now has. Job growth far surpassed expectations in January, and the labor force participation also grew, so you can be encouraged about the progress of our economy. It's going to be a whole new ball game.

But there is still much work to do. That I can tell you. Also this week, on the first day of Black History Month, I was pleased to host African American leaders at the White House. We are determined to deliver more opportunity, jobs and safety for the African-American citizens of our country. America can really never, ever rest until children of every color are fully included in the **American Dream**— so important. I think, probably, one of my most and maybe my most important goal. It is our mutual duty and obligation to make sure this happens.

At Dover Air Force Base on Wednesday I joined the family of Chief Special Warfare Operator William "Ryan" Owens as our fallen hero was returned home. A great man. Chief Owens gave his life for his country and for our people. Our debt to him and his family, a beautiful family, is eternal. God has truly blessed this nation to have given us such a brave and selfless patriot as Ryan. We will never forget him. We will never ever forget those who serve. Believe me.

And I will never forget that my responsibility is to keep you—the American people—**safe and free**.

That's why last week I signed an executive order to help keep terrorists out of our country. The executive order establishes a process to develop new vetting and mechanisms to ensure those coming into America love and support our people. That they have good intentions.

On every single front, we are working to deliver for American workers and American families. You, the law-abiding citizens of this country, are my total priority. Your safety, your jobs and your wages guide our decisions.

We are here to serve you, the great and loyal citizens of the United States of America.

The forgotten men and women will be never be forgotten **Again**. Because from now on, it's going to be **America First**. That's how I got elected, that's why you voted for me, and I will never forget it.

God Bless You, and God Bless America.

"America can really never,
ever rest until children of every color
are fully included
in the American Dream—
so important."

Chapter 19

04 February 2017

12:00 P.M. EST

THE VICE PRESIDENT: Thank you all. And thank you, Gene, thank you for your great leadership of the Federalists. Give Gene a round of applause for heaven's sake, please. The Federalist Society with -- distinction. (Applause.)

Thank you for the warm introduction.

To my friend -- Leonard Leo, everybody, is in the house. (Applause.)

Ambassador Gray, members of the Federalist Society, hon-ored guests, it's a privilege to be with you. It's a privilege to be with you here in this place, in Congress Hall at such a time as this in the life of our nation.

I bring you greetings, and I'm here today on behalf of the President of the United States of America, Donald Trump, who appreciates the Federalist Society -- (applause) -- and all that it stands for. (Applause.)

It's truly humbling to be in this position and to be in this place today. Thank you all of you, members of the Feder-alist Society, for your support and your hard work over the past year. It was quite a campaign, but it's already been quite an administration, am I right? (Laughter and applause.)

And I know the President feels the same way as I do, that we're here in no small part because of your commitment and the ideals of the Federalist Society to restore the **promise** of America.

And it's fitting that we're in Philadelphia today, in the shadow of Independence Hall, only steps away from where our Founding Fathers proclaimed ideals that have echoed throughout the ages. They declared these truths to be self-evident, that we are, all of us, created equal, and that we are endowed not by government, but that we are endowed, as the President himself recited this week at the National Prayer Breakfast, endowed by our Creator with the inalienable rights of life and liberty, and the pursuit of happiness. That principle is at the center of the **American Experience**, and it will always be. (Applause.)

The men who wrote these words will ever be honored in the American pantheon -- Thomas Jefferson, John Adams, James Madison, and so many more. The documents they drafted, the Declaration of Independence, the year in which they signed it, 1776, are now synonymous with freedom of the world. What they did that day is the greatest gift we have as sons and daughters of the United States. It's humbling to be so near to where they pledged to each other their lives, their fortunes, and their sacred honor.

Yet our Founders were not finished with their noble work, were they? In the words of Abraham Lincoln, they had labored to create an "apple of gold." Now they needed a "picture of silver" to frame it in, to "adorn" and to "preserve" the principles at the heart of our exceptional experiment in self-government. And so it would be 11 years later, in the summer of 1787, our Founding Fathers returned to Independence Hall. They came to craft a framework of government that would protect those timeless ideals -- the ideals that bind us together as a people and give us purpose as a nation.

They gave us the Constitution of the United States of America. (Applause.)

It was, it is, and I believe it will forever be the greatest charter of liberty our world has ever seen. It has fostered our nation's unparalleled success. And it is, to this day, the greatest bulwark against tyranny in history.

This is the Constitution that President Trump and I have both sworn to uphold. On January 20th, just over two weeks ago, we stood before the American people and before God, and we made solemn vows. In my oath of office, I simply promised to "support and defend the Constitution," as did the President. And I promise you, we will keep that oath. (Applause.)

People keep asking me what it was like up there on the stage. I tell people it was just very humbling -- it was humbling for me to be there. You see, my grandfather came to this country from a little town in Ireland called Tubercurry when he was about our son's age. He got on a boat, he crossed the Atlantic, and he went through Ellis Island and took a train to Chicago, Illinois, where he drove a bus for 40 years. He was the proudest man I ever knew. The fact that Richard Michael Cawley had the courage to cross that ocean is why Michael Richard Pence is now the Vice President of the United States of America.

It is, I expect, startling to him -- knowing me as well as he did -- (laughter) -- in more ways than one. I found myself thinking up on that stage what that Irishman must be thinking looking down from Glory, and I've only come to one conclusion: He was right. Not about me, he was right about America, where anybody can be anybody because of the system of liberty that we have enshrined in the Constitution and the founding documents of this nation. (Applause.)

That moment was made all the more special to me because of the man who administered my oath of office, Justice Clarence Thomas. (Applause.)

I'm privileged to have met Justice Thomas about a decade ago, when I was a member of Congress, and privileged to have a chance to get acquainted with a man of his conviction and his courage on the Supreme Court of the United States. I know everyone in this room holds Justice Thomas in the same high regard. Not only that, we want to aid him in his lonely fight -- his lonely fight too often on the Supreme Court -- and we can do that best by giving Justice Clarence Thomas another colleague on the bench who shares his courage and his commitment to our nation's guiding documents. And this we are doing. (Applause.)

You know, the American people elected President Trump I believe in significant part because of his vow to do just that --- to nominate someone to the Supreme Court in the mold of not only Justice Thomas, but also of the late and great Justice Antonin Scalia. (Applause.)

It was such a special night earlier this week when we were

joined not only by our nominee and his wife, but also by the widow of Justice Scalia and his son, who was with us there and shared that moment. Justice Antonin Scalia's devotion to the Constitution will be forever remembered by the people of the United States of America. (Applause.)

But this was President Trump's promise. And make no mistake about it, my friends in the Federalist Society, we're in the promise-keeping business in Washington, D.C. now.

Before I say any more, it behooves us to remember Justice Scalia's legacy and to honor his memory. We all knew the late Justice, some of you personally, others through his titanic impact on our nation's laws. The Federalist Society actually owes him a great deal. Justice Scalia was one of its first faculty mentors in the early 1980s, I'm told, at the University of Chicago. Our country owes a great deal to him, too. His incomparable opinions -- even more, his incisive dissents -- will stand the test of time, influencing future generations of lawyers through his wit and wisdom. As his successor said the other night, America misses Justice Scalia greatly. And I know we'll always cherish him in our hearts. Would you mind getting to your feet and just showing how much we appreciate the life and work and memory of the late Justice Antonin Scalia? (Applause.)

I mentioned before that last week, I had the great privilege to speak with the Justice's widow, Maureen. And the President had asked me to invite her to join us at the White House, as I said, for the Supreme Court announcement the next day. But during the conversation, I told her that President Trump was about to nominate a worthy replacement for her husband and before I could go any further, she stopped me and said, actually, that's not how the President puts it. She said, "The President actually told me that no one can replace my husband. They can only succeed him." (Laughter.)

Isn't that wonderful? And it's true, and we all know why. And that's why President Trump devoted so much energy to picking the best possible nominee. Last year, President Trump took the unprecedented step of releasing a list of the 21 men and women he was considering for the Supreme Court. There was full transparency literally every step of the way, unprecedented transparency in this process. Each individual the President named shared several key qualifications: sterling academic credentials, a brilliant legal mind, and an unwavering commitment to the Constitution of the United States.

Four days ago, as you all know, President Trump nominated someone who fits this description to a tee: Judge Neil M. Gorsuch. (Applause.)

My friends, I can say with the utmost confidence: Judge Gorsuch is a worthy successor to Justice Antonin Scalia. By the grace of God, and with what I know will be the tireless efforts of everyone in this room, I believe Neil Gorsuch soon take his seat as an associate justice on the Supreme Court of the United States. (Applause.)

When you get right down to it, Judge Gorsuch plain and simple is one of the most mainstream, respected, and exceptionally qualified Supreme Court nominees in American history.

But don't take my word for it. That actually was the conclusion of the American Bar Association in 2006. (Laughter.)

After President George W. Bush nominated him to the 10th Circuit Court of Appeals, the ABA gave him a unanimous rating of "well-qualified" -- which is the highest possible recommendation.

And the United States Senate agreed. Only two months after Neil Gorsuch's nomination to the court of appeals, the Senate confirmed him by a unanimous voice vote, and nearly a third of those senators, on both sides of the aisle, are still serving in the Senate today. A unanimous vote. As President Trump asked on Tuesday, "can you believe that?" (Laughter.)

Oh, yes, you can, when you look at Judge Gorsuch's record ever since. In his decade on the 10th Circuit, he has established himself as a fair and impartial judge who has been faithful to the Constitution. He is well-known by his peers as a keen legal thinker and, just as important, a clear legal writer. It's evident to all that he's a man also of high character and courage -- indispensable qualities for a jurist. Over the past few days it's been amazing to see the outpouring of support from those who know Judge Gorsuch and his work. Ed Whelan from the Ethics and Public Policy Center and a former clerk to Justice Scalia declared him a "dedicated originalist and textualist" who "writes with clarity, force, and verve."

The Wall Street Journal praised him as a "distinguished choice who will adhere to the original meaning of the Constitution."

And Leonard Leo, who of course is here, called him an "exceptional jurist."

By the way, Leonard, let me say again how much I and the

President appreciate your tireless work on behalf of our country and the Constitution. We are grateful for all you have done. (Applause.)

Now, I should also note that Judge Gorsuch is so well-liked that even those who disagree with him sing his praises. Norm Eisen, President Obama's former ethics czar, simply said Judge Gorsuch is "a great guy."

And Neal Katyal, the acting solicitor general under President Obama, endorsed Judge Gorsuch in the strongest possible terms. He called him "an extraordinary judge" who will "help restore confidence in the rule of law." That's what this is really all about, isn't it? Our constitutional order requires the rule of law, without exception. We are, after all, a nation of laws.

Judge Gorsuch firmly understands this. He has said on many occasions that judges must apply the law as written, without regard to their own politics or personal feelings. He put it well on Tuesday and movingly, saying "in our legal order it's for Congress and not the courts to write new laws." He added, "It is the role of judges to apply, not alter, the work of the people's representatives." And my favorite line sitting as I was on the front row was this one -- he said: "A judge who likes every outcome he reaches is very likely a bad judge, stretching for results he prefers rather than those the law demands."

I don't know about you, but that's my kind of Supreme Court justice. (Applause.)

But it's not just his words. Judge Gorsuch's record on the bench clearly demonstrates his fidelity to the wisdom of the Founders rather than the whims of our own day and age.

He has written more than 200 published opinions in his decade on the 10th Circuit. And if you read them all, and some have, which the President's team I promise you did, an unmistakable picture emerges: He is an originalist and a textualist who will pick up right where Justice Scalia left off.

Judge Gorsuch has such a long history of upholding the separation of powers and the checks and balances between the three branches. He also defends the Constitution's unique system of federalism, and he restricts the national government to the specific and enumerated powers enshrined in the Constitution, while leaving to the states much more sizeable control over their lives and destinies. These carefully calibrated mechanisms, so wisely designed by our Founding Fathers, are a strong foundation for the protection of the American people's fundamental liberties. By defending them, Judge Gorsuch has shown himself to be a true friend of our freedoms.

It should be abundantly clear that Judge Neil Gorsuch is indeed a worthy successor to Justice Antonin Scalia. He is cut from the same cloth. Our Constitution and our country will be stronger with him on the Supreme Court.

But we're not there yet, which is why I'm here. (Laughter.)

First, of course, we must abide by the Constitution and secure the "advice and consent of the Senate."

The morning after his nomination, I had the privilege of escorting Judge Gorsuch to Capitol Hill for the first time. I'm pleased to report in just a few short days he has already met with 12 senators in both political parties. And he making himself available to meet with all 100 members of the Senate -- if they're willing to meet with him.

Of course, several announced their opposition within minutes of his nomination. And now they're even threatening to filibuster procedure in the Senate to stop him. Make no mistake about it, this would be an unwise and an unprecedented act.

Never before in the history of our country has an associate justice nominee to the Supreme Court faced a successful filibuster, and Judge Neil M. Gorsuch should not be the first. (Applause.)

Now let me tell you, President Trump and I have full confidence that Judge Gorsuch will be confirmed. But rest assured, we will work with the Senate leadership to ensure that Judge Gorsuch gets an up or down vote on the Senate floor -- one way or the other. (Applause.)

This seat does not belong to any party, or any ideology, or any interest group. This seat on the Supreme Court belongs to the American people, and the American people deserve a vote on the floor of the United States Senate. (Applause.)

My friends, this is a historic time for our country. We are on the verge literally of reaffirming the supremacy of the Constitution on our nation's Supreme Court. We are giving a new voice to the age-old vision of our Founding Fathers. We are rededicating ourselves and our country to the timeless principles that they proclaimed only a few steps away from right where we're standing today.

Under President Trump's leadership, we are returning power to the American people, the rightful rulers of the greatest nation the world has ever known.

We have much work to do, but I'm confident with the grace of God, we will accomplish the task before us. So let me just close by saying thank you. Thank you to all of you for your work as men and women of the law, participants in the Federalist Society, your own fealty to the Constitution of the United States and the way you live that out in your lives and in your careers.

I must tell you that it's inspiring to be with you today. And I truly do believe that for all our nation has accomplished over these last 241 years, I'm absolutely confident that as we keep faith with the ideals that were first minted just a few steps away from here in our founding documents -- in that Declaration and in that Constitution -- the best days for America are yet to come.

Thank you very much and God bless you and may God bless. (Applause.)

END
1:22 P.M. EST

Chapter 20

REMARKS BY PRESIDENT TRUMP TO COALITION REPRESENTATIVES AND SENIOR U.S. COMMANDERS MACDILL AIR FORCE BASE TAMPA, FLORIDA

06 February 2017

1:48 P.M. EST

THE PRESIDENT: Thank you very much. (Applause.)

Thank you, everybody. Thank you very much. Thank you very much. That's so nice. A lot of **Spirit**. Great **Spirit** for this country. Thank you, all. We have tremendous **Spirit** and I want to thank you.

We had a wonderful election, didn't we? (Applause.)

And I saw those numbers -- and you like me, and I like you. That's the way it worked. (Laughter.)

I'm honored to be here today among so many of our really and truly great heroes. I want to begin by thanking General Votel and General Thomas for their distinguished leadership and service on behalf of our country. Very, very outstanding people. I'd also like to thank General Dunford, the Chairman of the Joint Chiefs of Staff. That's big stuff, when you have the Chairman. Where is -- Joe, stand up for a second. This is one of the great people. (Applause.)

Thank you.

Also, Commander Vogel and everyone serving at MacDill Air Force Base. Quite a place. And we're going to be loading it up with beautiful new planes and beautiful new equipment. You've been lacking a little equipment. We're going to load it up. You're going to get a lot of equipment. Believe me. (Applause.)

So importantly, also, let me thank all of the coalition partners and their representatives assembled here today. We proudly -- very proudly -- stand with you, and we will be fighting for your security. They're fighting for our security and freedom.

Let me recognize our great governor and a very good friend of mine, and somebody who endorsed me -- that makes him a better friend of mine. (Laughter.)

You know, if they don't endorse, believe me, if you're ever in this position, it's never quite the same, okay? (Laughter.)

You can talk, but it never means the same. But this man is a great, great governor and has done a fantastic job -- Rick Scott, governor, stand up please. (Applause.)

Thank you, Rick.

Finally, on behalf of the entire nation, let me express our gratitude to all members -- and I mean all members -- of our military serving in the United States Central Command and the United States Special Operations Command. We salute the Army, Marine Corps, Navy, Air Force, and Coast Guard, along with our civilian defense personnel, who are so important to the success of what we're doing.

Let me also recognize the military families and spouses who bravely shoulder the burdens of war. I want every military family in this country to know that our administration is at your service. We stand with you 100 percent. We will protect those who protect us, and we will never ever let you down. As your President, I have no higher duty than to protect the American people -- highest duty we have. I said it the other night. Great, great Supreme Court nominee -- you all saw that -- but I said to myself, perhaps the only thing more important to me definitely is the defense of our nation. The Supreme Court is so important, but we have to defend our nation. And we will do that, believe me. (Applause.)

We will do that. And each and every one of you is central to that mission.

The men and women serving at CENTCOM and SOCOM have poured out their hearts and souls for this country. They really experience things that very few people get to experience. You've shed your blood across the continents and the oceans. You've engaged the enemy on distant battlefields, toiled in the burning heat and bitter cold, and sacrificed everything so that we can remain safe and strong and free. Our administration will always honor our sacred bond to those who serve, and we will never ever forget you. Believe me, we will never ever forget you.

We will ensure that the men and women of our military have the tools, equipment, resources, training, and supplies you need to get the job done. You've seen me say we've been depleted. Our navy is at a point almost as low as World War I. That's a long time ago. That's a long time ago. It's not going to happen anymore, folks. It's not going to happen anymore -- not with me.

But we will ensure no taxpayer dollars are wasted. I have already saved more than $700 million when I got involved in the negotiation on the F-35. You know about that. And I want to thank Lockheed Martin and I want to thank Boeing, and I want to thank all of the companies that have really opened up. And when I say opened up, Rick Scott understands this very well -- opened up and cut their prices. Okay? Because that's what they did. And we've got that program, it's going to be back in really great shape from really being very troubled.

And we are going to be taking care of our great veterans. We will make a historic financial investment in the Armed Forces of the United States and show the entire world that America stands with those who stand in defense of freedom. We have your back every hour, every day, now and always. That also means getting our allies to pay their fair share. It's been very unfair to us. We strongly support NATO. We only ask that all of the NATO members make their full and proper financial contributions to the NATO Alliance, which many of them have not been doing. Many of them have not been even close, and they have to do that.

Central Command and Central [Special] Operations Command are at the very center of our fight against radical Islamic terrorism. America stands in awe of your courage. Those serving at CENTCOM have bravely fought across the theater of war in the Middle East, and bravely battled a vicious enemy that has no respect for human life. Today, we express our gratitude to everyone serving overseas, including all of our military personnel in Afghanistan.

SOCOM has dispatched its legendary warriors to the most

secret, sensitive and daring missions in defense of the United States of America. No enemy stands a chance against our Special Forces -- not even a chance. They don't have a chance, and that's the way we're going to keep it. And you're going to be better off because you're going to have the finest equipment known to man. Going to be better off.

For proof that our nation has been blessed by God, look no further than the men and women of the United States military. They are the greatest fighters and the greatest force of justice on the face of the Earth and that the world has ever known. The challenges facing our nation nevertheless are very large -- very, very large.

We're up against an enemy that celebrates death and totally worships destruction -- you've seen that. ISIS is on a campaign of genocide, committing atrocities across the world. Radical Islamic terrorists are determined to strike our homeland as they did on 9/11; as they did from Boston to Orlando, to San Bernardino. And all across Europe, you've seen what happened in Paris and Nice. All over Europe it's happening. It's gotten to a point where it's not even being reported and, in many cases, the very, very dishonest press doesn't want to report it. They have their reasons and you understand that.

So today, we deliver a message in one very unified voice: To these forces of death and destruction, America and its allies will defeat you. We will defeat them. We will defeat radical Islamic terrorism, and we will not allow it to take root in our country. We're not going to allow it. You've been seeing what's been going on over the last few days. We need strong programs so that people that love us and want to love our country and will end up loving our country are allowed in -- not people that want to destroy us and destroy our country. (Applause.)

Freedom, security and justice will prevail. In his first State of the Union message, President George Washington wrote that, "To be prepared for war is one of the most effectual means of preserving peace."

Almost 200 years later, as the General was also speaking about Ronald Reagan, he said that wisdom comes in three very, very strong words: "Peace through Strength."

I've said it many times during the campaign, speaking in front of tens of thousands of people at one sitting, and I'd always mention **America First** -- a phrase that you probably never heard, "**Make America Great Again.**" (Applause.)

Anybody ever heard that? (Applause.)

And *Peace through Strength*.

The men and women of the United States military provide the strength to bring peace to our troubled, troubled times. We stand behind you. We support your mission. We love our country. We are loyal to our people. We respect our flag. We celebrate our traditions. We honor our heroes. You are our heroes. And we are prepared to fight. And we pray for peace.

Thank you. God bless you, and God bless America. Thank you very much. Thank you. (Applause.)

END
2:00 P.M. EST

Chapter 21

07 February 2017

9:49 A.M. EST

THE PRESIDENT: Oh, the sheriffs are great people. Well, thank you very much. Law enforcement was a big subject in the campaign and a subject that was very well received. You have no idea how respected you are, sheriffs and, generally speaking, the leaders of law enforcement. Anybody involved in law enforcement, you have no idea how respected you are -- you don't get the honest facts from the press -- if you don't know how respected you are. So I just want to say that upfront.

I'm honored to welcome the National Sheriffs' Association. Your leadership is here, and I know the great job you do. I've known you and followed you for a long period of time. Your efforts and your officers are outstanding. I know so many sheriffs from my area -- some in particular -- and they're great friends and great people.

I just want to let you know that our job is to help you in law enforcement, and we're going to help you do your job. We're going to expand access to abuse-deterring drugs, which a lot of you have been talking about. They're out, and they're very hard to get. Stop the opioid epidemic. We've got to do it. It's a new thing. And, honestly, people aren't talking about it enough. It's a new thing, and it's a new problem for you folks. It's probably a vast majority of your crimes -- or at least a very big portion of your crimes are caused by drugs.

We're going to stop the border. We're going to stop -- we're not going to have the drugs pouring from the border like they have been. We will work with you on supporting your longstanding efforts to strengthen the bonds between the communities and the police, which is very important. And it's sort a new phenomenon to a certain extent, and it's happening more and more. And some great results out when you can strengthen the bonds.

We're committed to securing our borders to reduce crime, illegal drugs, human trafficking, especially in border counties. We have a lot of the border counties represented. We're also committed to working with law enforcement to stop terrorist attacks. You've been reading about that, been seeing about that -- they want to take a lot of our powers away. There are some people with a lot of the wrong intentions, and it's -- we've got a lot of bad people out there.

And, Dana, I just want to thank you on behalf of the government, on behalf of our country for leading a strong, strong effort in the courts. We really appreciate it, believe me. Because as you know, we don't have an attorney general. We have somebody who's phenomenal -- Jeff Sessions. He's going to be there hopefully soon. But I believe it's about a record for the length of time that they've delayed the Cabinet. These are Cabinet members that are phenomenal people. And we haven't had representation, and now we have excellent representation, fortunately, in Dana. And Jeff will be with you very shortly, hopefully. But we're having a hard time getting approvals. And it's only a delay tactic -- it's all politics.

One person came up to me, a senator, a Democratic senator who came up to me the other day and said, Jeff Sessions is a fantastic man. He's fabulous. He's a friend of mine. He's a great, great man and a great talent. And we're lucky to have him. I said, oh, great, I guess that means you're voting for him? No, I won't be voting that. (Laughter.)

He said, politics doesn't allow me to do that.

I thought it was a disgrace. If the press talks loud and hard enough, I'll have to tell you who said that to me. You don't want to hear it. You don't want to hear who said that? (Laughter.)

I didn't think you'd care. I didn't think you'd care. I'll probably tell you, actually. Anyway.

So we're going to be very tough on crime. So we're going to be very tough on the drugs pouring in, and that's a big part of the crime. We're going to be very strong at the border. We have no choice. And we're going to be building a wall. We're starting very soon. General Kelly will be working with a lot of you. And he's fantastic. He was the one who got approved very quickly along with General Mattis. He's very, very outstanding. And I very much appreciate that you're here today.

And, Sheriff, I really thank you for leading the effort. Your reputation is fantastic, and it's a great honor to know you. Maybe we can go around -- we'll let the press stay for a little while, unless you'd rather leave. Would the press rather stay? Just so you understand. This is a new phenomenon. You're on live television all over the world right now, so don't get nervous when you speak, okay? (Laughter.)

But I don't think these things have ever taken place before. But you are on live television, so if you don't want to say anything, you don't have to. But if you do, I think it's a good thing to say. So maybe we'll just go around the room.

SHERIFF WELSH: Well, Mr. President, thank you so much for having us here. I'm Sheriff Carolyn Welsh from Chester County, Pennsylvania, and proud to say Pennsylvania, the commonwealth, that put you over the top November 8th.

THE PRESIDENT: It's true. (Laughter.)

SHERIFF WELSH: We're very proud of that. We don't stop bragging about that.

THE PRESIDENT: You were a great support.

SHERIFF WELSH: Thank you. And I just want to thank you for, during the campaign and since the campaign, being such a strong, courageous supporter of law enforcement on the national -- on the federal level with the Border Patrol, on the state level, and the counties, municipalities, boroughs, and particularly with the elected sheriffs of the counties -- because we are the sheriff, we are the people's representative, and we are elected by the people, and we greatly appreciate your strong and continued support.

THE PRESIDENT: Thank you, Carolyn. There's a new sheriff in town.

SHERIFF WELSH: That's right.

THE PRESIDENT: I hear this so much. (Laughter.)

I hear this so much, Dana. They always use, "there's a new sheriff in town." So anyway.

SHERIFF EAVENSON: Sheriff Harold Eavenson from Rockwall County, Texas. We appreciate your support very much. Our county is probably about 85 percent Republican. So it was pretty easy for you --

THE PRESIDENT: They were very nice. I agree. They were very nice.

SHERIFF EAVENSON: And being in a border state, I have been to the border in Texas any number of times, been to the border in Arizona. I clearly understand the problem we have. And previously when we'd go to the border and hear what the ranchers and sheriffs have to say -- those border sheriffs and border ranchers, it was a 180 degrees from what we heard from the previous administration.

THE PRESIDENT: So you're seeing a big difference?

SHERIFF EAVENSON: We're very proud to have you as President.

THE PRESIDENT: And that's only two weeks. Okay? It's a very short period of time. I'm hearing it from a lot of people. People are calling in and they're -- and people I know that are in the area, they're saying it's like day and night. Because we're not playing games. We're not playing games. We're stopping the drugs from pouring into our country and poisoning our youth. So thank you very much. I appreciate it.

SHERIFF EAVENSON: You're welcome.

MR. THOMPSON: Mr. President, I'm Jonathan Thompson, the executive director and CEO of the National Sheriffs' Association. Let me tell you the difference of six months. I sat in this room, in this chair, and I was pleading -- I was begging for help. Today, you've invited us here to your home. You're offering help. You're delivering on that offer. And on behalf of our members across the country, thank you.

THE PRESIDENT: Thank you very much. It's so nice. I appreciate that.

SHERIFF STANEK: Mr. President, Rich Stanek from Hennepin County, Minneapolis, Minnesota.

First off, thank you very much. As Ms. Conway said, next time, up by three points in my state -- over the top.

THE PRESIDENT: Boy, we almost won your state. You know we weren't supposed to do very well in your state, and we won -- lost by one point. I say, if I went there one more visit we would have won. (Laughter.)

We would have won Minnesota. But it was very close.

SHERIFF STANEK: Many of us have your back, Mr. President.

THE PRESIDENT: Thank you, I know.

SHERIFF STANEK: And I just want to say that you hit on two topics that are near and dear to my heart. The first is opioids -- 144 people that died last year as a result of opioid overdose; 31 percent increase over the year before. We need help. Eighty-plus percent of the drugs come from south of the border. Everybody knows it. I know you will do something about it.

THE PRESIDENT: I will. It's already being done, believe me. It's a big, big difference. And we will do that, and you do have a big problem, and you have a big problem with the refugees pouring in, don't you?

SHERIFF STANEK: Yes, we do, sir. And we all asking if what you're doing, which is let the courts decide, do what we've been doing. Rule of law is strong and the proper vetting of individuals is really important to us.

THE PRESIDENT: Well, you know, the vetting is much, much tougher now. And we need this court case. It will be very helpful to keeping the wrong people out of our country. You understand that better than anybody. So I think we're going to have some good results.

SHERIFF STANEK: I do, sir.

THE PRESIDENT: It may take a little while. And you know, this is a very dangerous period of time because while everybody is talking and dealing, a lot of bad people are thinking about, hey, let's go in right now. But we're being very, very tough with the vetting -- tougher than ever before.

SHERIFF STANEK: Sir, I chaired the Homeland Security Committee for the National Sheriffs' Association. We heard from General Kelly yesterday, his message was right on the mark about carrying out your directives, and we appreciate that.

THE PRESIDENT: That used to be a political position, you know, what General Kelly is doing here right now. Homeland Security, if you remember -- it's like a political position. Not anymore. Now it's, in my opinion, one of truly most important positions. So he's doing a great job. Thank you very much.

SHERIFF STANEK: Thank you, sir.

THE PRESIDENT: Yes, sir.

SHERIFF GLICK: Mr. President, thank you. It's such an honor to be here. I'm Danny Glick, sheriff of Laramie County, Wyoming. You know, there are so many issues that you'll hear going around this table. One of the ones that probably isn't -- that people don't realize is EPA decisions that have affected our coal industry, our oil industry in the West. But beyond that, it increases the number of people that are jobless and thus increases our crime statistics. And it's starting to overwhelm us. We're very small out there for the most part, and we don't have the numbers of deputies, officers and law enforcement that can sometimes keep up with this. I appreciate what you've done and what you're planning in the future. I think it was very well publicized, and I just appreciate being here today.

THE PRESIDENT: Thank you, Sheriff. And I will tell you that the EPA -- you're right. I call it -- it's clogged the bloodstream of our country. People can't do anything. People are looking to get approvals for factories for 15 years, and then after the 15th year they get voted down after having spent a fortune. So that's going to end. We have one of our really great people -- as you know, Scott is looking to be approved by the Senate. We're still waiting for that one, too. It's a disgrace what's going on. But as soon as he gets involved, we're going to unclog the system.

And, by the way, people are going to get rejected, but they're going to get rejected quickly. But for the most part, they're going to be accepted when they want to do. We're going to bring the jobs back. And your state was very, very good to me, as you know. I mean, they were very, very good to me and I appreciate that. And just tell the people we're going to get the system unclogged and we're going to get it up.

As you know, I approved two pipelines that were stuck in limbo forever. I don't even think it was controversial. You know, I approved them -- I haven't even heard -- I haven't had one call from anybody saying, oh, that was a terrible thing you did. I haven't had one call. You know, usually, if I do something it's like bedlam, right? I haven't had one call from anybody. And a lot of jobs -- in the Keystone case, we have potentially 32,000 jobs almost immediately. And then, as you know, I did the Dakota pipeline and nobody called up to complain. Because it was unfair. Years of getting approvals, nobody showed up to fight it. This company spends a tremendous -- hundreds and hundreds of millions of dollars, and then all of a sudden, people show up to fight it. It's not fair to our companies. And I think everyone is going to be happy in the end, okay?

So I appreciate it very much, Sheriff. It's a great honor to have you here. Thank you. And say hello to your people. Yes, sir.

SHERIFF LAYTON: Good morning, Mr. President. I'm John Layton. I'm the sheriff of Marion County, Indiana, which is... (Laughter.)

THE PRESIDENT: You never met our great Vice President. (Laughter.)

SHERIFF LAYTON: I'm very proud of this man. And we as sheriffs -- this is, to me, it seems like it's unprecedented. I look back into the history of the NSA, long before myself, and I never have -- I could never find where -- not only did the President and now the Vice President, as well, has invited us into your house to share some concerns of ours --

THE PRESIDENT: And in about 10 minutes, you're going to see the Oval Office, too, which is -- that's the other thing, you know, people have had meetings here. I had the car companies, the biggest companies -- Ford, General Motors, Fiat -- and they were in this room often. And I said, oh, so you've seen the Oval Office? "No, we've never been invited to see the Oval Office." You know where the Oval Office is? Ten feet in that direction -- 10 feet.

SHERIFF LAYTON: Looking forward to it. (Laughter.)

THE PRESIDENT: Look, these are the biggest people that were going there -- these are the biggest people. So they were never invited to the Oval Office and they were only 10 feet away. You would think they would be invited. But you're going to see the Oval Office, okay?

SHERIFF LAYTON: Thank you, Mr. President. One of the main concerns was not just my office as sheriff, but across the nation -- the mentally ill in the jails, and the people that they're being really, for lack of a better term, warehoused in our jails across America because we don't have the facilities necessary to take care of them on the outside. And it ends up a lot of these people go to jail because the public or the police officer happens to be mad at them at the time, instead of they need to be in the jail for a very good reason. So we just appreciate you having the back of law enforcement. We do all feel that, as everyone with a badge knows, that you do have our backs and that we're looking forward to years of harmony and taking care of business with the people we serve.

THE PRESIDENT: Well, I appreciate it. And I will say that, in the recent election, law enforcement is with me. I mean, the numbers were staggering -- staggering. It wasn't like, gee, it's 51-49. Believe me, it was through the roof. Law enforcement and military also.

SHERIFF LAYTON: Absolutely.

THE PRESIDENT: I think, generally, people in uniform tend to like me. (Laughter.)

Explain that to me. Dana, explain that to me. (Laughter.)

So, Sheriff, thank you very much. And do you miss your former governor?

SHERIFF LAYTON: We do, we do.

THE PRESIDENT: You have a good new governor.

SHERIFF LAYTON: Holcomb is holding down the fort for us, though, but big shoes for him to fill.

THE PRESIDENT: Mike Pence has been fantastic.

SHERIFF LAYTON: Yes, he has.

THE PRESIDENT: Dana, I want to thank you for your service. Amazing the way you just stepped into the breach and have done such a good job. And let's see what happens with the court case.

MR. BOENTE: Well, Mr. President, thank you for the privilege to serve you and the Department of Justice and the American people. I'm very honored by it. And I want to thank all the sheriffs here, but I guess our local and state partners -- it's very important to federal law enforcement and all the agencies. And I know that Senator Sessions -- we're looking forward to him getting to the Department -- will make that an important priority. And he wants to strengthen that bond that we have with them because it's very, very important to law enforcement.

THE PRESIDENT: Yes, well, thank you very much. And, you know, one of the things that you know better than anybody is that we had a very good victory in Boston. So I said to everybody, why don't we use the Boston case? Why aren't we using the Boston case? Because the Boston victory was great, but it's statutorily.

MR. BOENTE: Judge Gordon, who wrote that decision, had a very good analysis where he referred to immigration law, and I thought it was a terrific opinion. And I think it's the right opinion.

THE PRESIDENT: And a highly respected judge, too. So I appreciate it. Thank you, Dana, very much. Appreciate it.

SHERIFF PAGE: Mr. President, I'm Sheriff Page from Rockingham County, North Carolina. And you did very well in North Carolina. (Laughter.)

And I just want to...

THE PRESIDENT: Go North Carolina.

SHERIFF PAGE: Hey! (Laughter.)

And I just want to say that we appreciate you being where you're at. The first responsibility of government is protecting its people. As we as elected by the people and you're elected by the people, we got that. When you say there's a new sheriff in town, we relate to that. You're about the rule of law. We haven't seen that in many years, and we appreciate that.

And I want to tell you something -- when General Kelly was speaking yesterday for the sheriffs, he made -- he was telling us about -- he went -- I saw something that I haven't seen before. He went to the border, he looked at the assets, and he asked the law enforcement down there, what's going on and what can we do to help fix the situation down here.

So you've got a good team. You're putting together a good team. You've got the support of sheriffs from across the country, and we appreciate what you're doing.

THE PRESIDENT: Well, thank you. And a funny story -- so when General Kelly was just sworn in, now Secretary Kelly, and I said, you want to have dinner tonight and we'll talk? "Sir, I'm heading to the border." I said, I like that better. (Laughter.)

We don't need to eat. I said, I like that better. So he's right on the ball, he's going to be fantastic. Because everybody has said the same thing.

Thank you. That's very nice.

SHERIFF PAGE: Thank you, sir.

SHERIFF MAHONEY: Good morning, Mr. President. Dave Mahoney, I'm the sheriff in Dane County, which is Madison, Wisconsin. I want to thank you for inviting our nation's sheriffs into the White House. You know, as the only elected law enforcement leaders in our community, we are the most engaged in our community's issues and concerns. And I think it's important. I think there's a strong message when the President of the United States invites our nation's sheriffs in to talk about those issues that are of importance in our community.

THE PRESIDENT: Has this ever happened before with the sheriffs?

PARTICIPANT: No, sir.

PARTICIPANT: No, sir.

THE PRESIDENT: It never happened?

PARTICIPANT: Never.

THE PRESIDENT: And yet the murder rate in our country is the highest it's been in 47 years, right? Did you know that? Forty-seven years. I used to use that -- I'd say that in a speech and everybody was surprised, because the press doesn't tell it like it is. It wasn't to their advantage to say that. But the murder rate is the highest it's been in, I guess, from 45 to 47 years. And you would think that you would be invited here, and you would think that you people would be able to solve -- had you -- if you ran Chicago, you would solve that nightmare, I tell you. I'll bet everybody in that room, especially Carolyn, right, would raise their hand. Because to allow -- I mean, literally -- hundreds of shootings a month, it's worse than some of the places that we read about in the Middle East, where you have wars going on. It's so sad. Chicago has become so sad a situation.

SHERIFF MAHONEY: I'm only three hours from downtown Chicago, and as Sheriff Stanek mentioned, the issues of heroin and opiate addiction -- I'm averaging 12, 15 overdoses a week in my community. And we need help from DEA, FBI, and our task forces. We need them to be adequately funded and led by leaders who want to work collectively with our nation's sheriffs.

THE PRESIDENT: How much of your crime is caused, do you think, by drugs generally?

SHERIFF MAHONEY: Eighty-percent?

THE PRESIDENT: Eighty percent. So without drugs, you would have a whole different ballgame.

SHERIFF MAHONEY: I have a jail, over 1,000 beds. Eighty percent suffer from chronic drug and alcohol addiction.

THE PRESIDENT: And when did it start, big league? Or has it been going on for many years?

SHERIFF MAHONEY: Well, I think heroin and opiates have overshadowed cocaine, which of course has been, since the eighties, our number-one drug of choice. Now it's prescription painkillers and --

THE PRESIDENT: And at a much higher level?

SHERIFF MAHONEY: At a higher level.

THE PRESIDENT: Much higher.

SHERIFF MAHONEY: The overdoses are at a much higher level.

THE PRESIDENT: Right, right.

PARTICIPANT: Mr. President, I hate to interrupt -- it used to take 90 days to take a load of heroin from the border to get it into the (inaudible) mainstream. Now it's taking 14 days.

THE PRESIDENT: Okay, well, we'll have it take infinity, okay? (Laughter.)

SHERIFF MAHONEY: I want to thank you too for seeking the input and guidance of our nation's sheriffs on issues like immigration. My community is looking for immigration reform, an expedited way for a good immigrant to obtain citizenship in this great country. And I appreciate the invitation today to join you, and look forward to working with you on many of these issues. Some we'll disagree on, but far more we're going to agree on.

THE PRESIDENT: Absolutely, you're right. I actually can't believe that we're having to fight to protect the security -- in a court system to protect the security of our nation. I can't even believe it. And a lot of people agree with us, believe me. There's a group of people out there -- and I mean much more than half of our country -- much, much more. You're not allowed to use the term "silent majority" anymore. You're not allowed, because they make that into a whole big deal.

But there's a group of people out there -- massive, massive numbers, far bigger than what you see protesting. And if those people ever protested, you would see a real protest. But they want to see our borders secure and our country secure, and they want to see people that can love our country come in, not people that are looking to destroy our country.

So anyway, thank you, Sheriff.

SHERIFF AUBREY: Sheriff John Aubrey, fifth-term sheriff, Jefferson County, Kentucky. Past president of National Sheriffs' Association. And my fellow sheriffs have brought up a number of points, and I'd like to add two to it that I know are on your plate and the administration's plate. The 1033 program, where we were sharing Department of Defense surplus material that helps us in our war. They were used in the war, and they helped us in our war. That got severely curtailed.

And the other thing is asset forfeiture. People want to say we're taking money and without due process. That's not true. We take money from dope dealers --

THE PRESIDENT: So you're saying -- okay, so you're saying the asset-taking you used to do, and it had an impact, right? And you're not allowed to do it now?

SHERIFF AUBREY: No, they have curtailed it a little bit. And I'm sure the folks are --

THE PRESIDENT: And that's for legal reasons? Or just political reasons?

SHERIFF AUBREY: They make it political and they make it

-- they make up stories. All you've got to do --

THE PRESIDENT: I'd like to look into that, okay? There's no reason for that. Dana, do you think there's any reason for that? Are you aware of this?

MR. BOENTE: I am aware of that, Mr. President. And we have gotten a great deal of criticism for the asset for-feiture, which, as the sheriff said, frequently was taking narcotics proceeds and other proceeds of crime. But there has been a lot of pressure on the department to curtail some of that.

THE PRESIDENT: So what do you do? So in other words, they have a huge stash of drugs. So in the old days, you take it. Now we're criticized if we take it. So who gets it? What happens to it? Tell them to keep it?

MR. BOENTE: Well, we have what is called equitable sharing, where we usually share it with the local police departments for whatever portion that they worked on the case. And it was a very successful program, very popular with the law enforcement community.

THE PRESIDENT: And now what happens?

MR. BOENTE: Well, now we've just been given -- there's been a lot of pressure not to forfeit, in some cases.

THE PRESIDENT: Who would want that pressure, other than, like, bad people, right? But who would want that pressure? You would think they'd want this stuff taken away.

SHERIFF AUBREY: You have to be careful how you speak, I

guess. But a lot of pressure is coming out of -- was coming out of Congress. I don't know that that will continue now or not.

THE PRESIDENT: I think less so. I think Congress is going to get beat up really badly by the voters because they've let this happen. And I think badly. I think you'll be back in shape. So, asset forfeiture, we're going to go back on, okay?

SHERIFF AUBREY: Thank you, sir.

THE PRESIDENT: I mean; how simple can anything be? You all agree with that, I assume, right?

PARTICIPANT: Absolutely, yeah.

THE PRESIDENT: Do you even understand the other side of it?

PARTICIPANT: No.

THE PRESIDENT: It's like some things...

PARTICIPANT: No sense.

THE PRESIDENT: Sort of like the Iran deal. Nobody even understands how a thing like that could have happened. It does nothing.

PARTICIPANT: You shouldn't be allowed to profit from the illegal proceeds. So if you're going to sell narcotics and sell illegal drugs in our country, you also cannot profit from that. And so we seize those profits.

THE PRESIDENT: So do we need any legislation or any executive orders for that, would you say, Dana -- to put that back in business?

MR. BOENTE: I don't think we need any executive orders. We just need kind of some encouragement to move in that direction.

THE PRESIDENT: Okay. Good. You're in charge. (Laughter.) I love that answer, because it's better than signing executive orders and then these people take it and they make it look so terrible, "oh, it's so terrible." I love it. You're encouraged.

PARTICIPANT: Thank you.

THE PRESIDENT: Good. Asset forfeiture. You're encouraged. Okay. Yes, sir.

MR. BITTICK: Mr. President, we appreciate you having us here today at the White House. My name is John Cary Bittick, and I'm a sheriff in Monroe County, Georgia. And I'm a past president of the National Sheriffs Association, as well. And I currently chair our governmental affairs committee. And I just want to thank you for the administration working actually on pieces of legislation and on political ideas with us. It's refreshing, and we are thoroughly enjoying it. We are currently working with Senator Grassley on some criminal justice reform issues. And the administration has been supporting us. And asset forfeiture is a big thing.

THE PRESIDENT: Okay, go for it. Just go for it. Dana will tell me if I can't or if. (Laughter.)

MR. BITTICK: Yes, sir. I think they got that message.

THE PRESIDENT: Okay, that's great.

MR. BITTICK: But we appreciate it, and we appreciate your ear. And we appreciate you taking the time to sit down and at least talk to us.

THE PRESIDENT: I appreciate it too. Thank you, John.

MR. BITTICK: Thanks for your support.

THE PRESIDENT: Thank you.

SHERIFF CHAMPAGNE: Thank you, Mr. President, Mr. Vice President. Greg Champagne, I am sheriff in St. Charles Parish, Louisiana, basically a suburban community outside of New Orleans. I have the honor of representing 3,088 sheriffs around the country. And you see the leadership of our organization. These are the leadership of past presidents and the future presidents of our agency. But more importantly than that, we all represent and oversee literally a few hundred thousand deputy sheriffs who are truly the backbone of law enforcement in this country. We have a bumper sticker the NSA puts out that says, "Sheriffs and deputies: The original homeland security." And so that is a force-multiplier.

Those men and women out there are the tip of the spear, and we stand ready to help and keep this community safe, because that's what we're all elected to do. So we thank you so much for having us.

THE PRESIDENT: Thank you very much. You're a great group of people.

We're going to go into the Oval Office. Does anybody have anything to -- not even a question, a statement, as to how we can bring about law enforcement in a very good, civil, lovely way, but we have to stop crime -- right? Would anybody like to make a statement?

PARTICIPANT: Mr. President, on asset forfeiture, we got a state senator in Texas who was talking about introducing legislation to require conviction before we can receive their forfeiture.

THE PRESIDENT: Can you believe that?

PARTICIPANT: And I told him that the cartel would build a monument to him in Mexico if he could get that legislation.

THE PRESIDENT: Who is the state senator? Want to give his name? We'll destroy his career. (Laughter.)
Okay, thank you.

PARTICIPANT: Mr. President, we have been invited to the White House before. We've sat at this table with the former administration. This is totally different. Not once did the President go around the room and ask the sheriffs what were issues that were important to us, he or she, in our parts of the country, but rather it was an outgoing message about gun control, about other things. You asked us what is important to us, whether it's mental health in the jails, opioid addiction. You hit it right off the bat. The border, immigration, vetting. We appreciate that. That has not happened before. We've been here before, but we've never had a President sit down and listen to what it is that we're facing representing our constituents and public safety across this country. And that's why we appreciate it. That's why we're here today.

THE PRESIDENT: You know, Bill Belichick, is a great guy, a friend of mine. And he was telling me -- somebody told me that he'll oftentimes, wanting to get a player, he'll go to the other players on the team -- he'll say, what do you think of this guy? You know, they all the different people. And he'll listen to them. And he's done very well, right? He's done very well. And essentially what they're -- we're talking to the people that know -- I'm not telling you, you're telling me. That came up this morning. I mean, that was a big statement. And I didn't realize it was all clogged. The system is all clogged. So we're going to unclog the system, and we're going to go right now into the Oval Office.

Would you like the press to come in with you, Mr. Vice President? Should we let them come in? Otherwise they're going turn around, waiting for the next meeting for six hours. They don't have such an easy job, I'll tell you. They don't have such an easy job.

Q   Mr. President, how far are you willing to take your travel ban fight?

THE PRESIDENT: Oh, we're going to take it through the system. It's very important. It's very important for the country, regardless of me or whoever succeeds at a later date. I mean, we have to have security in our country. We have to have the ability. When you take some place like Syria, when you take all of the different people pouring -- and if you remember, ISIS said, we are going to infiltrate the United States and other countries through the migration. And then we're not allowed to be tough on the people coming in? Explain that one.

So we'll see what happens. We have big court case. We're

well-represented. And we're going to see what happens.

Q   Is it going to go to the Supreme Court, you think?

THE PRESIDENT: It could. We will see. Hopefully it doesn't
have to. It's common sense. You know, some things are
law, and I'm all in favor of that. And some things are common sense. This is common sense.

Q   Mr. President, if it's unreported or under-reported --
"unreported" is the phrase you used yesterday -- but if it's
under-reported, why do you think the media is not reporting, or America is not caring about this type of...

THE PRESIDENT: I have to know, because I'm reported on
possibly more than anybody in the world -- I don't think
you have anything to say about that. I happen to know
how dishonest the media is. I happen to know stories
about me that should be good -- or bad -- you know; I
don't mind a bad story if it's true. But I don't like bad
stories that -- stories that should be a positive story when
they make them totally negative. I understand the total
dishonesty of the media better than anybody. And I let
people know it. I mean, the media is a very, very dishonest
arm, and we'll see what happens. Not everybody. And I
have to say that. I always preface it by saying, not everybody. But there's tremendous dishonest -- pure, outright
dishonesty from the media.

Let's go into the Oval Office.

(Meeting moves to Oval Office.)

THE PRESIDENT: So they said this is the first President
they've ever seen with all the papers on their desk. (Inau-

dible) cutting the price of the F-35 fighters. We have a lot of papers.

Okay, go ahead, folks.

PARTICIPANT: Mr. President, on behalf of 3,088 sheriffs in America, there is a new sheriff in town, and it's only fitting that we provide you with our sculpture. The first time the NSA has provided a sculpture to a non-law enforcement person. And there is a new sheriff in town -- for you.

THE PRESIDENT: Thank you so much. Thank you. (Applause.)

It's beautiful.

END
10:21 A.M. EST

"Stop the opioid epidemic.
We've got to do it.
It's a new thing."

Chapter 22

**REMARKS BY PRESIDENT TRUMP AT
MCCA WINTER
CONFERENCE
J.W. MARRIOTT
WASHINGTON, D.C.**

08 February 2017

9:18 A.M. EST

THE PRESIDENT: Thank you very much. This is -- great to be with people I truly feel comfortable with. Please sit down. They'll say I didn't get a standing ovation because they never sat down. (Laughter.)

And I say, I got one standing ovation because they never sat down.

But I want to thank you. I have great, great love for what you do and the way you do it. And when I'm with the police chiefs and I'm with the sheriffs of our country -- and these are the big ones. These are the really big ones. I just want to thank you very much. And I thought before I spoke about what we're really here to speak about, I would read something to you. Because you can be a lawyer, or you don't have to be a lawyer; if you were a good student in high school or a bad student in high school, you can understand this.

And it's really incredible to me that we have a court case that's going on so long. As you know, in Boston, we won it with a highly respected judge and a very strong opinion, but now we're in an era that, let's just say, they are interpreting things differently than probably 100 percent of the people in this room. I'd like to almost know; does anybody disagree when I read this.

But I'm going to read what's in dispute, what's in question. And you will see this -- it's INA 212(f) 8 U.S.C. 1182(f): "Suspension of entry or imposition of restrictions by the President" -- okay, now, this isn't just me, this is for Obama, for Ronald Reagan, for the President. And this was done, very importantly, for security -- something you people know more about than all of us. It was done for the security of our nation, the security of our citizens, so that people come in who aren't going to do us harm.

And that's why it was done. And it couldn't have been written any more precisely. It's not like, oh, gee, we wish it were written better. It was written beautifully. So just listen, here's what it says. This is what they're arguing: "Whenever the President finds that the entry of any aliens" -- okay, the entry, the entry of any aliens -- "or of any class of aliens" -- so any aliens, any class of aliens -- "into the United States" -- so the entry of people into the United States. Let's say, just to be precise, of aliens into the United States.

So any time -- "whenever the President finds that the entry of any alien or any class of aliens into the United States would be detrimental to the interests of the United States" -- right? So if I find, as President, that a person or group of people will be detrimental to the interests of the United States -- and certainly there's lots of examples that we have, but you shouldn't even have them, necessarily -- he may be -- and "he may by proclamation, and for such period as he shall deem necessary..." Now, the only mistake is they should have said "he or she." But hopefully, it won't be a she for at least another seven years. After that, I'm all -- (laughter and applause.) See? I just noticed that, actually. I just noticed it. I'm saying, whoa, this is not politically correct. It's correct, but it's not politically correct, you know, this is the old days.

He may by proclamation and for such period as he shall deem necessary -- so here it is, people coming in -- suspend the entry of all aliens. Right? That's what it says. It's not like -- again, a bad high school student would understand this. Anybody would understand this. Suspend the entry of all aliens or any class of aliens as immigrants or non-immigrants, or impose on the entry of aliens. Okay, so you can suspend the aliens, right? You can suspend the aliens from coming in -- very strong -- or impose on the entry of aliens any restrictions he may deem to be appropriate. Okay. So you can suspend, you can put restrictions, you can do whatever you want. And this is for the security of the country -- which, again, you're the chiefs, you're the sheriffs. You understand this.

And I listened to lawyers on both sides last night, and they were talking about things that had just nothing to do with it. I listened to a panel of judges, and I'll comment on that -- I will not comment on the statements made by certainly one judge. But I have to be honest that if these judges wanted to, in my opinion, help the court in terms of respect for the court, they'd what they should be doing. I mean, it's so sad.

They should be -- when you read something so simple and so beautifully written, and so perfectly written -- other than the one statement, of course, having to do with he or she -- but when you read something so perfectly written and so clear to anybody, and then you have lawyers and you watched -- I watched last night in amazement, and I heard things that I couldn't believe, things that really had nothing to do with what I just read.

And I don't ever want to call a court biased, so I won't call it biased. And we haven't had a decision yet. But courts seem to be so political, and it would be so great for our justice system if they would be able to read a statement and do what's right. And that has to do with the security of our country, which is so important.

Right now, we are at risk because of what happened. General Kelly is an extremely talented man and a very good man -- now Secretary Kelly, Homeland Security. We are doing our job. He's a great man. (Applause.)

We're doing our job. And one of the reasons you probably heard that we did it so quickly -- in fact, I said, let's give a one-month notice, and then law enforcement -- and General Kelly was so great because he said, we totally knew about it. We knew about everything. We do things well. We did things right.

But the law enforcement people said to me, oh, you can't give a notice, because if you give a notice that you're going to be really tough in one month from now, or in one week from now -- I suggested a month and I said, well, what about a week? They said, no, you can't do that, because then people are going to pour in before the toughness goes on. Do you people agree? I mean, you know more about law than anybody, law enforcement. (Applause.)

So I wanted to give, like, a month. Then I said, well, what about a week? They said, well, then you're going to have a whole pile of people perhaps -- perhaps -- with very evil intentions coming in before the restrictions.

So there it is, folks. It's as plain as you can have it. I didn't -- and I was a good student. I understand things. I comprehend very well, okay? Better than I think almost anybody. And I want to tell you, I listened to a bunch of stuff last night on television that was disgraceful. It was disgraceful. Because what I just read to you is what we have, and it just can't be written any plainer or better. And for us to be going through this -- and, by the way, a highly, highly respected judge in Boston ruled very strongly in our favor. You heard that.

In fact, I said to my people, why don't you use the Boston case? And there were reasons why they couldn't use the Boston case. This one came later for various reasons. But use the Boston case. And I won't read that, but there were statements made by that judge -- who, again, highly respected -- that were right on. They were perfect. They were perfect.

So I think it's sad. I think it's a sad day. I think our security is at risk today. And it will be at risk until such time as we are entitled and get what we are entitled to as citizens of this country. As chiefs, as sheriffs of this country, we want security.

One of the reasons I was elected was because of law and order and security. It's one of the reasons I was elect-ed. Also jobs and lots of other things. But I think one of the strongest reasons is security. And they're taking away our weapons one by one, that's what they're doing. And you know it and I know it, and you people have been very unhappy for a long period of time. And I can read the polls maybe better than anybody because it seems that I understood the polls a lot better than many of the pollsters understood the polls -- assuming they were honest polls, which I think probably many of them weren't. I really believe that. (Applause.)

But we need security in our country. We have to allow you folks to do your job. You're great people, great people. Great men and women. And we have to allow you to do your job. And we have to give you the weapons that you need. And this is a weapon that you need. And they're trying to take it away from you, maybe because of politics or maybe because of political views. We can't let that happen.

So with that, let's get on to business, right? It's really something. Thank you. (Applause.)

I want to thank Sheriff Sandra Hutchens and Chief Tom Manger for your leadership and, frankly, for the service. You have had great service. Everyone has told me about you two legendary people. All of us here today are united by one shared mission: to serve and protect the public of the United States.

During my campaign for President, I had the chance to spend time with law enforcement officials all across our country. They are the most incredible people you will ever meet. And I just wanted to say to all of them right now, from the bottom of my heart, thank you, thank you, thank you. (Applause.)

There are many actions we in the federal government can take to help improve safety in your communities. But I believe that community safety begins with moral leadership. Our police officers, sheriffs and deputies risk their lives every day. And they're entitled to an administration that has their back. (Applause.)

The first step in restoring **public safety** is affirming our confidence in the men and women charged with upholding our laws. And I'm going to add justices, judges in that category. And I'm very proud to have picked Judge Gorsuch, who I think is going to be an outstanding member of the Supreme Court -- outstanding. (Applause.)

So I'd like to begin my remarks with a declaration issued to all of you, and delivered to every member of the law enforcement community all across the United States. My message today is that you have a true, true friend in the White House. You have. (Applause.)

I stand with you. I support our police. I support our sheriffs. And we support the men and women of law enforcement. (Applause.)

Right now, many communities in America are facing a public safety crisis. Murders in 2015 experienced their largest single-year increase in nearly half a century. In 2016, murders in large cities continued to climb by double digits. In many of our biggest cities, 2016 brought an increase in the number of homicides, rapes, assaults and shootings. In Chicago, more than 4,000 people were shot last year alone, and the rate so far this year has been even higher. What is going on in Chicago?

We cannot allow this to continue. We've allowed too many young lives to be claimed -- and you see that, you see that all over -- claimed by gangs, and too many neighborhoods to be crippled by violence and fear. Sixty percent of murder victims under the age of 22 are African American. This is a national tragedy, and it requires national action. This violence must end, and we must all work together to end it.

Whether a child lives in Detroit, Chicago, Baltimore, or anywhere in our country, he or she has the right to grow up in **safety** and in peace. No one in America should be punished because of the city where he or she is born. Every child in America should be able to play outside without fear, walk home without danger, and attend a school without being worried about drugs or gangs or violence.

So many lives and so many people have been cut short. Their potential, their life has been cut short. So much potential has been side-lined. And so many **dreams** have been shattered and broken, totally broken. It's time to stop the drugs from pouring into our country. And, by the way, we will do that. And I will say this: General, now Secretary, Kelly will be the man to do it, and we will give him a wall. And it will be a real wall. (Applause.)

And a lot of things will happen very positively for your cities, your states, believe me. The wall is getting designed right now. A lot of people say, oh, oh, Trump was only kidding with the wall. I wasn't kidding. I don't kid. I don't kid. I watch this, and they say I was kidding. No, I don't kid. I don't kid about things like that, I can tell you. No, we will have a wall. It will be a great wall, and it will do a lot of -- will be a big help. Just ask Israel about walls. Do walls work? Just ask Israel. They work -- if it's properly done. It's time to dismantle the gangs terrorizing our citizens, and it's time to ensure that every young American can be raised in an environment of decency, dignity, love and support. You have asked for the resources, tools and support you need to get the job done. We will do whatever we can to help you meet those demands. That includes a zero tolerance policy for acts of violence against law enforcement. (Applause.)

We all see what happens. We all see what happens and what's been happening to you. It's not fair.

We must protect those who protect us. The number of officers shot and killed in the line of duty last year increased by 56 percent from the year before. Last year, in Dallas, police officers were targeted for execution — think of this. Who ever heard of this? They were targeted for execution. Twelve were shot and five were killed. These heroic officers died as they lived -– protecting the innocent, rushing into danger, risking their lives for people they did not even know, but for people that they were determined to save. Hats off to you people.

These slain officers are an eternal monument to all of the men and women who protect our streets and serve our public. We will not forget them, and we will not forget all of the others who made that final sacrifice in the line of duty.

God has blessed our nation to put these heroes among us. Those who serve in law enforcement work long hours. You work long hours. I know so many sheriffs, so many chiefs, so many police who work long hours and dangerous hours, oftentimes in difficult conditions and for not that much pay relative to what you're doing. They do it because they care.

We must work with them, not against them. They're working against you. For many years they've been working against you. We must support them, not undermine them. And instead of division and disunity -- and which is so much disunity -- we must build bridges of partnership and of trust. Those who demonize law enforcement or who use the actions of a few to discredit the service of many are hurting the very people they say that they want to help. When policing is reduced, crime is increased, and our poorest citizens suffer the most. And I see it all the time. When the number of police goes down, crime goes up.

To build needed trust between law enforcement and the communities they serve, it is not enough for us to merely talk to each other. We must listen to each other. All of us share the view that those in uniform must be held to the highest possible standard of conduct -- so important.

You're the role models to young Americans all across this country, many of whom want to go into law enforcement, many of whom want to be a sheriff or a police chief, many of whom -- they have great respect for you. Tremendous respect. You don't even realize it, but I will tell you, they have great respect and admiration for the people in this room and the people that you represent. And don't let anyone ever tell you different. Don't let the dishonest media try and convince you that it's different than that, because it's not. (Applause.)

That is why our commitment to law and law enforcement also includes ensuring that we are giving departments the resources they need to train, recruit and retain talent. As part of our commitment to safe communities, we will also work to address the mental health crisis. Prisons should not be a substitute for treatment. We will fight to increase access to life-saving treatment to battle the addiction to drugs, which is afflicting our nation like never ever before -- ever. (Applause.)

I've been here two weeks. I've met a lot of law enforcement officials. Yesterday, I brought them into the Oval Office. I asked a group, what impact do drugs have in terms of a percentage on crime? They said, 75 to 80 percent. That's pretty sad. We're going to stop the drugs from pouring in. We're going to stop those drugs from poisoning our youth, from poisoning our people. We're going to be ruthless in that fight. We have no choice. (Applause.)

And we're going to take that fight to the drug cartels and work to liberate our communities from their terrible grip of violence. You have the power and knowledge to tell General Kelly -- now Secretary Kelly -- who the illegal immigrant gang members are. Now, you have that power because you know them, you're there, you're local. You know the illegals, you know them by their first name, you know them by their nicknames. You have that power. The federal government can never be that precise. But you're in the neighborhoods -- you know the bad ones, you know the good ones.

I want you to turn in the bad ones. Call Secretary Kelly's representatives and we'll get them out of our country and bring them back where they came from, and we'll do it fast. You have to call up the federal government, Homeland Security, because so much of the problems -- you look at Chicago and you look at other places. So many of the problems are caused by gang members, many of whom are not even legally in our country.

And we will work with you on the frontlines to keep

America **safe** from terrorism, which is what I began this with. Terrorism -- a tremendous threat, far greater than people in our country understand. Believe me. I've learned a lot in the last two weeks. And terrorism is a far greater threat than the people of our country under-stand. But we're going to take care of it. We're going to win. We're going to take care of it, folks.

Let today be the beginning of a great national partner-ship. Let today serve as a great call to action. And let this moment represent a new beginning in relations between law enforcement and our communities. I want you to know the American public totally stands with you. I want you to know the American people support you. I want you to know how proud we are, truly proud, to know you.

We applaud your efforts. We thank you for your ser-vice. And we promise that you will always find an open door at the White House -- an open invitation to our great cops and sheriffs nationwide. They're great people. You are great people.

Thank you. God bless you. And God bless America. Thank you very much. Thank you. (Applause.)

END
9:44 A.M. EST

"One of the reasons I was elected was because of law and order and security."

Chapter 23

**REMARKS BY PRESIDENT TRUMP AND
INTEL CEO BRIAN KRZANICH ON U.S. JOBS
OVAL OFFICE**

08 February 2017

12:52 P.M. EST

THE PRESIDENT: You've never seen so much paper on a President's desk. (Laughter.)

That's because we're negotiating lots of deals for our country, which will be tremendous.

And I just want to introduce Brian Krzanich, who's the CEO of Intel, a great, great company. And Brian called a few weeks ago and said, we want to do a very big announcement having to do with our country, but also having to do mostly with Arizona, and the jobs and the great technology that will be produced.

So this is Brian. And, Brian, why don't you say a few words and maybe also talk about the product you're going to be making. It's amazing.

MR. KRZANICH: Yes. Thank you, Mr. President, for this. It's an honor to be here today representing Intel and to be able to announce our $7 billion investment in our newest, most advanced factory -- Fab 42 in Chandler, Arizona.

We'll be completing that factory to make the most advanced 7-nanometer semiconductor chips on the planet. Intel is very proud of the fact that the majority of our manufacturing is here in the U.S. and the majority of our research and development is here in the U.S., while over 80 percent of what we sell is sold outside of the U.S.

And we're consistently one of the top five exporters in the country and one of the top two research and development spenders in the United States.

And we've been able to do that even while the regulatory and tax policies have disadvantaged us in the past relative to the competition we have across the world.

And Fab 42 is an investment in Intel, but also the U.S.'s future in innovation and leadership in the semiconductor industry.

Fab 42 will employ approximately 3,000 direct high-paying, high-wage, high-tech jobs at its peak, and over 10,000 people in the Arizona area in support of the factory. And this factory will produce, as I said, the most powerful computer chips on the planet, powering the best computers, the best data centers, autonomous cars.

All of these devices are the most powerful computing devices on the planet.

And at Intel we have a simple saying that says, while other people predict the future, we build the future. And this factory is a great example of that.

I want to thank the President for this opportunity to be here today.

THE PRESIDENT: Thank you, Brian. And you have something over there. Show a little bit about the new product.

MR. KRZANICH: This is an example of the wafer that will be built in Fab 42. This is one of our newest 10-nanometer silicon wafers. Seven-nanometers will be built in Fab 42. And this is the future of computing.

THE PRESIDENT: That's great, thanks. Do you have any questions for Brian? I know you have none for me, so how about -- (laughter) --

Q   Are you going to bring back jobs? The other business you have outside the country, do you plan on bringing them back here?

MR. KRZANICH: This is actually expansion. This is about growth. So this position is actually about growth and new jobs in the U.S.

THE PRESIDENT: Great thing for Arizona. Unbelievable company and product, and we're very happy. And I can tell you the people of Arizona are very happy. It's a lot of jobs. Probably the investment -- what are you saying, your total investment will be what?

MR. KRZANICH: Total investment in just this factory is $7 billion. But if you take Arizona, we already have two other factories in Arizona. So we have several tens of billions of dollars of investments in factories in Arizona. We're the number-one private employer in Arizona.

Q   And how long have you been planning this investment?

MR. KRZANICH: We've been working on this factory for

several years. We held off actually doing this investment until now.

Q   Was there something that President Trump did or said that made you want to announce this here and now?

MR. KRZANICH: It's really in support of the tax and regulatory policies that we see the administration pushing forward that really make it advantageous to do manufacturing in the U.S.

THE PRESIDENT: Thank you, all.

END
12:56 P.M. EST

"...We're negotiating lots of deals for our country..."

Chapter 24

**Remarks by President Trump at Swearing-In of
Attorney General Sessions
Oval Office**

09 February 2017

11:01 A.M. EST

THE PRESIDENT: Thank you very much, everybody, for being here today. It is with great pride, very great pride, that I say these words to you right now: Attorney General Jeff Sessions. (Applause.)

Welcome to the White House. (Applause.)

I want to congratulate you, Jeff, your wife Mary, and your entire family. Jeff Sessions has been a federal prosecutor at the highest level and at the most respected level, a state attorney general, and then a U.S. senator for two decades. He has devoted his life to the cause of justice and believes deeply that all people are equals in the eyes of the law -- and very importantly for Jeff and for so many of us, also in the eyes of God.

He's a man of integrity, a man of principle, and a man of total, utter resolve. You just got a little witnessing of that. That resolve is what we need right now. America faces many challenges. We face the menace of rising crime and the threat of deadly terror. And it's not getting better, but it will get better very soon. It's going to get a lot better.

These dangerous times require a determined attorney general, which is what Jeff is. Jeff understands that the job of attorney general is to serve and protect the people of the United States, and that is exactly what he will do, and do better than anybody else can. He's trained better for it than anybody else. The level of respect that he has throughout this country as a former prosecutor, not even to mention being a long-time U.S. senator, is absolutely incredible.

He will be a great protector of the people. I'm signing three executive actions today designed to **restore safety** in America. These executive actions continue to deliver on my **campaign promises**.

First, I'm directing Department of Justice and Homeland Security to undertake all necessary and lawful action to break the back of the criminal cartels that have spread across our nation and are destroying the blood of our youth and other people, many other people.

Secondly, I'm directing Department of Justice to form a task force on reducing violent crime in America.

And thirdly, I'm directing the Department of Justice to implement a plan to stop crime and crimes of violence against law enforcement officers. It's a shame what's been happening to our great, truly great law enforcement officers. That's going to stop as of today.

Today's ceremony should be seen as a clear message to the gang members and drug dealers terrorizing innocent people. Your day is over. A new era of justice begins, and it begins right now.

I want to again thank and congratulate Mary and our new Attorney General, Jeff Sessions. I wish you God's wisdom and blessings in your journey. Mr. Vice President, would you please conduct the swearing-in. Thank you. Thank you very much for being here, everyone. (Applause.)

(The Attorney General is sworn in.)

ATTORNEY GENERAL SESSIONS: Mr. President, thank you for this great honor. It's something I never expected would happen in my life, but I do love the Department of Justice. I care about its traditions and its heritage. I had 15 years in that great department, and the honor to lead it now is something that I do not have words to express effectively.

There are a lot of things we need to do. First, we need to value and support and encourage the fabulous people who work there. I've worked with them over the years. I know how good they are, and their talents need to be directed at this nation's benefit in a lot of different ways. We have a crime problem. I wish the blip -- I wish the rise that we are seeing in crime in America today were some sort of aberration or a blip. My best judgement, having been involved in criminal law enforcement for many years is that this is a dangerous, permanent trend that places the health and safety of the American people at risk. We will deploy the talents and abilities of the Department of Justice in the most effective way possible to confront this rise in crime and to protect the people of our country.

We have an increased threat, since I was a United States attorney, from terrorism. Mr. President, you've spoken firmly on that. You've led this nation to say we're going to respond effectively to the threat of terrorism, and you can count on your Department of Justice to do so in an effective way. And you've said something that I believe and I think the American people believe -- that we need a lawful system of immigration; one that serves the interests of the people of the United States. That's not wrong, that's not immoral, that's not indecent. We admit a million people a year plus, lawfully, and we need to end this lawlessness that threatens the public safety, pulls down wages of working Americans.

It is an honor beyond words to serve under you and your leadership. You're putting together a great Cabinet, which is just a thrill for me to have the opportunity to join. And I look forward to making sure that every ounce of strength I have and that the people of the Department of Justice have is going to be focused on preserving and protecting the Constitution and the safety of this country. We will defend the laws of this country as passed by Congress. We will defend the lawful orders of the President of the United States with vigor and determination.

Thank you all for being here, I see a lot of good friends, and may God bless all our efforts. Thank you. (Applause.)

END
11:07 A.M. EST

"We will defend the lawful orders of the President of the United States with vigor and determination."

Chapter 25

Remarks by President Trump in Meeting with the
Aviation Industry
State Dining Room

09 February 2017

9:47 A.M. EST

THE PRESIDENT: Thank you for being here. Nothing like having meetings in the White House. Good place. Good place for meetings. Good place for a lot of things. People don't realize **I inherited a mess**. **A big mess**. I think they know. I think they understand.

Well, thank you all. I know so many of you through reading and through business magazines, and you've done an amazing job. And I want to congratulate you. I know you're under pressure from a lot of foreign elements and foreign carriers. I've been hearing that a little bit. At the same time, we want to make life good for them also. They come with big investments -- in many cases, those investments are made by their governments. But they are still big investments.

I'm thrilled to welcome the leaders of the airline industry to the White House. Your industry supports over 10 million well-paying U.S. jobs and creates almost $1 trillion in economic activity, which is really big stuff, really amazing. Last year, our airlines moved approximately 2 million people each day in our country, which is an incredible number of people. And they move them well -- despite the bad equipment that the airports give you in many cases, because they can't get approvals, and we had regulatory morass that's a disaster.

And I can tell you that a lot of the new equipment that already is obsolete the day they order it -- and that's according to people that know, including my pilot. I have a pilot who's a real expert, and he said, sir, the equipment they're putting on is just the wrong stuff. And we'll talk about that. Because if we're going to modernize our systems, we should be using the right equipment. And I know Mr. Tilden is nodding. You know what I mean. It's one thing to order equipment, but let's order the right equipment. Probably the wrong equipment costs more. You can probably buy the right equipment for less money. So we want to talk about that. Because my pilot, he's a smart guy, and knows what's going on. He said the government is using the wrong equipment and instituting a massive, multibillion-dollar project, but they're using the wrong type of equipment. So let's find out about that.

We want the traveling public to have the greatest customer service, with an absolute minimum of delays and with great convenience all at the lowest possible cost. We want to help you **realize these goals**, and we will indeed help you **realize these goals**. Airports are very important when you travel. Very important.

As an example, some of you were saying yesterday to me that you go to China, you go to Japan, they have fast trains all over the place. We don't have one. I don't want to compete with your business -- (laughter) -- but we don't have one fast train. And it's the same thing with our airports. Our airports used to be the best. Now they're at the bottom of the rung. We've spent $6 trillion -- think of it -- as of about two months ago, $6 trillion in the Middle East. We've got nothing. We've got nothing. We never even kept just even a little tiny oil well. Not one little one. I said, keep the oil. But we've spent right now $6 trillion in the Middle East. We have nothing. And we have an obsolete plane system, we have obsolete airports, we have obsolete trains. We have bad roads. We're going to change all of that, folks. You're going to be so happy with Trump. I think you already are.

So we want to help you **realize these goals** by rolling back burdensome regulations. And you people are regulated probably as much as almost anybody, although I can think of a couple of industries that are even worse. Lowering the overall tax burden on American businesses big league. That's coming along very well. Way ahead of schedule, I believe. And we're going to be announcing something, I would say, over the next two or three weeks that will be phenomenal in terms of tax, and developing our aviation infrastructure.

Again, I want to thank you all for being here. So I want this to be a meeting of substance. I want to be able to do things for you. The auto industry was in. They left, they said it was the best meeting they've ever had. I even took them into the Oval Office. The head of Ford, the head of General Motors, the head of Fiat, others -- they never saw the Oval Office. I said, you mean they never took you in? You see how far away it was from the room? Ten feet. It was 10 feet across the hallway, but they never got taken in. I took them in.

The auto companies are going to be making massive investments in Michigan and Ohio, in Pennsylvania, a lot of the places where jobs have left. So we're really happy

about that. They've been great. Ford is going to build
-- you know they cancelled a big plant in a certain place, I
won't say where -- a $2 billion plant, and they're building
it in the United States and they're expanding greatly. General Motors the same thing. They've been great. They've
been great. I think they'll continue to be great.

But we're also going to be great to them. We're going to
get rid of a lot of unnecessary regulation, and we're going
to make their life a lot easier. They're going to employ
a lot more people. So a lot of businesses are rushing
in. They're coming in big league.

So with that, I thought what I would do is perhaps we'll
start with Mr. Gray. We'll go around the room and just
quickly just say who you are and who you represent. The
biggest of the airlines are here.

STAFFER: Thank you, press.

THE PRESIDENT: And you can -- no, stay, stay, stay. Let
them see who's here. (Laughter.)

Everyone is so quick to get rid of the press. I think I am the
most open President ever. (Laughter.)

They want to get rid of the press. What, you don't want to
see who Mr. Gray is? (Laughter.)

Maybe I should have started with somebody else. (Laughter.)

Okay, you can stay. Yeah, stay. Stay for a while. See who's
here, right? Okay, good.

MR. GRAY: Well, thank you, Mr. President. I'm Myron Gray, and I represent the United Parcel Service.

MS. EVENS: I'm Ginger Evens, I'm the Commissioner of Aviation for the city of Chicago.

MR. FLYNN: Mr. President, Bill Flynn with Atlas Air.

MR. WIGINGTON: Rob Wigington, CEO for Nashville Airport Authority.

MR. CALIO: Nick Calio, Airlines for America. Thank you for having us.

MR. BASTIAN: Mr. President, Ed Bastian, CEO of Delta Airlines.

THE PRESIDENT: Great. Welcome. Delta is doing well.

MR. BASTIAN: Doing great, and you know we've been neighbors for a long time.

THE PRESIDENT: That's right. That's right, good.

MR. BASTIAN: Hopefully we've been good to you.

THE PRESIDENT: You've been very good. Thank you.

MR. HAYES: Mr. President, Robin Hayes, CEO of JetBlue Airways. (Inaudible.)

THE PRESIDENT: Good job.

MR. BRONCZEK: Mr. President, Dave Bronczek, FedEx.

THE PRESIDENT: By the way, Fred Smith was here yester-day.

MR. BRONCZEK: Yes, I know.

THE PRESIDENT: He's a great, great guy.

MR. KELLY: Gary Kelly, Southwest Airlines.

THE PRESIDENT: Great job.

MR. TILDEN: Brad Tilden, Alaska Air Group. And we're actually in the process of merging with Virgin America right now.

THE PRESIDENT: Okay, good.

MR. FOYE: Mr. President, Pat Foye, Executive Director of the Port Authority of New York and New Jersey.

THE PRESIDENT: Great. We spoke a long time ago.

MR. FOYE: Yes, sir.

THE PRESIDENT: And you did a good job.

MR. FOYE: Thank you.

THE PRESIDENT: Appreciate it.

MR. POTTER: Mr. President, Jack Potter, Metropolitan Washington Airports Authority.

MR. BURKE: Mr. President, Kevin Burke. I'm the President of Airports Council International-North America, which is every airports in the United States and Canada. Thank you for having us.

THE PRESIDENT: Thank you.

MR. VANECEK: Mr. President, Bill Vanecek. I'm the Director of Aviation for the Buffalo Niagara International Airport and Niagara Falls International Airport. I'm also the chairman of Airports Council International-NA.

THE PRESIDENT: Great.

MR. LOPANO: Mr. President, good morning. My name is Joe Lopano. I'm from Tampa International Airport.

MR. MUÑOZ: Oscar Muñoz with United Airlines. And Mr. Doug Parker from American couldn't be here today.

THE PRESIDENT: Okay. Thank you.

MS. FLINT: Good morning, Mr. President. Deborah Flint, the CEO of Los Angeles World Airports. LAX is the world's seventh largest airport and the country's third largest airport.

THE PRESIDENT: We'll make it number one worldwide. Let's make it number one. (Laughter.)

I didn't like the number. What is number one now in terms of service?

MS. FLINT: Atlanta.

THE PRESIDENT: That's good. We love the state of Georgia. I love Georgia -- I tell you that's for sure. So that's good.

PARTICIPANT: Number one in the world.

THE PRESIDENT: So let me ask you -- so what can we do to make your airlines better, to make your balance sheet better, to have you get more jobs and create more jobs, to have you win competition worldwide so you can start doing more business worldwide? Because I know you have a lot of competition, and a lot of that competition is subsidized by governments, big league. I've heard that complaint from different people in this room. Probably about one hour after I got elected I was inundated with calls from your industry, and many other industries, because it's a pretty unfair situation.

What can we do? Give me suggestions that we can make your life easier and that you can employ a lot more people.

MR. KELLY: Well, Mr. President, I'll lead this off.

THE PRESIDENT: Southwest Airlines.

MR. KELLY: Thank you very much for the opportunity to be here. We have never had a meeting like this, certainly in my years at Southwest Airlines. So we're very grateful for this opportunity.

THE PRESIDENT: I want to congratulate you because you have done an amazing job, really amazing job. You really have. So congratulations. Go ahead.

MR. KELLY: I think we're very well aligned with your philosophy. We would welcome tax reform. We would welcome regulatory reform. And very well aligned on the need for infrastructure investment.

The single biggest opportunity for aviation is to modernize the air traffic control system. We work very well with our partners in the airports around the table. I know them all and we serve all of these airports and --

THE PRESIDENT: You shouldn't know them too well. (Laughter.)

MR. KELLY: Well, they're our landlords. (Laughter.)

(Inaudible) the only landlord available. But we have billions of dollars' worth of airport projects underway around the country to continue to modernize the airports. We've spent billions of dollars on the air traffic control modernization but it's not making any meaningful progress.

THE PRESIDENT: I hear that. I hear we have the wrong system. I'm hearing that the United States government -- and is the gentleman who's the head of the FAA right now not a pilot? Or is that -- does he --

MR. KELLY: I don't know if he's a pilot or not.

THE PRESIDENT: I'd like to find out because I think it maybe would be good to have a pilot, like a really good pilot who knows what's going on. I've heard that, and, I don't know, it seems a little hard to believe because the complexity of your business is right up there, right?

MR. KELLY: Oh, very much so.

THE PRESIDENT: And I would think you need a very sophisticated person in that job, and somebody that, frankly --

being a pilot would be helpful, because I'm hearing you put the wrong -- I hear the government contracted this system that's the wrong system, and I hear that from pilots. So who would be better to tell me? But I hear we're spending billions and billions of dollars. It's a system that's totally out of whack. It's way over budget, it's way beyond schedule, and when it's completed, it's not going to be a good system. Other than that, it's okay. (Laughter.)

So what do you think about that, Gary?

MR. KELLY: Well, I agree with you. When you have a project that takes that long, it becomes outdated.

THE PRESIDENT: It's already outdated.

MR. KELLY: It's already outdated, no question. And we spent billions of dollars on this.

THE PRESIDENT: Has that been you or the government or both?

PARTICIPANT: Oh no, this is the federal -- FAA, air traffic control --

THE PRESIDENT: So when you say "we" -- "we" the government --

MR. KELLY: You're paying for it. You're ultimately -- the airlines and our customers are paying for it.

THE PRESIDENT: Why do the airlines allow that to happen where they put in a bad system? Not even antiquated -- and it's antiquated because it's taken so long. Why do the airlines allow a system that you know is bad from the beginning -- because you guys are pros -- why do they allow the government to put in the wrong system?

MR. KELLY: Well, we're not in control. And I think that's one of the things that we see as the path to having success, is we need to address the fundamental organization of the air traffic organization, not the safety and regulatory oversight -- that's a government function that needs to remain. But we believe that reforming the FAA by creating a non-for-profit corporation is the way to address the governments that you're speaking to, as well as the long-term financing.

THE PRESIDENT: Headed by the airlines? Headed by who? The board would be who?

MR. KELLY: The board would be represented by all the various constituents. So the government would have a seat, general aviation would have a seat, certainly the commercial airlines would have a seat. Everyone would --

THE PRESIDENT: Well, this wouldn't have happened then. You wouldn't be putting in a system -- a control system -- that is obsolete before they even signed the contract. And, by the way, overly expensive. More expensive than (inaudible).

MR. KELLY: You know, the interesting thing is I think that there is absolutely unanimous agreement that the system needs to be modernized and that it is well behind schedule. There is not agreement on the path forward to address that, and that's where we run into roadblocks. We want the government out of managing the air traffic control system so that it can be adequately managed, adequately financed, and we can get this done. We won

World War II in three-and-a-half years; we ought to be able to modernize air traffic control.

THE PRESIDENT: So how long would it take to -- because I'm hearing you have to scrap all of the billions of dollars that have been put in -- stupidly put in. How long would it take to come up with a great air traffic control system, the top anywhere in the world, the top of the line? How long would that take to do and how much would it cost?

MR. KELLY: The good news is, we don't have to scrap everything. We are still using fundamentally World War II-era ground-based radar to guide the aircraft from a navigation standpoint. We are not utilizing GPS satellite-delivered navigational tools. Those things exist. At least for Southwest Airlines, we have fully equipped all of our fleet to take advantage of that, but we're not getting those kinds of flight profiles written for each airport or each route.

THE PRESIDENT: So you'd save a lot of time, you'd save a tremendous amount of fuel.

MR. KELLY: We think that we're losing $25 billion a year as an industry. And I think the best example we can offer up to you -- the system is very safe, by the way. And our air traffic controllers are very fine men and women, and they do a fantastic job.

THE PRESIDENT: It's safe but it's very cautious. And it should be cautious.

MR. KELLY: Yes, it must be cautious.

THE PRESIDENT: But I notice the intervals when planes go out seem very, very long.

MR. KELLY: It used to be a 55-minute trip between Washington and New York, and today it's 80.

PARTICIPANT: Mr. President, it's not just about fuel -- it's about jobs. The partnership in New York City did a study that the cost of air traffic control congestion in New York and New Jersey alone is $75 billion over a period ending in 2028. Those are jobs that haven't been created and jobs that --

THE PRESIDENT: And what is the reason for that?

PARTICIPANT: It's the antiquated system, one, Mr. President. It's, two, the fact that New York/New Jersey is the busiest airspace in the world. And, three, frankly, that other countries, including Canada, have more efficient systems. Implementation and the funding NextGen is really critical. And this is not an act of (inaudible) -- this is about jobs.

PARTICIPANT: Sir, you asked why -- your question -- how did we let this happen to some degree.

THE PRESIDENT: Yeah.

PARTICIPANT: I've (inaudible) on telecom and railroads and some (inaudible) industry, and it's unfortunate that every time you go from one industry to the other, the regulatory burden continues or gets worse. So in this particular case, to be very frank and blunt, and to your point earlier, I think it's become political -- it's a political process, and so it's difficult for us to have control.

THE PRESIDENT: Not anymore it's not political. We're going to get --

PARTICIPANT: And you have the appointees that you --

THE PRESIDENT: -- at a reasonable price. So not any-more. Go ahead.

PARTICIPANT: I would take special care in reappointing the (inaudible) on the FAA. Whether or not it needs to be a pilot or not, I can't opine, but it would be nice to have people that actually have a thorough understanding of the business of aviation.

THE PRESIDENT: Is the head of the FAA a pilot? Does any-body know? Somebody should know.

PARTICIPANT: He's not.

THE PRESIDENT: He's not? He's not a pilot. I just think a non-pilot would not know the sophistication of this sys-tem, right? I mean, better to have a pilot -- because my pi-lot said it's a terrible system that they're installing; that the work they're doing now is a waste of tremendous amounts of money because the system is a bad system. That's com-ing from a pilot.

PARTICIPANT: Mr. President, when you talk about jobs, and you just recently asked about that, what we talked about just recently with the airlines is infrastructure in the sky, which is really antiquated. But you refer to infrastructure on the ground, the airports.

THE PRESIDENT: Both.

PARTICIPANT: Yeah, and the airports really are becoming antiquated, to your point. There is a system, there is a charge called a passenger-facility charge, which is a charge that's levied on every ticket. And it hasn't been increased in 16 years, so it's basically defunded.

THE PRESIDENT: How much is it?

PARTICIPANT: It's $4.50. That could be increased by a simple act of Congress, and it's not a U.S. tax. It's a user fee. So as a customer uses my airport in Tampa, the airlines collect that fee and they send it back to us in Tampa. It never comes to Washington and gets approved in the budget.

THE PRESIDENT: The problem is, I don't like raising fees or taxes -- I'll be honest. I mean, we're spending all this money overseas, we're giving away trillions of dollars to all these countries. All of the countries that trade with us are ripping us off. The last thing we have to do is raise the fee. I understand what you're saying, but $4.50 -- it's a lot when you look at all of the passengers.

If there were other ways of doing this -- because you're only hurting yourself by -- really, eventually, people are going to just stop flying because it's very expensive with all the taxes. I mean, there are other ways. We're spending so much money overseas, fighting wars, doing things, and, frankly, making horrible trade deals. So don't worry about the money. I'll be able to get the money. The money -- we're going to change things around.

END
10:07 A.M. EST

Chapter 26

09 February 2017

12:41 P.M. EST

THE PRESIDENT: Thank you all for coming. We had a couple of great meetings this morning -- the airline industry, we're going to get that one going. They've got a lot of problems but it's going to be good. We just had talks with Qatar and a couple of countries -- Afghanistan. I would say that that's a tough situation but we'll do something about it. We'll be having some -- we'll be giving you some pretty -- information -- pretty good information soon. We're going to have some good, big conversations with other world leaders over the next few hours. A lot of things happening, a lot of positive things.

I want to start by thanking Senator Manchin for having the courage to vote for somebody that's really very outstanding, really outstanding -- as good as they've seen in a long time. Nominating the justice to the Supreme Court, a justice, has always been considered one of the very important things that a President can do.

I guess I'm looking very much at defense and we're negotiating a lot of contracts with airlines and a lot of other people, but when you get right down to it, the F-35 Fighter is very important and all of the things we're doing are very important. But I've always considered, and I guess a lot of people have, the Supreme Court nominees to be right up there -- right up there. We'll take defense, number one, I think, Senator, we have to go with defense of our country, number one. And right after that, I suspect it's going to be Supreme Court justices.

And Judge Gorsuch is an exceptionally qualified nominee -- probably there's rarely been anybody that's been more qualified. He has impeccable academic and legal credentials. He went to Columbia -- very, very great student. He went to Harvard, top of his class. He went to Oxford, great student, great intellect. He has an outstanding record for 10 years on the bench. One of the great writers they say -- legal writers -- I've read some of the things that he's written and, believe me, he is a great, great writer. He'll respect and very much respect the Constitution, as written, and he will apply the law as written.

He's a mainstream judge, very much mainstream, and I urge you all to confirm him. He's been doing very well. A lot of people are liking him very much on the other side. And I think that, because of politics, perhaps they're not going to vote for him. I think that's a shame because that's not being honest.

I've had a couple of people tell me from the other side -- because, believe it or not, I have a lot of friends on the other side too -- and they think he's outstanding. And then they go on to tell me that perhaps they won't be able to do that. But that's one of the reasons that our country is in stagnation in so many different forms and so many different ways. I think it's very dishonest and I think it's very unfortunate.

But we'll see what happens. I think he's doing very well. And I know that some people are going to come on board and hopefully we can do this in a very quick and civil manner.

The Cabinet slowly is happening. Jeff Sessions just got -- you're very happy about that -- because Jeff is outstanding. And we just swore in Jeff Sessions as Attorney General, and I think he's going to be outstanding.

So I just want to thank you all for being here. We're going to have a good lunch and we're going to talk about our Supreme Court nominee, somebody who will do a fantastic job for many years to come. Thank you very much.

Q   Mr. President, any comment on Judge Gorsuch's comments about you, sir?

THE PRESIDENT: You misrepresented his comments.

Q   I just wanted to ask you what your thoughts were, Sir.

THE PRESIDENT: His comments were misrepresented. And what you should do is ask Senator Blumenthal about his Vietnam record that didn't exist after years of saying it did. So ask Senator Blumenthal about his Vietnam record. He misrepresented that just like he misrepresented Judge Gorsuch.

Thank you all very much.

END
12:45 P.M. EST

Chapter 27

09 February 2017

6:10 P.M. EST

THE VICE PRESIDENT: Thank you, General Caslen. Your wife informed me that it was not booing that I heard when you came up, but it was "Supe." (Laughter.)

Give this wonderful superintendent a round of applause, would you please? He deserves it, and the nation is proud of your service. (Applause.)

General Holland, General Jebb, Captain Villanueva, distinguished guests, and core of cadets of the United States Military Academy -- it is an extraordinary privilege for me to be with you tonight.

Two special guests are with me that I want to acknowledge. A man who I knew before he was even elected to the Congress, and now he is one of the most prominent members of the United States Senate; Senator Tim Scott is with us tonight just to be with all of you. Senator Scott, thank you for joining us this evening. (Applause.)

And my commanding officer is with us, as well. My wife of 31 years -- (laughter) -- Karen Pence is in the house. Would you make her feel welcome? (Applause.)

I'm very humbled to have raised my right hand just a few short weeks ago to accept the responsibilities and be Vice President of the United States of America.

And by the power vested in me, I hear by grant amnesty for all minor conduct offenses of those present. (Applause.)

I'm not sure I'll be asked back now. But it's really good to be with you all and, frankly, very humbling.

I came here on behalf of the President of the United States, your Commander-in-Chief, President Donald Trump, and I bring you his greetings and his gratitude. (Applause.)

I left the Oval Office when I headed to West Point this afternoon, and the President insisted that I send his greetings to all of you, his heartfelt thanks for your willingness to serve our great country.

But more than that, the President sends his commitment to you that President Donald Trump and this administration will stand with you as you stand to defend the United States of America. (Applause.)

I tell you it's the greatest privilege of my life to serve with the 45th President. But it's a special honor to serve with a President so dedicated to America's Armed Forces.

You know, being here tonight is a humbling experience for me, and it's very moving. You see, I'm not a soldier. My life did not take that path. But I am the son of a soldier and the proud father of a United States Marine.

My father, you'll be glad to know, Ed Pence, was member

of the United States Army. (Applause.)

My dad served in combat in Korea. And he's one of those people that earned some medals on this chest and came home and put them in the drawer. The best man I ever knew. He's been gone some three decades now in our family, but he's still the greatest influence on my life every day.

I'm not only the proud son of someone in the service, but my wife, Karen, and I are also the proud parents of a son who answered the call of duty. Our son is right now serving in the Marine Corps as a second lieutenant. And like all of you, his highest hope is to serve our country with great distinction. And on behalf of all of your parents, these parents say, you all make us proud. Give yourselves a round of applause, would you please? (Applause.)

I know your parents have the same faith that we have, that each one of you are going to continue this path you have chosen with great distinction. We have faith in you and faith in the principles you've come to serve.

We have faith because of those who have walked this same path as you, in ages past. The training that you're receiving here has been generations in the making. I just had a wonderful gathering with a number of your most distinguished and accomplished fellow cadets. And I heard their calling here was not just to serve the country, but to grow as leaders.

We're really standing -- we're standing where generations have stood -- on hallowed ground. If you think about it, for over 200 years, men and women from across our country have come to these grounds, driven here by that call to serve, that call to leadership -- of duty, honor, country.

They came here separately, in different eras, with different pasts. Yet they all left as one, didn't they? Forever bound to each other each one of you are, as brothers and sisters, gripping hands in the *Long Grey Line*. And the American people are proud of each and every one of you in this room.

That line remains unbroken to this day, and so long as it continues, everyone who calls our country home can know with absolute certainty that the United States of America -- our home, our homeland -- will be **safe**.

So it is humbling for me to be here, one of the people that has been benefited by those countless generations that have gone before. It's humbling especially to be where so many courageous Americans prepare to protect families like mine. And it's humbling to stand before all of you, who gladly follow in their footsteps.

You are all already true leaders, and you are all already patriots.

President Trump and I thank you. We thank you for answering the call to serve your country -- to put **America First**.

Now, President Trump has made a solemn promise to all of you and to everyone who wears the uniform. On Monday, he gave a speech earlier this week, in which he essentially promised to stand with and "protect those who protect us." He promised in his words to give you "the tools, the equipment, the resources, the training, and the supplies you need to get the job done." And he promised to "honor our sacred bond to those who serve." These are the President's **promises** to all of you. And make no mistake about it those **promises** will be kept in this administration. (Applause.)

That's really why I'm here tonight on the President's behalf. Honoring those who serve our country requires recognizing the men and women who achieve extraordinary things in the line of duty.

There's a passage in the Old Book. I try and open it up and read it every morning. It says, "If you owe debts, pay debts. If honor, then honor. If respect, then respect." And tonight marks the 40th Annual Lieutenant Henry O. Flipper Dinner, which is all about doing just that. It commemorates a man who we just heard overcame extraordinary adversity -- demonstrated leadership, self-discipline, and courage in service to this country.

The year 1877, only twelve years before, the horrible evil of slavery, that great stain on our experiment in self-government, had finally been eradicated in the fires of the Civil War. And out of those ashes emerged hope -- hope that America's **founding promise** of equality and freedom would finally be made real for all Americans.

It was in this hope that spurred Henry Flipper to write his congressman, James Freeman, to request an appointment to the finest military academy in the world. Henry's skill with the written word impressed Freeman, we are told, who determined that he was indeed worthy.

So came Henry Flipper to where we stand today. All who attend West Point face many trials, but Henry Flipper faced many more that we all understand by virtue of his willingness to challenge the status quo, challenge the injustices of his day.

He persevered through four years, making history as the First African American ever to graduate from the United States Military Academy. But as we just heard his struggles would continue. He was ejected from the Army only four years later after being accused of a crime he did not commit.

After Henry passed away, a band of patriotic Americans took up his cause. And thanks to their efforts, the Army righted this wrong by retroactively awarding Henry Flipper an honorable discharge in 1976. And you heard that President Clinton pardoned him in the years that followed.

The following year after he was honorably discharged, his alma mater began to celebrate his accomplishments with the first installment of the dinner we have here tonight. Fittingly, I'm told the first Henry O. Flipper Dinner was held 100 years after his ground-breaking graduation from West Point. Altogether fitting.

But the purpose of tonight, I'm told, is not just to remember Henry Flipper and his extraordinary courage and accomplishment, but it's held every year in the midst of African American History Month.

A week ago today, President Trump signed a proclamation honoring this occasion and declaring that "the history of African Americans exemplifies the resilience and the **spirit** that continue to make our Nation great."

We need only look at Henry Flipper's life to see this truth in this statement. But we should also look back to the generations of African Americans who have defended and died for this country as far back as the very hour of our nation's birth.

When I think of these brave men and women, I can't help but think of that famous painting, it's known as *Washington's Crossing*. It depicts George Washington and his band crossing the Delaware.

If you look closely, if you haven't looked at that painting, and it's one of my favorites, you'll see someone who is sometimes overlooked. Next to General Washington himself, immediately to his left, is a young African American solider.

The symbolism is profound. The painting was rendered by a German abolitionist who was determined to recognize the countless African Americans who fought side by side with our Founders in the pursuit of a **free** America -- of liberty and equality for all.

Men like Crispus Attucks, who perished in the Boston Massacre, or Lemuel Hayes, who fought at Lexington and Concord, or the dozens who enlisted in the First Rhode Island Regiment, just to name a few.

In New England, some African American patriots rose as high as the rank of colonel. Yet no matter their rank, they were, all of them, every bit as freedom-loving and dedicated to independence as George Washington himself.

Tonight I think of them -- but, of course, not only them. I think of the nearly 200,000 African Americans who fought for the Union in the Civil War and for the new birth of freedom that followed it.

I think of the Buffalo Soldiers we learned tonight that Henry Flipper was among them who actually helped tame the West. I think of the Tuskegee Airmen who flew for freedom in World War Two -- men like General Benjamin O. Davis, Jr., whose strength of character carried him through four difficult years at West Point, and who is now honored for his resolve with a barracks that bears his name. I think of all these heroes in this month, and many more I haven't mentioned, because they are the best of us.

And during this month, African American History Month, but not only this month, we remember them and we thank them for what they did. Their names and their sacrifices will never be forgotten. For they understood the **promise** of America -- the timeless ideals that bind us together as a people, and give us purpose as a nation.

That's why we are here tonight. We know in our hearts that America is extraordinary and that **our sacred birth-right** must be defended, no matter the cost. This gift has always inspired our fellow Americans to step up and serve, and I believe it always will.

It certainly inspired Henry Flipper and all those that we reflect on tonight. He persevered not just through four years at West Point, but over injustice itself. We remember and honor him tonight for his unyielding tenacity in the face of hardship.

Henry's life always be a model for those who find towering barriers standing before them waiting to be overcome. For 40 years now, the United States Corps of Cadets has chosen one of its own who has embodied Henry's courage, his leadership, his determination to let no obstacle stand in his way. And tonight that honor falls to Cadet Lars

Lofgren. (Applause.)

Cadet Lofgren personifies the legacy of Henry Flipper and all the other previous recipients of the Flipper Award. As all of you know, two years ago, Cadet Lofgren was tragically injured during a training exercise at Fort Campbell, Kentucky. Since that day, he has been paralyzed from the waist down. But he didn't let it stop him. Less than 12 months later, he participated -- I had to read this twice -- he participated in the 2016 Warrior Games, where he won an astounding seven medals. (Applause.)

Not only that, he then returned to West Point to complete his final year -- such is his love for America, for this great institution, and his sense of duty.

Cadet Lofgren, you are an inspiration to us all. You are truly a worthy recipient of the Henry Flipper Award. And I'm honored to be here tonight to be a part of watching you receive it. And tonight you will receive it from none other than one of Henry's descendants, Ken Davis. And we thank him so much for being with us today.

I know everyone joins me in congratulating Cadet Lofgren and the honor he gives us by being here tonight.

The legacy of Henry Flipper lives on in many others, including two distinguished guests we have with us tonight.

Pat Locke, who retired from the Army as a major, is here with us this evening. She's a trailblazer cut from the same cloth as Henry Flipper himself. In 1980, she departed from these grounds -- stand up and take a bow. Would you please? (Applause.)

Thank you, Major.

In 1980, she departed from these grounds as the first-ever, female African American graduate of West Point.

We also have with us Cadet Christian Nattiel. He is the first African American from West Point to receive the prestigious Rhodes Scholarship and will soon head to Oxford to teach them a thing or two. (Applause.)

All those whom I have recognized are heirs of a long and proud tradition that stretches back into the mists of American history. But they are not the only ones. It is this same tradition that really brings all of us here tonight and together.

Now, we've not come to West Point, nor did our forefathers, because of the color of our skin or the creed we profess. We gather because of our country -- a country that has given us so much, and to which we are now called to give in return.

One of my late father's favorite versus was: To whom much is given, much will be required.

And I know that every one of you that has stepped forward to be a part of this incredible tradition to serve your country feels that in your heart. You cadets before me have answered that call. You've stepped up, and soon you will go forth.

Last night was Post Night, I'm told, when the graduating seniors learned where they will be stationed. You will, all of you, do our country proud, so that future generations may yet call themselves sons and daughters of America. Let's give all of those who participated in Post Night a round of applause. (Applause.)

Your accomplishments here at West Point, your leadership speaks louder than anyone could at a dinner like tonight.

And your service is needed now more than ever. Beyond our nation's borders lies a world riven by conflict and oftentimes wracked by chaos. Evil abounds across the globe. Old enemies have reared their ugly heads once more, and new ones have arisen, too.

The forces of radical Islam terrorism seek to destroy not only our people, but our very way of life. The barbarians known as ISIS are brutally killing anyone who stands in the way of their attempts to establish a global caliphate. They will not stop until we stop them. And we will stop them. (Applause.)

The threats facing America have never been more numerous, it seems sometimes, more sophisticated, more zealous in their adherence to failed ideas that belong in the ash-heap of history.

But make no mistake about it: President Trump and this administration and this country will not rest until these enemies are destroyed and our nation is safe again. (Applause.)

And I promise you -- I promise you, those of you that are preparing to enter the service of the United States of America on your graduation of West Point, we will not relent in our effort until we have rebuilt the arsenal of democracy and ensured that our soldiers, sailors, airmen, Marines, and Coast Guard have the resources and the training they need to accomplish their mission, protect our families, and come home safe to theirs. That is our promise. (Applause.)

Rest assured, I can testify from what I see in him every day, America has a President and a Commander-in-Chief who loves the armed forces and will stand with you every day. I've seen his dedication to you more times than I can count. In fact, I see it literally on a daily basis.

Under his leadership, I can **promise** you three things. First, know that President Trump and I will always have your backs. You will have everything you need, and more, to defeat those who confront our nation and threaten our freedom, and to protect this country.

Secondly, know that you and your families in the days ahead will always have our prayers, and the prayers of the American people will go with you as you serve. Of this I'm confident.

And last, know that we will always support you, not second-guess you, and we will never call your courageous service or your sacrifice a failure.

Before I leave, I can't help but recall the words that the General just shared with me. We took a stroll, didn't we, General, down a block to see that MacArthur statue? And I polished his boot. (Laughter.)

Before I left the Oval Office this afternoon, the President told me, you have to go down to the MacArthur statue. We did.

And I read those words that were I think first spoken in

this very room, and they're words that really represent the foundation of the past, present, and the future of this extraordinary institution and the tradition that you've embraced -- duty, honor, country.

MacArthur said: "Those three hallowed words reverently dictate what you ought to be, what you can be, and what you will be. They are your rallying points to build courage when courage seems to fail, to regain faith when there seems to be little cause for faith, to create hope when hope becomes forlorn."

Stirring words on a cold night, they warmed my heart because I knew I'd be looking out on a roomful of men and women who were living out that every single day.

You know to serve with President Trump is to serve with someone who has boundless confidence in the American people and boundless optimism about America's future. And it's an honor to be with you tonight.

But let me say what the President would say if he was here, that looking out at your shining faces, seeing your dedication to America, we're more confident than ever that the best days for America are yet to come.

Thank you. God bless you. God bless West Point. And God bless the United States of America.

END
7:33 P.M. EST

Chapter 28

10 February 2017

11:27 A.M. EST

THE VICE PRESIDENT: Good morning. On behalf of President Donald Trump, it will be my great privilege today to administer the oath of office to America's new Secretary of Health and Human Services, Dr. Tom Price. (Applause.)

We're grateful to be joined by colleagues and friends to mark this important occasion in the life of our administration and no less extent in the life of this nation.

The American people can be proud of having the finest health care in the world.

But we all have known the challenges in recent years since the passage of the Affordable Care Act.

President Trump has made it the top priority of this new Congress to repeal and replace the Affordable Care Act with health care reform that will lower the cost of health insurance without growing the size of government.

And finding someone to lead Health and Human Services who brings a background in medicine, a background in health care, a background in budgetary issues in the Congress of the United States, who understands the unique challenges of state officials in programs like Medicaid was easily met when he made the decision to name Dr. Tom Price as the new Secretary of Health and Human Services.

Dr. Price is uniquely qualified to step into this leading role during this time of reform in the life of health care in America.

For nearly 20 years, Tom Price worked in private practice as an orthopedic surgeon in the Atlanta area, mending broken bones, giving people the hope and the health to lead lives to the fullest.

You passed on your wisdom by training rising generations of physicians at a local college and hospital -- an impressive career in health care.

But your patients weren't the only ones that benefitted by your leadership and by your example. You would carry your leadership qualities into the Georgia State Senate where you served for eight years, becoming the majority leader of the Georgia State Senate, and helping to steer a time of real reform and renewal in the state of Georgia.

Then it was on to Congress where I first met Dr. Price. He would serve in the Congress now for more than 12 years -- chairman of the Budget Committee, but without question emerging as the most principled expert on health care policy in the House of Representatives, if not the entire Congress.

And now President Trump has transformed you with leading the Department of Health and Human Services on behalf of the American people.

And as Secretary, we're both confident that you will bring that experience as a physician, that experience at the state level, and that singular experience at the national level to ensure that President Trump's vision for a health care system in this country that works for every American will become a reality in the years ahead.

So with that, on behalf of President Trump, is it my great privilege to administer to you the oath of office.

(The Oath is administered.) (Applause.)

END
11:31 A.M. EST

Chapter 29

**REMARKS BY PRESIDENT TRUMP AND
PRIME MINISTER ABE OF JAPAN IN
JOINT PRESS CONFERENCE
EAST ROOM**

10 February 2017

1:08 P.M. EST

PRESIDENT TRUMP: Thank you very much. Prime Minister Abe, on behalf of the American people, I welcome you to the very famous White House. You honor us with your presence. This is one of our earliest visits from a foreign leader, and I am truly glad that it could be from such an important and steadfast ally.

The bond between our two nations, and the friendship between our two peoples, runs very, very deep. This administration is committed to bringing those ties even closer. We are committed to the security of Japan and all areas under its administrative control, and to further strengthening our very crucial alliance.

The U.S.-Japan alliance is the cornerstone of peace and stability in the Pacific region. It is important that both Japan and the United States continue to invest very heavily in the alliance to build up our defense and our defensive capabilities, which, under our mutual leadership, will become stronger and stronger, and, as time goes by, ultimately they will be impenetrable.

We face numerous challenges, and bilateral cooperation is

essential. Our country is committed to being an active and fully engaged partner. We will work together to promote our shared interests, of which we have many in the region, including freedom from navigation and of navigation, and defending against the North Korean missile and nuclear threat, both of which I consider a very, very high priority.

On the economy, we will seek a trading relationship that is free, fair and reciprocal, benefitting both of our countries. The vibrant exchange between us is a true blessing.

Japan is a proud nation with a rich history and culture, and the American people have profound respect for your country and its traditions. I also want to take this opportunity, Mr. Prime Minister, to thank you and the people of Japan for hosting our armed forces.

Working together, our two countries have the ability to bring greater harmony, stability and prosperity to the Pacific region and beyond, improving countless lives in the process. We are committed to that goal -- highly committed.

Prime Minister Abe, on behalf of the United States of America, I thank you for being with us today. We will soon be traveling to the great state of Florida, where I know we will have a long and very successful talk, negotiations, and a very, very productive weekend.

Mr. Prime Minister.

PRIME MINISTER ABE: (As interpreted.) This is the fourth time in six months for me to visit the United States. The last time was in Pearl Harbor, Hawaii at the end of last year. I am indeed sincerely grateful for the always heartwarming welcome accorded to me by the American people.

I would also like to express my sincere gratitude to President Trump. Donald, you must have been very busy in this very important period of 100 days after your inauguration. And thank you very much for inviting me over to the White House.

My name is Abe, but in the United States some people mistakenly pronounce my name as "Abe." But that is not bad, because even in Japan everybody knows the name of that great President, that a farmer and carpenter's son can become a President.

And that fact, 150 years ago, surprised the Japanese, who were still under the shogunate rule. The Japanese opened their eyes to democracy. The United States is the champion of democracy.

Donald, President, you are excellent businessman, but you have never been in the Congress or been a governor. You have not experienced being in the public office. But you have fought the uphill struggle and fight for more than a year in the election campaign to become a new President. And this is the dynamism of democracy. I would like to celebrate and congratulate Donald being sworn in as the President.

The United States is a country having the largest number of chances, opportunities in the world. That has always been the case right now, as well as going forward. This will never change.

And that is the reason why automotive industries and other Japanese businesses have built factories all over the

United States, to engage in local production here. Last year, from Japan to the United States, there have been more than $150 billion of new investment being made into the United States. And those Japanese businesses have created a large number of jobs. The mutually beneficial economic relations have been built by Japan and the United States. With President Trump taking on the leadership, I'm sure there will be -- major-scale infrastructure investment will be made, including the fast-speed train.

Those of you who have rode on the Japanese Shinkansen, I'm sure you would appreciate the speed, the comfort and safety with the latest maglev technology.

From Washington, D.C. to New York, where Trump Tower exists, only one hour would it take if you ride the maglev train from Washington, D.C. to New York. Japan, with our high level of technical capability, we will be able to contribute to President Trump's growth strategy. There will be even more new jobs being born in the United States.

And to further deepen these bilateral economic relations between Deputy Prime Minister Aso and Vice President Pence, there will be a cross-sectoral dialogue to be held. And we have agreed on this.

And furthermore, in Asia Pacific, where we see dramatic growth to expand free trade and investment, this will be a big chance for both Japan and the United States. But, of course, it must be done in a fair manner. Never should a state-owned company, backed by state capital, should not make any economic intervention. Free ride on intellectual property should not be condoned. In Asia Pacific region, with Japan and U.S. taking on the leadership to create free and fair market based upon rules, should be built. I and

President Trump have confirmed on our strong will to do so.

The cornerstone of peace and prosperity in Asia Pacific, that is the strong Japan-U.S. alliance. And this is unwavering ties between our two countries. I and President Trump will work together to further strengthen our alliance. We have shared this strong resolve.

As we see increasingly difficult security environment, we have confirmed that U.S.-Japan Security Pact Article 5 will be applied to Senkaku Islands. The United States will strengthen its presence in the region. And under the banner of the proactive contribution to peace, Japan will play a greater role. At the same time, we will maintain the deterrence and also to proceed on reducing the impact we had fought through on the realignment of the U.S. forces in Japan.

And Henoko's -- relocation to Henoko of the impasse Futenma is the only solution. And Japan and U.S. will continue to work closely on this.

On North Korea, we would strongly demand North Korea to abandon nuclear and ballistic missile program, and not to make any more provocations. And we have completely agreed on the importance of the early solution for the abduction issue in East China Sea, South China Sea, and Indian Ocean -- everywhere we need to maintain the freedom of navigation and rule of law. And such international order there must be maintained.

Japan and United States have confirmed that we will strongly protest any use of force, as well as coercion to change the status quo. I and the President will address not only bilateral but regional issues. And we have had a very frank exchange of views on the peace and prosperity of the world that we should contribute, for any form of terrorism should be strongly condemned. And we will cooperate in our fight against terrorism. Japan will, of course, exercise a commensurate role in this regard. And furthermore, the regional conflict of the refugees, of poverty and infectious diseases -- there are many challenges faced by the world, which will be a serious issue to threaten the peace and stability for Japan as well as the United States.

But Japan and the United States and the international community must work hand in hand in order to solve these questions. Of course, there are disagreements, but we should not close down dialogue just by pointing to the differences and ignoring the common interests and common goals. We need to have dialogue because there are disagreements. What we mostly desire -- what is most desired by those who are challenging the existing international order is to just focus on differences. We should not close the dialogue of Japan -- have for four years that I have consistently followed through on our foreign policy.

Now, whatever the challenge and difficulty ahead of us, I and Trump -- President Trump will continue our dialogue to seek shared solutions. And after lunch, I am looking forward for a weekend in Florida with Donald. We will play golf together. My scores in golf is not up to the level of Donald at all, but my policy is never up, never in, always aiming for the cup -- never cut to just the goal with short-cuts and short chops. Those are the words never found in my dictionary. (Laughter.)

But in a relaxed atmosphere, I hope to take time to discuss with Donald on the future of the world, future of the region, and future of Japan and the United States.

Thank you.

PRESIDENT TRUMP: Thank you very much. We'll take a few questions, unless you don't want to ask any questions, if that's possible. Maybe we'll start -- where is Daniel Halper, New York Post? Daniel.

Q Thank you, Mr. President. I'm curious about yesterday's ruling in the 9th Circuit Court. Has it caused you to rethink your use of executive power? And how will you respond? And will you sign new executive orders and perhaps a new travel ban?

And, Mr. Prime Minister, I'm curious about your reaction to America's withdrawal from the Trans-Pacific Partnership, the TPP.

Do you think that that's weakened America's position in Asia? And how do you think -- how do you envision any sort of trade deal with the President working out?

PRESIDENT TRUMP: Well, your question was unrelated to what we're here for today, but I'll answer it. We are going to keep our country safe, we are going to do whatever is necessary to keep our country safe. We had a decision which we think we'll be very successful with. It shouldn't have taken this much time because safety is a primary reason. One of the reasons I'm standing here today is the security of our country. The voters felt that I would give it the best security. So we'll be doing something very rapidly having to do with additional security for our country. You'll be seeing that sometime next week.

In addition, we will continue to go through the court process, and ultimately I have no doubt that we'll win that particular case.

PRIME MINISTER ABE: (As interpreted.) Now, in the world, we are also facing the issues of the refugees and terrorism. We need to work closely together on these global issues. Japan have always played our own role, but going forward, we will continue to work with the international community to execute our responsibility in a commensurate manner. And each of our country has immigration control scheme, as well as policy on immigration, as well as refugees. These are to do with domestic affairs of that country, so I would refrain from making any comments.

PRESIDENT TRUMP: Okay. Blake Berman, Fox. Blake Berman.

Q   Thank you, Mr. President. I'd like to pick up where Daniel left off, if you don't mind. You said earlier this week -- and I'm quoting for you -- you said, "I've learned a lot in the last two weeks, and terrorism is a far greater threat than the people of our country understand, but we're going to take care of it."

Based off of what you have learned, and now knowing that your executive order is at least temporarily on hold, do you still feel as confident now as you have been at any point, that you and the administration will be able to protect the homeland?

And, Mr. Prime Minister, thank you. I would just like to pick off again on what Daniel had asked about TPP. Do you feel it's a mistake that the United States has at least signaled its intention to withdraw from the deal? Thank you, both.

PRESIDENT TRUMP: I feel totally confident that we will have tremendous security for the people of the United States. We will be extreme vetting, which is a term that I developed early in my campaign because I saw what was happening. And while I've been President, which is just for a very short period of time, I've learned tremendous things that you could only learn, frankly, if you were in a certain position, namely, President. And there are tremendous threats to our country. We will not allow that to happen, I can tell you that right now. We will not allow that to happen.

So we'll be going forward. We'll be doing things to continue to make our country **safe.** It will happen rapidly. And we will not allow people into our country who are looking to do harm to our people. We will allow lots of people into our country that will love our people and do good for our country. It's always going to be that way, at least during my administration, I can tell you that.

PRIME MINISTER ABE: (As interpreted.) On TPP -- oh, of course, we are fully aware of President Trump's decision. On economic issues, we will be discussing at the working lunch to follow. As for Japan and United States, trade and investment, as well as economic relations, how can we develop and grow our relationship. As I have already mentioned, Deputy Prime Minister Aso and Vice President Pence will create a new framework for dialogue, and I am quite optimistic that the good results will be seen from the dialogue.

Now, for the free and fair common set of rules to be created for the free trade regime in the region, and that was the purpose of TPP, and that importance have not changed. I, myself, believe that.

Q (As interpreted.) Thank you. My name is Hara from NHK. I have a question to Prime Minister Abe. Now, for the automotive market in Japan, as well as foreign exchange of Japan, in the prior remarks there have been discrepancy in your positions. So at the summit meeting, what were the discussions? And were you able to narrow down the gap?

And President Trump had said that he will make the United States a great country. What is meant by the "great country"? And, Prime Minister, what do you mean when you say United States is a great ally for you?

PRIME MINISTER ABE: Now with the birth of the Trump administration, a new genesis will be built between Japan and U.S. in economic relations. In order to put forward such strong message, I have proposed to launch a new framework for economic dialogue, and we were able to agree on this.

As for sectorial discussions, we will be having a discussion at our working lunch. In any case, between President Trump and I, myself, on Japan and U.S. economic relations, we will -- we have already agreed that we will have Vice President Pence and Deputy Prime Minister Aso to discuss fully on the economic relations between our two countries. And we are looking forward for the good results to ensue from the debate between the experts.

As for the foreign exchange, we will have -- Secretary of Treasury and the Minister of Finance will continue the close communication.

For the United States to become a great nation, the various roles played by the United States and the responsibility to go with it, the world over is faced with increasing uncertainty. That United States will become a great America and become a great and strong ally would be good for Japan. And for Japan and U.S. alliance to be further strengthened would be good not only for our two nations, but also contribute to the peace and prosperity of the Asia Pacific and United States to become even greater. We will welcome that.

PRESIDENT TRUMP: Thank you. I will say that -- and you've seen it -- ever since I won the election and became President-elect, I've been telling companies, car companies and other companies -- many companies: Come back into the United States. And they've been coming back in. And big announcements are going to be made over the next short period of time. Some of you already know what those announcements are.

We lost a lot of our factories, a lot of our plants. And those factories and those plants will be coming back. And jobs will be coming back to Michigan and Ohio and Pennsylvania and North Carolina, and so many other places where we've lost so many jobs. And those are the people that were so good to me, and now I'm being good to them. So we've had a tremendous number of announcements. We've had Ford and General Motors and many, many others -- Intel yesterday made a major announcement. And they did that because of what is happening with our tax structure, which is going along very well. And we'll be having some very big news over the next short period of time.

But we are a nation of tremendous potential. And the expression "**Make America Great Again**," I will tell you -- and I will add very strongly and with great assurance, it will be greater than ever before.

And I just want to thank the Prime Minister for a friend-ship. We developed a great friendship when we met in New York City, at Trump Tower. We spoke for a long, long period of time. And when I greeted him today at the car, I was saying -- I shook hands, but I grabbed him and hugged him because that's the way we feel. We have a very, very good bond -- very, very good chemistry. I'll let you know if it changes, but I don't think it will. (Laughter.)

So I just want to thank the Prime Minister for being here. We're going to be meeting your wife in a very short period of time, and I look very much forward to that. And I want to thank everybody in the room. We're going to have a tremendous relationship, long-term relationship of mutual benefit with Japan.

Thank you all very much. Thank you. Thank you, Mr. Prime Minister.

PRIME MINISTER ABE: One more.

PRESIDENT TRUMP: Yes, certainly. Go ahead.

Q (As interpreted.) Thank you very much. From Sankei Shimbun, my name is Takita. I have a question to President Trump. Obama administration, under the rebalance to Asia, have emphasized Asia.

But China is taking hard-line stance in South China Sea, as well as China Sea.

And North Korea has went on with the missiles and nuclear development. So some countries in Asia are concerned over commitment of United States in Asia. So against this backdrop, as was mentioned earlier, for the Trump administration, for the situations in Asia, how would you respond to the increasing difficulty here?

And, President, you have repeatedly stated about China taking on the currency -- foreign exchange policies which are not good for the United States. Do you think that eventually it will change in the future?

PRESIDENT TRUMP: I had a very, very good conversation, as most of you know, yesterday with the President of China. It was a very, very warm conversation. I think we are on the process of getting along very well. And I think that will also be very much of a benefit to Japan. So we had a very, very good talk last night and discussed a lot of subjects. It was a long talk. And we are working on that as we speak. We have conversations with various representatives of China, I believe, that that will all work out very well for everybody -- China, Japan, the United States, and everybody in the region.

As far as the currency devaluations, I've been complaining about that for a long time. And I believe that we will all eventually -- and probably very much sooner than a lot of people understand or think -- we will be all at a level playing field, because that's the only way it's fair. That's the only way that you can fairly compete in trade and other things. And we will be on that field, and we will all be working very hard to do great for our country. But it has to be fair. And we will make it fair.

I think the United States is going to be an even bigger

player than it is right now, by a lot, when it comes to trade. A lot of that will have to do with our tax policy, which you'll be seeing in the not-too-distant future. We'll have an incentive-based policy much more so than we have right now. Right now we don't even know -- nobody knows what policy we have. But we're going to have a very much incentive-based policy. We're working with Congress, working with Paul Ryan, working with Mitch McConnell. And I think people are going to be very, very impressed.

We're also working very much -- and this has a lot to do with business -- on health care, where we can get great health care for our country at a much-reduced price, both to the people receiving the health care and to our country.

Because our country is paying so much, and Obamacare, as you know, is a total and complete disaster. So we're going to end up with tremendous health care at a lower price. And I think people are going to be extremely happy.

Difficult process, but once we get going -- and, as you know, Tom Price was just approved a few hours ago. So we finally have our Secretary, and now we get down to the final strokes.

Again, I want to thank everybody for being here. I want to thank Mr. Prime Minister. What an honor, what a great honor it is. And let's go to Florida. (Applause.)

END
1:37 P.M. EST

Chapter 30

10 February 2017

Transcript:

My fellow Americans,
This week our hearts are with the people of Louisiana and Mississippi. Families have lost their homes, businesses, and livelihoods after devastating tornadoes swept through many, many communities.

My administration will make sure they have the support that they need and really desperately want. We're going to take care of them. It's remarkable to see Americans across the country come together to help families rebuild their lives. That is the beauty of the **American Spirit** – there's nothing like it.

There is a **great spirit** all over the country – and that **spirit** is what we will need to rebuild America to, as I have said so often, **Make America Great Again**.

On Tuesday, I was pleased to host at the White House the CEO of Intel, who announced that Intel will invest $7 billion dollars in a new manufacturing facility in Arizona – creating thousands of new American jobs. That's what we want, new American jobs, and good jobs.

Intel decided to move forward with this project because they know we are totally committed to lifting the regulatory and tax burdens that are hurting American innovation and companies.

In fact, we are in the process right now of working on a major tax reform that will massively reduce taxes on our workers and businesses. We want to make it much easier to do business in America – and that's what we are going to do. We are going to make it also much harder for companies to leave. They're not just going to say bye-bye and fire everybody. There will be consequences.

I want America to be the great jobs magnet of the world – but we can't do that if we don't stop the wasteful rules and excessive taxes that make it impossible for companies to compete. Every hour of every day, my Administration is focused on creating jobs for our people and I mean good jobs. More jobs, better jobs, higher-paying jobs – that's our mission.

This week, I also met with Sheriffs and Police Chiefs from across the country. I pledged to them that we would stand with the incredible men and women of law enforcement – and so too will our great new Attorney General, Jeff Sessions.

My administration is committed to your security, which is why we will continue to fight to take all necessary and legal action to keep terrorists, radical and dangerous extremists from ever entering our country. We will not allow our generous system of immigration to be turned against us as a tool for terrorism and truly bad people. We must take firm steps today to ensure that we are **safe** tomorrow.

We will defend our country, protect our Constitution, and deliver real prosperity for our people.

God bless you, God bless America. Have a great week.

Chapter 31

10 February 2017

PRESIDENT TRUMP: Hello everybody. Everything good?

Press conference good. I think it was great. Really good.

Are you comfortable?

UNKNOWN PERSON: Talk about some things you said (audio unclear).

PRESIDENT TRUMP: Some What?

UNKNOWN PERSON: What you said at the press conference?

PRESIDENT TRUMP: Sure.

UNKNOWN PERSON: You spoke about, you were going to win this court battle against the immigration and the travel ban and you also – (interrupted by the President).

PRESIDENT TRUMP: The unfortunate part is that it takes time statutorily. It takes a little time. But we will win that battle, but we also have a lot of other options including just filing a brand new order on Monday.

UNKNOWN PERSON: Is that your plan?

PRESIDENT TRUMP: Could very well be. But I would like to keep you, you know, I would like to surprise you. We need speed for - reasons of security, so it could very well be that we do that.

UNKNOWN PERSON: What are the changes that you are looking at?

PRESIDENT TRUMP: Very little, just in honor of the decision, we will perhaps do that. We will see; but on Monday or Tuesday.

UNKNOWN PERSON: You talked about new security measures. Is that separate from potentially, writing a new

PRESIDENT TRUMP: We are going to have very, very strong vetting. I call it extreme vetting and we are going to have strong security in our country.

We are going to have people come into our country that want to be her[e] for good reasons.

UNKNOWN PERSON: What do you make about reports that General Flynn had conversation with the Russians about sanction before you were sworn in?

PRESIDENT TRUMP: I don't know about it. I haven't seen it. What report is that? I have not seen it.

UNKNOWN PERSON: The Washington Post is reporting that he talked to the Ambassador to Russia, before you were Inaugurated, about sanctions.

PRESIDENT TRUMP: I haven't see that. I'll look at that.

UNKNOWN PERSON: What is your response to the Iranian President, who earlier today, told people that any – any nation that threatens the nation of Iran is going to regret it eventually?

PRESIDENT TRUMP: He better be careful.

Thank you, thank you very much.

Chapter 32

13 February 2017

12:13 P.M. EST

PRESIDENT TRUMP: I'm honored to be here with Prime Minister Trudeau, whose father I knew and respected greatly. And he gave me a picture of myself and your father, and what a great picture. I will keep that in very special place -- at the Waldorf Astoria, together.

We're going to launch the Canada-United States Council for Advancement of Women Entrepreneurs. We have some of the great ones in this room -- and business leaders. We have so many great women leaders around the table today, and we're going to go through your names exactly, because many of you I know, some of you I don't, so I want to find out all about you.

Women, as you know, I can say that from my past life, I had so many women executives who were phenomenal -- phenomenal -- and really helped me a great deal in business. So it was really fantastic. They play a tremendously important role, women in our economy.

Women are the primary source of income in 40 percent of American households and households with children under the age of 18.

In order to create economic growth and lots of very good, well-paying jobs, we must ensure that our economy is a place where women can work and thrive. And I think that's happening in the United States much more so, and Ivanka is very much involved in this. And I appreciate you being involved in it.

And I know, Justin, in Canada it's happening big league, and it's very important. We need policies that help to keep women in the workforce and to address the unique barriers faced by female entrepreneurs -- and they are unique. We need to make it easier for women to manage the demands of having both a job and a family, and we also need to make it easier for women entrepreneurs to get access to capital. And I guess pretty much all entrepreneurs, we have to help them out, because the system is not working so well for entrepreneurs getting capital. But it's in particular difficult for women, so we're going to get access to markets and access to networks.

And I look forward to hearing your advice. We're going to go around the table, and I want to really learn something today. And again, it's a great honor to be with you. And, Justin, I can say on behalf of our country, it's an honor to be with you.

PRIME MINISTER TRUDEAU: Thank you, Donald, for welcoming us. And I'm really excited about launching this, sitting around the table here with a number of successful executives who just happen to be women. One of the things that I've been lucky enough to do over the past year in New York and Beijing and across Canada is sit down with women CEOs, women executives to talk about both their successes and the challenges they're facing that are particular, but also how, of course, we create more paths to success for women across our community and across our society.

Whenever I sit down with a woman executive, I know that she has had to overcome significant barriers that exist, and therefore is likely to have greater insight into how to help reduce those barriers for others, but also be a formidable contributor to the success of business and her economy.

So I think for me, it's not just about doing the right thing, it's about understanding that women in leadership positions is a very powerful leverage for success, for business, for communities, and for our entire economy.
(Speaks in French.)

It's a great pleasure to sit with you now and to hear from your extraordinary leadership.

PRESIDENT TRUMP: Thank you, Mr. Prime Minister. So how about we start with Ivanka, we go around the room. Ivanka, you might just want to say a couple of words.

MS. TRUMP: Welcome. I'm honored to be here, and really looking forward to hearing from each of you who serve as tremendous role models for me and so many other business leaders. (Inaudible)

Our countries can lend some tremendously valuable perspective as we think about the unique challenges that entrepreneurs, women in the workforce, female small-business owners are confronted with each and every day. And as we think about how we level the playing field for this generation and for the next.

So thank you for being here. And I look forward to hearing from you today.

MR. FARRELL: Thank you. I'm Dawn Farrell and I'm from a company called TransAlta, which is located in Alberta, where you're going to build the Keystone Pipeline.

PRESIDENT TRUMP: A big chunk of it, that's right.

MS. FARRELL: So thanks for the opportunity to contribute to this important dialogue, and a dialogue that we've had for 100 -- over hundreds of years. My company is in the business of making electricity. We generate electricity from coal, natural gas, and also from renewable sources -- wind, hydro and solar. We have operations in Canada, the United States and in Australia.

And, really, for us to excel, we have to be excellent at operations, engineering, finance and trading, and we have to excel in the public policy dialogue that happens around energy. And I'll talk about that as part of today, because we've done some excellent work with the Trudeau government.

Now, future jobs in our space absolutely depend on growth. There's no question of that. And I truly believe for there to be future opportunities for women, we have to have growth, because the more jobs there are, the more opportunities. And collaborations like this where we break down barriers and simplify, and build trust and build confidence -- because I think businesses invest when there's confidence. And my hope is that's what comes out of here.

Now, for us, having operations in Canada and the United

States makes us absolutely more competitive. Our Centralia operation, which is in Washington State, is one of the most competitive plants. They have twice won our most coveted award for plant of the year. But the reality is, teams of people from the United States and teams of people from Canada cross the border often to work with each other to share and to -- so that we can excel as a company overall. So it's huge --

PRESIDENT TRUMP: That's good. Well, we're going to go around. Thank you. Good job. Boy, she did a hell of a job. (Laughter.)

Wow, no wonder she's successful. (Laughter.)

Monique, thank you.

MS. LEROUX: Monique Leroux. I am the Chair of the Board of the Quebec Investment Fund and the Chair of the Economy Council of the Province. I'm also a Board member of large, global corporations like S&P Global, Michelin, and Couche-Tard, which is a very interesting Canadian company. Each of those organizations, of course, have significant businesses in the U.S. and also employs a lot of people in this country.

I feel really honored and privileged to be part of the Council. I would like to thank you for this great opportunity.

PRESIDENT TRUMP: Thank you.

MS. LEROUX: We have long history of cooperation, and I think that for the woman agenda it will contribute a lot for our great countries.

PRESIDENT TRUMP: Thank you, Monique. Appreciate it.

MS. LEE: My name is Tina Lee. I'm CEO of T&T Supermarket. We're Canada's largest Asian supermarket chain. I employ 5,000 staff and serve 500,000 people across the country every week.

PRESIDENT TRUMP: Wow. Fantastic.

MS. LEE: Thank you.

PRESIDENT TRUMP: Thank you.

MS. STEPHENSON: I'm Carol Stephenson. I'm on the Board of Directors at General Motors, and I don't think that General Motors needs any introduction. (Laughter.)

PRESIDENT TRUMP: No, we had -- Mary Barra was here last week, and she's terrific.

MS. STEPHENSON: She is.

PRESIDENT TRUMP: Thank you. Thank you very much.

MS. LUNDGREN: I'm Tamara Lundgren. I'm the President and CEO of Schnitzer Steel Industries, which is one of the world's largest recyclers of metal products, sold to steel mills around the world. I also sit on the Board of Parsons Corporation, which has been a big participant in the public-private partnerships in Canada. And I sit on the Board of Ryder, which goes back and forth between the U.S. and Canada over 400 times every day. And lastly, I'm the Chair of the Board of the Portland branch of the 12th District Federal Reserve Board.

PRESIDENT TRUMP: Very good. Thank you very much.

MS. ALLAN: Hello, Elyse Allan. I'm Vice President of GE, as well as GE's operations in Canada. And we're a digital industrial company. We have business in 190 countries in the world.

PRESIDENT TRUMP: Right. That's good. Good, thank you.

MS. VERSCHUREN: I'm Annette Verschuren. I'm the CEO of NRStor, which is an energy storage development company. Half of my career I've worked with U.S. based companies -- Home Depot, (inaudible) and Michaels -- craft store. I think that our countries are so absolutely bound together by our people, our resources, our trade.

Linda Hasenfratz and I worked for many years on North American competitiveness and found ways in which we could get products and services and people through the border efficiently because, as you know, we're the biggest trading partners in the world.

PRESIDENT TRUMP: Well, we're going to be working on that very closely over the next very short period of time. There are some new things happening that can be very good. Thank you very much.

MS. SWEET: Hello, I'm Julie Sweet. I'm CEO of North America for Accenture, responsible for both the U.S. and Canadian businesses.

PRESIDENT TRUMP: Thank you.

MS. HASENFRATZ: Hi, I'm Linda Hasenfratz. I'm CEO of Linamar Corporation. We're a diversified manufacturing company.

We have 57 plants and 25,000 employees around the world, including right here in the U.S. and, of course, also heavily invested in Canada. We've doubled our workforce in the U.S. over the last five years. We've also doubled our workforce in Canada over the last five years and have a lot of exciting opportunities for growth. We're mainly in the auto parts and access equipment sectors.

PRESIDENT TRUMP: Thank you very much. Thank you, everybody.

END
12:24 P.M. EST

[NOTE: For further information on Women Entrepreneurs see the Mastercard Index of Women Entrepreneurs 2017.]

Chapter 33

13 February 2017

2:16 P.M. EST

PRESIDENT TRUMP: Prime Minister Trudeau, on behalf
of all Americans, I thank you for being with us today. It is
my honor to host such a great friend, neighbor, and ally at
the White House, a very special place. This year, Canada
celebrates the 150th year of Confederation. For Americans, this is one of the many milestones in our friendship,
and we look forward -- very much forward, I must say -- to
many more to come.

Our two nations share much more than a border. We
share the same values. We share the love, and a truly
great love, of freedom. And we share a collective defense. American and Canadian troops have gone to battle
together, fought wars together, and forged the special
bonds that come when two nations have shed their blood
together -- which we have.

In these dangerous times, it is more important than ever
that we continue to strengthen our vital alliance. The
United States is deeply grateful for Canada's contribution
to the counter-ISIS effort. Thank you. And we continue to
work in common, and in common cause, against terrorism,
and work in common cooperation toward reciprocal trade

and shared growth.

We understand that both of our countries are stronger when we join forces in matters of international commerce. Having more jobs and trade right here in North America is better for both the United States and is also much better for Canada. We should coordinate closely -- and we will coordinate closely -- to protect jobs in our hemisphere and keep wealth on our continent, and to keep everyone safe.

Prime Minister, I pledge to work with you in pursuit of our many shared interests. This includes a stronger trading relationship between the United States and Canada. It includes safe, efficient, and responsible cross-border travel and migration. And it includes close partnership on domestic and international security.

America is deeply fortunate to have a neighbor like Canada. We have before us the opportunity to build even more bridges, and bridges of cooperation and bridges of commerce. Both of us are committed to bringing greater prosperity and opportunity to our people.

We just had a very productive meeting with women business leaders from the United States and Canada, where we discussed how to secure everything that we know the full power of women can do better than anybody else. We know that. I just want to say, Mr. Prime Minister, that I'm focused and you're focused on the important role women play in our economies. We must work to address the barriers faced by women and women entrepreneurs, including access to capital, access to markets, and, very importantly, access to networks.

In our discussion today we will focus on improving the ways our government and our governments together can benefit citizens of both the United States and Canada, and, in so doing, advance the greater peace and stability of the world.

Mr. Prime Minister, I look forward to working closely with you to build upon our very historic friendship. There are incredible possibilities for us to pursue, Canada and the United States together. Again, thank you for joining us, and I know our discussions will be very, very productive for the future of both countries.

Mr. Prime Minister.

PRIME MINISTER TRUDEAU: Thank you, Mr. President. Good afternoon, everyone. Thank you very much for joining us.

I'd first like to start by extending my sincere thanks to President Trump for inviting me down to Washington. Any day I get to visit our southern neighbors is a good day in my book, particularly when it's so nice and warm compared to what it is back home. We are suffering under a significant winter storm that's hitting our Atlantic provinces particularly harsh, so I just want to send everyone back at home my thoughts as they shovel out, and impress on everyone to stay safe.

(As interpreted from French.) The President and myself have had a very productive first meeting today. We had the opportunity to get to know one another better, and, more importantly, we had the opportunity to talk about the unique relationship between Canada and the United States.

(In English.) Ends on both sides of the 49th parallel have understood that the bond between our nations is a special one. No other neighbors in the entire world are as fundamentally linked as we are. We've fought in conflict zones together, negotiated environmental treaties together, including 1991's historic Air Quality Agreement. And we've entered into ground-breaking economic partnerships that have created good jobs for both of our peoples.

Canadians and Americans alike share a common history as well as people-to-people ties that make us completely and totally integrated. Our workers are connected by trade, transportation and cross-border commerce. Our communities rely on each other for security, stability and economic prosperity. Our families have long lived together and worked together. We know that, more often than not, our victories are shared. And just as we celebrate together, so too do we suffer loss and heartbreak together.

Through it all, the foundational pillar upon which our relationship is built is one of mutual respect. And that's a good thing, because as we know, relationships between neighbors are pretty complex and we won't always agree on everything. But because of our deep, abiding respect for one another, we're able to successfully navigate those complexities and still remain the closest of allies and friends. Make no mistake -- at the end of the day, Canada and the U.S. will always remain each other's most essential partner.

And today's conversations have served to reinforce how important that is for both Canadians and Americans. As we know, 35 U.S. states list Canada as their largest export market, and our economies benefit from the over $2 billion in two-way trade that takes place every single day. Millions of good, middle-class jobs on both sides of the border depend on this crucial partnership. Maintaining strong economic ties is vital to our mutual success, and we're going to continue to work closely together over the coming years so that Canadian and American families can get ahead.

(As interpreted from French.) As we know, 35 U.S. states list Canada as their largest export market and our economies benefit from the over $2 billion in two-way trade that takes place every single day. Millions of good, middle-class jobs on both sides of the border depend on this crucial partnership. Maintaining strong economic ties is vital to our mutual success, and we're going to continue to work closely together over the coming years so that Canadian and American families can get ahead.

(In English.) I'd like to highlight just a few of the specifics that President Trump and I discussed today. At the end of the day, the President and I share a common goal. We both want to make sure that hardworking folks can go to work at a good job, put food on the table for their families, and save up to take a vacation every once in a while. That's what we're trying to do here.

Today, we reiterated that our nations are committed to collaborating on energy infrastructure projects that will create jobs while respecting the environment. And, as we know, investing in infrastructure is a great way to create the kind of economic growth that our countries so desperately need.

In that same vein, we know that ensuring equal opportunities for women in the workforce is essential for growing the economy and maintaining American and Canadian competitiveness on the world stage. As such, the President and I have agreed to the creation of the Canada-United States Council for Advancement of Women Entrepreneurs and Business Leaders. This initiative is more than just about dollars and cents. This is about ensuring that women have access to the same opportunities as men, and prioritizing the support and empowerment of women who are senior business leaders and entrepreneurs. In doing so, we'll grow the Canadian and American economies, and help our businesses prosper.

(As interpreted from French.) Finally, President Trump and myself have agreed to work together to fight against the traffic of opioids across our border. The rise of illegal use of opioids in our society is nothing less than a tragedy. We will do everything we can to ensure the safety of Canadians and Americans.

Ladies and gentlemen, President Trump, I know that if our countries continue to work together, our people will greatly benefit from this cooperation.

(In English.) History has demonstrated time and again that in order to tackle our most pressing issues, both foreign and domestic, we must work with our closest allies, learn from each other, and stand in solidarity as a united voice. With a level of economic and social integration that is unmatched on the world stage, Canada and the United States will forever be a model example of how to be good neighbors. Winston Churchill once said, "That long Canadian frontier from the Atlantic to the Pacific Oceans, guarded only by neighborly respect and honorable obligations, is an example to every country, and a pattern for the future of the world." That, my friends, is the very essence of the Canada-U.S. relationship.

I look forward to working with President Trump over the coming years to nurture and build upon this historic partnership. Once again, it's a tremendous pleasure to be here in Washington. Merci beaucoup.

PRESIDENT TRUMP: Okay, we'll take a couple of questions. Scott Thuman. Scott.

Q   Thank you, Mr. President. You just spoke about the desire to build bridges, although there are some notable and philosophical differences between yourself and Prime Minister Trudeau. I'm curious, as you move forward on issues from trade to terrorism, how do you see this relationship playing out? And are there any specific areas with which during your conversations today you each decided to perhaps alter or amend your stances already on those sensitive issues like terrorism and immigration?

And, Prime Minister Trudeau, while only in its infancy so far, how do you see this relationship compared to that under the Obama administration?

PRESIDENT TRUMP: Well, we just began discussions. We are going to have a great relationship with Canada, maybe as good or better, hopefully, than ever before. We have some wonderful ideas on immigration. We have some, I think, very strong, very tough ideas on the tremendous problem that we have with terrorism. And I think when we put them all together, which will be very, very quickly -- we have a group of very talented people -- we will see some very, very obvious results. We're also doing some cross-border things that will make it a lot easier for trade and a lot better and a lot faster for trade.

We have -- through technology, we have some really great

ideas, and they'll be implemented fairly quickly.

PRIME MINISTER TRUDEAU: One of the things we spoke about was the fact that security and immigration need to work very well together. And certainly Canada has emphasized security as we look towards improving our immigration system and remaining true to the values that we have. And we had a very strong and fruitful discussion on exactly that.

There's plenty that we can draw on each other from in terms of how we move forward with a very similar goal, which is to create free, open societies that keep our citizens safe. And that's certainly something that we're very much in agreement on.

Tonda MacCharles.

Q   Good afternoon, Mr. President and Mr. Prime Minister. And, Mr. Prime Minister, could you answer in English and French for us, please?

A little bit of a follow-on on my American colleague's question. President Trump, you seem to suggest that Syrian refugees are a Trojan horse for potential terrorism, while the Prime Minister hugs refugees and welcomes them with open arms. So I'd like to know, are you confident the northern border is secure?

PRESIDENT TRUMP: You can never be totally confident. But through the incredible efforts -- already I see it happening -- of formerly General Kelly, now Secretary Kelly, we have really done a great job. We're actually taking people that are criminals -- very, very hardened criminals in some cases, with a tremendous track record of abuse and problems -- and we're getting them out. And that's what I said I would do. I'm just doing what I said I would do when we won by a very, very large Electoral College vote. And I knew that was going to happen. I knew this is what people were wanting. And that wasn't the only reason, that wasn't my only thing that we did so well on. But that was something was very important. And I said we will get the criminals out, the drug lords, the gang members. We're getting them out.

General Kelly, who is sitting right here, is doing a fantastic job. And I said at the beginning we are going to get the bad ones -- the really bad ones, we're getting them out. And that's exactly what we're doing.

I think that in the end everyone is going to be extremely happy. And I will tell you right now, a lot of people are very, very happy right now.

PRIME MINISTER TRUDEAU: Canada has always understood that keeping Canadians safe is one of the fundamental responsibilities of any government. And that's certainly something that we're very much focused on.

At the same time, we continue to pursue our policies of openness towards immigration, refugees, without compromising security. And part of the reason we have been successful in doing that over the past year -- welcoming close to 40,000 Syrian refugees -- is because we have been coordinating with our allies, the United States and around the world, to demonstrate that security comes very seriously to us. And that's something that we continue to deal with.

(As interpreted from French.) It is clear that if you want

to have a healthy and secure society or safe society, you have to make sure that you maintain -- that you focus on security. And we have welcomed refugees from Syria. We have been very successful, but we have always taken our responsibility toward security very seriously. And our allies, including the United States, understand this focus very well. And they have done so since the very beginning.

PRESIDENT TRUMP: Caitlin Collins (ph), please.

Q   Thank you. President Trump, now that you've been in office and received intelligence briefings for nearly one month, what do you see as the most important national security matters facing us?

And, Prime Minister Trudeau, you've made very clear that Canada has an open-door policy for Syrian refugees. Do you believe that President Trump's moratorium on immigration has merit on national security grounds?

PRESIDENT TRUMP: Okay. Thank you. Many, many problems. When I was campaigning, I said it's not a good situation. Now that I see it -- including with our intelligence briefings -- we have problems that a lot of people have no idea how bad they are, how serious they are, not only internationally, but when you come right here.

Obviously, North Korea is a big, big problem, and we will deal with that very strongly. We have problems all over the Middle East. We have problems just about every corner of the globe, no matter where you look. I had a great meeting this weekend with Prime Minister Abe of Japan and got to know each other very, very well -- extended weekend, really. We were with each other for long periods of time, and our staffs and representatives.

But on the home front, we have to create borders. We have to let people that can love our country in, and I want to do that. We want to have a big, beautiful, open door, and we want people to come in and come in our country. But we cannot let the wrong people in, and I will not allow that to happen during this administration. And people -- citizens of our country want that, and that's their attitude, too.

I will tell you, we are getting such praise for our stance, and it's a stance of common sense -- maybe a certain toughness, but it's really more than toughness, it's a stance of common sense -- and we are going to pursue it vigorously. And we don't want to have our country have the kinds of problems that you're witnessing taking place not only here but all over the world. We won't stand for it. We won't put up with it. We're just not going to let it happen. We're going to give ourselves every bit of chance so that things go well for the United States. And they will go well. Thank you.

PRIME MINISTER TRUDEAU: Canada and the United States have been neighbors a long time, and Canadians and Americans have stood together, worked together at home and around the world. We've fought and died together in battlefields in World War I and World War II, in Korea, in Afghanistan. But there have been times where we have differed in our approaches, and that's always been done firmly and respectfully.

The last thing Canadians expect is for me to come down and lecture another country on how they choose to govern themselves. My role and our responsibility is to continue to govern in such a way that reflects Canadians' approach and be a positive example in the world.

Richard Latendresse.

Q   Thank you, Mr. Prime Minister. I'll ask my question in French first and then, for you, I'll -- again in English.

(As interpreted from French.)

Mr. Prime Minister, if I heard you correctly, you said that Canadian businesses, Canadian workers are concerned for their businesses and for their work and jobs concerning the renegotiation of NAFTA. So what guarantees did you get from this government that we will keep our jobs and our businesses in the renegotiation of NAFTA?

(In English.) Mr. President, again, during the last three months, you have denounced NAFTA. You have talked over and over about the Mexican portion of the agreement, very little about the Canadian one. My question is in two short part is, is Canada a fair trader? And when you talk about changes to NAFTA concerning Canada, are you talking about big changes or small changes? Thank you.

PRIME MINISTER TRUDEAU: (As interpreted.) First of all, Richard, thank you for your question. It is a real concern for many Canadians because we know that our economy is very dependent on our bonds, our relationship with the United States. Goods and services do cross the border each way every single day, and this means a lot of millions of jobs for Canadians, and good jobs for Canadians. So we are always focusing on these jobs, but there are also good jobs, millions of jobs, in the United States that depend on those relationships between our two countries.

So when we sit down as we did today, and as our teams will be doing in the weeks and months to come, we will be talking about how we can continue to create good jobs for our citizens on both sides of the border. And during this exercise, we continue to understand that we have to allow this free flow of goods and services, and we have to be aware of the integration of our economies, which is extremely positive for both our countries. And this is the focus that we will have in the coming weeks and months to come.

(In English.) Canadians are rightly aware of the fact that much of our economy depends on good working relationships with the United States, a good integration with the American economy. And the fact is, millions of good jobs on both sides of the border depend on the smooth and easy flow of goods and services and people back and forth across our border.

And both President Trump and I got elected on commitments to support the middle class, to work hard for people who need a real shot at success. And we know that by working together, by ensuring the continued effective integration of our two economies, we are going to be creating greater opportunities for middle-class Canadians and Americans now and well into the future.

PRESIDENT TRUMP: I agree with that 100 percent. We have a very outstanding trade relationship with Canada. We'll be tweaking it. We'll be doing certain things that are going to benefit both of our countries. It's a much less severe situation than what's taking place on the southern border. On the southern border, for many, many years, the transaction was not fair to the United States. It was an extremely unfair transaction. We're going to work with Mexico, we're going to make it a fair deal for both parties. I think that we're going to get along very well with

Mexico; they understand and we understand.

You probably have noticed that Ford is making billions of dollars of new investments in this country. You saw Intel the other day announce that because of what I've been doing and what I'm doing in terms of regulation -- lowering taxes, et cetera -- they're coming in with billions and billions of dollars of investment, and thousands of thousands of jobs. General Motors, likewise, is expanding plants and going to build new plants. Fiat Chrysler was at a meeting where they're doing the same. Jack Ma -- we have so many people that want to come into the United States. It's actually very exciting.

I think it's going to be a very exciting period of time for the United States and for the workers of the United States, because they have been truly the forgotten man and forgotten women. It's not going to be forgotten anymore, believe me.

So our relationship with Canada is outstanding, and we're going to work together to make it even better. And as far as the southern border is concerned, we're going to get that worked out. We're going to make it fair, but we are going to make it so that everybody is happy. It's very important to me.

Thank you. Thank you very much.
Thank you, ladies and gentlemen.
Thank you very much. (Applause.)

END
2:42 P.M. EST

Chapter 34

**REMARKS BY PRESIDENT TRUMP AT SWEARING-IN CEREMONY
FOR TREASURY SECRETARY MNUCHIN
OVAL OFFICE**

13 February 2017

8:42 P.M. EST

THE PRESIDENT: It is my great honor tonight to present to
the American people our new Treasury Secretary of the
United States, Steven Mnuchin.

Steven, I want to congratulate you. A lot of people wanted
that position, Steven. A lot of people. A lot of very successful people. But I've known you for a long time, and I
know how smart you are and how great you will be for our
country. So congratulations to you, to Louise, and to your
whole family.

Americans should know that Steven -- our nation's financial system is truly in great hands. With him, we're going
to have no problem, believe me. Once again, with this
appointment, I am following through on my promise to
appoint only the very best and the very brightest.

Steven is a financial legend with an incredible track record
of success. I've watched this over the years. He's been my
friend for many, many years. Everything he's touched has
turned to gold. He's done an amazing job. And that's what
we want for our country.

He has distinguished himself through decades of achievement in finance and in banking, and has a degree of skill, talent, and insight that few will ever be able to match. He has spent his entire career making money in the private sector, and that's okay -- especially when you're Secretary of Treasury. That's what we want. Now he will go to work on behalf of the American taxpayer.

To all citizens I say: Steven will be your champion, and a great champion. He will fight for middle-class tax reductions, financial reforms that open up lending and create millions of new jobs, and fiercely defend the American tax dollar and our financial security. And he will also defend our manufacturing jobs from those who cheat and steal and rob us blind. It won't be that anymore. We won't have that anymore. Countries and others won't be able to take advantage of us. **It's a whole new era.**

Steven knows the system and he will help ensure that Wall Street plays by the rules. He will use his insights to get the best possible result, most importantly for the American worker. They've been treated very unfairly for a long time. Not anymore. He will put his skills to work for America's working families, and he will help **make America the greatest jobs magnet** on the face of the Earth. It will truly be for our country, for the first time in a long time, a rising tide that lifts all boats and that lifts all ships.

Steven, I want to again congratulate you and Louise on this unbelievably high honor. This is one of the great honors. I know you will carry your office with dedication, integrity and passion -- tremendous passion. You have much -- very important work ahead for the American citizens, and you will have absolutely no problem. He'll work 24 hours a day -- I know him. He'll work 28 hours a day, if they give the extra four hours. He will be very, very special.

So I'd like to just say, so importantly, God bless you, God bless America, and congratulations. Thank you, Steven. (Applause.)

(The Secretary is sworn in.)

SECRETARY MNUCHIN: Mr. President, I want to thank you for this extraordinary opportunity to serve you and the country as the Secretary of Treasury. It has been a great experience to travel around the country with you for the last year, seeing so many parts of this country and meeting hundreds of business leaders.

I share your economic vision and goals, and committed to working with you to enact policies, to grow the economy, and make better economic opportunities for all Americans. I would also like to thank Vice President Pence for the honor of swearing me in and for all your support in this job. There have been so many people that have helped me in this process, and I want to thank them all as they helped prepare me for the role of Secretary. And I want to thank them.

It's a great honor to follow in the footsteps of Alexander Hamilton and so many great Treasury Secretaries. I look forward to working with the entire great staff of the Treasury Department. I am committed to using the full powers of this office to create more jobs, to combat terrorist activities and financing, and to **Make America Great Again**. Thank you. (Applause.)

END
8:49 P.M. EST

Chapter 35

14 February 2017

10:50 A.M. EST

THE PRESIDENT: Well, I am delighted to welcome everybody to the White House. And Betsy DeVos, who has gone through -- our new Education Secretary -- she went through an interesting moment. And you're going to do a fantastic job, and I know you would have done it again if you had to do it again, right? (Laughter.)

SECRETARY DEVOS: Probably.

THE PRESIDENT: She had no doubt that final night, waiting for the vote. So I just want to congratulate you. You showed toughness and genius.

As I said many times in my campaign, we want every child in America to have the opportunity to climb the ladder to success. I want every child also to have a **safe** community, and we're going to do that very much. We're going to be helping you a lot -- a great school and some day to get a really well-paying job or better, or better; own their own company. And a lot of people are looking at that.

But it all begins with education, and that's why we're here this morning. And I'm here also to celebrate a little bit with Betsy because we started this journey a long time ago, having to do with change and so many other good things with education. And I'm so happy that that all worked out.

Right now, too many of our children don't have the opportunity to get that education that we all talk about. Millions of poor, disadvantaged students are trapped in failing schools and this crisis -- and it really is a crisis -- of education and communities working together but not working out. And we're going to change it around, especially for the African American communities. It's been very, very tough and unfair. And I know that's a priority and it's a certainly a priority of mine.

That's why I want every single disadvantaged child in America, no matter what their background or where they live, to have a choice about where they go to school. And it's worked out so well in some communities where it's been properly run and properly done. And it's a terrific thing.

Charter schools, in particular, have demonstrated amazing gains and results. And you look at the results -- we have cases in New York City that have been amazing in providing education to disadvantaged children and the success of so many different schools that I can name throughout the country that I got to see during the campaign. I went to one in Las Vegas; it was the most unbelievable thing you've ever seen. And they've done a fantastic job.

So there are many such schools and we want to do that on a large-scale basis. We can never lose sight of the connection between education and jobs. I'm bringing a lot of jobs back. We're bringing a lot of big plants back into the country -- everyone said it was impossible. And before I even took office, we started the process and tremendous numbers of plants are coming back into this country -- car plants and other plants. And I have meetings next week with four or five different companies, big ones that are going to bring massive numbers of jobs back.

So we're doing it from the jobs standpoint, but education only makes it better. Our goal is a clear and very **safe** community, great schools, and we want those jobs that are high-paying jobs -- we've lost a lot of our best jobs to other countries and we're going to bring them back.

So I'm going to do my job, and Betsy, at the education level, will do her job. And just to do it very, very formally, I want to congratulate you on having gone through a very tough trial and a very unfair trial, and you won. And there's something very nice about that. And I'll tell you the real winner will be the children -- I guess a couple of adults (inaudible) -- but will be the children of this country. And I just want to congratulate you.

SECRETARY DEVOS: Thank you, Mr. President.

THE PRESIDENT: Perhaps we'll go around the room. And everybody knows our fantastic Vice President, Mike Pence. But if we went around the room, it would be very nice. So why don't we start? Betsy, you might want to say a few words to us.

SECRETARY DEVOS: Well, Mr. President and Mr. Vice President, I am just very honored to have the opportunity to serve America's students, and I'm really excited to be here today with parents and educators representing traditional public schools, charter public schools, home-schools, private schools, a range of choices. And we're eager to listen and learn from you your ideas for how we can ensure that all of our kids have an equal opportunity for a high-quality, great education and therefore an opportunity for the future.

So again, I just wanted to have the opportunity to serve, and looking forward to fulfilling the **mission** that you set forward.

THE PRESIDENT: It's our honor -- believe me, Betsy.

Kenneth.

MR. SMITH: Ken Smith, educator helping at-risk kids get through school. Vice President, it actually has the largest application of jobs for America's graduates in the country. And in a minute we'll talk about that as a solution.

THE PRESIDENT: Great. Good.

Laura.

MS. PARRISH: Laura Parrish, I'm from Falls Church, Virginia. I home-school my 10- and my 13-year-old.

THE PRESIDENT: Good. Very good.

Mary.

MS. RINER: My name is Mary. I'm a charter school parent here in D.C., and considered the best school in America.

THE PRESIDENT: You think, huh? (Laughter.)

MS. RINER: I know.

THE PRESIDENT: I like that.

MS. RINER: According to U.S. News & World Report.

THE PRESIDENT: Really? Is that right? Wow.

Jennifer.

MS. COLEMAN: I am Jennifer Coleman. I am from Prince William County, Virginia. I am the mother of six, and I home-school my oldest four; they are grades kindergarten through seven. And before that I was a private school teacher.

THE PRESIDENT: Very good.

MR. CIRENZA: Bartholomew Cirenza. I'm a parent of seven, and my kids have gone through both private and public school, and I see differences, and --

THE PRESIDENT: Big difference.

MR. CIRENZA: Big difference.

THE PRESIDENT: Okay.

MS. BAUMANN: Good morning, I'm Julie. I teach special education at a public school in New Jersey.

THE PRESIDENT: Very good. Thank you.

MS. QUENNVILLE: Hi, I'm Jane Quennville, and I'm a principal of a special-ed center in Virginia serving children ages five through twenty-two with autism and physical and medically fragile conditions.

THE PRESIDENT: How is that going?

MS. QUENNVILLE: Well --

THE PRESIDENT: Have you seen an increase in the autism with the children?

MS. QUENNVILLE: Yes, yes. In fact, our school has shifted its population -- saw more children with autism, definitely.

THE PRESIDENT: So what's going on with autism? When you look at the tremendous increases, really, it's such an incredible -- it's like really a horrible thing to watch, the tremendous amount of increase. Do you have any idea? And you're seeing it in the school?

MS. QUENNVILLE: Yes, I think -- I mean, I think the statistics, I believe, are 1 in 66, 1 in 68 children are diagnosed with autism.

THE PRESIDENT: And now it's going to be even lower --

MS. QUENNVILLE: Probably.

THE PRESIDENT: Which is just amazing. Well, maybe we can do something.

MS. BONILLA: I am Carol Bonilla. I teach Spanish in a private elementary school in Arlington. I teach the students in fourth through eighth grade.

THE PRESIDENT: Very good. Thank you.

MS. VIANA: Good morning, Mr. Vice President, Mr. President. My name is Aimee Viana. I'm the parent of two children -- fifth grade and second grade -- and I live right outside of Raleigh, North Carolina in Cary, and I'm also a former educator in public and private schools.

THE PRESIDENT: Fantastic. Thank you. So thank you all very much. Let's get going.

END
10:58 P.M. EST

Chapter 36

14 February 2017

2:18 P.M. EST

THE PRESIDENT: Well, thank you very much. This is a big signing, a very important signing.

And this is H.J. Resolution 41, disapproving the Securities and Exchange Commission's rule on disclosure of payments by resource extraction issuers. It's a big deal.

And I want to thank Speaker Paul Ryan for being here. He's been tremendous. Jeb Hensarling very, very important and really worked hard. Representative Bill Huizenga and all of the friends -- Peter -- all of my friends are up here. And we really appreciate it.

This is one of many that we've signed, and we have many more left. And we're bringing back jobs big league, we're bringing them back at the plant level; we've bringing them back at the mine level. The energy jobs are coming back. And it's -- you see what's going on with the stock market. They know that we know what we're doing, so it's going up.

So I think what I'm going to do, if I might, can I ask you to say a few words?

REPRESENTATIVE HUIZENGA: My pleasure, Mr. President.

THE PRESIDENT: Bill Huizenga.

REPRESENTATIVE HUIZENGA: So this is the first CRA that has been signed by the President. I'm very pleased to be the author of House Joint Resolution 41.

Over 20 years, there's been 56,000 rules that have been put in place with very little legislative input or oversight, and it's time that changed.

And I'm very thankful to the President, the Speaker, our Chairman Hensarling for being able to make this happen. And we think this is a good first step. So I'm very pleased. Thank you.

THE PRESIDENT: I'll sign it -- we may have to give him the pen. Congratulations. Great job. You've done a fantastic job.

(The President signs H.J. Resolution 41.)

THE PRESIDENT: A lot of people going back to work now. (Applause.)

He's working on Obamacare -- it's going to be very soon. Right?

SPEAKER RYAN: Yes.

THE PRESIDENT: Thank you all very much.

END
2:20 P.M. EST

Chapter 37

15 February 2017

10:40 A.M. EST

THE PRESIDENT: So it's nice to see we have some great retailers here today and we're going to go around the room and we'll all introduce ourselves. Some of you I've read about on the covers of business magazines and it's great to have you here. Thank you very much.

I'm pleased to host all of you at the White House. The CEOs -- you're some of the great CEOs of our country and the biggest in the retail industry, which is very important to the country in supporting millions and millions of jobs -- really one of the great job producers. Probably, would you say, almost number one? Pretty close, right?

MR. KUSHNER: I agree.

THE PRESIDENT: It is number one.

There's a lot of confidence in our economy right now. There's a great confidence level. You've been seeing that in the stock market. You've been seeing that in businesses. And you've been seeing that at every chart that's taken. There's evidence also by the jobs report that just came out for January -- 227,000 jobs added. My administration remains very focused on the issues that will encourage economic growth -- that's what we're all about. We have a lot of plants moving back into various states, including the state of Ohio, the state of Michigan, Pennsylvania. You have a lot of companies moving back in, coming back into the country, bringing the jobs with them.

We're cutting regulations big league. We are really cutting them by massive amounts. The auto industry just left a week ago -- they were here in the same room -- and they are very happy with what we're doing and everyone is. I think just about every -- the financial industry. We're having a lot of the different industries in and we're cutting regulations in just about every industry. In fact, I can't think of any that we're not. If I do, we have a major story, okay, because I think just every industry we're cutting, some more than others. You have a very, very big regulatory problem and we're going to take care of that because I want more jobs. We're doing that because we want more jobs.

As you know, the overregulation costs our economy an estimated $2 trillion a year, which is incredible -- $2 trillion -- and it costs your businesses a lot of money, tremendous amounts of money and time. I've taken executive action to create a permanent structure of regulatory reduction by creating one and one. So basically, for every one regulation, two are out. So we knock out two. So we put in one, but to put in one, you have to knock out two. That's the least of it, but it's an important symbol.

In addition to reducing government regulations, we'll also reform our tax code to help middle-income families and American businesses grow and thrive. Tax reform is one of the best opportunities to really impact our economy. So we're doing a massive tax plan. It's coming along really well. It will be submitted in the not-too-distant future, and it will be not only good and simpler; it will be -- you're talking about big numbers of savings. And we're talking also middle income and very much for business. And the business is for middle income because you can employ a lot of people. So we hope you're going to do that.

We're going to provide tax relief for families. We're going to simplify very greatly the tax code -- it's too complicated. We're going to bring down the number of alternatives, and I think it's going to be just a much, much simpler tax code. In fact, H&R Block probably won't be too happy -- that's one business that might not be happy with what we're doing. Other than H&R Block, I think people are going to love it.

We're going to lower the rates very, very substantially for virtually everybody in every category, including personal and business. And I just want to go around the room. I'd like you to introduce yourself and then I'll tell you a little bit more, and you're going to tell me what you're looking for. But we want jobs. We want jobs brought back to the country. We want them brought back fast. We want you to expand your stores. And you'll tell me why you will or why you won't. And tell me why you won't -- we'll work on you a little bit, right, Vice President Mike Pence? (Laughter.)

So go ahead.

MS. SOLTAU: I'm Jill Soltau. I'm with JoAnn Fabric and Craft Stores.

MR. PECK: Art Peck with The Gap.

THE PRESIDENT: Good. Very good.

MR. JOLY: Hubert Joly with Best Buy.

THE PRESIDENT: Good. Great store.

MR. RHODES: I'm Bill Rhodes with AutoZone.

MR. CORNELL: Brian Cornell with Target.

THE PRESIDENT: Good. The Tar-get -- right? (Laughter.)

MR. PESSINA: Stefano Pessina, Walgreens Boots Alliance.

MR. SANDFORT: Greg Sandfort with Tractor Supply.

THE PRESIDENT: Yes.

MR. ELLISON: Marvin Ellison with J.C. Penney.

THE PRESIDENT: I read a good report on you. (Laughter.)

Good job.

MR. ELLISON: Thank you. (Laughter.)

THE PRESIDENT: So maybe we go around the room a little bit. I guess we can let the press go now, right? Do you suggest that? Go ahead. Thank you all very much.

END
10:46 A.M. EST

Chapter 38

REMARKS BY PRESIDENT TRUMP AND
PRIME MINISTER NETANYAHU OF ISRAEL IN
JOINT PRESS CONFERENCE
[AS PREPARED BY WHITE HOUSE STENOGRAPHER IN
REAL TIME]
EAST ROOM

15 February 2017

12:15 P.M. EST

PRESIDENT TRUMP: Thank you very much. Thank you. Today I have the honor of welcoming my friend, Prime Minister Benjamin Netanyahu, to the White House. With this visit, the United States again reaffirms our unbreakable bond with our cherished ally, Israel. The partnership between our two countries built on our shared values has advanced the cause of human freedom, dignity and peace. These are the building blocks of democracy.

The state of Israel is a symbol to the world of resilience in the face of oppression -- I can think of no other state that's gone through what they've gone -- and of survival in the face of genocide. We will never forget what the Jewish people have endured.

Your perseverance in the face of hostility, your open democracy in the face of violence, and your success in the face of tall odds is truly inspirational. The security challenges faced by Israel are enormous, including the threat of Iran's nuclear ambitions, which I've talked a lot about. One of the worst deals I've ever seen is the Iran deal. My administration has already imposed new sanctions on Iran, and I will do more to prevent Iran from ever developing -- I mean ever -- a nuclear weapon.

Our security assistance to Israel is currently at an all-time high, ensuring that Israel has the ability to defend itself from threats of which there are unfortunately many. Both of our countries will continue and grow. We have a long history of cooperation in the fight against terrorism and the fight against those who do not value human life. America and Israel are two nations that cherish the value of all human life.

This is one more reason why I reject unfair and one-sided actions against Israel at the United Nations -- just treated Israel, in my opinion, very, very unfairly -- or other international forums, as well as boycotts that target Israel. Our administration is committed to working with Israel and our common allies in the region towards greater security and stability. That includes working toward a peace agreement between Israel and the Palestinians.

The United States will encourage a peace and, really, a great peace deal. We'll be working on it very, very diligently. Very important to me also -- something we want to do. But it is the parties themselves who must directly negotiate such an agreement. We'll be beside them; we'll be working with them.

As with any successful negotiation, both sides will have to make compromises. You know that, right? (Laughter.)

PRIME MINISTER NETANYAHU: Both sides.

PRESIDENT TRUMP: I want the Israeli people to know that

the United States stands with Israel in the struggle against terrorism. As you know, Mr. Prime Minister, our two nations will always condemn terrorist acts. Peace requires nations to uphold the dignity of human life and to be a voice for all of those who are endangered and forgotten.

Those are the ideals to which we all, and will always, aspire and commit. This will be the first of many productive meetings. And I, again, Mr. Prime Minister, thank you very much for being with us today.

Mr. Prime Minister, thank you.

PRIME MINISTER NETANYAHU: President Trump, thank you for the truly warm hospitality you and Melania have shown me, my wife Sara, our entire delegation. I deeply value your friendship. To me, to the state of Israel, it was so clearly evident in the words you just spoke -- Israel has no better ally than the United States. And I want to assure you, the United States has no better ally than Israel.

Our alliance has been remarkably strong, but under your leadership I'm confident it will get even stronger. I look forward to working with you to dramatically upgrade our alliance in every field -- in security, in technology, in cyber and trade, and so many others. And I certainly welcome your forthright call to ensure that Israel is treated fairly in international forums, and that the slander and boycotts of Israel are resisted mightily by the power and moral position of the United States of America.

As you have said, our alliance is based on a deep bond of common values and common interests. And, increasingly, those values and interests are under attack by one malevolent force: radical Islamic terror. Mr. President, you've shown great clarity and courage in confronting this challenge head-on. You call for confronting Iran's terrorist regime, preventing Iran from realizing this terrible deal into a nuclear arsenal. And you have said that the United States is committed to preventing Iran from getting nuclear weapons. You call for the defeat of ISIS. Under your leadership, I believe we can reverse the rising tide of radical Islam. And in this great task, as in so many others, Israel stands with you and I stand with you.

Mr. President, in rolling back militant Islam, we can seize an historic opportunity -- because, for the first time in my lifetime, and for the first time in the life of my country, Arab countries in the region do not see Israel as an enemy, but, increasingly, as an ally. And I believe that under your leadership, this change in our region creates an unprecedented opportunity to strengthen security and advance peace.

Let us seize this moment together. Let us bolster security. Let us seek new avenues of peace. And let us bring the remarkable alliance between Israel and the United States to even greater heights.

Thank you. Thank you, Mr. President.

PRESIDENT TRUMP: Thank you. Again, thank you. We'll take a couple of questions. David Brody, Christian Broadcasting. David.

Q   Thank you, Mr. President, Mr. Prime Minister. Both of you have criticized the Iran nuclear deal, and at times even called for its repeal. I'm wondering if you're concerned at all as it relates to not just the National Security Advisor, Michael Flynn, who is recently no longer here, but also some of those events that have been going on with communication in Russia -- if that is going to hamper this deal at all, and whether or not it would keep Iran from becoming a nuclear state.

And secondly, on the settlement issue, are you both on the same page? How do you exactly term that as it relates to the settlement issue? Thank you.

PRESIDENT TRUMP: Michael Flynn, General Flynn is a wonderful man. I think he's been treated very, very unfairly by the media -- as I call it, the fake media, in many cases. And I think it's really a sad thing that he was treated so badly. I think, in addition to that, from intelligence -- papers are being leaked, things are being leaked. It's criminal actions, criminal act, and it's been going on for a long time -- before me. But now it's really going on, and people are trying to cover up for a terrible loss that the Democrats had under Hillary Clinton.

I think it's very, very unfair what's happened to General Flynn, the way he was treated, and the documents and papers that were illegally -- I stress that -- illegally leaked. Very, very unfair.

As far as settlements, I'd like to see you hold back on settlements for a little bit. We'll work something out. But I would like to see a deal be made. I think a deal will be made. I know that every President would like to. Most of them have not started until late because they never thought it was possible. And it wasn't possible because they didn't do it.

But Bibi and I have known each other a long time -- a smart man, great negotiator. And I think we're going to make a deal. It might be a bigger and better deal than people in this room even understand. That's a possibility. So let's see what we do.

PRIME MINISTER NETANYAHU: Let's try it.

PRESIDENT TRUMP: Doesn't sound too optimistic, but -- (Laughter.)

He's a good negotiator.

PRIME MINISTER NETANYAHU: That's the "Art of the Deal." (Laughter.)

PRESIDENT TRUMP: I also want to thank -- I also want to thank -- Sara; could you please stand up? You're so lovely and you've been so nice to Melania. I appreciate it very much. (Applause.)

Thank you.

Your turn.

PRIME MINISTER NETANYAHU: Yes, please. Go ahead.

Q   Thank you very much. Mr. President, in your vision for the new Middle East peace, are you ready to give up the notion of two-state solution that was adopted by previous administration? And will you be willing to hear different ideas from the Prime Minister, as some of his partners are asking him to do, for example, annexation of parts of the West Bank and unrestricted settlement construc- tions? And one more question: Are you going to fulfill your promise to move the U.S. embassy in Israel to Jerusa- lem? And if so, when?

And, Mr. Prime Minister, did you come here tonight to tell the President that you're backing off the two-state solution?

Thank you.

PRESIDENT TRUMP: So I'm looking at two-state and one-state, and I like the one that both parties like. (Laughter.)

I'm very happy with the one that both parties like. I can live with either one.

I thought for a while the two-state looked like it may be the easier of the two. But honestly, if Bibi and if the Palestinians -- if Israel and the Palestinians are happy, I'm happy with the one they like the best.

As far as the embassy moving to Jerusalem, I'd love to see that happen. We're looking at it very, very strongly. We're looking at it with great care -- great care, believe me. And we'll see what happens. Okay?

PRIME MINISTER NETANYAHU: Thank you. I read yesterday that an American official said that if you ask five people what two states would look like, you'd get eight different answers. Mr. President, if you ask five Israelis, you'd get 12 different answers. (Laughter.)

But rather than deal with labels, I want to deal with substance. It's something I've hoped to do for years in a world that's absolutely fixated on labels and not on substance. So here's the substance: There are two prerequisites for peace that I laid out two years -- several years ago, and they haven't changed.

First, the Palestinians must recognize the Jewish state. They have to stop calling for Israel's destruction. They have to stop educating their people for Israel's destruction.

Second, in any peace agreement, Israel must retain the overriding security control over the entire area west of the Jordan River. Because if we don't, we know what will happen -- because otherwise we'll get another radical Islamic terrorist state in the Palestinian areas exploding the peace, exploding the Middle East.

Now, unfortunately, the Palestinians vehemently reject both prerequisites for peace. First, they continue to call for Israel's destruction -- inside their schools, inside their mosques, inside the textbooks. You have to read it to believe it.

They even deny, Mr. President, our historical connection to our homeland. And I suppose you have to ask yourself: Why do - - why are Jews called Jews?

Well, the Chinese are called Chinese because they come from China. The Japanese are called Japanese because they come from Japan. Well, Jews are called Jews because they come from Judea. This is our ancestral homeland. Jews are not foreign colonialists in Judea.

So, unfortunately, the Palestinians not only deny the past, they also poison the present. They name public squares in honor of mass murderers who murdered Israelis, and I have to say also murdered Americans. They fund -- they pay monthly salaries to the families of murderers, like the family of the terrorist who killed Taylor Force, a wonderful young American, a West Point graduate, who was stabbed to death while visiting Israel.

So this is the source of the conflict -- the persistent Palestinian refusal to recognize the Jewish state in any boundary; this persistent rejection.

That's the reason we don't have peace. Now, that has to change. I want it to change. Not only have I not abandoned these two prerequisites of peace; they've become even more important because of the rising tide of fanaticism that has swept the Middle East and has also, unfortunately, infected Palestinian society.

So I want this to change. I want those two prerequisites of peace -- substance; not labels -- I want them reinstated. But if anyone believes that I, as Prime Minister of Israel, responsible for the security of my country, would blindly walk into a Palestinian terrorist state that seeks the destruction of my country, they're gravely mistaken.

The two prerequisites of peace -- recognition of the Jewish state, and Israel's security needs west of the Jordan -- they remain pertinent. We have to look for new ways, new ideas on how to reinstate them and how to move peace forward. And I believe that the great opportunity for peace comes from a regional approach from involving our newfound Arab partners in the pursuit of a broader peace and peace with the Palestinians.

And I greatly look forward to discussing this in detail with you, Mr. President, because I think that if we work together, we have a shot.

PRESIDENT TRUMP: And we have been discussing that, and it is something that is very different, hasn't been discussed before. And it's actually a much bigger deal, a much more important deal, in a sense. It would take in many, many countries and it would cover a very large territory. So I didn't know you were going to be mentioning that, but that's -- now that you did, I think it's a terrific thing and I think we have some pretty good cooperation from people that in the past would never, ever have even thought about doing this. So we'll see how that works out.

Katie from Townhall. Where's Katie? Right there. Katie.

Q   Thank you, Mr. President. You said in your earlier remarks that both sides will have to make compromises when it comes to a peace deal. You've mentioned a halt on settlements. Can you lay out a few more specific compromises that you have in mind, both for the Israelis and for the Palestinians?

And, Mr. Prime Minister, what expectations do you have from the new administration about how to either amend the Iran nuclear agreement or how to dismantle it altogether, and how to overall work with the new administration to combat Iran's increased aggression, not only in the last couple of months but the past couple of years as well?

PRESIDENT TRUMP: It's actually an interesting question. I think that the Israelis are going to have to show some flexibility, which is hard, it's hard to do. They're going to have to show the fact that they really want to make a deal. I think our new concept that we've been discussing actually for a while is something that allows them to show more flexibility than they have in the past because you have a lot bigger canvas to play with. And I think they'll do that.

I think they very much would like to make a deal or I

wouldn't be happy and I wouldn't be here and I wouldn't be as optimistic as I am. I really think they -- I can tell you from the standpoint of Bibi and from the standpoint of Israel, I really believe they want to make a deal and they'd like to see the big deal.

I think the Palestinians have to get rid of some of that hate that they're taught from a very young age. They're taught tremendous hate. I've seen what they're taught. And you can talk about flexibility there too, but it starts at a very young age and it starts in the school room. And they have to acknowledge Israel -- they're going to have to do that. There's no way a deal can be made if they're not ready to acknowledge a very, very great and important country. And I think they're going to be willing to do that also. But now I also believe we're going to have, Katie, other players at a very high level, and I think it might make it easier on both the Palestinians and Israel to get something done.

Okay? Thank you. Very interesting question. Thank you.

PRIME MINISTER NETANYAHU: You asked about Iran. One thing is preventing Iran from getting nuclear weapons -- something that President Trump and I think are deeply committed to do. And we are obviously going to discuss that.

I think, beyond that, President Trump has led a very important effort in the past few weeks, just coming into the presidency. He pointed out there are violations, Iranian violations on ballistic missile tests. By the way, these ballistic missiles are inscribed in Hebrew, "Israel must be destroyed." The Palestinian -- rather the Iranian Foreign Minister Zarif said, well, our ballistic missiles are not intended against any country. No. They write on the missile in Hebrew, "Israel must be destroyed."

So challenging Iran on its violations of ballistic missiles, imposing sanctions on Hezbollah, preventing them, making them pay for the terrorism that they foment throughout the Middle East and beyond, well beyond -- I think that's a change that is clearly evident since President Trump took office. I welcome that. I think it's -- let me say this very openly: I think it's long overdue, and I think that if we work together -- and not just the United States and Israel, but so many others in the region who see eye to eye on the great magnitude and danger of the Iranian threat, then I think we can roll back Iran's aggression and danger.

And that's something that is important for Israel, the Arab states, but I think it's vitally important for America. These guys are developing ICBMs. They're developing -- they want to get to a nuclear arsenal, not a bomb, a hundred bombs. And they want to have the ability to launch them everywhere on Earth, and including, and especially, eventually, the United States.

So this is something that is important for all of us. I welcome the change, and I intend to work with President Trump very closely so that we can thwart this danger.

PRESIDENT TRUMP: Great. Do you have somebody?

PRIME MINISTER NETANYAHU: Moav (ph)?

Q   Mr. President, since your election campaign and even after your victory, we've seen a sharp rise in anti-Semitic incidents across the United States. And I wonder what you say to those among the Jewish community in the States, and in Israel, and maybe around the world who believe and feel that your administration is playing with xenophobia and maybe racist tones.

And, Mr. Prime Minister, do you agree to what the President just said about the need for Israel to restrain or to stop settlement activity in the West Bank? And a quick follow-up on my friend's questions -- simple question: Do you back off from your vision to the end of the conflict of two-state solution as you laid out in Bar-Ilan speech, or you still support it? Thank you.

PRESIDENT TRUMP: Well, I just want to say that we are very honored by the victory that we had -- 306 Electoral College votes. We were not supposed to crack 220. You know that, right? There was no way to 221, but then they said there's no way to 270. And there's tremendous enthusiasm out there.

I will say that we are going to have peace in this country. We are going to stop crime in this country. We are going to do everything within our power to stop long-simmering racism and every other thing that's going on, because lot of bad things have been taking place over a long period of time.

I think one of the reasons I won the election is we have a very, very divided nation. Very divided. And, hopefully, I'll be able to do something about that. And, you know, it was something that was very important to me.

As far as people -- Jewish people -- so many friends, a daughter who happens to be here right now, a son-in-law, and three beautiful grandchildren. I think that you're going to see a lot different United States of America over the next three, four, or eight years. I think a lot of good things are happening, and you're going to see a lot of love. You're going to see a lot of love. Okay? Thank you.

PRIME MINISTER NETANYAHU: I believe that the issue of the settlements is not the core of the conflict, nor does it really drive the conflict. I think it's an issue, it has to be resolved in the context of peace negotiations. And I think we also are going to speak about it, President Trump and I, so we can arrive at an understanding so we don't keep on bumping into each other all the time on this issue. And we're going to discuss this.

On the question you said, you just came back with your question to the problem that I said. It's the label. What does Abu Mazen mean by two states, okay? What does he mean? A state that doesn't recognize the Jewish state? A state that basically is open for attack against Israel? What are we talking about? Are we talking about Costa Rica, or are we talking about another Iran?

So obviously it means different things. I told you what are the conditions that I believe are necessary for an agreement: It's the recognition of the Jewish state and it's Israel's -- Israel's -- security control of the entire area.

Otherwise we're just fantasizing. Otherwise we'll get another failed state, another terrorist Islamist dictatorship that will not work for peace but work to destroy us but also destroy any hope -- any hope -- for a peaceful future for our people.

So I've been very clear about those conditions, and they haven't changed. I haven't changed. If you read what I said eight years ago, it's exactly that. And I repeated that again, and again, and again. If you want to deal with labels, deal with labels. I'll deal with substance.

And finally, if I can respond to something that I know from personal experience. I've known President Trump for many years, and to allude to him, or to his people -- his team, some of whom I've known for many years, too. Can I reveal, Jared, how long we've known you? (Laughter.)

Well, he was never small. He was always big. He was always tall.

But I've known the President and I've known his family and his team for a long time, and there is no greater supporter of the Jewish people and the Jewish state than President Donald Trump. I think we should put that to rest.

PRESIDENT TRUMP: Thank you very much. Very nice. I appreciate that very much.

PRIME MINISTER NETANYAHU: Thank you.

END
12:42 P.M. EST

Chapter 39

16 February 2017

10:53 A.M. EST

THE PRESIDENT: Thank you all for being here. I had a lot of good discussions this morning. I'm negotiating a lot of contracts that are saving billions and billions of dollars for the American people and for all of us, and I'm very proud of it.

You know, the F-35 fighter jet, the Air Force One program, which was totally out of control and now it's back where it's supposed to go, and many other things. In addition, I had a very good phone call this morning about a major plant that's moving back into the United States. We'll be talking about it soon.

And what I do have is a little free time at about 12 o'clock. So I don't think the press will want to show up, but I think I'll have a press conference probably at 12 o'clock in the East Room. We had a little time in between things. So if the press would like to show up -- will anybody show up to that press conference? (Laughter.)

Historically, they didn't care about these things. For me, they show up. So I think 12 o'clock in the East Room of the White House we'll have a press conference.

I just want to thank you folks for coming today. This was good. This was scheduled a long time ago -- some of my very, very early supporters. And I've been your support- er also. We're doing really well. The fake-news media doesn't like talking about the economy; I never see any- thing about the stock market sets new records every day. I never see it. But I think the people understand it.

We're giving a speech in Melbourne, Florida on Saturday. I think it's going to be around 4 o'clock. and I hear the tickets, you can't get them, but that's okay. It's better than you have too many, right? So it's going to be great. I look forward to that. So that will be Melbourne at 4 o'clock.

I really appreciate you folks. You folks have been so great. And right from the beginning, and, Tom, right at the beginning. Just about every one of you, right at the beginning. Some of you were a little after the begin- ning. (Laughter.)

But we forgive. But we forgive.

Let's go around, just for the media, and you'll introduce yourselves and then we'll start talking, and I'll see the me- dia back at 12 o'clock.

Chris?

CONGRESSMAN COLLINS: Well, Mr. President, we're all honored to be here. This is really our Trump caucus recon- vening for the first time in a little bit, but our first meeting was the first part of March. Duncan Hunter and I both en- dorsed you on February 24th, a week from tomorrow. So it's the one-year anniversary. But this is the Trump caucus, reconvening, and we're just so honored you're taking time out of your busy schedule to be with us.

THE PRESIDENT: These are real friends.

CONGRESSMAN COLLINS: Western New York.

THE PRESIDENT: Thank you. That's right.

CONGRESSMAN HUNTER: Duncan Hunter, Mr. President, from San Diego, California.

CONGRESSMAN CRAMER: Kevin Cramer from North Dakota.

CONGRESSMAN SHUSTER: Bill Shuster from Western Pennsylvania and chairman of the transportation committee.

THE PRESIDENT: That's right. We're going to give you some money for transportation. That's good. Good territory.

CONGRESSMAN REED: Mr. President, Tom Reed. It was a pleasure to travel with you to Florida.

THE PRESIDENT: That's right.

CONGRESSMAN REED: Congratulations.

THE PRESIDENT: Thank you. Thank you.

CONGRESSMAN MARINO: Mr. President, Tom Marino from Williamsburg, Pennsylvania. And please indulge me for 30 seconds. I have something for you.

THE PRESIDENT: Uh oh. (Laughter.)

PARTICIPANT: Something for you to sign, I think he means. (Laughter.)

THE PRESIDENT: I think this is great.

CONGRESSMAN MARINO: This is a portrait by an engineer -- a gentleman, Joe Padmerino (ph), who... 60-some-years-old. Never voted. Never registered. He registered for you and voted for you, and he asked me to give this to you. There's a nice letter there. I'm sorry, Mr. Vice President -- but that's that. I'll set this over here.

THE PRESIDENT: That's beautiful. Thank you.

CONGRESSMAN MARINO: (Inaudible.)

THE PRESIDENT: He's a talented guy, I can see that.

CONGRESSMAN MARINO: And the other thing here is --

THE PRESIDENT: It's nice.

CONGRESSMAN MARINO: -- the chairman and CEO of Little League World Series baseball here.

THE PRESIDENT: Right.

CONGRESSMAN MARINO: And, Mr. Vice President, I kind of figured that you would be here as well, so this is from the New York team last year that was in the World Series. That's for you. And this is a jersey that -- an original jersey of the New York team in the World Series last year. And this is for you as well.

THE PRESIDENT: Thank you very much. (Laughter and applause.)

Okay. All right. Thank them for me.

CONGRESSMAN MARINO: I will do that.

THE PRESIDENT: Thank them for me. Rick, we know who you are.

CONGRESSMAN DESJARLAIS: Scott DesJarlais from Tennessee. And I just want you to know that Tennessee was falling behind in March -- and we're excited about the work you're doing. We know that health care and tax reform has to be done this year, and we like the work you're doing, and we need you to help us.

THE PRESIDENT: We're going to get it done. And the health care is going really well. And now that we finally have Tom, Tom Price -- so that's a big thing. I mean, we couldn't get him.

We are going to be announcing -- I guess I'll do it at 12 o'clock -- a new Secretary of Labor, who is really phenomenal. So that will be at 12 o'clock. And we're getting -- I mean, this is the slowest in history, the approval of a Cabinet. And these people are outstanding people. The man I'll be announcing for Labor is a star, great person. A great person.

And so I look forward to that. But I appreciate everything you've done. You've been fantastic, and I appreciate that. Thank you.

CONGRESSMAN KELLY: Mr. President, good to see

you. Mike Kelly.

THE PRESIDENT: I know, Mike.

CONGRESSMAN KELLY: From right above Pittsburgh, up near Erie. Thanks so much. What an exciting summer we had together.

THE PRESIDENT: We did okay.

CONGRESSMAN KELLY: We did better than okay.

THE PRESIDENT: We took an area that wasn't a big Republican area, and we swamped them, right? (Laughter.)

CONGRESSMAN KELLY: We did. We did. Thirty-four years since Erie actually voted for a Republican.

THE PRESIDENT: Wow.

CONGRESSMAN KELLY: Thanks to you.

THE PRESIDENT: Well, thank you very much.

CONGRESSMAN KELLY: Yes, sir.

CONGRESSMAN LONG: Billy Long, Missouri 7th. And I'm co-chair of the Congressional Study Group on Japan. I'm going to be leading the delegation to Japan Saturday, meeting with Prime Minister Abe on Monday.

THE PRESIDENT: He's a great guy.

CONGRESSMAN LONG: So if you will tell me how many golf balls he lost in Florida. I don't know how many House of Representative golf balls to take. (Laughter.)

THE PRESIDENT: He played well, I'll tell you. And you know, we played with Ernie Els. I called up Billy -- I said, see if you can get me somebody good to play with; I have the Prime Minister of Japan who wants to play golf. So we get to the front of the club, and Ernie Els is waiting for us. He said, when you're ready. So we had a good time.

No, he played very nicely, and he's a great guy. You're going to like him. I like him.

CONGRESSMAN LONG: Oh, yeah, I've met him the last three or four years -- met with him there. He's a great guy. And I knew you all would hit it off because you're both people persons and a great personalities.

THE PRESIDENT: Well, we had a good feeling.

CONGRESSMAN LONG: So I knew you guys would get along good.

THE PRESIDENT: Well, I always said about President Obama, it's great to play golf, but play golf with heads of countries. And, by the way, people like yourself, when you're looking for votes, don't play with your friends who you play with every week. (Laughter.)

Does that make sense?

CONGRESSMAN LONG: Yeah, it does.

THE PRESIDENT: I hit it off with the Prime Minister. He is a fabulous guy. He's -- loves his country. And we spoke all day long and well into the night. As you know, they launched a missile in North Korea, and we were discussing that. So it was really something.

But have a good time over there.

CONGRESSMAN LONG: I will.

THE PRESIDENT: And give him my regards.

CONGRESSMAN LONG: Ambassador Sasae was in my district for two full days, and he mentioned he was with you down there to play golf.

THE PRESIDENT: He was.

CONGRESSMAN LONG: He's another great guy -- he and his wife both.

THE PRESIDENT: They're all good.

CONGRESSMAN LONG: One last quick thing. Fran Drescher, from "The Nanny" --

THE PRESIDENT: Right.

CONGRESSMAN LONG: -- said you were on "The Nanny" one time. She has a request with her battle for cancer that you have a cancer board that has one non-medical person. So she wanted me to put her name in the hat for that. My daughter came through a successful cancer battle.

THE PRESIDENT: She's fought hard. She's fought hard. Yes. You know what, if you would, Billy, why don't you give me that request? And we'll see if we can do that.

CONGRESSMAN LONG: We will. I'll give it to your people. Thank you.

THE PRESIDENT: Marsha.

CONGRESSWOMAN BLACKBURN: Yes, I'm Marsha Blackburn from Tennessee. I Chair the Telecommunications and Technology Subcommittee of Energy and Commerce. And we are looking forward to broadband expansion. Go broadband!

THE PRESIDENT: We're going to get it.

CONGRESSWOMAN BLACKBURN: Yes. All right.

THE PRESIDENT: Thank you very much, everybody. I'll see you at 12 o'clock if you want. If you don't want, don't be there. (Laughter.)

If you don't show up, I won't be offended. (Laughter.)

Q   Are you going to find some of those leakers, Mr. President?

THE PRESIDENT: We're going to find the leakers. We're going to find the leakers. They're going to pay a big price for leaking. It's all about the leakers. You know the Russians are just a muse -- it's all about the leakers.

END
11:01 A.M. EST

Chapter 40

16 February 2017

12:55 P.M. EST

THE PRESIDENT: Thank you very much. I just wanted to begin by mentioning that the nominee for Secretary of the Department of Labor will be Mr. Alex Acosta. He has a law degree from Harvard Law School, was a great student. Former clerk for Justice Samuel Alito. And he has had a tremendous career. He's a member, and has been a member, of the National Labor Relations Board, and has been through Senate confirmation three times, confirmed -- did very, very well. And so Alex, I've wished him the best. We just spoke. And he's going to be -- I think he'll be a tremendous Secretary of Labor.

And also, as you probably heard just a little while ago, Mick Mulvaney, former congressman, has just been approved -- weeks late, I have to say that. Weeks, weeks late. Office of Management and Budget. And he will be, I think, a fantastic addition. Paul Singer has just left. As you know, Paul was very much involved with the anti-Trump, or, as they say, "Never Trump." And Paul just left and he's given us his total support. And it's all about unification. We're unifying the party, and hopefully we're going to be able to unify the country. It's very important to me. I've been talking about that for a long time, but it's very, very important to me. So I want to thank Paul Singer for being here and for coming up to the office. He was a very strong opponent, and now he's a very strong ally. And I appreciate that.

I think I'll say a few words, and then we'll take some questions. And I had this time -- we've been negotiating a lot of different transactions to save money on contracts that were terrible, including airplane contracts that were out of control and late and terrible. Just absolutely catastrophic in terms of what was happening. And we've done some really good work. We're very proud of that.

And then right after that, you prepare yourselves and we'll do some questions -- unless you have no questions. That's always a possibility.

I'm here today to update the American people on the incredible progress that has been made in the last four weeks since my inauguration. We have made incredible progress. I don't think there's ever been a President elected who, in this short period of time, has done what we've done.

A new Rasmussen poll, in fact -- because the people get it; much of the media doesn't get it. They actually get it, but they don't write it -- let's put it that way. But a new Rasmussen poll just came out just a very short while ago, and it has our approval rating at 55 percent and going up. The stock market has hit record numbers, as you know. And there has been a tremendous surge of optimism in the business world, which is -- to me means something much different than it used to. It used to mean, oh, that's good. Now it means that's good for jobs. Very different. Plants and factories are already starting to move back into the United States and big league -- Ford, General Motors, so many of them.

I'm making this presentation directly to the American people with the media present, which is an honor to have you this morning, because many of our nation's reporters and folks will not tell you the truth and will not treat the wonderful people of our country with the respect that they deserve. And I hope going forward we can be a little bit different, and maybe get along a little bit better, if that's possible. Maybe it's not, and that's okay too.

Unfortunately, much of the media in Washington, D.C., along with New York, Los Angeles, in particular, speaks not for the people but for the special interests and for those profiting off a very, very obviously broken system.

The press has become so dishonest that if we don't talk about it, we are doing a tremendous disservice to the American people -- tremendous disservice. We have to talk about it to find out what's going on, because the press honestly is out of control. The level of dishonesty is out of control.

I ran for President to represent the citizens of our country. I am here to change the broken system so it serves their families and their communities well. I am talking, and really talking, on this very entrenched power structure, and what we're doing is we're talking about the power structure, we're talking about its entrenchment. As a result, the media is going through what they have to go through to oftentimes distort -- not all the time -- and some of the media is fantastic, I have to say; they're honest and fantastic. But much of it is not -- the distortion. And we'll talk about it, and you'll be able to ask me questions about it.

But we're not going to let it happen, because I'm here

again to take my message straight to the people. As you know, our administration inherited many problems across government and across the economy.

To be honest, **I inherited a mess -- it's a mess -- at home and abroad. A mess.** Jobs are pouring out of the country. You see what's going on with all of the companies leaving our country, going to Mexico and other places -- low-pay, low-wages. Mass instability overseas, no matter where you look. The Middle East, a disaster. North Korea -- we'll take care of it, folks. We're going to take care of it all. **I just want to let you know I inherited a mess.**

Beginning on day one, our administration went to work to tackle these challenges. On foreign affairs, we've already begun enormously productive talks with many foreign leaders -- much of it you've covered -- to move forward toward stability, security, and peace in the most troubled regions of the world, which there are many.

We've had great conversations with the United Kingdom -- and meetings -- Israel, Mexico, Japan, China, and Canada. Really, really productive conversations. I would say far more productive than you would understand. We've even developed a new council with Canada to promote women's business leaders and entrepreneurs. It's very important to me, very important to my daughter Ivanka.

I have directed our defense community, headed by our great general, now Secretary Mattis -- he's over there now, working very hard -- to submit a plan for the defeat of ISIS, a group that celebrates the murder and torture of innocent people in large sections of the world. It used to be a small group, and now it's in large sections of the world. They've spread like cancer. ISIS has spread like cancer. Another mess I inherited.

And we have imposed new sanctions on the nation of Iran, who's totally taken advantage of our previous admin-istration. And they're the world's top sponsor of terror-ism. And we're not going to stop until that problem is properly solved. And it's not properly solved now. It's one of the worst agreements I've ever seen drawn by anybody.

I've ordered plans to begin for the massive rebuilding of the United States military. I've had great support from the Senate. I've had great support from Congress gener-ally. We've pursued this rebuilding in the hopes that we will never have to use this military. And I will tell you that is my -- I would be so happy if we never had to use it. But our country will never have had a military like the military we're about to build and rebuild. We have the greatest people on Earth in our military, but they don't have the right equipment. And their equipment is old. I used it, I talked about it at every stop. Depleted -- it's depleted. It won't be depleted for long.

And I think one of the reasons I'm standing here instead of other people is that, frankly, I talked about we have to have a strong military. We have to have strong law enforcement also. So we do not go abroad in the search of war. We really are searching for peace, but it's peace through strength.

At home, we have begun the monumental task of return-ing the government back to the people on a scale not seen in many, many years. In each of these actions, **I'm keeping my promises to the American people**. These are **cam-paign promises**. Some people are so surprised that we're having strong borders. Well, that's what I've been talking about for a year and a half -- strong borders. They're so surprised -- "oh, you're having strong borders." Well, that's what I've been talking about to the press and to everybody else.

One promise after another after years of politicians lying to you to get elected. They lie to the American people in order to get elected. Some of the things I'm doing probably aren't popular, but they're necessary for security and for other reasons. And then coming to Washington and pursuing their own interests, which is more important to many politicians.

I'm here following through on what I pledged to do. That's all I'm doing. I put it out before the American people. Got 306 Electoral College votes. I wasn't supposed to get 222. They said there's no way to get 222; 230 is impossible. Two hundred and seventy, which you need, that was laughable. We got 306 because people came out and voted like they've never seen before. So that's the way it goes. I guess it was the biggest Electoral College win since Ronald Reagan.

In other words, the media is trying to attack our administration because they know we are **following through on pledges that we made**, and they're not happy about it for whatever reason. But a lot of people are happy about it. In fact, I'll be in Melbourne, Florida, five o'clock on Saturday, and I heard -- just heard that the crowds are massive that want to be there.

I turn on the TV, open the newspapers, and I see stories of chaos. Chaos! Yet, it is the exact opposite. This administration is running like a fine-tuned machine, despite the fact that I can't get my Cabinet approved, and they're outstanding people. Like Senator Dan Coates whose there -- one of the most respected men of the Senate -- he can't get approved. How do you not approve him? He's been a colleague, highly respected -- brilliant guy, great guy, everybody knows it -- but waiting for approval.

So we have a wonderful group of people that's working very hard, that's being very much misrepresented about, and we can't let that happen. So if the Democrats, who have -- all you have to do is look at where they are right now -- the only thing they can do is delay, because they've screwed things up royally, believe me.

Let me list to you some of the things that we've done in just a short period of time. I just got here. I got here with no Cabinet. Again, each of these actions is a **promise** I made to the American people. So we'll go over just some of them, and we have a lot happening next week and in the weeks coming.

We've withdrawn from the job-killing disaster known as Trans-Pacific Partnership. We're going to make trade deals, but we're going to have one-on-one deals -- bilateral. We're going to have one-on-one deals.

We've directed the elimination of regulations that undermine manufacturing, and called for expedited approval of the permits needed for America and American infrastructure, and that means plants, equipment, roads, bridges, factories. People take 10, 15, 20 years to get disapproved for a factory. They go in for a permit -- it's many, many years. And then at the end of the process -- they spend tens of millions of dollars on nonsense -- and at the end of the process, they get rejected. Now, they may be rejected with me, but it's going to be a quick rejection. It's not going to take years. But mostly, it's going to be an acceptance. We want plants built, and we want factories built, and we want the jobs. We don't want the jobs going to other countries.

We've imposed a hiring freeze on nonessential federal workers. We've imposed a temporary moratorium on new federal regulations. We've issued a game-changing new rule that says for each one new regulation, two old regulations must be eliminated. Makes sense. Nobody has ever seen regulations like we have. If you go to other countries and you look at industries they have, and you say, let me see your regulations, and they're a fraction, just a tiny fraction of what we have. And I want regulations because I want safety, I want all environmental situations to be taken properly care of. It's very important to me. But you don't need four or five or six regulations to take care of the same thing.

We've stood up for the men and women of law enforcement, directing federal agencies to ensure they are protected from crimes of violence. We've directed the creation of a task force for reducing violent crime in America, including the horrendous situation -- take a look at Chicago and others -- taking place right now in our inner cities. Horrible. We've ordered the Department of Homeland Security and Justice to coordinate on a plan to destroy criminal cartels coming into the United States with drugs. We're becoming a drug-infested nation. Drugs are becoming cheaper than candy bars, and we're not going to let it happen any longer.

We've undertaken the most substantial border security measures in a generation to keep our nation and our tax dollars safe, and are now in the process of beginning to build a promised wall on the southern border. Met with General, now Secretary, Kelly yesterday and we're starting that process. And the wall is going to be a great wall, and it's going to be a wall negotiated by me. The price is going to come down, just like it has on everything else I've negotiated for the government. And we're going to have a wall that works. We're not going to have a wall like they have now, which is either nonexistent or a joke.

We've ordered a crackdown on sanctuary cities that refuse to comply with federal law and that harbor criminal aliens, and we've ordered an end to the policy of catch and release on the border. No more release, no matter who you are -- release. We've begun a nationwide effort to remove criminal aliens, gang members, drug dealers, and others who pose a threat to public safety. We are saving American lives every single day. The court system has not made it easy for us. And we've even created a new office in Homeland Security dedicated to the forgotten American victims of illegal immigrant violence, of which there are many.

We've taken decisive action to keep radical Islamic terrorists out of our country. Though parts of our necessary and constitutional actions were blocked by a judge's, in my opinion, incorrect and unsafe ruling, our administration is working night and day to keep you safe -- including reporters safe -- and is vigorously defending this lawful order. I will not back down from defending our country. I got elected on defense of our country. And I keep my campaign promises. And our citizens will be very happy when they see the result. They already are. I can tell you that. Extreme vetting will be put in place, and it already is in place in many places. In fact, we had to go quicker than we thought because of the bad decision we received from a circuit that has been overturned at a record number. I've heard 80 percent -- I find that hard to believe; that's just a number I heard -- that they're overturned 80 percent of the time. I think that circuit is in chaos and that circuit is, frankly, in turmoil. But we are appealing that and we are going further.

We're issuing a new executive action next week that will comprehensively protect our country, so we'll be going along the one path and hopefully winning that. At the same time, we will be issuing a new and very comprehensive order to protect our people, and that will be done some time next week, toward the beginning or middle at the latest part.

We've also taken steps to begin construction of the Keystone Pipeline and Dakota Access Pipelines -- thousands and thousands of jobs -- and put new "**Buy American**" measures in place to require American steel for American pipelines. In other words, they build a pipeline in this country and we use the powers of government to make that pipeline happen. We want them to use American steel. And they're willing to do that, but nobody ever asked before I came along. Even this order was drawn and they didn't say that. And I'm reading the order, I'm saying, why aren't we using American steel? And they said, that's a good idea. We put it in.

To drain the swamp of corruption in Washington, D.C. I've started by imposing a five-year lobbying ban on White House officials and a lifetime ban on lobbying for a foreign government.

We've begun preparing to repeal and replace Obamacare. Obamacare is a disaster, folks. It's a disaster. You can say, oh, Obamacare -- I mean, they fill up our alleys with people that you wonder how they get there, but they're not the Republican people that our represent-atives are representing. So we've begun preparing to repeal and replace Obamacare and are deep in the midst of negotiations on a very historic tax reform to bring our jobs back. We're bringing our jobs back to this country big league. It's already happening, but big league.

I've also worked to install a Cabinet over the delays and ob-struction of Senate Democrats. You've seen what they've done over the last long number of years. That will be one of the great Cabinets ever assembled in American histo-ry. You look at Rex Tillerson -- he's out there negotiating right now. General Mattis I mentioned before, General Kelly. We have great, great people. Mick is with us now. We have great people.

Among their responsibilities will be ending the bleeding of jobs from our country and negotiating fair trade deals for our citizens. Now, look, fair trade -- not free -- fair. If a country is taking advantage of us, we're not going to let that happen anymore. Every country takes advantage of us, almost. I may be able to find a couple that don't. But for the most part, that would be a very tough job for me to do.

Jobs have already started to surge. Since my election, Ford announced it will abandon its plans to build a new factory in Mexico and will instead invest $700 million in Michigan, creating many, many jobs. Fiat-Chrysler announced it will invest $1 billion in Ohio and Michigan, creating 2,000 new American jobs. They were with me a week ago. You know -- you were here. General Motors, likewise, committed to invest billions of dollars in its American manufacturing operation, keeping many jobs here that were going to leave. And if I didn't get elected, believe me, they would have left. And these jobs and these things that I'm announcing would never have come here.

Intel just announced that it will move ahead with a new plant in Arizona that probably was never going to move ahead with. And that will result in at least 10,000 American jobs. Walmart announced it will create 10,000 jobs in the United States just this year because of our various plans and initiatives. There will be many, many more. Many more. These are a few that we're naming. Other countries have been taking advantage of us for decades -- decades and decades and decades, folks. And we're not going to let that happen anymore. Not going to let it happen.

And one more thing. I have kept my **promise** to the American people by nominating a justice of the United States Supreme Court, Judge Neil Gorsuch, who is from my list of 20, and who will be a true defender of our laws and our Constitution -- highly respected, should get the votes from the Democrats -- you may not see that, but he'll get there one way or the other. But he should get there the old-fashioned way, and he should get those votes.

This last month has represented an unprecedented degree of action on behalf of the great citizens of our country. Again, I say it -- there has never been a presidency that's done so much in such a short period of time. And we haven't even started the big work that starts early next week. Some very big things are going to be announced next week.

So we're just getting started. We will be giving a speech, as I said, in Melbourne, Florida, at 5:00 p.m. I hope to see you there. And with that, I'd just say, God bless America, and let's take some questions.

Mara. Mara, go ahead. You were cut off pretty violently at our last news conference.

Q   Did you fire Mike Flynn?

THE PRESIDENT: Mike Flynn is a fine person, and I asked for his resignation. He respectfully gave it. He is a man who -- there was a certain amount of information given to Vice President Pence, who is with us today. And I was not happy with the way that information was given.

He didn't have to do that, because what he did wasn't wrong, what he did in terms of the information he saw. What was wrong was the way that other people, including yourselves in this room, were given that information, because that was classified information that was given illegally. That's the real problem. And you can talk all you want about Russia, which was all a fake news, fabricated deal to try and make up for the loss of the Democrats, and the press plays right into it. In fact, I saw a couple of the people that were supposedly involved with all of this -- they know nothing about it. They weren't in Russia, they never made a phone call to Russia, they never received a phone call. It's all fake news. It's all fake news.

The nice thing is I see it starting to turn, where people are now looking at the illegal, Mara -- and I think it's very important -- the illegal giving out classified information. And let me just tell you, it was given out, like, so much. I'll give you an example. I called, as you know, Mexico. It was a very confidential, classified call, but I called Mexico. And in calling Mexico, I figured, oh, well, that's -- I spoke to the President of Mexico, had a good call. All of a sudden it's out for the world to see. It's supposed to be secret. It's supposed to be either confidential or classified in that case. Same thing with Australia. All of a sudden people are finding out exactly what took place.

The same thing happened with respect to General Flynn. Everybody saw this, and I'm saying -- the first thing I thought of when I heard about it is, how does the press get this information that's classified? How do they do it? You know why? Because it's an illegal process, and the press should be ashamed of themselves. But, more important-ly, the people that gave out the information to the press should be ashamed of themselves. Really ashamed. Yes, go ahead.

Q   Why did you keep your Vice President in the dark for almost two weeks?

THE PRESIDENT: Because when I looked at the informa-tion, I said, I don't think he did anything wrong. If any-thing, he did something right. He was coming into office, he looked at the information. He said, huh, that's fine, that's what they're supposed to do. They're supposed to be -- and he didn't just call Russia. He called and spoke to, both ways -- I think there were 30-some-odd coun-tries. He's doing the job.

You know, he was just doing his job. The thing is he didn't tell our Vice President properly, and then he said he didn't remember. So either way, it wasn't very satisfactory to me. And I have somebody that I think will be outstanding for the position, and that also helps, I think, in the making of my decision.

But he didn't tell the Vice President of the United States the facts, and then he didn't remember. And that just wasn't acceptable to me.

Yes.

Q   President Trump, since you brought up Russia, I'm looking for some clarification here. During the campaign, did anyone from your team communicate with members of the Russian government or Russian intelligence? And if so, what was the nature of those conversations?

THE PRESIDENT: Well, the failing New York Times wrote a big, long front-page story yesterday. And it was very much discredited, as you know. It was -- it's a joke. And the people mentioned in the story -- I notice they were on television today saying they never even spoke to Russia. They weren't even a part, really -- I mean, they were such a minor part -- I hadn't spoken to them. I think the one person; I don't think I've ever spoken to him. I don't think I've ever met him. And he actually said he was a very low-level member of, I think, a committee for a short period of time. I don't think I ever met him. Now, it's possible that I walked into a room and he was sitting there, but I don't think I ever met him. I didn't talk to him, ever. And he thought it was a joke.

The other person said he never spoke to Russia, never received a call. Look at his phone records, et cetera, et cetera. And the other person, people knew that he'd represented various countries, but I don't think he represented Russia -- but knew that he represented various countries. That's what he does. I mean, people know that. That's Mr. Manafort, who's, by the way -- who's, by the way, a respected man. He's a respected man. But I think he represented the Ukraine, or Ukraine government, or somebody. But everybody -- people knew that. Everybody knew that. So these people -- and he said that he has absolutely nothing to do and never has with Russia. And he said that very forcefully. I saw his statement. He said it very forcefully. Most of the papers don't print it because that's not good for their stories.

So the three people that they talked about all totally deny it. And I can tell you, speaking for myself, I own nothing in Russia. I have no loans in Russia. I don't have any deals in Russia. President Putin called me up very nicely to congratulate me on the win of the election. He then called me up extremely nicely to congratulate me on the inauguration, which was terrific. But so did many other leaders -- almost all other leaders from almost all other countries. So that's the extent.

Russia is fake news. Russia -- this is fake news put out by the media. The real news is the fact that people, probably from the Obama administration because they're there -- because we have our new people going in place right now. As you know, Mike Pompeo is now taking control of the CIA. James Comey at FBI. Dan Coats is waiting to be approved. I mean, he is a senator, and a highly respected one. And he's still waiting to be approved. But our new people are going in.

And just while you're at, because you mentioned this, Wall Street Journal did a story today that was almost as disgraceful as the failing New Times's story yesterday. And it talked about -- you saw it, front page. So, Director of National Intelligence just put out -- acting -- a statement: "Any suggestion that the United States intelligence community" -- this was just given to us -- "is withholding information and not providing the best possible intelligence to the President and his national security team is not true."

So they took this front-page story out of The Wall Street Journal -- top -- and they just wrote the story is not true. And I'll tell you something, I'll be honest -- because I sort of enjoy this back and forth, and I guess I have all my life, but I've never seen more dishonest media than, frankly, the political media. I thought the financial media was much better, much more honest. But I will say that I never get phone calls from the media. How do they write a story like that in The Wall Street Journal without asking me? Or how do they write a story in The New York Times, put it on front page? That was like that story they wrote about the women and me -- front page. Big massive story. And it was nasty.

And then they called. They said, "We never said that. We like Mr. Trump." They called up my office -- we like Mr. Trump; we never said that. And it was totally -- they totally misrepresented those very wonderful women, I have to tell you -- totally misrepresented. I said, give us a retraction. They never gave us a retraction. And, frankly, I then went on to other things. Go ahead.

Q   Mr. President --

THE PRESIDENT: You okay?

Q   I am. Just wanted to get untangled. Very simply, you said today that you had the biggest electoral margins since Ronald Reagan with 304 or 306 electoral votes. In fact, President Obama got 365 in 2008.

THE PRESIDENT: Well, I'm talking about Republican. Yes.

Q   President Obama, 332. George H.W. Bush, 426 when he won as President. So why should Americans trust --

THE PRESIDENT: Well, no, I was told -- I was given that information. I don't know. I was just given. We had a very, very big margin.

Q   I guess my question is, why should Americans trust you when you have accused the information they receive of being fake when you're providing information that's fake?

THE PRESIDENT: Well, I don't know. I was given that information. I was given -- actually, I've seen that information around. But it was a very substantial victory. Do you agree with that?

Q   You're the President.

THE PRESIDENT: Okay, thank you. That's a good answer. Yes.

Q   Mr. President, thank you so much. Can you tell us in determining that Lieutenant General Flynn -- there was no wrongdoing in your mind, what evidence was weighed? Did you have the transcripts of these telephone intercepts with Russian officials, particularly Ambassador Kislyak, who he was communicating with? What evidence did you weigh to determine there was no wrong doing? And further than that, sir, you've said on a couple of occasions this morning that you were going to aggressively pursue the sources of these leaks.

THE PRESIDENT: We are.

Q   Can we ask what you're doing to do? And also, we've heard about a review of the intelligence community headed by Stephen Feinberg. What can you tell us about that?

THE PRESIDENT: Well, first of all, about that, we now have Dan Coats, hopefully soon Mike Pompeo and James Comey, and they're in position. So I hope that we'll be able to straighten that out without using anybody else. The gentleman you mentioned is a very talented man, very successful man. And he has offered his services, and it's something we may take advantage of. But I don't think we'll need that at all because of the fact that I think that we're going to be able to straighten it out very easily on its own.

As far as the general is concerned, when I first heard about it, I said, huh, that doesn't sound wrong. My counsel came -- Don McGahn, White House Counsel -- and he told me, and I asked him, and he can speak very well for himself. He said he doesn't think anything is wrong. He really didn't think -- it was really what happened after that, but he didn't think anything was done wrong. I didn't either, because I waited a period of time and I started to think about it. I said, well, I don't see -- to me, he was doing the job.

The information was provided by -- who I don't know -- Sally Yates -- and I was a little surprised because I said, doesn't sound like he did anything wrong there. But he did something wrong with respect to the Vice President, and I thought that was not acceptable. As far as the actual making the call -- in fact, I've watched various programs and I've read various articles where he was just doing his job. That was very normal. At first, everybody got excited because they thought he did something wrong. After they thought about it, it turned out he was just doing his job.

So -- and I do -- and, by the way, with all of that being said, I do think he's a fine man.

Yes, Jon.

Q   On the leaks, sir --

THE PRESIDENT: Go ahead, finish off, then I'll get you, Jon.

Q   Sorry, what will you do on the leaks? You have said twice today --

THE PRESIDENT: Yes, we're looking at it very, very seriously. I've gone to all of the folks in charge of the various agencies, and we're -- I've actually called the Justice Department to look into the leaks. Those are criminal leaks. They're put out by people either in agencies. I think you'll see it stopping because now we have our people in. You know, again, we don't have our people in because we can't get them approved by the Senate. We just had Jeff Sessions approved in Justice, as an example. So we are looking into that very seriously. It's a criminal act.

You know what I say -- when I was called out on Mexico, I was shocked. Because all this equipment, all this incredible phone equipment. When I was called out on Mexico, I was -- honestly, I was really, really surprised. But I said, you know, it doesn't make sense, that won't happen. But that wasn't that important to call, it was fine. I could show it to the world and he could show it to the world -- the President who is a very fine man, by the way. Same thing with Australia. I said, that's terrible that it was leaked but it wasn't that important. But then I said, what happens when I'm dealing with the problem of North Korea? What happens when I'm dealing with the problems in the Middle

East? Are you folks going to be reporting all of that very, very confidential information -- very important, very -- I mean, at the highest level, are you going to be reporting about that too?

So I don't want classified information getting out to the public. And in a way, that was almost a test. So I'm dealing with Mexico. I'm dealing with Argentina. We were dealing on this case with Mike Flynn. All this information gets put into the Washington Post and gets put into the New York Times. And I'm saying, what's going to happen when I'm dealing on the Middle East? What's going to happen when I'm dealing with really, really important subjects like North Korea? We've got to stop it. That's why it's a criminal penalty.

Yes, Jon.

Q   Thank you, Mr. President. I just want to get you to clarify just a very important point. Can you say definitively that nobody on your campaign had any contacts with the Russians during the campaign? And, on the leaks, is it fake news or are these real leaks?

THE PRESIDENT: Well, the leaks are real. You're the one that wrote about them and reported them. I mean, the leaks are real. You know what they said -- you saw it. And the leaks are absolutely real. The news is fake because so much of the news is fake.

So one thing that I felt it was very important to do -- and I hope we can correct it, because there is nobody I have more respect for -- well, maybe a little bit -- than report-ers, than good reporters. It's very important to me, and especially in this position. It's very important. I don't mind bad stories. I can handle a bad story better than anybody as long as it's true. And over a course of time, I'll make mistakes and you'll write badly and I'm okay with that. But I'm not okay when it is fake. I mean, I watch CNN -- it's so much anger and hatred and just the hatred. I don't watch it anymore because it's very good -- he's saying no. It's okay, Jim. It's okay, Jim. You'll have your chance. But I watch others too. You're not the only one, so don't feel badly.

But I think it should be straight. I think it should be -- I think it would be, frankly, more interesting. I know how good everybody's ratings are right now, but I think that actually would be -- I think that it would actually be better. People -- I mean, you have a lower approval rate than Congress. I think that's right. I don't know, Peter, is that one right? Because you know, I think they have lower -- I heard, lower than Congress.

But honestly, the public would appreciate it. I'd appreciate it. Again, I don't mind bad stories when it's true. But we have an administration where the Democrats are making it very difficult. I think we're setting a record, or close to a record in the time of approval of a Cabinet. I mean, the numbers are crazy. When I'm looking -- some of them had them approved immediately. I'm going forever, and I still have a lot of people that we're waiting for.

And that's all they're doing, is delaying. And you look at Schumer and the mess that he's got over there, and they have nothing going. The only thing they can do is delay. And you know, I think they'd be better served by approving and making sure that they're happy and everybody is good. And sometimes, I mean -- I know President Obama lost three or four, and you lose them on the way. And that's okay. That's fine.

But I think they would be much better served, Jon, if they just went through the process quickly. This is pure delay tactics. And they say it, and everybody understands it. Yeah, go ahead, Jim.

Q   The first part of my question on contacts. Do you definitively say that nobody--?

THE PRESIDENT: Well, I had nothing to do with it. I have nothing to do with Russia. I told you, I have no deals there. I have no anything.

Now, when WikiLeaks, which I had nothing to do with, comes out and happens to give -- they're not giving classified information. They're giving stuff -- what was said at an office about Hillary cheating on the debates -- which, by the way, nobody mentions. Nobody mentions that Hillary received the questions to the debates.

Can you imagine -- seriously, can you imagine if I received the questions? It would be the electric chair, okay? "He should be put in the electric chair." You would even call for the reinstitution of the death penalty, okay? Maybe not you, Jon.

Yes, we'll do you next, Jim. I'll do you next. Yes?

Q   Thank you, Mr. President. I just want to clarify one other thing.

THE PRESIDENT: Sure.

Q   Did you direct Mike Flynn to discuss the sanctions with

the Russian ambassador?

THE PRESIDENT: No, I didn't. No, I didn't.

Q (Inaudible.) (Off mic.)

THE PRESIDENT: No, I didn't.

Q   Did you fire him because (inaudible) --

THE PRESIDENT: Excuse me -- no, I fired him because of what he said to Mike Pence, very simple. Mike was doing his job. He was calling countries and his counterparts. So it certainly would have been okay with me if he did it. I would have directed him to do it if I thought he wasn't doing it. I didn't direct him but I would have directed him because that's his job.

And it came out that way -- and, in all fairness, I watched Dr. Charles Krauthammer the other night say he was doing his job. And I agreed with him. And since then I've watched many other people say that.

No, I didn't direct him, but I would have directed him if he didn't do it, okay?

Jim.

Q   Mr. President, thank you very much. And just for the record, we don't hate you, I don't hate you. If you could pass that along.

THE PRESIDENT: Okay. Well, ask Jeff Zucker how he got his job, okay?

Q   If I may follow up on some of the questions that have taken place so far, sir.

THE PRESIDENT: Well, not too many. We do have other people. You do have other people, and your ratings aren't as good as some of the other people that are waiting.

Q   They're pretty good right now, actually.

THE PRESIDENT: Okay. Go ahead, Jim.

Q   If I may ask, sir, you said earlier that WikiLeaks was revealing information about the Hillary Clinton campaign during the election cycle. You welcomed that at one point.

THE PRESIDENT: I was okay with it.

Q   You said you loved WikiLeaks. At another campaign press conference, you called on the Russians to find the missing 30,000 emails. I'm wondering, sir, if you --

THE PRESIDENT: Well, she was actually missing 33,000, and then that got extended with a whole pile after that, but that's okay.

Q   Maybe my numbers are off a little bit too.

THE PRESIDENT: No, no, but I did say 30,000, but it was actually higher than that.

Q   If I may ask you, sir, it sounds as though you do not have much credibility here when it comes to leaking if that is something that you encouraged in the campaign.

THE PRESIDENT: Okay, fair question. Ready?

Q   So if I may ask you that -- if I may ask a follow-up --

THE PRESIDENT: No, no, but are you -- let me do one at a time. Do you mind?

Q   Yes, sir.

THE PRESIDENT: All right. So in one case you're talking about highly classified information. In the other case you're talking about John Podesta saying bad things about the boss. I will say this: If John Podesta said that about me and he was working for me, I would have fired him so fast your head would have spun. He said terrible things about her. But it wasn't classified information.

But in one case you're talking about classified. Regardless, if you look at the RNC, we had a very strong -- at my suggestion -- and I give Reince great credit for this -- at my suggestion, because I know something about this world, I said I want a very strong defensive mechanism. I don't want to be hacked. And we did that, and you have seen that they tried to hack us and they failed.

The DNC did not do that. And if they did it, they could not have been hacked. But they were hacked, and terrible things came. And the only thing that I do think is unfair is some of the things were so -- they were -- when I heard some of those things, I said -- I picked up the papers the next morning, I said, oh, this is going to front page. It wasn't even in the papers.

Again, if I had that happen to me, it would be the biggest story in the history of publishing or the head of newspapers. I would have been the headline in every newspaper. I mean, think of it. They gave her the questions for the debate, and she should have reported herself. Why didn't Hillary Clinton announce that, "I'm sorry, but I have been given the questions to a debate or a town hall, and I feel that it's inappropriate, and I want to turn in CNN for not doing a good job"?

Q   And if I may follow up on that, just something that Jonathan Karl was asking you about -- you said that the leaks are real, but the news is fake. I guess I don't under-stand. It seems that there is a disconnect there. If the information coming from those leaks is real, then how can the stories be fake?

THE PRESIDENT: Well, the reporting is fake. Look, look --

Q   And if I may ask -- I just want to ask one other ques-tion.

THE PRESIDENT: Jim, you know what it is? Here's the thing. The public isn't -- they read newspapers, they see television, they watch. They don't know if it's true or false because they're not involved. I'm involved. I've been involved with this stuff all my life. But I'm involved. So I know when you're telling the truth or when you're not.

I just see many, many untruthful things. And I tell you what else I see. I see tone. You know the word "tone." The tone is such hatred. I'm really not a bad per-son, by the way. No, but the tone is such -- I do get good ratings, you have to admit that. The tone is such hatred.

I watched this morning a couple of the networks, and I have to say "Fox & Friends" in the morning, they're very honorable people. They're very -- not because they're good, because they hit me also when I do something wrong. But they have the most honest morning show. That's all I can say. It's the most honest. But the tone, Jim. If you look -- the hatred. I mean, sometimes -- sometimes somebody gets --

Q (Off mic.)

THE PRESIDENT: Well, you look at your show that goes on at 10 o'clock in the evening. You just take a look at that show. That is a constant hit. The panel is almost always exclusive anti-Trump. The good news is he doesn't have good ratings. But the panel is almost exclusive anti-Trump. And the hatred and venom coming from his mouth, the hatred coming from other people on your network.

Now, I will say this. I watch it. I see it. I'm amazed by it. And I just think you'd be a lot better off -- I honestly do. The public gets it, you know. Look, when I go to rallies, they turn around, they start screaming at CNN. They want to throw their placards at CNN.

I think you would do much better by being different. But you just take a look. Take a look at some of your shows in the morning and the evening. If a guest comes out and says something positive about me, it's brutal.

Now, they'll take this news conference. I'm actually having a very good time, okay? But they'll take this news conference -- don't forget that's the way I won. Remember, I used to give you a news conference every time I made a speech, which was like every day.

Q (Off mic.)

THE PRESIDENT: No, that's how I won. I won with news conferences and probably speeches. I certainly didn't win by people listening to you people, that's for sure.

But I am having a good time. Tomorrow they will say, Donald Trump rants and raves at the press. I'm not ranting and raving. I'm just telling you, you're dishonest people. But -- but I'm not ranting and raving. I love this. I'm having a good time doing it. But tomorrow the headlines are going to be: Donald Trump Rants and Raves. I'm not ranting and raving.

Q   If I may just --

THE PRESIDENT: Go ahead.

Q   One more follow-up because --

THE PRESIDENT: Should I let him have a little bit more? What do you think, Peter?

Q   Just because of this --

THE PRESIDENT: Peter, should I have let him have a little bit more? Sit down. Sit down.

Q   Just because of the attack --

THE PRESIDENT: We'll get it.

Q   Just because of the attack of fake news and attacking our network, I just want to ask you, sir --

THE PRESIDENT: I'm changing it from fake news, though.

Q   Doesn't that undermine --

THE PRESIDENT: Very fake news now. (Laughter.)

Q   But aren't you --

THE PRESIDENT: Yes, go ahead.

Q   Real news, Mr. President. Real news.

THE PRESIDENT: And you're not related to our new --

Q   I am not related, sir, no. (Laughter.)

I do like the sound of Secretary Acosta, I must say.

THE PRESIDENT: I looked -- you know, I looked at
that name. I said, wait a minute, is there any relation
there? Alex Acosta.

Q   I'm sure you checked that out, sir.

THE PRESIDENT: No, I checked it. I said -- they said, no,
sir. I said, do me a favor, go back and check the family tree.

Q   But aren't you concerned, sir, that you are undermining the people's faith in the First Amendment freedom of
the press, the press in this country when you call stories
you don't like "fake news"? Why not just say it's a story I
don't like?

THE PRESIDENT: I do that.

Q   When you call it fake news, you're undermining confidence --

THE PRESIDENT: No, I do that. No, no, I do that.

Q   -- in our news media.

THE PRESIDENT: Here's the thing.

Q   Isn't that important?

THE PRESIDENT: Okay, I understand -- and you're right about that except this. See, I know when I should get good and when I should get bad. And sometimes I'll say, wow, that's going to be a great story, and I'll get killed. I know what's good and bad. I'd be a pretty good reporter -- not as good as you. But I know what's good. I know what's bad.

And when they change it and make it really bad -- something that should be positive. Sometimes something that should be very positive, they'll make okay. They'll even make it negative. So I understand it because I'm there. I know what was said. I know who is saying it. I'm there. So it's very important to me.

Look, I want to see an honest press. When I started off today by saying that it's so important to the public to get an honest press. The press -- the public doesn't believe you people anymore. Now, maybe I had something to do with that, I don't know. But they don't believe you.

If you were straight and really told it like it is, as Howard Cosell used to say, right? Of course, he had some questions also. But if you were straight, I would be your biggest booster, I would be your biggest fan in the world -- including bad stories about me. But if you go -- as an example, you're CNN -- I mean, it's story after story after story is bad. I won. I won. And the other thing: Chaos. There's zero chaos. We are running -- this is a fine-tuned machine. And Reince happens to be doing a good job. But half of his job is putting out lies by the press.

I said to him yesterday, this whole Russia scam that you guys are building so that you don't talk about the real subject, which is illegal leaks. But I watched him yesterday working so hard to try and get that story proper. And I'm saying, here's my Chief of Staff, a really good guy, did a phenomenal job at RNC. I mean, we won the election, right? We won the presidency. We got some senators. We got some -- all over the country, you take a look, he's done a great job.

And I said to myself, you know -- and I said to somebody that was in the room -- I said, you take a look at Reince, he's working so hard just putting out fires that are fake fires. They're fake. They're not true. And isn't that a shame, because he'd rather be working on health care. He'd rather be working on tax reform, Jim. I mean that. I would be your biggest fan in the world if you treated me right. I sort of understand there's a certain bias, maybe by Jeff or somebody -- for whatever reason. And I understand that. But you've got to be at least a little bit fair. And that's why the public sees it -- they see it. They see it's not fair. You take a look at some of your shows and you see the bias and the hatred. And the public is smart. They understand it.

Okay, yeah, go ahead.

Q   We have no doubt that your latest story is (inaudible). But for those who believe that there is something to it, is there anything that you have learned over these last few weeks that you might be able to reveal that might ease their concerns that this isn't fake news? And secondly --

THE PRESIDENT: I think they don't believe it. I don't think the public would. That's why the Rasmussen poll just has me through the roof. I don't think they believe it. Well, I guess one of the reasons I'm here today is to tell you the whole Russian thing -- that's a ruse. That's a ruse. And, by the way, it would be great if we could get along with Russia, just so you understand that. Now, tomorrow you'll say, Donald Trump wants to get along with Russia, this is terrible. It's not terrible -- it's good.

We had Hillary Clinton try and do a reset. We had Hillary Clinton give Russia 20 percent of the uranium in our country. You know what uranium is, right? It's this thing called nuclear weapons and other things. Like, lots of things are done with uranium, including some bad things. Nobody talks about that. I didn't do anything for Russia. I've done nothing for Russia. Hillary Clinton gave them 20 percent of our uranium. Hillary Clinton did a reset, remember, with the stupid plastic button that made us all look like a bunch of jerks? Here, take a look. He looked at her like, what the hell is she doing with that cheap plastic button? Hillary Clinton -- that was a reset. Remember? It said "reset."

Now, if I do that, oh, I'm a bad guy. If we could get along with Russia, that's a positive thing. We have a very talented man, Rex Tillerson, who is going to be meeting with them shortly. And I told him, I said, I know politically it's probably not good for me. Hey, the greatest thing I could do is shoot that ship that's 30 miles offshore right out of the water. Everyone in this country is going to say, oh, it's so great. That's not great. That's not great. I would love to be able to get along with Russia.

Now, you've had a lot of Presidents that haven't taken that tact. Look where we are now. Look where we are now. So, if I can -- now, I love to negotiate things. I do it really well and all that stuff, but it's possible I won't be able to get along with Putin. Maybe it is. But I want to just tell you, the false reporting by the media, by you people -- the false, horrible, fake reporting makes it much harder to make a deal with Russia. And probably Putin said, you know -- he's sitting behind his desk and he's saying, you know, I see what's going on in the United States, I follow it closely; it's got to be impossible for President Trump to ever get along with Russia because of all the pressure he's got with this fake story. Okay? And that's a shame.

Because if we could get along with Russia -- and, by the way, China and Japan and everyone -- if we could get along, it would be a positive thing, not a negative thing.

Q   Tax reform --

Q   Mr. President, since you --

THE PRESIDENT: Tax reform is going to happen fairly quickly. We're doing Obamacare -- we're in final stages. We should be submitting the initial plan in March, early March, I would say. And we have to, as you know, statutorily and for reasons of budget, we have to go first. It's not like -- frankly, the tax would be easier, in my opinion, but for statutory reasons and for budgetary reasons, we have to submit the health care sooner. So we'll be submitting health care sometime in early March, mid-March. And after that, we're going to come up -- and we're doing very well on tax reform. Yes.

Q   Mr. President, you mentioned Russia. Let's talk about

some serious issues that have come up in the last week that you have had to deal with as President of the United States.

THE PRESIDENT: Okay.

Q   You mentioned the vessel, the spy vessel, off the coast of the United States.

THE PRESIDENT: Not good.

Q   There was a ballistic missile test that many interpreted as a violation --

THE PRESIDENT: Not good.

Q   -- of the agreement between the two countries. And a Russian plane buzzed a U.S. destroyer.

THE PRESIDENT: Not good.

Q   I listened to you during the campaign --

THE PRESIDENT: Excuse me, excuse me, when did it happen? It happened when -- if you were Putin right now, you would say, hey, we're back to the old games with the United States. There's no way Trump can ever do a deal with us because the -- you have to understand, if I was just brutal on Russia right now, just brutal, people would say, you would say, oh, isn't that wonderful. But I know you well enough. Then you would say, oh, he was too tough, he shouldn't have done that. Look, of all --

Q   I'm just trying to find out your orientation to those --

THE PRESIDENT: Wait a minute. Wait, wait. Excuse me just one second.

Q   I'm just trying to find out what you're doing to do about them, Mr. President.

THE PRESIDENT: All of those things that you mentioned are very recent, because probably Putin assumes that he's not going to be able to make a deal with me because it's politically not popular for me to make a deal. So Hillary Clinton tries to reset, it failed. They all tried. But I'm different than those people. Go ahead.

Q   How are you interpreting those moves? And what do you intend to do about them?

THE PRESIDENT: Just the way I said it.

Q   Have you given Rex Tillerson any advice or counsel on how to deal?

THE PRESIDENT: I have. I have. And I'm so beautifully represented. I'm so honored that the Senate approved him. He's going to be fantastic.

Yes, I think that I've already --

Q   Is Putin testing you, do you believe, sir?

THE PRESIDENT: No, I don't think so. I think Putin probably assumes that he can't make a deal with me anymore because politically it would be unpopular for a politician to make a deal. I can't believe I'm saying I'm a politician, but I guess that's what I am now. Because, look, it would be much easier for me to be tough on Russia, but then we're not going to make a deal.

Now, I don't know that we're going to make a deal. I don't know. We might, we might not. But it would be much easier for me to be so tough -- the tougher I am on Russia, the better. But you know what, I want to do the right thing for the American people. And to be honest, secondarily, I want to do the right thing for the world.

If Russia and the United States actually got together and got along -- and don't forget, we're a very powerful nuclear country and so are they. There's no upside. We're a very powerful nuclear country and so are they. I've been briefed. And I can tell you, one thing about a briefing that we're allowed to say because anybody that ever read the most basic book can say it: Nuclear holocaust would be like no other. They're a very powerful nuclear country and so are we.

If we have a good relationship with Russia, believe me, that's a good thing, not a bad thing.

Q   So when you say they're not good, do you mean that they are --

THE PRESIDENT: Who did I say is not good?

Q   No, when I read off the three things that have recently happened and each one of them you said they're not good.

THE PRESIDENT: No, it's not good, but they happened.

Q   But do they damage the relationship? Do they undermine this country's ability to work with Russia?

THE PRESIDENT: They all happened recently, and I under-stand what they're doing, because they're doing the same thing. Now, again, maybe I'm not going to be able to do a deal with Russia, but at least I will have tried. And if I don't, does anybody really think that Hillary Clinton would be tougher on Russia than Donald Trump? Does anybody in this room really believe that? Okay.

But I tell you one thing: She tried to make a deal. She had the reset. She gave all the valuable uranium away. She did other things. You know, they say I'm close to Russia. Hillary Clinton gave away 20 percent of the ura-nium in the United States. She's close to Russia. I gave -- you know what I gave to Russia? You know what I gave? Nothing.

Q   Can we conclude there will be no response to these particular provocations?

THE PRESIDENT: I'm not going to tell you anything about what response I do. I don't talk about military response. I don't say I'm going into Mosul in four months. "We are going to attack Mosul in four months." Then three months later: "We are going to attack Mosul in one month." "Next week, we are going to attack Mosul." In the meantime, Mosul is very, very difficult. Do you know why? Because I don't talk about military, and I don't talk about certain oth-er things. You're going to be surprised to hear that. And, by the way, my whole campaign, I'd say that. So I don't have to tell you --

Q   There will be a response?

THE PRESIDENT: I don't want to be one of these guys that say, "Yes, here's what we're going to do." I don't have to do that.

Q   There will be a -- in other words, there will be a response, Mr. President?

THE PRESIDENT: I don't have to tell you what I'm going to do in North Korea. Wait a minute. I don't have to tell you what I'm going to do in North Korea. And I don't have to tell you what I'm going to do with Iran. You know why? Because they shouldn't know. And eventually you guys are going to get tired of asking that question. So when you ask me, what am I going to do with the ship -- the Russian ship, as an example -- I'm not going to tell you. But hopefully, I won't have to do anything. But I'm not going to tell you. Okay.

Q   Thanks.

Q   Can I just ask you -- thank you very much, Mr. President -- the Trump --

THE PRESIDENT: Where are you from?

Q   BBC.

THE PRESIDENT: Okay. Here's another beauty.
Q   That's a good line. Impartial, free, and fair.

THE PRESIDENT: Yeah, sure.

Q   Mr. President --

THE PRESIDENT: Just like CNN, right?

Q   Mr. President, on the travel ban -- we could banter

back and forth. On the travel ban, would you accept that that was a good example of the smooth running of government, that fine-tuned --

THE PRESIDENT: Yeah, I do. I do. And let me tell you about the travel --

Q   Were there any mistakes in that?

THE PRESIDENT: Wait, wait, wait. I know who you are. Just wait. Let me tell you about the travel ban. We had a very smooth rollout of the travel ban, but we had a bad court. We got a bad decision. We had a court that's been overturned -- again, maybe wrong, but I think it's 80 percent of the time. A lot. We had a bad decision. We're going to keep going with that decision. We're going to put in a new executive order next week sometime. But we had a bad decision. That's the only thing that was wrong with the travel ban.

You had Delta with a massive problem with their computer system at the airports. You had some people that were put out there, brought by very nice buses, and they were put out at various locations. Despite that, the only problem that we had is we had a bad court. We had a court that gave us what I consider to be, with great respect, a very bad decision. Very bad for the safety and security of our country. The rollout was perfect.

Now, what I wanted to do was do the exact same executive order but said one thing -- and I said this to my people: Give them a one-month period of time. But General Kelly, now Secretary Kelly, said, if you do that, all these people will come in, in the month -- the bad ones. You do agree, there are bad people out there, right? They're not everybody that's like you. You have some bad people out there.

So Kelly said, you can't do that. And he was right. As soon as he said it, I said, wow, never thought of it. I said, how about one week? He said, no good. You got to do it immediately, because if you do it immediately, they don't have time to come in. Now, nobody ever reports that, but that's why we did it quickly.

Now, if would have done it a month, everything would have been perfect. The problems is we would have wasted a lot of time, and maybe a lot of lives, because a lot of bad people would have come into our country.

Now, in the meantime, we've vetting very, very strongly. Very, very strongly. But we need help, and we need help by getting that executive order passed.

Q   Just a brief follow-up. And if it's so urgent, why not introduce --

THE PRESIDENT: Yes, go ahead.

Q   Thank you. I just was hoping that we could get a yes-or-no answer on one of these questions involving Russia. Can you say whether you are aware that anyone who advised your campaign had contacts with Russia during the course of the election?

THE PRESIDENT: Well, I told you, General Flynn obviously was dealing. So that's one person. But he was dealing -- as he should have been --

Q   During the election?

THE PRESIDENT: No, no, nobody that I know of.

Q   So you're not aware of any contacts during the course of the election?

THE PRESIDENT: Look, look, how many times do I have to answer this question?

Q   Can you just say yes or no on it?

THE PRESIDENT: Russia is a ruse. Yeah, I know you have to get up and ask a question, so important. Russia is a ruse. I have nothing to do with Russia, haven't made a phone call to Russia in years. Don't speak to people from Russia. Not that I wouldn't, I just have nobody to speak to. I spoke to Putin twice. He called me on the election -- I told you this -- and he called me on the inauguration, and a few days ago. We had a very good talk, especially the second one -- lasted for a pretty long period of time. I'm sure you probably get it because it was classified, so I'm sure everybody in this room perhaps has it. But we had a very, very good talk. I have nothing to do with Russia. To the best of my knowledge, no person that I deal with does.

Now, Manafort has totally denied it. He denied it. Now, people knew that he was a consultant over in that part of the world for a while, but not for Russia. I think he represented Ukraine or people having to do with Ukraine, or people that -- whoever. But people knew that. Everybody knew that.

Q   But in his capacity as your campaign manager, was he in touch with Russian officials during the election?

THE PRESIDENT: I have -- you know what, he said no. I can

only tell you what he -- now, he was replaced long before the election. You know that, right? He was replaced long before the election. When all of this stuff started coming out, it came out during the election.

But Paul Manafort, who's a good man also, by the way -- Paul Manafort was replaced long before the election took place. He was only there for a short period of time.

How much longer should we stay here, folks? Five more minutes, is that okay? Five?

Q   Mr. President, on national security --

THE PRESIDENT: Wait, let's see, who's -- I want to find a friendly reporter. Are you a friendly reporter? Watch how friendly he is. Wait, wait -- watch how friendly he is. Go ahead. Go ahead.

Q   So, first of all, my name is (inaudible) from (inaudible) Magazine. And (inaudible). I haven't seen anybody in my community accuse either yourself or any of the -- anyone on your staff of being anti-Semitic. We have an understanding of (inaudible).

THE PRESIDENT: Thank you.

Q   However, what we are concerned about, and what we haven't really heard be addressed is an uptick in anti-Semitism and how the government is planning to take care of it. There have been reports out that 48 bomb threats have been made against Jewish centers all across the country in the last couple of weeks. There are people who are committing anti-Semitic acts or threatening to --

THE PRESIDENT: You see, he said he was going to ask a very simple, easy question. And it's not. It's not. Not a simple question, not a fair question. Okay, sit down. I understand the rest of your question.

So here's the story, folks. Number one, I am the least anti-Semitic person that you've ever seen in your entire life. Number two, racism -- the least racist person. In fact, we did very well relative to other people running as a Republican.

Q (Inaudible.)

THE PRESIDENT: Quiet, quiet, quiet. See, he lied about -- he was going to get up and ask a very straight, simple question. So you know, welcome to the world of the media. But let me just tell you something -- that I hate the charge. I find it repulsive. I hate even the question because people that know me -- and you heard the Prime Minister, you heard Netanyahu yesterday -- did you hear him, Bibi? He said, I've known Donald Trump for a long time, and then he said, forget it.

So you should take that, instead of having to get up and ask a very insulting question like that.
Yeah, go ahead. Go ahead.

Q Thank you. I'm Lisa from the PBS --

THE PRESIDENT: See, it just shows you about the press, but that's the way the press is.

Q Thank you, Mr. President. Lisa Desjardins from the PBS Newshour.

THE PRESIDENT: Good.

Q On national security and immigration, can you give us more details on the executive order you planned for next week, even its broad outlines? Will it be focused on specific countries?

THE PRESIDENT: It's a very fair question.

Q   And in addition, on the DACA program for immigration, what is your plan? Do you plan to continue that program or to end it?

THE PRESIDENT: We're going to show great heart. DACA is a very, very difficult subject for me, I will tell you. To me, it's one of the most difficult subjects I have, because you have these incredible kids, in many cases -- not in all cases. In some of the cases they're having DACA and they're gang members and they're drug dealers too. But you have some absolutely incredible kids -- I would say mostly -- they were brought here in such a way -- it's a very, very tough subject.

We are going to deal with DACA with heart. I have to deal with a lot of politicians, don't forget, and I have to convince them that what I'm saying is right. And I appreciate your understanding on that.

But the DACA situation is a very, very -- it's a very difficult thing for me. Because, you know, I love these kids. I love kids. I have kids and grandkids. And I find it very, very hard doing what the law says exactly to do. And you know, the law is rough. I'm not talking about new laws. I'm talking the existing law is very rough. It's very, very rough. As far as the new order, the new order is going to be very much tailored to what I consider to be a very bad decision, but we can tailor the order to that decision and get just about everything, in some ways more. But we're tailoring it now to the decision. We have some of the best lawyers in the country working on it. And the new executive order is being tailored to the decision we got down from the court. Okay?

Q   Mr. President, Melania Trump announced the reopening of the White House Visitors Office.

THE PRESIDENT: Yes.

Q   And she does a lot of great work for the country as well. Can you tell us a little bit about what First Lady Melania Trump does for the country? And there is a unique level of interest in your administration, so by opening the White House Visitors Office, what does that mean to you?

THE PRESIDENT: Now, that's what I call a nice question. That is very nice. Who are you with?

Q   (Inaudible.)

THE PRESIDENT: Good. I'm going to start watching. Thank you very much.

Melania is terrific. She was here last night. We had dinner with Senator Rubio and his wife, who is, by the way, lovely. And we had a really good discussion about Cuba because we have very similar views on Cuba. And Cuba was very good to me in the Florida election as you know, the Cuban people, Americans.

And I think that Melania is going to be outstanding. That's

right, she just opened up the Visitors Center -- in other words, touring of the White House.

She, like others that she's working with, feels very, very strongly about women's issues, women's difficulties, very, very strongly. And she's a very, very strong advocate. I think she's a great representative for this country.

And a funny thing happens because she gets so unfairly maligned. The things they say -- I've known her for a long time. She was a very successful person. She was a very successful model. She did really well.

She would go home at night and didn't even want to go out with people. She was a very private person. She was always the highest quality that you'll ever find.

And the things they say -- and I've known her for a long time -- the things they say are so unfair. And actually, she's been apologized to, as you know, by various media because they said things that were lies.

I'd just tell you this: I think she's going to be a fantastic First Lady. She's going to be a tremendous representative of women and of the people. And helping her and working with her will be Ivanka, who is a fabulous person and a fabulous, fabulous woman. And they're not doing this for money. They're not doing this for pay. They're doing this because they feel it, both of them.

And Melania goes back and forth, and after Barron finishes school -- because it's hard to take a child out of school with a few months left -- she and Barron will be moving over to the White House. Thank you. That's a very nice question.

Go ahead.

Q   Mr. President.

THE PRESIDENT: Yes. Oh, this is going to be a bad question but that's okay.

Q   No, it's not going to be a bad question.

THE PRESIDENT: Good, because I enjoy watching you on television.

Q   Well, thank you so much. Mr. President, I need to find out from you -- you said something as it relates to inner cities. That was one of your platforms during your campaign.

THE PRESIDENT: Fix the inner cities, yes.

Q   Fixing the inner cities. What will be that fix and your urban agenda, as well as your HBCU executive order that's coming out this afternoon? See, it wasn't bad, was it?

THE PRESIDENT: That was very professional and very good.

Q   I'm very professional.

THE PRESIDENT: We'll be announcing the order in a little while, and I'd rather let the order speak for itself. But it will be something I think that will be very good for everybody concerned. But we'll talk to you about that after we do the announcement.

As far as the inner cities, as you know, I was very strong on the inner cities during the campaign. I think it's probably what got me a much higher percentage of the African

American vote than a lot of people thought I was going to get. We did much higher than people thought I was going to get and I was honored by that, including the Hispanic vote, which was also much higher. And, by the way, if I might add, including the women's vote, which was much higher than people thought I was going to get.

So we are going to be working very hard on the inner cities having to do with education, having to do with crime. We're going to try and fix as quickly as possible -- you know it takes a long time. It's taken 100 years or more for some of these places to evolve, and they evolved many of them very badly.

But we're going to be working very hard on health and health care; very, very hard on education. And also, we're going to working in a stringent way, and a very good way, on crime.

You go to some of these inner city places, and it's so sad when you look at the crime. You have people -- and I've seen this, and I've sort of witnessed it. In fact, in two cases, I have actually witnessed it. They lock themselves into apartments, petrified to even leave, in the middle of the day. They're living in hell. We can't let that happen. So we're going to be very, very strong.

It's a great question, and it's a very difficult situation, because it's been many, many years. It's been festering for many, many years. But we have places in this country that we have to fix.

We have to help African American people that, for the most part are stuck there -- Hispanic American people. We have Hispanic American people that are in the inner cities, and they're living in hell.

I mean, you look at the numbers in Chicago. There are two Chicagos, as you know. There's one Chicago that's incredible, luxurious and all, and safe. There's another Chicago that's worse than almost any of the places in the Middle East that we talk about, and that you talk about every night on the newscasts. So we're going to do a lot of work on the inner cities. I have great people lined up to help with the inner cities.

Q   Well, when you say -- when you say the inner cities, are you going to include the CBC, Mr. President, in your conversations with your urban agenda, your inner city agenda, as well as your --

THE PRESIDENT: Am I going include who?

Q   Are you going to include the Congressional Black Caucus and the Congressional Hispanic Caucus, as well as --

THE PRESIDENT: Well, I would. I tell you what, do you want to set up the meeting? Do you want to set up the meeting?

Q   No, no, no.

THE PRESIDENT: Are they friends of yours?

Q   I'm just a reporter.

THE PRESIDENT: No, go ahead, set up the meeting.

Q   I know some of them, but I'm sure they're watching right now.

THE PRESIDENT: Let's go set up a meeting. I would love to meet with the Black Caucus. I think it's great -- the Congressional Black Caucus. I think it's great.

I actually thought I had a meeting with Congressman Cummings, and he was all excited, and then he said, oh, I can't move, it might be bad for me politically, I can't have that meeting. I was all set to have the meeting. You know, we called him and called him, and he was all set. I spoke to him on the phone. Very nice guy.

Q I hear he wanted that meeting with you as well.

THE PRESIDENT: He wanted it. But we called, called, called, called -- they can't make a meeting with him. Every day, I walked in, I said, I would like to meet with him.

Because I do want to solve the problem. But he probably was told by Schumer or somebody like that -- some other lightweight -- he was probably told -- he was probably told, don't meet with Trump, it's bad politics. And that's part of the problem of this country.Okay, one more. Go ahead.

Q Yes, Mr. President, two questions --

THE PRESIDENT: No, no. One question. Two, we can't handle. This room can't handle two. Go ahead, give me the better of your two.

Q (Inaudible) it's not about your personality or your beliefs. We're talking about (inaudible) around the country, some of it by supporters in your name. What do you --

THE PRESIDENT: And some of it -- and can I be honest with you? And this has to do with racism and horrible things that are put up. Some of it written by our opponents. You do know that. Do you understand that? You don't think anybody would do a thing like that. Some of the signs you'll see are not put up by the people that love or like Donald Trump, they're put up by the other side, and you think it's like playing it straight. No. But you have some of those signs, and some of that anger is caused by the other side. They'll do signs and they'll do drawings that are inappropriate. It won't be my people. It will be the people on the other side to anger people like you. Okay. Go ahead.

Q   You are the President now. What are you going to do about it?

THE PRESIDENT: Who is that? Where is that? Oh, stand up. You can --

Q   What are you going to do about the tensions that have been discussed?

THE PRESIDENT: Oh, I'm working on it. No, I'm working on it very hard.

Q   Are you going to give a speech?

THE PRESIDENT: No, no, look. Hey, just so you understand, we had a totally divided country for eight years, and long before that, in all fairness to President Obama.

Long before President Obama, we have had a very divided. I didn't come along and divide this country. This country was seriously divided before I got here.

We're going to work on it very hard. One of the questions that was asked -- I thought it was a very good question

-- was about the inner cities. I mean, that's part of it. But we're going to work on education. We're going to work on lack [sic]-- you know, we're going to stop -- we're going to try and stop the crime. We have great law enforcement officials. We're going to try and stop crime. We're not going to try and stop, we're going to stop crime.

But it's very important to me. But this isn't Donald Trump that divided a nation. We went eight years with President Obama, and we went many years before President Obama. We lived in a divided nation. And I am going to try -- I will do everything within my power to fix that.

I want to thank everybody very much. It's a great honor to be with you. Thank you. Thank you very much. (Applause.)

END
2:13 P.M. EST

"But tomorrow the headlines are going to be: Donald Trump Rants and Raves."

Chapter 41

ROOSEVELT ROOM

16 February 2017

3:43 P.M. EST

THE PRESIDENT: Okay. We had an exciting news conference before. And some people loved it. I think nobody hated it, but it was -- I think it was very productive. And thank you all for being there, that was very nice. And thank you, all of the wonderful politicians, but -- right, Mitch, especially the miners that are with us, right? So I just want to thank you. Seriously. (Applause.)

We appreciate it. We appreciate it very much.

And this is our second bill signing this week as we continue to work for the American people. This is H.J. Resolution 38, and that will eliminate another terrible job-killing rule, saving many thousands of American jobs, especially in the mines, which I've been promising you. The mines are a big deal. I've had support from some of you folks right from the very beginning, and I won't forget it. I went to West Virginia and I -- we had 17,000, 18,000 people that couldn't get into that big arena, right? You were a few of them. But that was some day and some night.

I want to thank Senate Majority Leader Mitch McConnell, House Speaker Paul Ryan, House Majority Leader Kevin

McCarthy, House Natural Resources Committee Chairman Rob Bishop -- thank you, Rob -- and Representative Bill Johnson, who worked very hard on this bill. And they really did, they worked very hard. This was a tough one.

I also want to thank the great members of Congress who have joined us today. We have a lot of them. In eliminating this rule, I am continuing to keep my **promise** to the American people to get rid of wasteful regulations that do nothing -- absolutely nothing -- but slow down the economy, hamstring companies, push jobs to other countries -- which is happening all over, although I must tell you, we've stopped it.

You've seen all the factories, all the plants that are moving back. They're going back to a lot of places. So you know that, right, fellas? They're moving back fast. Ford, General Motors, Fiat -- so many. Very happy.

Compliance costs for this rule would be over $50 million a year for the coal industry alone, and it's unnecessary. I want to also thank the incredible coal miners who are with us today. I think we can maybe thank them the most, right, for – political leaders. (Applause.)

You folks have put up with a lot. And you know, in other countries, they love their coal. Over here, we haven't treated it with the respect it deserves. Even for defense, having that coal is a very important thing for us. So I want to thank you all.

This rule we're eliminating it's a major threat to your jobs, and we're going to get rid of that threat immediately. We're going to fight for you like I promised I would in the campaign. And you were very good to me, and I'm going to be even better to you, I promise you that.

And we're going to fight for, also, low-energy prices for all Americans. There's a spirit of optimism rising across the country. It's going to continue to grow as we sign more and more bills. We're going to make our nation more than competitive -- not just competitive, we're going to be more than competitive. And we're going to win at many, many industries. We're already starting back with the automobile industry. We had the airline industry in the other day. They have rules and regulations that by the time they get through it, it's -- nothing left, and they have to get rid of a lot of jobs. We had a great meeting, actually.

We had the unions in. We had the workers in. We had a lot of people in, and they were all very excited about what's happening. And I haven't looked yet at the stock market, but it's been going up at record clips. We have a tremendous streak going on. And that's only because of the optimism. They feel the optimism. And that optimism is creating a lot of jobs.

So it's an honor to have everybody with us, and, in particular, the miners. We appreciate everything you've done, fellas. Thank you very much.

Would anybody like to say a few words? How about one of the miners saying a few words? I hear these guys all the time. I hear Rand all the time. (Laughter.)

Come on. Who'd like to -- come on, Mike.

MR. NELSON: President Trump, we thank you very much for everything you've done for us. Everything that you're doing for our industry is very much needed. I've been mining in this industry for 40 years, and this is a very exciting time for our industry. Thank you very much.

THE PRESIDENT: Thank you very much.

SENATOR MANCHIN: Tell him where you're from, Mike.

MR. NELSON: I'm from Morgantown, West Virginia, but I work at the Marion County Coal Company.

THE PRESIDENT: How did I do in that area?

MR. NELSON: Oh, you did great. (Laughter and applause.)

THE PRESIDENT: Good. Good. Say something.

CONGRESSWOMAN CAPITO: Well, President Trump --

THE PRESIDENT: You're a -- you represent.

CONGRESSWOMAN CAPITO: Yes. Representing West Virginia as the Senator, and Senator Manchin and I, and we have our congressional delegation here -- Congressman Jenkins, Congressman McKinley, and Congressman Mooney. This is a lifeline to us, and these miners, they mine in West Virginia. It's a source of pride for us as a state that we've been able to power this country, and that we've had the opportunity to provide the energy to this country. And thank you for being a partner with us and being a leader, President Trump, in this. We believe in this, and we believe in your commitment to making sure American miners get back to work. Thank you.

THE PRESIDENT: Thank you. (Applause.)

SENATOR PAUL: This is a big day for Kentucky. We want to thank President Trump for getting rid of this job-killing regulation. It was scheduled to cost us thousands of more jobs. Nobody seemed to care about Kentucky, but I can promise you, Eastern Kentucky voted about 75 percent for Donald J. Trump. (Applause.)

SENATOR MANCHIN: Let me just say something very quickly. There's not a miner here that's not an environmentalist. So when people say that we don't want to do the right thing -- there's a balance between the environment and the economy, these miners would be the first ones to tell you. They're out in the woods, they're hunting, they're fishing, they're doing everything possible. All they want is the respect that -- basically they've given us the country we have because of the hard work of them and their fathers and grandfathers and all of their family has done.

So I'm so proud. These are all West Virginians too. Makes it even prouder for all of us. So thank you. God bless you.

LEADER MCCONNELL: Well, Mr. President, you know that the last eight years brought a depression -- a depression -- to Eastern Kentucky, and our folks are so excited to have a pro-coal President. And we thank you so much for being on our side. (Applause.)

THE PRESIDENT: Anybody else? Come on. Sure. Absolutely. You deserve it.

LEADER MCCONNELL: Thank you, Mr. President.

THE PRESIDENT: You deserve it. Come on up.

PARTICIPANT: Well, Mr. President, this is an example

of what you talked about so much during your campaign. This is what is going to **Make America Great Again**. This is the legislative branch and you working together to keep the promise that you made to put coal miners back to work and to save the coal industry. If we had not overturned this rule, we were looking at nearly 70,000 jobs across the country, and about 80 percent of our coal reserves being unavailable. So thank you for your willingness to work with us to get this done. It's very, very important to the coal miners of this country and to our electricity grid. Thank you, Mr. President. (Applause.)

PARTICIPANT: As a 45-year miner, I'm very proud to be in this historic building, and I am very proud to be here with my President of the United States, who keeps his word. And we thank you very much, sir.

THE PRESIDENT: It's a great honor. (Applause.)

So I want to thank everybody. And tell your friends back in West Virginia and Kentucky and all the other places where we worked -- Wyoming --

SENATOR HEITKAMP: North Dakota.

REPRESENTATIVE JORDAN: Ohio.

THE PRESIDENT: North Dakota. Ohio.

REPRESENTATIVE LAMBORN: Colorado.

THE PRESIDENT: You're right about that. They have been fantastic. Everybody's been -- actually, everybody's been great, and we appreciate it very much. Special people. Special workers. We're bringing it back, and we're bringing it back fast. We didn't have to wait a long period of time. It's been very few days since I've been here, and I think this is long ahead of schedule, right? Wouldn't you say even --

SENATOR MANCHIN: Absolutely.

THE PRESIDENT: Even you might say -- (laughter) -- this is about four-years faster than they thought would have happened. So it's my honor. And, fellas, go back to work, all right? I think we'll take them into the Oval Office, right? Let's take them into the Oval Office. Let's have a little tour, okay? They've probably been there many times before. (Laughter.)

Come on. Come with me. Good.

Thank you, everybody. Thank you, very much.

AIDE: Sign the Bill here.

THE PRESIDENT: Oh. (Laughter.)

I could have gotten away with it.

PARTICIPANT: It's the important part.

(The President signs the Bill.)

END
3:53 P.M. EST

Chapter 42

16 February 2017

6:42 P.M. EST

THE VICE PRESIDENT: Good evening. Please be seated.
On behalf of the President of the United States, it will be
my great privilege tonight to administer the oath of office
to the next Director of the Office of Management and
Budget Mick Mulvaney. (Applause.)

Grateful to be joined by family and friends, but most especially grateful to be joined by Pam Mulvaney. Pam, thank
you for being here and thank you for your family's commitment to the United States in this new chapter.

We also have with us a distinguished group of guests.
Senator Mike Enzi, chairman of the Senate Committee on
the Budget, is with us today. Mr. Chairman, thank you for
being with us today.

Senator Ron Johnson, also on the budget committee. And
the Congressman's good friends Senator Tom Cotton,
Representative Mark Meadows, Representative Justin
Amash, and of course, his fellow South Carolinians --
Senator Lindsey Graham and Senator Tim Scott and
Representative Joe Wilson. That's quite a turnout, and I
know it means the world to the President, as it does to

our new director. Give all these members a round of applause. (Applause.)

In Congressman Mick Mulvaney, President Trump has nominated someone with an extraordinary record in public and private life. He once described himself as a serial entrepreneur, starting no fewer than four businesses over the course of his life. And along the way, he established himself as a principled, results-driven leader. And he'll be bringing those leadership qualities and his well-earned reputation for fiscal responsibility to his new role leading the Office of Management and Budget.

These qualities have served him well in public office. In 2006, he won a seat in South Carolina's House of Representatives, followed two years later by a seat in the state senate. Two years after that, he ran for the United States Congress on a promise of faithfully serving the good people of the Palmetto State. I had the great pleasure of knowing Congressman Mulvaney as a member of Congress, and I couldn't be more enthusiastic at the President's decision to task him to lead this vitally important agency and our national budget.

He quickly established himself in the Congress, as I saw first-hand, as one of the leading fiscal experts on Capitol Hill. He work[s] on the House committees on financial services, oversight, and government reform only added to that sterling reputation. A happy warrior on behalf of fiscal responsibility, Mick Mulvaney will bring those very same qualities to the Office of Management and Budget.

Mick, President Trump has asked you to lead the Office of Management and Budget, a vital role in a day and age of deficits and debt. And we're both very confident that your leadership, your integrity, and your commitment to protecting America's fiscal and economic future will serve all the people of the United States with great distinction.

Thank you for stepping up at this time in the life of our nation. And behalf of President Trump, it now is my great privilege to administer to you the oath of office.

(The Oath is administered.) (Applause.)

END
6:47 P.M. EST

Chapter 43

PRESIDENT TRUMP'S WEEKLY ADDRESS
17 FEBRUARY 2017
THE PRESIDENT'S WEEKLY ADDRESS AIRED TODAY ON
FACEBOOK LIVE AND IS NOW AVAILABLE TO WATCH ON
YOUTUBE.

Transcript:

My fellow Americans,
We have taken major steps during the first few weeks of
my Administration to remove wasteful regulations and get
our people back to work. I have been saying I was going to
do that for a long time.

This week I signed two pieces of legislation to remove
burdens on our economy, continue to keep my **promises** to
the American People and so much more.

I signed House Joint Resolution 38, which eliminates an
anti-coal regulation put forward by unelected bureaucrats.
Our coal miners have been treated horribly, and we are going to turn that around - and we are going to turn it around
quickly. We are going to fight for lower energy prices for all
Americans as part of the deal.

That's why I also signed a resolution to eliminate a cost-
ly regulation Dodd-Frank imposed on American energy
companies. By stopping this regulation, we are able to save
American companies and workers millions and millions of
dollars in job-killing compliance costs.

But to truly succeed as a country, we must realize the full

potential of women in our economy.

That is why I was thrilled to host the White House's Women's Business Leaders Roundtable—very exciting, great women.

As President, I am committed to ensuring that women entrepreneurs have equal access to the capital, markets, and networks of support that they need, and I mean really need. And it's going to happen. This is a priority for my Administration. I campaigned on helping women in the workforce, and we are going to deliver on that **promise**, believe me.

In fact, as part of my first official meeting with Canadian Prime Minister Justin Trudeau this week, we announced the creation of the Joint United States-Canada Council for Advancement of Women Entrepreneurs and Business Leaders. Actually, very exciting.

The United States also reaffirmed our unbreakable bond this week with our cherished ally, Israel. It was an honor to welcome my friend, Prime Minister Benjamin Netanyahu to the White House.

I affirmed to the Prime Minister America's commitment to working with Israel and our allies and partners toward greater security and stability. The threat of terrorism—and believe me it is a threat—must be confronted and defeated and we will defeat it.

We share with Israel a deep conviction that we must protect all innocent human life.

So as you head into the President's Day weekend, the

American people should know that we are working tire-lessly on your behalf. We are not here for the benefit of bureaucrats, consultants, or pundits—we are here to work for you, and only for you, the American people.

Thank you, God Bless you and God Bless America.

Chapter 44

17 February 2017

1:31 P.M. EST

THE PRESIDENT: Thank you, Dennis. And I have to say, I love South Carolina. I love it. (Applause.)

Remember we came down -- all together, we came down, and this was going to be a place that was tough to win, and we won in a landslide. This was a good one. (Applause.)

So I want to thank the people of South Carolina and your Governor -- tremendous guy. He supported us right from the beginning. So I'd like to thank Governor McMaster for the incredible job. He's right here someplace. Thank you very much. You have been fantastic.

And I have to say also, that is one beautiful airplane. (Applause.)

Congratulations to the men and women here who have built it. What an amazing piece of art. What an amazing piece of work.

Thank you, Dennis, for the invitation to be with you today. You know, in the old days, when I made this speech I got paid a lot of money. Now I have to do it for nothing. (Laughter and applause.)

Not a good deal, but that's okay. We love it.

It's wonderful to be back in South Carolina, especially with your new governor. Where is Henry? He's around here someplace. Where is he? Stand up, Henry. Proud of you. He helped us so much. (Applause.)

And I want to also thank your former Governor, Nikki Haley, who is doing an awfully good job for us. (Applause.)

She's representing America very well as our Ambassador to the United Nations. She is doing a spectacular job. It's early, but she has just been really great.

We're here today to celebrate American engineering and American manufacturing. We're also here today to celebrate jobs. Jobs. (Applause.)

This plane, as you know, was built right here in the great state of South Carolina. Our goal as a nation must be to rely less on imports and more on products made right here in the U.S.A. (Applause.)

It's amazing to think that a little over 113 years ago, next door, in North Carolina, Orville Wright was the first man to sail the skies in a very little airplane. The 1903 Wright Flyer was made of mostly wood and cloth. It was so small that Orville's brother, Wilbur, could not join him on the flight. He was always very upset about that. The flight lasted all of 12 seconds, but it was incredible.

That flight was a testament to the **American Spirit**. I see that same **Spirit** everywhere I travel in the country. I saw that **Spirit** all throughout the campaign. We have the greatest people anywhere in the world. We have the greatest **Spirit**, and you just look at what's going on to-day in our country -- you look at what's happening with jobs. You look at what's happening with plants moving back into our country. All of a sudden, they're coming back. And they're going to be very happy about it, believe me. (Applause.)

They're going to be very, very happy. (Applause.)

As your President, I am going to do everything I can to unleash the power of the **American Spirit** and to put our great people back to work. (Applause.)

This is our mantra: **Buy American and Hire American**. (Applause.)

We want products **Made in America**, **Made by American Hands**. You probably saw the Keystone pipeline I approved recently, and the Dakota. And I'm getting ready to sign the bill. I said, where is the pipe made? And they told me not here. I said, that's good -- add a little sentence that you have to buy American steel. (Applause.)

And you know what? That's the way it is. It's the way it's going to be.

We are going to fight for every last American job. We've come a long way since the Wright Brothers and their first flight more than a century ago. Your plane is made of carbon fiber. It seats 330 passengers. It's 18 feet longer than the previous version of the 787. And this airplane can fly for half a day before it touches the ground. The name says it all: *Dreamliner.* Great name. Our country is all about making **dreams** come true.

Over the last number of years, that hasn't been necessarily the case, but we're going to make it the case **Again**. (Applause.)

That's what we do in America —- we **dream** of things, and then we build them. We turn vision into reality, and we will be doing a lot more of that, believe me, in the months and years to come. (Applause.)

I also want to say a word to all of the members of the armed forces who are here with us today in this record crowd. (Applause.)

South Carolina has a long, very, very, proud military tradition and history. We salute all South Carolina military families, and we salute all the men and women who wear the uniform. (Applause.)

We are going to fully rebuild our military -- by the way, do you care if we use the F-18 Super Hornets? (Applause.)

Or do you only care about -- what do you think? Well -- (jet flies overhead) -- thought that was a Super Hornet. (Laughter.)

We are looking seriously at a big order, and we'll see how that -- you know the problem is that Dennis is a very, very tough negotiator. (Laughter.)

But I think we may get there.

We're also working on the Air Force One project, which was a difficult project for previous administrations. But it looks like we're getting closer and closer. (Applause.)

And we're going to ensure that our great service members have the tools, equipment, training and resources they need to get the job done. (Applause.)

As George Washington said, being prepared for war is the best way to prevent it. And that's really what it is: The best way to prevent war, being prepared. Peace through strength. We build a military might so great -- and we are going to do that -- that none will dare to challenge it. None. (Applause.)

We will ensure our men and women in uniform have the latest, the most cutting edge systems in their arsenal. Right now it's not that way. It will be that way very, very soon. Believe me. You will be an important player in this effort.

Boeing has built many important aircraft -- including, as I said, the F-18 Super Hornet, the F-15 Strike Eagle, and the Apache helicopter, just to name a few. (Applause.)

And I'm being very, very serious -- the new Air Force One, that plane, as beautiful as it looks, is 30 years old. Can you believe it? What can look so beautiful at 30? An airplane. (Laughter.)

I don't know. Which one do we like better folks? Tell me. (Applause.)

On every front, we are going to work for the American people. Nowhere in our focus -- and I mean this so strongly -- and our focus has to be so strong, but my focus has been all about jobs. And jobs is one of the primary reasons

I'm standing here today as your President, and I will never, ever disappoint you. Believe me. I will not disappoint you. (Applause.)

I campaigned on the **promise** that I will do everything in my power to bring those jobs back into America. We wanted to make much easier -- it has to be much easier to manufacture in our country and much harder to leave. I don't want companies leaving our country, making their product, selling it back, no tax, no nothing, firing everybody in our country. We're not letting that happen anymore, folks. Believe me. There will be a very substantial penalty to be paid when they fire their people and move to another country, make the product, and think that they're going to sell it back over what will soon be a very, very strong border. Going to be a lot different. It's going to be a lot different. (Applause.)

Already American industry will come roaring back. And believe me if we -- not me, I'm a messenger -- if we didn't have this victory, we wouldn't be even talking about it. To achieve that goal, we're going to massively reduce job-crushing regulations -- already started; you've seen that -- that send our jobs to those other countries. We are going to lower taxes on American business so it's cheaper and easier to produce product and beautiful things like airplanes right here in America. (Applause.)

We are going to enforce -- very strongly enforce our trade rules and stop foreign cheating. Tremendous cheating. Tremendous cheating. We want products made by our workers, in our factories, stamped with those four magnificent words: **Made in the USA**. (Applause.)

AUDIENCE: U-S-A! U-S-A! U-S-A!

THE PRESIDENT: Since November, jobs have already begun to surge. We're seeing companies open up factories in America. We're seeing them keep jobs at home. Ford, General Motors, Fiat-Chrysler -- just to name a very, very few. So many more already. They are keeping and bringing thousands of jobs back in country because the business climate, they know, has already changed.

In Arizona, Intel announced it will open a new plant that will create 10,000 American jobs. They are spending billions of dollars. (Applause.)

We will see more and more of that across the country as we continue to work on reducing regulations, cutting taxes -- including for the middle class, including for everyone, and including for business -- and creating a level playing field for our workers. When there is a level playing field, and I've been saying this for a long time, American workers will always, always, always win. But we don't have a level playing field. Very shortly, you will have a level playing field **Again**. (Applause.)

Because when American workers win, America as a country wins -- big league wins.

That's my message here today. America is going to start winning **Again** -- winning like never, ever before. We are not going to let our country be taken advantage of anymore in any way, shape or form. We love America, and we are going to protect America. We love our workers, and we are going to protect our workers. We are going to fight for our jobs, we are going to fight for our families and we are going to fight to get more jobs and better-paying jobs for the loyal citizens of our country. Believe me. (Applause.)

You've heard me say it before, and I will say it again: From now on, it's going to be **America First**. (Applause.)

Working together as a unit, there is nothing we cannot accomplish -- no task too large, no dream too great, no goal beyond our reach. Just like you built this incredible airplane behind me -- both of them, when you think about it -- we are going to rebuild this country and ensure that every forgotten community has the bright future it deserves. And by the way, those communities are forgotten no longer. The election took care of that. (Applause.)

And we will pass on to our children the freedom and prosperity that is their **American birthright**. Our children will inherit from us a nation that is **strong**, that is **proud** and that is totally **free**. And each of you will be part of creating that **New American Future**.

I want to thank you, South Carolina. I want to thank the great people of South Carolina. God bless you, may God bless the United States of America, and God bless Boeing. (Applause.)

Thank you, everybody. Thank you.

END
1:47 P.M. EST

Chapter 45

REMARKS BY THE VICE PRESIDENT AT THE MUNICH SECURITY CONFERENCE

MUNICH, GERMANY

18 February 2017

THE VICE PRESIDENT: Thank you, Ambassador Ischinger. Chancellor Merkel, Secretary General, distinguished colleagues, and honored guests, I bring greetings on behalf of the 45th President of the United States, Donald Trump. In my still new capacity as Vice President, I am honored and humbled to have the privilege to address this important annual forum.

I'm also pleased to have with me two members of the President's Cabinet, one of which you've already heard from, our Secretary James Mattis, of the Department of Defense, and Secretary John Kelly, of Homeland Security. We're also joined by a distinguished delegation of United States Senators and Congressmen, led by Senator John McCain. Please join me in welcoming my fellow Americans here with us today. (Applause.)

It's an honor to be with you all.

Founded in 1963, the Munich Security Conference has long played an important role in international affairs, bringing together political, economic, and social leaders from both sides of the Atlantic to promote peace and prosperity for our nations and our peoples.

History will attest that when the United States and Europe are peaceful and prosperous, we advance the peace and prosperity of the entire world.

Now, the President asked me to be here today to bring his greetings -- and a message.

Today, on behalf of President Trump, I bring you this assurance. The United States of America strongly supports NATO and will be unwavering in our commitment to this transatlantic alliance. (Applause.)

We've been faithful for generations -- and as you keep faith with us, under President Trump we will always keep faith with you.

Now, the fates of the United States and Europe are intertwined. Your struggles are our struggles. Your success is our success, and ultimately, we walk into the future together.

This is President Trump's promise: We will stand with Europe, today and every day, because we are bound together by the same noble ideals -- freedom, democracy, justice, and the rule of law.

So strong is our bond that over the past century, Americans have poured forth from our land to help defend yours. It's remarkable to think that this year marks the 100th anniversary of the United States' entry into World War One.

More than two decades later, in the fires of World War Two, we fought to defeat dictatorship and keep the flame of freedom alive in Europe and across the entire world.

Tens of thousands of my fellow countrymen now rest here for eternity. Tens of thousands more still stand guard here in Europe to this day.

So lest anyone doubt the United States' commitment to Europe and the importance of your defense, they need only look to our nation's investment in your peace and prosperity, in your safety and security, yesterday and to-day. And it has been an investment of treasure, yes, but so much more than that, America has sent you our best and bravest. (Applause.)

Our shared values and our shared sacrifices are the source of the United States' enduring bond to the nations and peoples of Europe. We honor that history by doing our part -- all of us -- to ensure the horrors of war never return to this continent.

For generations, we have worked side by side with you to strengthen and defend your democracies. Together, we formed the North Atlantic Treaty Organization in 1949 to defend our shared heritage and shared principles, such as sovereignty, territorial integrity, and self-determina-tion. We confronted the menace of Communism, which threatened to overwhelm Europe and the world in its heartless, inhuman embrace. We stood together in 1990 as this very nation reunited and Eastern Europe chose free-dom, free markets, and democracy.

I saw that choice first-hand as a young man. In 1977, at the age of 18, I traveled through Europe with my older brother, and we found ourselves in West Berlin. I marveled at the streets, the people, and the bustling commerce of a city renewed just 30 years after the ravages of war.

Then we crossed through Checkpoint Charlie. The vibrant color of the free world fell away, replaced by the dour greys of still-bombed-out buildings and the shadow of repression hanging over the people.

In that moment, I came face to face with the choice facing the Western World -- the choice between freedom and tyranny.

By the grace of God, and through the leadership of Reagan, Thatcher, Kohl, Mitterrand, Havel, Walesa, the wall fell, communism collapsed, and freedom prevailed.

The fall of the Soviet Union ushered in an opportunity for unprecedented peace and prosperity on both sides of the Atlantic. But the end of that era only marked the beginning of another. The collapse of communism has been followed by the rise of new adversaries and new threats.

Rogue nations developing nuclear weapons now jeopardize the safety of the entire world. Radical Islamic terrorism has fixated on the destruction of Western civilization. In the early days of this new century, that enemy struck ruthlessly at our nation's capital and our greatest city.

With the smoke still rising from Ground Zero and the Pentagon, the strength of our alliance shone forth. Just as the United States stood with Europe through the end of the 20th century, Europe stood tall with the United States at the outset of the 21st. And the American people will be forever grateful.

Again I had the privilege to see our bond first hand. Only two weeks after those horrific attacks on 9/11, as a member of Congress I traveled to Germany to participate in an international conference on terrorism. I'll never forget what I saw as we arrived at the American Embassy in Berlin -- a wall of flowers, 10-feet high, surrounded it; fragrant tokens of condolences, support, and prayers of your people for ours.

That image will forever be etched in my heart and mind. But the support of the European community went well beyond acts of kindness. For the first and only time in its history, NATO invoked Article 5 of the North Atlantic Treaty, fulfilling our commitment to confront our common enemies together, and the American people will never forget it.

In the global war against radical Islamic terrorists, we have been bound by shared sacrifice. For the past decade and a half, the nations of NATO and many other allies have answered the call to rid the world of this great evil. From Afghanistan to Iraq to many other conflicts across the globe, our sons and daughters have served together and fought together on the field of battle.

Thousands of our citizens, coming from every corner of this alliance and beyond, have given their lives in this struggle. Fighting alongside U.S. service members under NATO's mandate, more than 1,100 brave men and women from allied nations have fallen in Afghanistan since 2001. The Afghanis have lost many more in order to free their homeland and keep it free today.

No matter which country they hailed from, these heroes gave the last full measure of their devotion in the cause of our peace and our security. And I hope each one of you will assure their families, the families of their fallen that the American people will never forget their service and sacrifice on our behalf. (Applause.)

Now, those sacrifices, which continue to this day, are the surest sign of our enduring commitment to each other and our future together.

On President Trump's behalf, that future is exactly what I came here to address.

If the past century has taught us anything, it's that peace and prosperity in Europe and the North Atlantic can never be regarded as achieved; it must be continually maintained through shared sacrifice and shared commitment.

Peace only comes through strength.

President Trump believes we must be strong in our military might, able to confront any and all who would threaten our freedom and our way of life. We must be strong in our conviction that our cause is just and that our way of life is worth defending. If we lose the will to do our part to defend ourselves, we jeopardize our shared heritage of freedom.

Under President Trump's leadership, I can assure you, the United States will be strong -- stronger than ever before. We will strengthen our military, restore the arsenal of democracy, and working with many of the members of the Congress who are gathered here today, we're going to provide our soldiers, sailors, airmen, Marines, and Coast Guard with renewed resources to defend our nation and our treaty allies from the known threats of today and the unknown threats of tomorrow.

As we speak, the United States is developing plans for

significant increases in military spending to ensure that the strongest military in the world is stronger still.

We will meet our obligations to our people to provide for the common defense, and we'll continue to do our part to support our allies in Europe and in NATO.

But Europe's defense requires your commitment as much as ours. Our transatlantic alliance has at its core two principles that are central to its mission. In Article 5, we pledged to come to each other's aid in the event of an attack.

And to be ready, if and when that day comes, in Article 3 we vowed in that treaty to contribute our fair share to our common defense. The promise to share the burden of our defense has gone unfulfilled for too many for too long, and it erodes the very foundation of our alliance.

When even one ally fails to do their part, it undermines our ability to come to each other's aid. At that Wales summit in 2014, all 28 members of NATO declared their intention to move towards a minimum security commitment of 2 percent of their gross domestic product on defense within the decade.

In the words of the summit's declaration, such investments were necessary in "meeting NATO's capability targets and filling NATO's capability shortfalls."

As of this moment, the United States and only four other NATO members meet this basic standard. Now, while we commend the few nations that are on track to achieve that goal, the truth is that many others, including some of our largest allies, still lack a clear and credible path to meeting this minimum goal.

Let me be clear on this point, the President of the United States expects our allies to keep their word to fulfill this commitment, and for most that means the time has come to do more. (Applause.)

We must shoulder this responsibility together because the dangers we face are growing and changing every day. The world is now a more dangerous place than at any point since the collapse of communism a quarter century ago. The threats to our safety and security span the globe, from the rise of radical Islamic terrorism, to the threats posed by Iran and North Korea, and to many others who threaten our security and our way of life.

The rise of adversaries new and old demands a strong response from all of us.

In the east, NATO has markedly improved its deterrent posture by stationing four combat-ready multinational battalions in Poland and the Baltic States.

In the wake of Russian efforts to redraw international borders by force, rest assured the United States, along with the United Kingdom, Canada, and Germany, will continue its leadership role as a framework nation in the Enhanced Forward Presence Initiative, and we will support other critical joint actions to support this alliance. (Applause.)

And with regard to Ukraine, we must continue to hold Russia accountable and demand that they honor the Minsk Agreements, beginning by de-escalating the violence in eastern Ukraine.

And know this: The United States will continue to hold Russia accountable, even as we search for new common ground, which, as you know, President Trump believes can be found.

To the south, upheavals in Africa and the Middle East have sent violence rippling in every direction, reaching not only Europe but also the United States.

Today, the leading state sponsor of terrorism continues to destabilize the Middle East, and thanks to the end of nuclear-related sanctions under the Joint Comprehensive Plan of Action, Iran now has additional resources to devote to these efforts.

Let me be clear again: Under President Trump, the United States will remain fully committed to ensuring that Iran never obtains a nuclear weapon capable of threatening our countries, our allies in the region, especially Israel. (Applause.)

Throughout the Middle East, radical Islamic terrorists have found safe havens and secured vast resources that have allowed them to launch attacks here in Europe and inspire attacks in the United States.

Driven by evil, they target their own communities, their fellow Muslims, indiscriminately killing or enslaving those who reject their apocalyptic mania.

From Yemen to Libya, Nigeria to Syria, the rise of extremist groups ranging from ISIS and al-Qaeda, to al-Shabaab and Boko Haram endanger millions, including many faith-based peoples whose roots in their homelands extend into the mists of history.

ISIS is perhaps the greatest evil of them all. It showed a savagery unseen in the Middle East since the Middle Ages.

As President Trump has made clear, the United States will fight tirelessly to crush these enemies -- especially ISIS and its so-called caliphate -- and consign them to the ash heap of history, where they belong. (Applause.)

Last month, the President ordered the development of a comprehensive plan to utterly defeat ISIS. President Trump has no higher priority than the safety and security of the American people and ensuring the security of our treaty allies.

To confront the threats facing our alliance today, NATO must build upon its 20th century tactics and continue to evolve to confront the crises of today and tomorrow.

Last summer President Trump called on NATO to step up its efforts to disrupt terrorist plots before they ever reach our borders. And we've made great progress in expanding cooperation and information sharing between our intelligence and security services in recent years. But we must do more -- much more.

Consistent with the President's call, we are heartened to see that NATO has taken steps to increase focus on counter-terrorism and collaboration. The appointment of a new intelligence chief, charged with facilitating collaboration on counterterrorism, marks a positive strategic shift in NATO's ability to fulfill its mission.

Going forward, we must intensify our efforts to cut off terrorists' funding, increase our cyber capabilities. We must be as dominant in the digital world as we are in the physical world. (Applause.)

We must always stay at least one step ahead of our adversaries. For our shared goal of peace and prosperity can only be achieved through superiority and strength.

For our part, thanks to President Trump, the United States will be stronger than ever before. Our leadership of the free world will not falter, even for a moment. Our strength, and that of this alliance, is not derived solely from our strength of arms, though. It's borne of our shared principles, the principles and ideals that we cherish -- freedom, democracy, justice, and the rule of law. These are the wellspring of the United States' strength and of Europe's strength.

They spring from that timeless notion that our unalienable rights -- of life and liberty -- are not granted to us by sovereigns, or governments, or kings. They are, as the American Founders observed, endowed by our Creator. Marshalling the will to confront the evils of the 21st century will require faith, faith in these timeless ideals.

And as President Trump has said in his Inaugural Address, it's important to know: "We do not seek to impose our way of life on anyone, but rather to let it shine as an example for everyone to follow."

This then is our cause. It's why NATO exists. It's why, after so many centuries of strife and division, Europe is unified. The United States has been faithful to Europe for generations, and we will keep the faith that drove our forefathers to sacrifice so much in defense of our shared heritage.

We share a past, and after all we've been through, we

share a future. Today, tomorrow, and every day hence be confident that the United States is now and will always be your greatest ally. (Applause.)

Be assured, President Trump and the American people are fully devoted to our transatlantic union.

Our choice today is the same as it was in ages past: security through shared sacrifice and strength, or an uncertain future characterized by disunity and faltering will.
Well, the United States chooses strength. The United States chooses friendship with Europe and a strong North Atlantic alliance.

And in the name of all the sacrifices of the generations who have gone before, who have fought and bled and died for this alliance, with confidence in all of you, and firm reliance on Providence, I know the best days for America, for Europe, and for the free world are yet to come.

Thank you for the honor of joining you today and God bless you all. (Applause.)

END

Chapter 46

REMARKS BY PRESIDENT TRUMP AND FIRST LADY MELANIA TRUMP AT MAKE AMERICA GREAT AGAIN RALLY ORLANDO MELBOURNE INTERNATIONAL AIRPORT MELBOURNE, FLORIDA

18 February 2017

5:46 P.M. EST

MRS. TRUMP: Thank you. (Applause.)

Thank you. Let us pray. (A prayer is given.)

Good afternoon. It is my honor and great pleasure to stand here before you as the First Lady of the United States. (Applause.)

The America we envision is one that works for all Americans and where all Americans can work and succeed -- a nation committed to greater civility and unity between people from all sides of the political divide.

I will always stay true to myself and be truthful to you, no matter what the opposition is saying about me. (Applause.)

I will act in the best interest of all of you. I'm committed to creating and supporting initiatives dear to my heart, which will have impact on women and children all around the world. (Applause.)

My husband is creating a country of great safety and prosperity. Ladies and gentlemen, I'm proud to introduce the President of the United States, Donald Trump. (Applause.)

THE PRESIDENT: Thank you, everybody. (Applause.)

Thank you all. I didn't know that Melania was going to be saying the Lord's Prayer, but I thought that was very beautiful. Thank you. (Applause.)

Thank you.

It's so great to be here in Florida, my second home, with you. This is a state I truly love. This is a state where we all had great victory together. Thank you. (Applause.)

It's now been one month since my inauguration, and I am here to tell you about our incredible progress in **Making America Great Again**. (Applause.)

And I'm also here to tell you about our plans for the future. And they're big and they're bold, and it's what our country is all about, believe me. (Applause.)

I'm here because I want to be among my friends and among the people. (Applause.)

This was a great MOVEMENT -- a MOVEMENT like has never been seen before in our country, or probably anywhere else. This was a truly great MOVEMENT, and I want to be here with you, and I will always be with you, I **promise** you. (Applause.)

I want to be in a room filled with hardworking American patriots who love their country, who salute their flag, and who pray for a better future. (Applause.)

I also want to speak to you without the filter of the fake news. (Applause.)

The dishonest media, which has published one false story after another, with no sources, even though they pretend they have them -- they make them up in many cases -- they just don't want to report the truth, and they've been calling us wrong now for two years. They don't get it, but they're starting to get it, I can tell you that. (Applause.)

They've become a big part of the problem. They are part of the corrupt system.

Thomas Jefferson, Andrew Jackson and Abraham Lincoln, and many of our greatest Presidents, fought with the media and called them out, oftentimes on their lies. When the media lies to people, I will never, ever, let them get away with it. I will do whatever I can that they don't get away with it. (Applause.)

They have their own agenda, and their agenda is not your agenda. (Applause.)

In fact, Thomas Jefferson said, "Nothing can [now] be believed which is seen in a newspaper." "Truth itself," he said, "becomes suspicious by being put into that polluted vehicle." That was June 14th -- my birthday --- (laughter and applause) -- 1807.

But despite all their lies, misrepresentations and false stories, they could not defeat us in the primaries and they could not defeat us in the general election, and we will continue to expose them for what they are. And, most importantly, we will continue to WIN, WIN, WIN. (Applause.)

We are not going to let the fake news tell us what to do, how to live, or what to believe. We are **free** and independent people, and we will make our own choices. (Applause.)

We are here today to speak the truth, the whole truth, and nothing but the truth. I hear your demands, I hear your voices, and I promise you I will deliver. **I promise** that. (Applause.)

And, by the way, you've seen what we've accomplished in a very short period of time. The White House is running so smoothly. So smoothly. (Applause.)

And believe me, I -- and we -- INHERITED ONE BIG MESS. That, I can tell you. But I know that you want safe neighborhoods where the streets belong to families and communities, not gang members and drug deals who are right now, as I speak, being thrown out of the country and they will not be let back in. (Applause.)

We will have strong borders **Again**. (Applause.)

And I mean that. And you've seen it on television. You've seen it on television.

General Kelly, now Secretary Kelly, he's really doing the job. You're seeing it. The gang members -- bad, bad people. I said it day one. And they're going out, or they're being put in prison. But for the most part, get them the hell out of there. Bring them back to where they came from. (Applause.)

The fact is, you want great schools for your children, you want good, high-paying jobs for yourselves and for your loved one, and for the future of your families. You want a health care system -- and, by the way, we are going to be submitting in a couple of weeks a great health care plan that's going to take the place of the disaster known as Obamacare. (Applause.)

It will be repealed and replaced. And for those people, the people that are put into rooms where Republicans are talking about the plan, and it wouldn't matter what they say -- for those people, just so you understand, our plan will be much better health care at a much lower cost, okay? (Applause.)

Nothing to complain about. Obamacare, remember, it is a disaster.

You want low-cost American energy also, which means lifting the restrictions on oil, on shale, on natural gas, and on clean -- very clean coal. We're going to put the miners back to work. The miners go back to work. (Applause.)

You want us to enforce our immigration laws and to defend our borders. You want fair trade deals and a level playing field. We don't have a level playing field. Because you understand that when American workers win, America as a country wins, and wins big. And every country over the last long period of time has been taking advantage of the stupidity of our politicians. It's not going to happen any longer. (Applause.)

You want lower taxes, less regulation, millions of new jobs, and more products stamped with those beautiful, beautiful words: "**Made in the USA.**" (Applause.)

You want to make it easier for companies to do business

in America and harder for companies to leave. We don't want companies saying, "Everybody is fired, we're moving to another country, we're going to make the product, sell it across the border, and isn't wonderful?"

Not going to happen anymore. We're going to have strong borders. And when they want to sell that product back across our border, they're going to pay a 35 percent tax. And you know what? They're never going to leave. They will never, ever leave. (Applause.)

And you've seen that because I've already displayed it for the last two months, even before I got into office. They're not leaving. And if they do, they're going to pay a very, very big price for terminating the relationship to our workers.

You want a government that serves the people -- not the donors and not the special interests. In short, you want a government that keeps its **promises**. A great **Spirit** of optimism is sweeping -- and you see it -- it's sweeping all across the country. Look at what's happening to the stock market. Look at what's happening to every poll when it comes to optimism in our country. It's sweeping across the country. And, in fact, every day for the last long period of days, the stock market, meaning companies, have been hitting new highs. They're going to start hiring. It's going to be A NEW DAY IN AMERICA. You're going to be **Proud Again**. (Applause.)

Jobs are already starting to pour back in. They're coming back in like you haven't seen in a long time. Ford, General Motors, Fiat-Chrysler are bringing in and bringing back thousands of jobs, investing billions of dollars because of the new business climate that we are creating in our country.

In Arizona, Intel -- great company -- just announced it will open a new plant that will create at least 10,000 brand-new, beautiful American jobs. (Applause.)

I've followed through on my **promise** to withdraw from the job-killing disaster known as the Trans-Pacific Partnership -- TPP. We have just terminated our relationship to it. We're going to have tremendous trade deals all over the world, but they're going to be bilateral or, as we would say, one-on-one. None of these deals where we get caught in quick sand, where we get mired in and we can't do anything about it, like, by the way, NAFTA and so many others. And my administration has begun plans to crack down on foreign cheating and currency manipulation, which is killing our companies and really, really hurting our workers. We're going to end it. (Applause.)

Within a few days of taking the Oath of Office, I've taken steps to begin the construction of the Keystone and the Dakota Access pipelines. (Applause.)

Anywhere from 30,000 to 40,000 jobs. And very importantly, as I was about to sign it, I said, who makes the pipe? Who makes the pipe? Something this audience understands very well, right? Simple question. The lawyers put this very complex document in front. I said, who makes the pipe? They said, sir, it can be made anywhere. I said, not anymore. So I put a little clause on the bottom: The pipe has to be made in the United States of America if we're going to have pipelines. (Applause.)

We believe in two simple rules. And I can tell you, everybody in this massive -- this is a massive hangar; this is for the big planes. And, by the way, do you think that one media group back there, that one network, will show this crowd? Not one. Not one.

AUDIENCE: Booo --

THE PRESIDENT: Not one. They won't show the crowd. You know, coming in on the plane -- and that plane represents so much -- and just so you know, they were close to signing a $4.2 billion deal to have a new Air Force One. Can you believe this? I said, no way. I said, I refuse to fly in a $4.2 billion airplane. (Applause.)

I refuse. So I got Boeing in -- and it is actually -- a lot of people don't know -- the Air Force One project is actually two planes. Why they need two planes, we'll have to talk about that. But they have two planes. But we've got that price down by over a billion dollars. And I probably haven't spoken, to be honest with you, for more than an hour on the project. But I got the generals in, who are fantastic. I got Boeing in. But I told Boeing it's not good enough, we're not going to do it -- the price is still too high.

On the F-35 fighter jet, we were hundreds of billions of dollars over budget, seven years late. Great plane. Lockheed Martin -- a great plane. So think of it: They're seven years late, they're hundreds of -- billions of dollars over budget. Other than that, by the way, the project is going extremely well. And I got the folks in from Lockheed Martin, who are terrific people and a terrific product, by the way. I also got Boeing in. I said, do me a favor, give me a competing offer. And now they're competing and fighting, and we've gotten hundreds of millions of dollars off the price of a plane that was going to be ordered. In other words, if my opponent got in, there would have been no calls made to Lockheed and Boeing. They would have signed contracts. So they're going to make plenty of money but it's going to be a lot less than they would have made without Trump. That, I can tell you. And you might as well know about it -- (applause) because nobody talks. And, by the way, that's for fighter jets -- one of the biggest orders in the history of aviation, the order for the F-35 you've been reading about it -- because it was a disaster under the last administration. A disaster. And now we have it running beautifully.

In fact, when the Prime Minister of Japan -- Prime Minister Abe, who's great; great guy -- when he came over, he said, thank you. I said, for what? "You saved us many, many millions of dollars on the F-35 fighter jet." Because when I negotiated, I took our allies into the same negotiation. So the first thing he did was he thanked me for saving them money, and that's good. Okay? That's good. (Applause.)

I know the media will never thank me, so at least Japan is thanking me, right? (Applause.)

But we believe in two simple rules: **Buy American and Hire American**. We believe in them. (Applause.)

We've just issued a new order which requires that for every one new regulation, two old regulations must be eliminated. (Applause.)

And, by the way, a new director was just approved. Can you imagine the length of time it's taking the Democrats? And I actually think it's an embarrassment to them. But this is getting to be record-setting territory. These are incredible people.

Scott Pruitt was just approved, just now approved, for the Environmental Protection Agency. He'll do so good. (Applause.)

He'll do so good. But he won't have projects going 10 and 12 years and then getting rejected. And they may be rejected, but they'll be rejected quickly. But for the most part, they're going to be accepted, they're going to be environmentally friendly, and he is going to be a great Secretary. He will be amazing. So we're very happy. That took place yesterday.

That's going to be a big difference, because they were clogging up the veins of our country with the environmental impact statements and all of the rules and regulations. It was impossible to navigate for companies. And what did it really mean? Forget about the companies. What did it mean? It meant no jobs. It meant companies leaving our country and going to foreign countries to do things that they'd rather do here. So we're going to have a whole big situation. We are going to unfree all of those companies. They are going to be -- they're going to have freedom. They're going to be able to build what they want to build. It will be environmentally friendly. And we're going to start producing jobs like you've never seen before. That's going to happen. That was a big thing. (Applause.)

We're standing up for the incredible men and women, always, of law enforcement. (Applause.)

We're standing up. And I can tell you, the military and law enforcement, they stood up big. I don't say for me -- I'm the messenger, folks; I'm the messenger. They stood up for us in this last election. We got numbers that nobody believed were possible, from law enforcement and from military -- basically people that where uniforms like us. Isn't that nice?

And I saw this man on television just now. You -- I just saw him on television. He said, "I love Trump. Let Trump do what he has to do." That's my guy, right there. (Applause.)

It's true. Come here. Come here. No, I just -- I'm coming in. That's okay. Let him up. Let him up. I'm not worried about him. I'm only worried he's going to give me a kiss. I'm not worried about anything else. This guy is so great. He was one of many people -- they're interviewing people in the line -- and I have to say, there's a tiny group of protestors out there, and they were given as much publicity as this massive room packed with people. But they interviewed this man. Come on up here. Come on up. This guy is great. Hop over the fence. Come on. He can do it. This guy is in good shape. Look at him. Look at this guy. Come on. This guy is great. Don't worry about it. No, no, no come here. They're going to throw -- come on up. Come on. Come here. (Applause.)

This guy -- so he's been all over television, saying the best things, and I see him standing. Didn't you get here like at four in the morning?

AUDIENCE MEMBER: I did, sir.

THE PRESIDENT: Say a couple of words to this crowd. (Applause.)

AUDIENCE MEMBER: Mr. President, thank you, sir. We, the people, our MOVEMENT, is the reason why our President of the United States is standing here in front of us today. (Applause.)

When President Trump, during the election, **promised** all these things that he was going to do for us, I knew he was going to do this for us. (Applause.)

Mr. President, thank you so much, sir.

THE PRESIDENT: A star is born. A star is born. (Applause.)

Thank you. That's fine.

AUDIENCE: U-S-A! U-S-A! U-S-A!

THE PRESIDENT: I wouldn't say that Secret Service was thrilled with that. (Laughter.)

But we know our people, right? We know our people. (Applause.)

He's a great guy. And so many others. I see some others, they're being interviewed. I see them over here. They started -- they came at four in the morning. The media will give them no credit. The media, as I told you, they won't show this crowd. Look at that -- all the way outside. This is as big a hangar as you get. All the way outside, way back to the fences. Amazing. I want to thank you. But I want to thank everybody.

So I've directed the Department of Justice to take a firm, firm stance to protect our cops, sheriffs and police from crimes of violence against them. (Applause.)

We will work with our police, not against our police. Our police do a great job, and they've never been troubled like they're troubled now. It's very unfair what's happening. So we want to cherish our law enforcement, and we will always protect those who protect us.

We've directed the creation of a task force for reducing violent crime in America, including our inner cities. We're going to make our inner cities **Safe Again**. Look at what's going on. Look at what's happening in Chicago. Hundreds of shootings, hundreds of deaths. I'll tell you, what's happening in Chicago and many other places. Safety is a civil right, and we will fight to **Make America** totally **Safe Again**. I've ordered the Department of Homeland Security and the Department of Justice to coordinate on a plan to destroy transnational criminal cartels, which are all over the United States, and we are going to stop the drugs from pouring into your country, into your community, into your cities, and poisoning our youth. We're stopping it. (Applause.)

We're stopping it.

We've taken historic action to secure the southern border, and I've ordered the construction of a great border wall, which will start very shortly. (Applause.)

And I've taken decisive action to keep radical Islamic terrorists the hell out of our country. (Applause.)

So you probably read where we want to enforce the laws as existing, and so we signed an order a couple of weeks ago, and it was taken over by a court, originally by a judge, and then a --

AUDIENCE: Booo --

THE PRESIDENT: Yeah. It's very sad. And, you know, the

reason is for protection and safety. So the statute is so plain and so clear. I said last week -- I was speaking to a great group of sheriffs, the sheriffs group in Washington, and I said, if you have a college education, you can understand it; if you have a high school education, you can understand it; if you were a bad student in high school, you can understand it. And I was told -- I'll check, but I found it hard to believe -- in an over 30-page decision by the appellate court, three judges -- and you could tell by the way they were reacting, because it was broadcast on television, and everything we do gets a lot of people watching. So you could tell by the way that phone call went, it wasn't looking good. And when they wrote their decision, as I understand it -- maybe I'm wrong -- but they didn't write the statute they were making the decision about, because every word of the statute is a total kill for the other side.

So I thought I'd read it, and here's what it says. This is what it says: "Whenever the President finds that the entry of any aliens or any class of aliens into the United States" -- okay, so essentially, whenever somebody comes into the United States, right -- if it "would be detrimental to the interests of the United States" -- okay, now you know the countries we're talking about, and these were countries picked by Obama; they weren't even picked -- they were picked by Obama -- "he may" -- so the President may -- "by proclamation and for such period as he shall deem necessary" -- now, because it's old, it should have said he or she, right? They were not politically correct when they drew this. In fact, that's the only thing that was actually wrong with it. He or she -- but I don't think the women care too much about that, right? I don't think so.

By the way, we did very well with women. (Applause.)

You know, my wife said, when some of these phony polls were put out -- you know, the CNN poll was so far off -- the phony polls. But when some of these -- she said, what's wrong with you and women? We did very nicely with women. We did nicely with a lot of groups that they didn't think we were going to do so nicely with. I guess we had to. That's why we're all here tonight, right? (Applause.)

So, and it goes, "...and for such period as he shall deem necessary, suspend the entry of all aliens or any class of aliens as immigrants or non-immigrants, or impose on the entry of aliens any restrictions he may deem to be appropriate." So basically it says the President has the right to keep people out if he feels it's not in the best interest of our country. Right? (Applause.)

Unbelievable. Unbelievable. And I listened to these judges talk and talk and talk. So unfair.

So we'll be doing something over the next couple of days. We don't give up. We never give up. (Applause.)

We had a court that I disagree with, I disagree with big league. And, by the way, whether you read it or whether you watch it on television, when other lawyers come on many of them can't even understand. They're saying, how do you come up with that decision? It cannot be more simple. So they're ruling on what I just read you, and they don't even quote it in their ruling -- because you can't, because it's too obvious. So we will do something next week. I think you'll be impressed. Let's see what happens.

Here's the bottom line: We've got to keep our country safe. You look at what's happening. We've got to keep our country safe. (Applause.)

You look at what's happening in Germany. You look at what's happening last night in Sweden. Sweden? Who would believe this? Sweden? They took in large numbers. They're having problems like they never thought possible. You look at what's happening in Brussels. You look at what's happening all over the world. Take a look at Nice. Take a look at Paris. We've allowed thousands and thousands of people into our country, and there was no way to vet those people. There was no documentation. There was no nothing.

So we're going to keep our country **safe**. (Applause.)

And we all have heart, by the way. And what I want to do is build safe zones in Syria and other places so they can stay there and live safely until their cities and their country -- that mess that I was left by Obama and everybody else. Folks, we were left a mess like you wouldn't believe. But we're going to build safe zones. We're going to have those safe zones. You know, we do owe $20 trillion, okay? So we're going to have the Gulf States pay for those safe zones. They have nothing but money. And we're going to do it that way, instead of taking massive numbers -- tens of thousands of people -- into our country, and we don't know anything about those people.

We want people to come into our country, but we want people that love us. We want people that can cherish us and their traditions of our country. We want people that are going to be great for our country. We don't want people with bad, bad ideas. We don't want that.

I've also directed the defense community, headed by General, and now Sec -- oh, you know, he said it -- he said it -- and now Secretary "Mad Dog" Mattis. (Applause.)

To develop a plan to totally destroy ISIS. (Applause.)

I have ordered the Department of Defense to begin plans for the great rebuilding of the United States military. (Applause.)

We will pursue peace through strength. Our military is badly depleted. You have planes in the military where the father flew them and now the son is flying them, they're so old. We make the best equipment anywhere in the world. We're going to start using our best and most modern equipment. (Applause.)

And we're going to make sure that our veterans have the care they need when they come home. (Applause.)

We love our veterans. (Applause.)

We're going to do a great job for our veterans. Our veterans have been very, very sadly treated. These are our great, great people. We owe them so much. Our veterans are going to be taken care for once and for all. Our system and our country has let down our veterans. We are not going to let that go on any further. You wait until you see what we're going to be doing for our great veterans. Thank you, veterans, for all -- who's here? Who's a veteran? (Applause.)

We're going to take care of our veterans.

We're going to downsize the bloated bureaucracy and make government lean and accountable. We are going to drain the swamp in Washington, D.C. (Applause.)

AUDIENCE: Drain the swamp! Drain the swamp! Drain

the swamp!

THE PRESIDENT: I've already imposed -- I'm not sure they're too happy about it -- a five-year lobbying ban on executive branch officials, and a lifetime ban on lobbying for a foreign government. (Applause.)

And there's another major **promise** I have kept to the American people: I've nominated a fantastic justice to replace the late, great Justice Scalia. (Applause.)

His name is Judge Neil Gorsuch. (Applause.)

And he comes from my list of 20 very, very highly-qualified judges. He's incredible, and he has an incredible résumé. He's respected by all. His education is as good as it can get. His writings are truly amazing. He will be a true defender of our Constitution.

So let's tell the Senate Democrats to support his nomination for the good of the country. Because what's happening with the Democrats -- no wonder they're doing so badly. No wonder they're doing so badly. You take a look. Race after race -- I just want to tell you, in case you didn't read it -- of course, you're reading the fake news -- but the Democrats were supposed to win the presidency. That didn't happen. They were supposed to take over the Senate. That didn't happen. And they were supposed to take over, potentially, even the House. It was going to be, four weeks out, the greatest defeat in the modern history of American politics. And it was -- but it was for the Democrats, not for the Republicans. (Applause.)

So we have to tell the Democrats -- because they're doing the wrong thing for the American people -- to stop their tactics of delay and obstruction and destruction. They got to get on with it.

My administration is also pushing ahead strongly with very historic tax reform. We are working to lower tax rates on the middle class, to reduce tax rates, big league, on businesses, and to make our tax code more fair and very simple for all Americans, so it's understandable by everyone. (Applause.)

Senate Democrats should work with us to lower taxes and bring back our jobs. But the Democrats want to increase your taxes very, very substantially. We're not going to let that happen. It's also time for the Senate Democrats to take responsibility for Obamacare, and to work with us to replace it with new reforms that reverse this nationwide health care tragedy. It's a tragedy. You look at some states -- Arizona -- up 116 percent. And your deductibles have gotten so high that you can never use it. Obamacare doesn't work. It's become totally unaffordable. Remember they said to health care -- it's unaffordable. It doesn't work. And I said to the Republicans, I said, you want to do something great politically? Don't do anything. Sit back for two years, let it explode; the Democrats will come and beg for us to do something. But we can't do that to the American people. We have to fix it, and we will. (Applause.)

We need members of both parties to join hands and work with us to pass a $1 trillion infrastructure plan to build new roads, and bridges, and airports, and tunnels, and highways, and railways all across our great nation.

You are all part of this incredible movement -- this movement that we talk about so much, that's been written about on the cover of every magazine all over the world. It's a movement that is just sweeping -- it's sweeping across our country. It's sweeping, frankly, across the globe. Look at Brexit. Look at Brexit. Much smaller example, but it's still something you can look at.

People want to take back control of their countries, and they want to take back control of their lives and the lives of their family. (Applause.)

The nation-state remains the best model for human happiness, and the American nation remains the greatest symbol of liberty, of freedom, and justice on the face of God's Earth. (Applause.)

And now we have **Spirit** like we've never had before. It's now that we have our sacred duty, and we have no choice, and we want this choice to defend our country, to protect its values, and to serve its great, great citizens. (Applause.)

Erasing national borders does not make people **safer** or more prosperous -- it undermines democracy and trades away prosperity. We're giving it away. The so-called global elite have done very well for themselves, but have left working families with shrinking wages, really -- I mean, they are shrinking. Eighteen years ago, many of you in this room made more money working one job than you're making right now working two and three jobs. (Applause.)

Instead of peace, we've seen wars that never end and conflicts that never seem to go away. We don't fight to win. We fight politically correct wars. We don't win anymore. We don't win at trade. We don't win in any capacity. We don't win anymore. We're going to start winning again, believe me. (Applause.)

And we have the chance now, working together, to deliver change for the ages -- this will be change for the ages, change like never before; to pursue real peace, real stability and real prosperity. We want to secure our borders and protect our workers; to rebuild our military and our infrastructure; to fix our schools and restore safety to our neighborhoods; to bring hope and opportunity to our inner cities; to ensure a level playing field for all women in the workforce; to reform our tax code and remove the regulations that undermine growth and innovation; and to replace chasms of distrust with new bridges of opportunity and cooperation.

We must ignore the tired echoes of yesterday's fights. We're fighting battles that no longer help us. We're fighting battles that other people aren't treating us fairly in the fight. I'm a NATO fan, but many of the countries in NATO, many of the countries that we protect, many of these countries are very rich countries. They're not paying their bills. They're not paying their bills. They have to help us. No longer are we chained down by the discredited approaches of the past. No longer must we listen to those who have nothing to brag about but failure. New circumstances demand new solutions.

Americans have fought and won wars together. Our heroes have shed their blood together and lost their lives. Our citizens have raised their children together, fought for justice together, and shared common hopes and **dreams** from one generation to the next, stretching back to the first day of our American Independence.

This is our legacy. It belongs to all of you. And it belongs to every man, woman, and child in our nation. (Applause.)

Now is the time to call upon these deep ties in the name of bold action. Let us move past the differences of party and find a new loyalty rooted deeply in our country.

We are all brothers and all sisters. We share one home, one destiny, and one glorious American flag. (Applause.)

We're united together by history and by providence.

We will **Make America Strong Again, I promise**.

We will **Make America Proud Again**.

We will **Make America Safe Again**.

And we will **Make America Great Again**

-- greater than ever before. (Applause.)

May God bless you, and may God bless the United States of America. Thank you. Thank you. (Applause.)

END
6:34 P.M. EST

Chapter 47

REMARKS BY THE VICE PRESIDENT AND NATO SECRETARY GENERAL STOLTENBERG AT A JPA
NATO HEADQUARTERS
BRUSSELS, BELGIUM

20 February 2017

4:13 P.M. CET

SECRETARY GENERAL STOLTENBERG: (In progress) took office, and just a few days after your great speech in Munich where you so clearly declared the strong commitment and the unwavering support of the United States to the transatlantic bond.

And we welcome that because we see the strong commitment of the United States to the transatlantic bond, not only in words but also in deeds. These days the United States is deploying new forces -- additional forces -- to Europe, which is of great importance for the security of Europe and which demonstrates the strong transatlantic commitment of the United States. And we are very grateful for this commitment.

You also stressed that just as the U.S. stood with Europe, Europe stood tall with the United States. And we have to remember that the only time that the alliance has involved our collective defense clause, Article 5, was after an attack on the United States. And this was more than just a gesture. Several hundred thousands of Canadian and European troops have served in Afghanistan, and more than a thousand have paid the ultimate price.

The bond between the United States and NATO -- between the United States and Europe embodied in the NATO alliance is very important today because we live in times of turmoil and instability, and then we need a strong alliance more than ever. And we are stronger when we stand together.

During our meeting, we discussed our progress in the fight against terrorism. NATO continues to train security forces in Afghanistan. We have started to train security forces and officers in Iraq. And we support the U.S.-led coalition against ISIL with AWACS surveillance planes.

But we agree that the alliance can and should do more in the fight against terrorism. We also agree on the importance of higher defense spending and fairer burden sharing in NATO. This is has been my top priority since I took office. Europeans cannot ask the United States to commit to Europe's defense if they are not willing to commit more themselves.

And they are committing more. In 2016, after many years of cuts, we turned a corner. Defense spending increased across Europe and Canada by 3.8 percent in real terms, or U.S. $10 billion. But we still have a long way to go, so all allies must speed up their efforts to spend 2 percent of GDP on defense.

This will be an important point when allied leaders meet here in Brussels in May. So, Mr. Vice President, thank you for our excellent discussion. We agree that NATO is the most successful alliance in history because NATO has been able to adapt and change when the world is changing. And we agree that we must continue to change to keep our people safe. U.S. leadership remains indispensable. So I really look forward to working with you and to welcoming President Trump in Brussels in May.

So please, you have the floor.

THE VICE PRESIDENT: Thank you, Mr. Secretary General. It is a privilege to meet with you today to bring greetings on behalf of President Donald Trump and also to have the opportunity for a thorough and substantive discussion of the issues facing NATO and our historic alliance.

It has been a busy weekend for me. As I prepare to head back to the United States, I'm grateful. I'm grateful to have had the opportunity to speak on Saturday about our shared security issues at the Munich Security Conference. And I appreciate your encouraging words about the message of the United States at that conference.

And I also was pleased to be able to hold a series of productive bilateral meetings with leaders from all across the world.

It was also deeply moving for me and my family to return to Dachau, the very first concentration camp, and to be accompanied by a survivor by the name of Abba Naor. I had first visited that camp in 1977. I wanted my daughter to see it. And we went there and walked through that historic memorial.

Abba told me that he arrived at Dachau as a 17-year-old boy. He told me of the nightmarish existence that he experienced there. But then he spoke words that resonate with our alliance. He said: "Then the Americans came." Those words touched my heart, and they speak volumes about the history and importance of the North Atlantic alliance and of NATO, more of which I'll address momentarily. But I thank you again for your hospitality in this historic place at this important time.

I was also grateful today to meet with the leadership of the European Union. And on behalf of President Trump, I express the commitment of the United States to continued cooperation and partnership with the EU.

While we have our differences on some issues, I reiterated this point in all of my meetings with the EU leadership and appreciated the cordial and substantive discussions that we had.

But on Saturday, as the Secretary General mentioned, at the Munich Security Conference, I brought a message from President Trump -- the message is the same one I bring to you today.

It is my privilege here at the NATO Headquarters to express the strong support of President Trump and the United States of America for NATO and our transatlantic alliance. The United States has been a proud and faithful member of NATO since its founding in 1949. This alliance plays a crucial role in promoting peace and prosperity in the North Atlantic and, frankly, in the entire world.

The United States' commitment to NATO is clear. As we speak, President Trump and our administration are developing plans to ensure that the strongest military in the world in the United States becomes stronger still.

Let me assure you, Mr. Secretary, that in the United States, we're about the process of strengthening our military and restoring the arsenal of democracy. Working with members of Congress, we intend to increase military funding to make it possible for us to provide for the common defense for the people of the United States, but also meet the obligations that we have with our treaty allies, including in this historic treaty.

America -- therefore I can say with confidence: America will do our part. But Europe's defense requires Europe's commitment as much as ours.

At the Wales Summit in 2014, all 28 members of the NATO alliance declared their intention to move towards a minimum security investment of 2 percent of their gross domestic product on defense within a decade.

As a candidate for office, President Trump actually called attention repeatedly to the fact that for too long, for too many, this burden has not been shared fairly among our NATO allies. And that must come to an end.

At this moment, the United States and only four other NATO members meet this basic standard. And while we commend the few nations that are on track and have met the obligation, the truth is that many others, including some of our largest allies, still lack a clear and credible path to meet this minimum goal.

So let me say again what I said this last weekend in Munich, the President of the United States and the American people expect our allies to keep their word and to do more in our common defense. And the President expects real progress by the end of 2017.

As Secretary of Defense James Mattis said here in Belgium just a few short days ago, if you're a nation that meets the

2 percent target, we need your help encouraging other nations to do likewise. If you have a plan to get there, as he said, our alliance needs you to accelerate it. And if you don't yet have a plan, these are my words not his: Get one. It is time for actions, not words.

And let me thank specifically the Secretary General for your outspoken leadership on this issue. As you and I discussed privately and you've discussed with the President, the world needs NATO's strength and leadership now more than ever before. And we are grateful, Mr. Secretary General, that you join us in calling for immediate and steady progress on all of our NATO allies' commitment to our common defense.

The truth is the rise of adversaries new and old demands a strong response from this alliance. In the east, NATO has embarked on improvement in its deterrent posture by stationing four combat-ready multinational battalions in Poland and the Baltic States.

And as I assured the Secretary General in our meeting today, in the wake of Russian efforts to redraw international borders by force, the United States will continue its leadership role in the Enhanced Forward Presence Initiative and other critical joint actions.

With regard to Ukraine, as I said before, our alliance will continue to hold Russia accountable and demand that they honor the Minsk Agreements, beginning with de-escalating violence in eastern Ukraine.

For the sake of peace and for the sake of innocent human lives, we urge both sides to abide by the ceasefire that began today. And we pray for peace in Ukraine.

Be assured, the United States, as well, will continue to hold Russia accountable, even as we search for new common ground, which President Trump firmly believes can be found.

As I said in Munich, though, NATO's continued leadership is also necessary in the fight against radical Islamic terrorism; this, another item that as a candidate for office, President Trump first raised.

As a candidate a year ago, he called on NATO to evolve by expanding counterterrorism operations. And we're encouraged to see under your leadership NATO is in the process of doing just that. It's hard to speak of these issues in the abstract as I stand here in Brussels, just now almost a year ago that three horrific suicide bombings occurred, 33 innocent victims, including four Americans, hundreds more injured. I just want to assure the people of Brussels and all the people of Europe that your pain is our pain, your loss our loss. And it's precisely why the President believes it's essential that NATO continue on this new path of evolving and expanding its mission to be more effective in counterterrorism.

We will work tirelessly with our NATO allies to ensure security in our countries and yours. But adapting to these new and ever-shifting challenges must remain a central focus of our collaboration and cooperation. Our alliance needs to intensify efforts to cut off terrorist funding and increase cyber capabilities. We must be -- as I said before, we must be as dominant in the digital world as we are in the physical world. And the United States is committed to continuing to work with our NATO allies to achieve that objective for the security of all the nations in our alliance.

By building on tactics from the last century with these new century opportunities and challenges, NATO will be better prepared to confront and overcome the new adversaries of the 21st century.

Under President Trump's leadership, the United States, I can assure you, is fully committed to NATO's noble mission. We are grateful for your leadership, Mr. Secretary General. And I know the President looks forward to working closely with you to advance our shared objectives. A strong NATO means a safer world. And the United States of America looks forward to continuing to work with our partners in NATO to achieve just that.

So, Mr. Secretary, thank you very much for your hospitality and for your leadership.

Q   Vice President, you've given your assurances today here in Brussels to European leaders that the U.S. is committed to working with Europe. President Trump has said very different things. He's said that the EU is a vehicle for Germany, that the U.K. was smart to get out, and he expected other countries to follow. Who should European leaders listen to -- you or President Trump? Can they be certain that what you say, the assurances you give, won't be contradicted in a tweet or a statement at a press conference tomorrow?

And, Secretary General, who do you listen to? And are you concerned about differences in what you hear?

VICE PRESIDENT PENCE: Well, thank you for the question. Let me say it's my great privilege to serve as Vice President for the 45th President of the United States. And the President directed me to go to Munich and to come here to Brussels with a very specific message: To go to Munich to the Munich Security Conference and make it very clear, as I do so again today here at NATO's Headquarters, that the United States is expressing strong support for NATO, even as we challenge NATO and challenge our allies to evolve to the new and widening challenges and further meet their responsibilities in this ever-changing, ever-complicated world of threats.

But with regard to the EU, the President also directed me to come here to Brussels. And I had the great privilege of meeting with leaders of the Europe Union throughout the morning, and to express the desire of the United States to continue cooperation and partnership with the European Union.

We respect the determination of the people of Great Britain, as manifested in Brexit. And we respect the judgement of the peoples of Europe in the European Union. And as I said today through many leaders, we look forward to working across the Channel with all parties in the years ahead on behalf of peace and prosperity.

SECRETARY GENERAL STOLTENBERG: I have heard exactly the same firm message from the President of the United States in two phone calls; from the Vice President in meetings today and in Munich; and from Secretary Mattis -- Tillerson, and Kelly. They all conveyed the same message that the United States is firmly committed to the transatlantic partnership and have an unwavering support for the NATO alliance.

And I welcome that very much -- both the very clear statements from all leaders in the new administration, but also the fact that this is not only something we see in words, but we also see it in deeds.

For the first time in many years, we see an increase of U.S. military presence in Europe. And we are deploying new battle groups. The U.S. is deploying a new brigade. And we see on the ground more U.S. presence in Europe. So this is a commitment in words, but also in deeds.

When it comes to the European Union, I would like to underline the importance of the enhanced cooperation between NATO and the European Union. We have actually been able to bring that to a new level, implementing many different issues -- or measures. And we signed the joint declaration between President Tusk, President Juncker, and me in Warsaw and are now following up on implementing that.

We are working closer on hybrid, on cyber, on addressing how to build the capacity in our neighborhood, and how to stabilize our neighborhood, our areas where we work together with the European Union. And I think, actually, the NATO-EU cooperation is even more important now because we live in times with turmoil and unpredictability, and then we need a strong cooperation between NATO and the European Union, and I welcome the very strong U.S. support for that approach.

Q   Thank you. Mr. Vice President, I wanted to ask you about the dismissal of General Flynn recently. Did you feel like you were misled by members of the Trump adminis-tration? Or were you frustrated that you were left out of the loop on this situation? And what assurances have you received from President Trump that something like this will not happen again?

And for Mr. Secretary General, both you and the Trump administration have talked about the need for additional funding for defense. What are the consequences for inaction by NATO members? Is there any scenario in which the Article V commitments might be considered conditional if NATO members do not fulfill their defense spending obligations?

VICE PRESIDENT PENCE: Thank you, Ken. Let me say, I am very grateful for the close working relationship I have with the President of the United States. I would tell you that I was disappointed to learn that the facts that had been conveyed to me by General Flynn were inaccurate. But we honor General Flynn's long service to the United States of America, and I fully support the President's decision to ask for his resignation. It was the proper decision. It was handled properly and in a timely way.

And I have great confidence in the national security team of this administration going forward. The combination of Secretary Mattis, of Director Pompeo at the CIA, of Secretary Kelly at Homeland Secretary I think gives the American people great confidence that the team in this administration is providing the leadership and the direction to those agencies and also to the President of the United States to advance the security of our people.

GENERAL SECRETARY STOLTENBERG: Our collective defense clause, our collective defense commitment is unconditional. It's absolute, and it's the core of the NATO alliance. And I welcome the very strong commitment of the United States to this transatlantic bond and to this collective defense clause.

At the same time, I fully support what has been underlined

by President Trump and by Vice President Pence today, the importance of burden-sharing. And I think we have to remember that this is not only something that the U.S. is asking for, it's actually something that 28 Allies agreed. The leaders from 28 NATO-allied countries sat around the same table in 2014 and agreed to stop the cuts, to gradually increase defense spending, and then to meet the 2 percent target within a decade.

And the good news is that we are moving in the right direction. After many years of decline, after many years of defense cuts across Europe and Canada, we saw that in 2015 we stopped the cuts, the first year after we made the pledge. And then, in 2016, we had a significant increase of 3.8 percent in real terms, or $10 billion.

There is a long way to go, and much remains to be done, but at least we have turned a corner and we have started to move in the right direction. I am encouraged by that, and I expect all allies to make good on the promise that they made in 2014 to increase defense spending and to make sure to have a fairer burden-sharing.

Q   A question to the Vice President and the Secretary General. The German Foreign Minister has called the 2 percent goal too ambitious, and said that more spending would not necessarily lead to more security. Are you disappointed by that? And what would be the consequence if a country like Germany would not hold up to the 2 percent goal?

And a question to the Vice President, if I may. President Trump has repeatedly talked about his war with the press. Since NATO is an alliance of values, can you assure the allies that the freedom of press is not under threat in the United States? Thank you.

GENERAL SECRETARY STOLTENBERG: All allies have committed to the defense investment pledge, meaning to stop the cuts and to start to increase. And that also includes Germany, and it has also been clearly expressed from Germany that they are committed to the defense investment pledge we made together in 2014.

The good thing is that Germany has started to increase defense spending. In 2017, there will be a significant increase in German defense spending, with around or by -- around 8 percent. So, of course, Germany, as many other allies, have a long way to go. And some allies will meet the 2 percent target within a year or two. Romania declared last week that they will meet the 2 percent target this year. Lithuania and Latvia will soon be able to meet the 2 percent target also within a year or two.

So we are really making progress. Germany has started to increase defense spending. And again, I expect all allies to keep the pledge they made together as leaders in 2014.

VICE PRESIDENT PENCE: Let me say again: The President and I, our administration, are very grateful for the Secretary General's focus on burden-sharing and for our NATO allies, whether it be Germany or other countries, to meet the commitment that treaty allies made to one another. I think it's a demonstration of President Trump's leadership that before taking office he was speaking about the fact that the United States provides more than 70 percent of the cost of NATO today, and we are committed to continue to do our part, but that the time has come for our NATO allies to step forward. And the Secretary General's strong message on this is in all of our collective interest.

I will tell you that I had very productive discussions with Chancellor Merkel. We spoke about just this issue. And we look forward to a continued dialogue. Our hope is that we will have a date very soon where Chancellor Merkel will come to the White House. I expect the President will talk with her about it, as well. But this is simply about all of us doing what we all said we would do -- to provide for our common defense. And in the ever-changing threat environment in which we live, that's more important now than ever.

With regard to your second question, rest assured that both the President and I strongly support a free and independent press. But you can anticipate that the President and all of us will continue to call out the media when they play fast and loose with the facts. And the truth is that we have in President Trump someone who has a unique ability to speak directly to the American people. And when the media gets it wrong, I promise you President Trump will take his case straight to the American people to set the record straight.

Q   Mr. Vice President, you said the U.S. commitment to the EU was steadfast and enduring. Is the administration opposed to further disintegration of the EU, further countries exiting? And on NATO, what is the or else? If there isn't more defense spending this year, would you recommend cutting the European Reassurance Initiative? Would you cut back on exercises? What's the or else?

VICE PRESIDENT PENCE: Well, I think your second question is a very fair one. What is the "or else"? I think when Secretary Mattis was here, he spoke very plainly here at NATO's headquarters about the frustration of the American people, that as our country continues to make investments in Europe's security, we see European countries falling behind. The President really put this issue front and center, before the American people in his campaign for President. And, frankly, it struck a very resonant chord.

And so I don't know what the answer is to "or else," but I know that the patience of the American people will not endure forever; that the commitment that we have made to one another, that the American people are keeping with the people of Europe and NATO, is a commitment that the President of the United States and the American people expect our allies in Europe to keep, as well. But failing that, questions about the future we'll just leave in the future as hypotheticals.

But I have to tell you, with the Secretary General's strong leadership, having made the issue of burden-sharing his top priority, having a partnership with so many countries across NATO who, in my meetings over this weekend, have expressed a desire to step forward and keep their word, I'm very encouraged about the progress. What you see happening here is in a very real sense the result of American leadership. In President Trump we have a President who is stepping forward, he's expressing American leadership not just on the issue of funding, but also on his call last year that NATO should evolve to widen its tactics to include counterterrorism as a major focus. And NATO has begun to do that. The United States looks forward to supporting that.

With regard to the European Union, my message very simply was that the United States is committed to continuing our partnership with the European Union. And I wanted to make that very clear. We understand the relationship between our economies. We understand the deep heritage of member states in the European Union with people in the United States of America. Looking for ways that we could reassure this weekend leaders of the European Union of our commitment to ongoing cooperation and that maintaining that partnership in the years ahead is hopefully a resonant message that came through, and it's my great privilege to be here to deliver it.

SECRETARY GENERAL STOLTENBERG: Let me just add that the focus of the alliance is on how can we make sure that we succeed in delivering on what we agreed about fairer burden-sharing and increased defense spending. And, therefore, I will not speculate so much about "or else," what will happen if we don't succeed. But we heard a very firm and clear message from the United States. We heard it from the President, we heard it from the Vice President, and from Secretary Mattis at the defense ministerial meeting.

So I think that just underlines the importance of making sure that we move, that we succeed in increasing defense spending across Europe and Canada. And the good thing is that we have started; 3.8 percent real increase in 2016 is a significant step, but is only one step in the right direction. We need much more.

Let me also add that we need both to spend more, but we also need to spend better. So the focus of the alliance, the focus of the defense ministers, but also in our cooperation with the European Union, is how can we increase efficiency, how can we develop cooperation, how can we make sure that we address the fragmentation of especially European defense industry so we can reduce costs and get more out of the money we invest in our defense.

But there is no way we can choose between either spend more or better. We need to spend both more and better. So what we committed in 2014 was not either to spend more or to spend better, but it was to spend 2 percent of GDP in a better way, and we are addressing both things, and we are moving forward on both tracks.

END
4:44 P.M. CET

Chapter 48

20 February 2017

PRESIDENT TUSK: Mr. Vice President, dear friends, let me first of all thank you for this meeting. We all truly needed it.

Too much has happened over the past month and in your country and you; too many new and sometimes surprising opinions have been voiced over -- in this time about our relations and our common security for us to pretend that everything is as it used to be.

And thank you for being so open and frank with me, Mr. Vice President. Today I heard words which are promising for the future, words which explain a lot about the approach of the new administration in Washington.

I repaid our guest by offering honesty in my assessment of the situation. I shared our concerns and hopes. Given that I am an incurably pro-American European who is fanatically devoted to transatlantic cooperation, I could afford to be outspoken even more.

I asked the Vice President directly if he shared my opinions on three key matters: international order, security, and the attitude of the new American administration towards the European Union.

Firstly, I expressed my belief that maintaining order based on the rules of international law where brute force and egoism do not determine everything lies in the interest of the West; and that maintaining that order can only be enforced through a common, mutually supportive and decisive policy of the whole of the Western community. And for millions of people around the world, the predictability and stability of our approach provides the guarantee of, at the very least, hope that chaos, violence, and arrogance will not triumph in the global dimension.

Referring to some statements made in Munich just two days ago, I would like to say clearly that the reports of the death of the West have been greatly exaggerated. Whoever wants to demolish that order, anticipating a post-West order must know that in its defense we remain determined.

Secondly, our security is based on NATO and the closest possible transatlantic cooperation. We must work together to modernize the forms of this cooperation. Some of them should, indeed, be improved. But we should also, I believe, agree on one thing: The idea of NATO is not obsolete, just like the values, which lay at its foundation are not obsolete.

Let us discuss everything, starting with financial commitment -- but only to strengthen our solidarity, never to weaken it.

Thirdly, we are counting, as always, on the past; on the United States' whole-hearted and unequivocal -- let me repeat unequivocal -- support for the idea of a united Europe. The world would be a decidedly worst place if Europe were not united.

Americans know best what great value it is to be united, and that becoming divided is the prelude to a fall. It is in the interest of us all to prevent the disintegration of the West.

And as for our continent, in this respect, we will not invent anything better than the European Union.

In reply to these three methods, I heard today from Vice President Pence three times, yes. After such a positive declaration, both Europeans and Americans must simply practice what they preach.

On Saturday in Munich, you mentioned that during your trip across Europe in 1977 with your older brother, you found yourselves at some point in West Berlin, marveling at what you saw; then crossing through Checkpoint Charlie only to see the shadow of repression hanging over people. If you know, I had been living under this shadow for over 30 years. What I vividly remember from my own past is how after martial law was imposed in Poland on December 13, 1981, President Ronald Reagan urged all Americans to light a solidarity candle on Christmas Eve, as he did himself.

It is not difficult to imagine how this moving message of American solidarity with the oppressed Polish nation against, as Reagan said, the forces of tyranny and those who incite them from without, helped bring back hope and the determination not to give in.

In your speech, you also highlighted the historic role of some American and European leaders including Vaclav Havel and Lech Walesa. I was lucky to cooperate closely with the two of them in difficult times. Similarly to us, they all believed in the purpose of cooperation and solidarity between Europe and the U.S. We cannot let their efforts go to waste.

After today's talks, it will be easier for me to believe that we will fulfill this task.

Thank you.

VICE PRESIDENT PENCE: Thank you, President Tusk. Thank you for your warm hospitality today.

And thank you for those eloquent words and your personal courage and leadership. It's an honor to meet you and on behalf of the President of the United States to bring greetings. And I may make a note never to follow you at a podium again. (Laughter.)

So thank you again for your eloquence.

Last night I was honored to have dinner with the Prime Minister of Belgium. This morning I met with the European Union's High Representative Mogherini. And this morning, a very constructive and productive conversation with President Tusk, and it's an honor to be here.

This afternoon, I will meet with President Juncker of the European Commission before taking meetings at NATO at returning to Washington, D.C.

Saturday, as President Tusk said, I was pleased to address the Munich Security Council to speak about the importance of the strategic alliance the United States entered upon so many years ago in the North American Treaty Organization.

But the President did ask me to come here to Brussels, to the home of the European Union, and deliver an additional message. And so today it is my privilege on behalf of President Trump to express the strong commitment of the United States to continued cooperation and partnership with the European Union.

Whatever our differences, our two continents share the same heritage, the same values, and above all, the same purpose: to promote peace and prosperity through freedom, democracy, and the rule of law. And to those objectives we will remain committed.

This has been the European Union's goal since before its formal founding in 1993. What began as a modest Western European trade agreement in 1951 has grown into a commitment to the four freedoms: freedom of movement -- goods, capital, services, and people; a common currency; and a common approach to foreign and security policy. And what began 60 years ago with the Treaty of Rome among six Western European nations has grown to encompass north and south, east and west; and you welcomed new states after the end of the Cold War.

With this union and in cooperation with the United States, history will attest that when the United States and Europe are peaceful and prosperous, we do advance the peace and prosperity of all the world.

Our economies are the world's largest -- accounting for half of the world's economic output. Transatlantic commerce supports 14 million jobs on both continents and improves the lives and well-being of all of our citizens.

And so today we reaffirm our commitment to free, fair, and

flourishing economies that undergird our success, and to cooperation in achieving that.

Maintaining and strengthening our economic vitality will require hard but necessary choices. Renewed growth means improved peace and prosperity for all. We must be strong, and we must be united, as well, in our efforts to confront threats to Europe's security and stability.

It's heartbreaking to reflect that now nearly a year ago, here in Brussels, in the heart of the European Union, three horrific suicide bombings and attacks took place, killing 33 innocent victims, including four Americans, injuring hundreds more.

Let me say to this community, the European community, your losses at the hands of barbaric terrorists are felt equally in every household and every heart in America. And you have our condolences and our determination to continue to do all that we can in partnership with the European Union and with all of our allies in Europe to ensure that such attacks never happen again.

We seek to take measures, and we call upon the European community to join with the United States in continuing to intensify our efforts to counter the threat of radical Islamic terrorism here on the continent.

Now, this will require greater coordination and intelligence sharing among EU member states and between the EU and the North Atlantic Treaty Organization. And let me assure you, the United States is committed to continuing and expanding our collaboration on the collective security of all of our peoples.

The safety and security of your union and our people depends on that increased collaboration in the global fight against terrorism. And the United States will remain a full partner with the EU and with all of our European allies to accomplish that.

In addition to confronting terrorism together, clearly we must stand strong in defense of the sovereignty and territorial integrity of nations in Europe. In the wake of Russian efforts to redraw international borders by force, we will continue to support efforts in Poland and the Baltic States through NATO's Enhanced Forward Presence Initiative.

And with regard to Ukraine, the United States will continue to hold Russia accountable and demand that Russia honor the Minsk Agreements, beginning by de-escalating the violence in eastern Ukraine.

We urge both sides -- we urge both sides -- to abide by the cease-fire that was scheduled to begin today. And in the interest of peace and in the interest of innocent human lives, we hope and pray that this cease-fire takes hold. While the United States will continue to hold to hold Russia accountable, at President Trump's direction, we will also search in new ways for new common ground with Russia, which President Trump believes can be found.

The United States' commitment to the European Union is steadfast and enduring.

President Tusk, President Trump and I look forward to working together with you and the European Union to deepen our political and economic partnership. We are separated by an ocean, but we are joined by a common heritage and by a common commitment to freedom, to democracy, and to the rule of law. And we're confident that that bond will endure and grow in the years ahead as we meet our future together.

Thank you again for your hospitality, Mr. President. And thank you all.

END

Chapter 49

20 February 2017

2:52 P.M. EST

THE PRESIDENT: So I just wanted to announce -- we've been working all weekend very diligently, very hard -- that General H.R. McMaster will become the National Security Advisor. He's a man of tremendous talent and tremendous experience. I watched and read a lot over the last two days. He is highly respected by everybody in the military. And we're very honored to have him. He also has also known for a long time General Keith Kellogg, who I also have gotten to know and he's a terrific man, and they're going to be working together. And Keith is going to be Chief of Staff, and I think that combination is something very, very special.

I met with many other people. Tremendous respect for the people I met with. I know John Bolton we're going to be asking to work with us in a somewhat different capacity. John is a terrific guy. We had some really good meetings with him. He knows a lot. He has a good number of ideas that I must tell you I agree very much with. So we'll be talking to John Bolton in a different capacity. And we'll be talking to some of the other generals that I've met that I have really, really paid a lot of respect for.

So I think with that, I'd like to ask H.R. to say a couple of words. I'd like to ask Keith to say a couple of words. And then I'll see you back in Washington. We're leaving right now for Washington and the White House.

General.

LT. GENERAL MCMASTER: Mr. President, thank you very much. I'd just like to say what a privilege it is to be able to continue serving our nation. I'm grateful to you for that opportunity, and I look forward to joining the National Security team and doing everything I can to advance and protect the interests of the American people. Thank you very much, sir.

THE PRESIDENT: You're going to do a great job.

LT. GENERAL MCMASTER: Thank you, sir.

THE PRESIDENT: General.

LT. GENERAL KELLOGG: Mr. President, thank you for the opportunity to serve. I'm very honored by it and privileged by it. And I'm very honored and privileged to serve alongside H.R. McMaster, who I've known for years as well. He's a great statesman, he's a great soldier. Thank you, sir.

THE PRESIDENT: And so are you. Thank you very much. What a privilege. This is a great team. We're very, very honored. Our country is lucky to have two people like this. And, frankly, after having met so many of the people in the military, we're lucky to have all of them.
So thank you all very much. I'll see you back in Washington. We're leaving now. Thank you.

Q   Did Vice President Pence play a role in helping you?

THE PRESIDENT: He did. He did.

END
2:55 P.M. EST

Chapter 50

Remarks by President Trump at
the National Museum of
African American History and Culture

Washington, D.C.

21 February 2017

9:54 A.M. EST

THE PRESIDENT: Thank you very much, everybody. It's a great honor to be here. This was some beautiful morning and what a job they've done, like few others have been able to do.

I am very, very proud of Lonnie Bunch. The work and the love that he has in his heart for what he's done is -- I always talk about you need enthusiasm, you need really love for anything you do to do it successfully. And, Lonnie, you are where? Come on. Where's Lonnie? You should be up here, Lonnie. Come on.

And David -- we have to get David up here, too. David Skorton is tremendous and he was singing Lonnie's praises all morning long. So you two should at least be here. So we appreciate it very much.

And David Rubenstein, who is here someplace, he is -- come on, David, you have to get up here, David. You certainly deserve it. He's a very, very successful guy who spends money doing great things, and he's been a great help to so many different groups and this one in particular.

Thank you. It's a privilege to be here today. This museum is a beautiful tribute to so many American heroes -- heroes like Sojourner Truth, Harriet Tubman, Frederick Douglass, Booker T. Washington, Rosa Parks, the Greensboro students, and the African American Medal of Honor recipients, among so many other really incredible heroes.

It's amazing to see. I went to -- we did a pretty comprehensive tour, but not comprehensive enough. So, Lonnie, I'll be back. I told you that. Because I could stay here for a lot longer, believe me. It's really incredible.

I'm deeply proud that we now have a museum that honors the millions of African American men and women who built our national heritage, especially when it comes to faith, culture and the unbreakable **American Spirit**. My wife was here last week and took a tour, and it was something that she's still talking about. Ivanka is here right now. Hi, Ivanka. And it really is very, very special. It's something that, frankly, if you want to know the truth, it's doing so well that everybody is talking about it.

I know President Obama was here for the museum's opening last fall. And I'm honored to be the second sitting President to visit this great museum. Etched in the hall that we passed today is a quote from Spottswood Rice, a runaway slave who joined the Union Army. He believed that his fellow African Americans always looked to the United States as the promised land of universal **freedom**. Today and every day of my presidency, I pledge to do everything I can to continue that **promise of freedom** for African Americans and for every American. So important. Nothing more important.

This tour was a meaningful reminder of why we have to

fight bigotry, intolerance and hatred in all of its very ugly forms. The anti-Semitic threats targeting our Jewish community and community centers are horrible and are painful, and a very sad reminder of the work that still must be done to root out hate and prejudice and evil.

I want to thank a great friend of mine, Dr. Ben Carson, and his beautiful family -- Candy and the whole family -- for joining us today. It was very special to accompany him and his family for the first time seeing the Carson exhibit. First time. I'm so proud of you. I love this guy. He's a great guy. Really a great guy. And he can tell you better than me, but I'll tell you what, we really started something with Ben. We're very, very proud of him. Hopefully, next week he'll get his approval, about three or four weeks late -- and you're doing better than most, right? But the Democrats, they'll come along. I have no doubt they'll come along. But Ben is going to do a fantastic job at HUD. I have absolutely no doubt he will be one of the great -- ever -- in that position.

He grew up in Detroit, and had very little. He defied every statistic. He graduated from Yale, and he went on to University of Michigan's medical school. He became a brilliant -- totally brilliant -- neurosurgeon, saved many lives, and helped many, many people. We're going to do great things in our African American communities together. Ben is going to work with me very, very closely. And HUD has a meaning far beyond housing. If properly done, it's a meaning that's as big as anything there is, and Ben will be able to find that true meaning and the true meaning of HUD as its Secretary. So I just look forward to that. I look forward to watching that. He'll do things that nobody ever thought of.

I also want to thank Senator Tim Scott for joining us today. Friend of mine -- a great, great senator from South Carolina. I like the state of South Carolina. I like all those states where I won by double, double, double digits. You know, those states. But South Carolina was one, and Tim has been fantastic how he represents the people. And they love him.

I also want to profoundly thank Alveda King for being here, and as we saw her uncle's wonderful exhibit, and he certainly deserves that. Mrs. King -- and by the way, Ms. King, I can tell you this personally because I watch her all the time, and she is a tremendous fighter for justice. And so, Alveda, thank you very much.

MS. KING: Thank you, sir.

THE PRESIDENT: Come up here for a second.

MS. KING: Yes, sir. Thank you.

THE PRESIDENT: I have been watching you for so long, and you are so incredible. And I wanted to thank you for all the nice things you say about me.

MS. KING: Thank you, sir.

THE PRESIDENT: Not everybody says nice things, but she's special.

MS. KING: I love you and your family. You're the best. You're great.

THE PRESIDENT: Thank you. Come here.

MS. KING: Thank you. Thank you.

THE PRESIDENT: Thank you, darling. Appreciate it.

So with that, we're going to just end this incredible beginning of a morning. But engraved in the wall very nearby, a quote by the Reverend Martin Luther King, Jr. In 1955, he told the world, "We are determined...to work and fight until justice runs down like water, and righteousness like a mighty stream."

And that's what it's going to be. We're going to bring this country together, maybe bring some of the world together, but we're going to bring this country together. We have a divided country. It's been divided for many, many years, but we're going to bring it together. I hope every day of my presidency we will be honoring the determination and work towards a very worthy goal.

And for Lonnie, and David, and David, and Ben, and Alveda, and everybody, I just want to -- I just have to say that what they've done here is something that can probably not be duplicated. It was done with love and lots of money, right Lonnie? (Laughter.)

Lots of money. We can't avoid that. But it was done with tremendous love and passion, and that's why it's so great. So thank you all very much for being here, I appreciate it. And congratulations. This is a truly great museum. Thank you. (Applause.)

END
10:03 A.M. EST

Chapter 51

22 February 2017

12:39 P.M. EST

THE PRESIDENT: Thank you all. This will be somewhat of an informal meeting. I want to congratulate Mick Mulvaney, who's been confirmed finally -- we waited a long time -- by the Senate. And he's going to be an absolutely great director. Total confidence in Mick. Known him for a long time. He loves those budgets.

Unfortunately, the budget we're inheriting -- essentially inheriting -- is a mess. The finances of our country are a mess. But we're going to clean them up. Things that we've been doing, including negotiating deals that have already been negotiated, so you call it re-negotiating -- on airplanes and lots of other things, military items -- we'll end up either getting many more planes free, or we're going to save a lot of money. But we've already saved a lot; billions and billions of dollars have been saved.

We have enormous work to do as the national debt doubled over the last eight years. Our debt has doubled over a short period of time. I want the American people to know that our budget will reflect their priorities. We'll be directing all of our departments and agencies to protect every last American and every last tax dollar. No more wasted money.

We're going to be spending the money in a very, very careful manner. Our moral duty to the taxpayer requires us to make our government leaner and more accountable. We must do a lot more with less. And we must stop the improper payments and the abuses, negotiate better prices, and look for every last dollar of savings.

We've already imposed hiring freezes on nonessential government workers, and part of our commitment is to continue to do that for the American taxpayer. We have appointed a Cabinet that knows how to manage dollars wisely. I've known many of the folks for a long time. They've been tremendous winners -- whether it's Steve or Gary or another Steve, right here. And that's why I will direct them to manage the country's dollars and your dollars very wisely. We won't let your money be wasted anymore. We're going to run government smoothly, efficiently, and on behalf of the very hardworking taxpayers -- something that the taxpayers haven't seen in a long time. I will be holding everybody accountable for that, and I have no doubt that this group -- in particular, this group will do a fantastic job.

I want to congratulate Steve Mnuchin as our new Secretary of the Treasury. He's going to be outstanding. Tremendous track record -- he has a tremendous track record. I have great confidence in him.

So we're going to continue on, and we're going to take this budget, which is -- in all fairness, I've only been here for four weeks, so I can't take too much of the blame for what's happened. But it is absolutely out of control, and we're going to do things that are going to be tremendous over the years. We have to take care of our military. We have no choice, we have to take care of our military. It needs work; it's very depleted. And we have to take care of a lot of other things.

Healthcare is moving along nicely. It's being put into final forms. As you know, before we do the tax -- which is actually very well finalized -- but we can't submit it until the healthcare, statutorily or otherwise. So we're doing the healthcare. Again, moving along very well. Sometime during the month of March, maybe mid- to early March we will be submitting something that I think people will be very impressed by.

And with that, we're going to have a little meeting. And I think the press knows pretty much all of the people at the table, so thank you very much. We appreciate it.

END
12:43 P.M. EST

Chapter 52

22 February 2017

2:46 P.M. EST

THE VICE PRESIDENT: Thank you, Governor
Greitens. Would you give another round of applause for
a great, new, dynamic governor here in Missouri inspiring
people all across America with his leadership? (Applause.)

Thank you for that kind introduction, Governor
Greitens. And congratulations on your election last
year. You're already off to the races, and President Trump
and I thank you for your great leadership for the people of
Missouri. (Applause.)

Thank you all for coming out today. It actually gets cold in
Indiana in February. (Laughter.)

But I guess it's different here in Missouri. I'm very honored that you all would take time in the middle of a busy
week to hear a few words from me and on behalf of our
great President. And I do bring greetings on behalf of the
45th President of the United States of America, Donald
Trump. (Applause.)

And on his behalf I'm here, and on his behalf I'm also

grateful to see in the audience a number of distinguished leaders. Your great congresswoman representing Missouri with such great distinction -- Congresswoman Ann Wagner and Congressman Blaine Luetkemeyer are here. Give them both a big round of applause. (Applause.)

Thank you, it's a privilege to have you here.

I also want to thank all the small business owners who are with us today, including our host Doug Fabick and the Fabick family – 100-years in business here in Missouri creating jobs and opportunities. (Applause.)

Congratulations.

I enjoyed our discussion earlier today, and I appreciate your candid feedback, Doug, and the candid feedback that we got from other business leaders and job creators all across this region. And on that note, let me say thank you to all the great employees here at Fabick Cat for coming out today. Hardworking men and women, you're the ones that make companies like this grow. You are the strength in the American economy, and you're going to lead an American comeback. (Applause.)

As President Trump has said so many times, it was too long that we had forgotten men and women in this country. Well, the forgotten men and women, the men and women who carry this economy on their shoulders everyday are forgotten no more. And on behalf of President Trump, I thank all the hardworking men and women of Fabick Cat who are here today. Thanks for doing a great job for this country and this community. (Applause.)

Now, before we get started I'd like to address something

that happened here in St. Louis over the weekend. On Monday morning, America awoke to discover that nearly 200 tombstones were toppled in a nearby Jewish grave-yard.

Speaking just yesterday, President Trump called this a "hor-rible and painful" act, and so it was. That along with other recent threats to Jewish community centers around the country -- he declared it all a "sad reminder of the work that still must be done to root out hate and prejudice and evil."

We condemn this vile act of vandalism and those who per-petrate it in the strongest possible terms. (Applause.)

And let me say it's been inspiring to people all across this country to see the way the people of Missouri have rallied around the Jewish community with compassion and sup-port. You have inspired the nation with your kindness and your care. (Applause.)

It just so happens three days ago, my wife and my daugh-ter were overseas. We saw firsthand what happens when hatred runs rampant in a society. We were near Munich, Germany, where we visited the very first Nazi concentra-tion camp ever to be constructed, a place called Dachau.

We were accompanied by a survivor of Dachau, a 93-year-old man named Abba Naor, who told me he had arrived there as a 17-year-old boy. He described, as we walked through that memorial, the hellish life he endured -- toiling away as a slave while those around were taken away, one by one, never to return.

By the grace of God, he survived, and now he tells his story so that the world will never forget.

But before we left, he spoke words that touched my heart and I'll always carry with me throughout my life, and they resonate with this moment today. He spoke of that hellish existence in the waning days of the war, and then he looked up at me with a smile, and he said: "Then the Americans came." (Applause.)

He spoke of the kindness of those American soldiers who liberated that camp, and he pointed a finger at me and told me when you go back, you thank every one of those soldiers for what they did for me and for my people and for my country.

Would you join me in a round of applause for every man and woman here who has worn the uniform of a United States of America? We are proud of you, and we are grateful to you. (Applause.)

The American solider fought to end the hatred and violence against the Jewish people across Europe then, and as President Trump said yesterday, American will always, in his words, "fight bigotry, intolerance, and hatred in all its ugly forms" -- wherever it will arise. **That's the American Way**. (Applause.)

Now, thank you for letting me share that from my heart. But let me get on to what I came here to talk to you about. It is great to be back in Missouri. (Applause.)

I was here last September for a rally, and it was absolutely electric. Two months later, the Show Me State showed America what it was made of when you helped make Donald Trump the 45th President of the United States of

America. Thank you, Missouri. (Applause.)

The President and I will always be grateful for what you did for us and what you did for this country. America's small businesses were actually some of our biggest supporters. Small business owners across the land saw in this businessman who would become President someone who had the ideas and the energy and the vision to **Make America Great Again**. Hardworking Americans who make small businesses successful, folks like everyone here today, rallied behind this cause, and we brought real change to our nation's capital.

Fabick Cat is a true American success story. As I mentioned before, a family-owned business owned and operated since its founding back in 1917. Today -- thanks to all of you -- Fabick Cat has 1,100 employees at 37 locations throughout the Midwest. So many people rely on what you do. And, frankly, Doug, what you and the family has done here for a hundred years has made Missouri great, and it's going to be a part of **Making America Great Again**. (Applause.)

And I want to tell you, to all the small business owners who are here today, just know that President Trump is your biggest fan. (Applause.)

I'll make you a **promise**: President Trump is the best friend America's small businesses will ever have. (Applause.)

He asked me to be here today to tell you how much he appreciates what you do for the country.

Make no mistake about it, America finally has a President who's going to support and fight for you every single day. You know, both of us know that small business-es are the engine of our economy. They're the beating heart that creates jobs and prosperity and growth.

I grew up in a small business and in a small town, a fami-ly-owned business in Columbus, Indiana. I went to work at one of my dad's gas stations when I was only 14 years or age. I was a gas station attendant. For those of you under 30, just imagine. (Laughter.)

Just imagine if when you pulled into a gas station, some-body ran out with their name on their shirt, pumped your gas, washed your windows, checked you tires and didn't charge you any more money for it. (Laughter.)

That's what I did for a living, and I was proud to do it, proud to be a part of a family business, proud to be a part of small-business America.

As the world knows, the President grew up in a family busi-ness, too. We both, I can tell you, know the sacrifices that are required to make a family small business work -- the long hours, the hard work. And we both know this simple fact: When small business is strong, America is strong, and the American economy thrives. (Applause.)

That's why President Trump wants to help you become stronger than ever before. What he said on the campaign trail about strengthening small business is what we're already doing in the White House. On day one, we went right to work on a plan to cut taxes for working families, small businesses and family farms. He signed legislation to roll back reams of red tape and regulation issued under the Obama administration. He instructed every agency and department in Washington, D.C., also to identify two regulations to get rid of before they issue another ream of red tape. We're rolling back taxes and we're rolling back red tape already in Washington, D.C., thanks to you. (Applause.)

The President also knows that the rule of law is the heart of a growing free-market economy and he's taken decisive action to end illegal immigration, strengthen our borders and uphold the immigration laws of America. (Applause.)

And I'm glad to say businesses are already reacting to President Trump's "**Buy American and Hire American**" vision with optimism, investment, and a belief in our country again. Have you noticed it? I mean, from GM, to U.S. Steel, to IBM, to so many other companies, they're already announcing their intention to keep jobs here, to create news ones, tens of thousands of them. As Ford Motor Company's chief executive put it, even before the President took his oath of office, their investments are a "vote of confidence in the agenda of President Donald Trump." (Applause.)

So let's talk about that agenda. Let me say, if you take nothing else from what I tell you today, know this: The nightmare of Obamacare is about to end. (Applause.)

Despite the best efforts of liberal activists at many town halls around the country, the American people know the truth: Obamacare has failed, and Obamacare must go. (Applause.)

This failed law is crippling the American economy and crushing the American worker. We all know the broken promises of Obamacare; they're almost too many to count. They told you the cost of insurance would go down. They told you if you like your doctor, you can keep them. They told you your health plan -- you could keep that too. Well, none of it was true.

Americans are now paying $3,000 more a year for health insurance on average. Last year alone, premiums skyrocketed by a stunning 25 percent, and millions of Americans have lost their plans and their doctors since the outset of the Affordable Care Act. Higher cost, fewer choices, worse care -- that's Obamacare. And that's got to end.

Small businesses like those represented here today know exactly what I'm talking about. The last few years it's been harder to get ahead. Obamacare has only made it harder still -- if not impossible in some cases. One of the business leaders I just talked to talked about the weight of Obamacare on his nearly 700 employees, and the difficulty that it's placed on them and on their families. Obamacare is a job-killer and everybody in America knows it. And we're about to change all that. We're going to repeal Obamacare once and for all. Get rid of its mandates and its taxes and its intrusion on your lives and on your businesses. (Applause.)

And best of all, at the same time we repeal Obamacare, Obamacare is going to be replaced with something that actually works, something that brings freedom and individual responsibility back to American healthcare. (Applause.)

Now, President Trump and I want every American to have access to quality and affordable health insurance, which is why we're designing a better law. A market-driven law that reforms and improves how health care is provided in this country. We're working right now with leaders in Congress to lower the cost of health insurance by giving Americans the freedom to purchase health insurance across state lines the way you purchase life insurance and the way you purchase car insurance. (Applause.)

We're working with Congress to make sure that Americans with preexisting conditions have health insurance and don't have any fear of losing that health insurance. And we're working with Congress to give states the flexibility -- Governor Greitens, where'd you go? We're working with Congress to make sure we give states and governors like your great governor the flexibility they need to care for the least fortunate and their healthcare needs the way it will work in Missouri and the way that will work in each individual state. (Applause.)

Despite the scare tactics from the liberal left, the President and I are committed -- make it clear here -- we're committed to an orderly transition to a better healthcare system in America -- one that lowers the cost of health insurance, unleashes innovation, and puts the American people first. In all those concepts -- innovation, putting people first -- those are all the same principles that got Fabick Cat to 100 years. And it's what actually works in American business. And we truly do believe those free-market principles -- individual responsibility and a consumer choice -- can make the best healthcare system in America married to the best health insurance system in America, as well. (Applause.)

If they can work for America's business, they'll work in American healthcare.

But our agenda doesn't just stop there. I'll guarantee there isn't anyone here who can make sense of America's tax code, including me. (Laughter.)

There's an old joke that says the tax code is about 10 times the size of the Bible but with none of the good news. (Laughter and applause.)

It's a good line, but it's hardly a laughing matter. Truth is, our country's tax system these days penalizes success. It makes it far too hard for hardworking people and small businesses to achieve the **American Dream**. It takes too much money out of your pockets. It stifles job growth, wage growth, economic growth, and every other type of growth you need to get ahead.

Now, rest assured, when President Trump and I get done, before we get to this summertime, we're going to cut taxes across the board for working families, small businesses, and family farms -- and get this economy moving again. (Applause.)

We want you to keep more of your hard-earned money, plain and simple. You know how to spend your paycheck better than any politician in Washington, D.C., ever could. By the same token, you also know how to run your businesses and your own lives better than any bureaucrat -- that's why, as I mentioned before, we're going to keep on working together, and President Trump and I are going to keep rolling back senseless regulations that are strangling businesses and stifling our country's potential.

Everyone here knows the tremendous burden of red tape and regulation. Complying with these monstrous costs costs time and money to businesses that would be better spent hiring more good people and growing businesses and improving worker benefits. Our administration is working with Congress to repeal these job-killing, big-government regulations issued in the last administration in particular. We're going to rein in unelected bureaucrats so they can't cripple the economy from the comfort of their taxpayer-funded desks in Washington, D.C. (Applause.)

And before I close, if you haven't noticed it yet, let me remind you that we actually all elected a builder as the 45th President of the United States. (Applause.)

And under President Donald Trump, we're going to rebuild America. (Applause.)

President Trump has called attention to our nation's crumbling infrastructure like no contemporary person in public life. Rest assured, we're going to work with the Congress to make historic investments in infrastructure so that we have the best roads, the best bridges, the best highways, and the best airports in the best nation on Earth. (Applause.)

Every dollar we invest in infrastructure is a dollar we invest in America's future and in our prosperity. And when we do that, let's be clear: We're going to rebuild America, and we're going to **Hire American**, and we're going to **Buy American** when we rebuild this country. (Applause.)

We're going to rebuild America with American workers and American tools. (Applause.)

In fact, I'm pleased to announce President Trump has already taken action in this regard. Some of you may have noticed, just last month, after years of senseless delays, President Trump authorized the construction of the Keystone pipeline and the Dakota pipelines for our energy future and to create American jobs. (Applause.)

That's what it means to rebuild our infrastructure and put America back to work.

So, ladies and gentlemen, make no mistake about it. Our economy is going to grow faster than ever before and faster than you can imagine. We're already hearing from those who oppose these policies, though. People are out there opposing tax cuts, opposing slashing outdated regulations, opposing repealing Obamacare, and most of all, they seem to want to oppose the President's effort to give power back to the American people. We're hearing from these people every day, and the national media is more than willing to give them a platform each and every day.

So all I ask of all of you here in Missouri is let America hear from you. (Applause.)

In the days ahead, I promise you, President Trump and I are going to work with the Congress and we're going to drive forward our best efforts to turn this country around, create good-paying jobs at home, and a safer and more prosperous America. But America needs to hear from small business, from hardworking Americans who work in small business. The people who know we can do better. The people who know we can be more prosperous and know we can get this economy working for every American **Again**.

So let your voice be heard. Talk to a neighbor over a backyard fence. Stop somebody at the grocery store. Get online, on Facebook, send an email to a friend. But just send them a note and say, I ran into Mike the other day. (Laughter.)

They're doing exactly what they said they were going to

do, and I believe it works. And we need to support this President and this administration. That's what you've got to tell them. (Applause.)

So thanks for coming out on this sunny day in February. (Laughter.)

As my friend and our President likes to say, with boundless faith in the American people and faith in God who has ever watched over this land. (Applause.)

We will **Make America Safe Again**.

We will **Make America Prosperous Again**.

And with your help, and with God's help, and with this great new President, we will **Make America Great Again**.

Let's go get it done. Thank you. God bless you, Missouri. (Applause.)

END
3:08 P.M. EST

Chapter 53

23 February 2017

10:57 A.M. EST

THE PRESIDENT: Well, thank you very much. It's a great honor to have everybody. And some of the great people in the world of business, many of you I know -- many of you I know from reading all of our wonderful magazines and business magazines, in particular. So it's an honor to have you with us today.

Bringing manufacturing back to America, creating high-wage jobs was one of our campaign promises and themes, and it resonated with everybody. It was really something what happened. States that hadn't been won in many, many years were -- they came over to our fold. A lot of it had to do with the jobs, and other reasons -- but jobs. And I'm delivering on everything that we've said.

In fact, people are saying they've never seen so much happen in 30 days of a presidency. We've delivered on a lot.

And I think Mark can explain, and Mark can probably say some of the things we're doing for the auto industry. We're going to be doing for many of the industries.

As you know, the United States lost one-third of our manufacturing jobs since NAFTA. That's an unbelievable number and statistic. And 70,000 factories closed since China joined the WTO -- 70,000 factories. So when I used to give that statistic, I used to talk about and I always thought it was a typo. I said, it has to be a typo. I tell Wilbur -- Wilbur, that can't be right -- 70,000. Think of it, 70,000 factories. So you say, what are we doing?

My administration's policies and regulatory reform, tax reform, trade policies will return significant manufacturing jobs to our country. Everything is going to be based on bringing our jobs back, the good jobs, the real jobs. They've left, and they're coming back. They have to come back.

You've already seen companies such as Intel, Ford. Mark has been great. GM, Walmart, Amgen, Amazon, Fiat -- they came the other day; they're going to make a tremendous investment in the country. Carrier and many others announced significant new investments in the United States. For example, Ford is doing 700 million in Michigan, creating 700 new jobs -- is a vote of confidence. It was actually stated a vote of confidence. We have many other companies doing the same thing. Carrier, as you know -- and I got involved very late, almost like by two years late -- but many of the jobs that were leaving for Mexico, they're bringing back at least 800 jobs they're bringing back. And they actually never got to leave. I have no idea what they did with the plant in Mexico, but we'll have to ask them, because it was largely built.

General Motors is investing $1 billion in U.S. plants, adding or keeping 7,000 jobs. And it's going to be investing a lot more than that over the next fairly short period. Lockheed Martin has -- they've just announced 1,800 new jobs, and U.S. plants are doing a great job, and we started negotiating with them a little bit on the F-35. They cut their price a little bit. Thank you very much. She's tough. (Laughter.)

But it worked out well I think for everybody. And I think I have to say this: Marillyn, you've gotten a lot of credit, because what you did was the right thing. So we appreciate it. She cut her price over $700 million, right? By over $700 million. You think Hillary would have asked for $700 million? (Laughter.)

Oh, boy, I hope you -- I assume you wanted her to win. But you know what? You're going to do great and you're going to make more planes. It's going to work out the same, or better.

Walmart announced plans to create 10,000 jobs, and all of those jobs are going to be in the United States. Sprint and SoftBank is putting in $50 billion because of our election in the United States, over the next four years, to create 50,000 jobs. They've been terrific, by the way. And we have many others. Many of you are in the room, and you know exactly what I'm talking about. We have many, many other companies. And we're very happy.

Today we have 24 CEOs from the largest manufacturing companies in the country and even in the world. They represent people just in this room, nearly $1 trillion of sales and 2 million employees, large majorities of which are in the United States. They share our commitment to bringing manufacturing back and to create jobs in this country, which has been the biggest part of my campaign. I would say the border, a big part. Military strength, big part. And jobs, big part. I don't want to say which is most important. I guess we always have to say defense is maybe the most important.

But many of you take care of our defense, you make great products. Nobody makes the products that we do for our military. Nobody. And, in fact, a couple of countries who were not allowed to buy from us, I gave them -- hello, Jeff -- I gave them authorization -- you can only buy from us. I want them to buy from us. They were getting planes from other countries because our -- and they're allies. But they're going to be buying from us from now on.

And I just want to thank all of my people. My staff has been amazing. Gary, as you know -- you all know Gary from Goldman, Gary Cohn. And we're really happy -- just paid $200 million in tax in order to take this job, by the way. (Laughter.)

Which is very much unlike Gary. But he's great. And he'll be criticized by the media because he's getting paid $197,000. They'll say he really wanted that money -- which he gave up. I think he gave up -- did you give that up, Gary? I think so.

MR. COHN: Yes.

PARTICIPANT: It was one of those things.

THE PRESIDENT: It was one of those things. That's right. (Laughter.)

I want to thank -- Wilbur has been so fantastic. I've known Wilbur for so long, and he's a great guy, great negotiator, but a very fair negotiator. And he's going to be doing things that -- the deals we have with other countries are unbelievably bad. We don't have any good deals. In fact, I'm trying to find a country where we actually have a surplus of trade as opposed to -- everything is a deficit.

With Mexico, we have $70 billion in deficits, trade deficits, and it's unsustainable. We're not going to let it happen. Can't let it happen. We're going to have a good relationship with Mexico, I hope. And if we don't, we don't. But we can't let that happen -- $70 billion in trade deficits. And that doesn't include the drugs that pour across the border, like water. So we can't let that happen. With China, we have close to a $500-billion trade deficit. So we have to do something. I spoke to the President, I spoke to many people. We're going to work on that very, very hard, and we're going to do things that are the proper things to do.

But I actually said to my people: Find a country where we actually do well. So far, we haven't found that country. It's just losses with everybody, and we're going to turn that around.

I want to thank Jared Kushner, who has been so involved in this, and all of my guys. We have a great team. We have a team of all-stars. And we've been credit -- we've really been given credit for that. Right now, Rex, who, as you know, he's in Mexico -- I said, that's going to be a tough trip, because we have to be treated fairly by Mexico. That's going to be a tough trip. But he's over there with General Kelly, who's been unbelievable at the border. You see what's happening at the border. All of a sudden for the first time we're getting gang members out, we're getting drug lords out. We're getting really bad dudes out of this country and at a rate that nobody has ever seen before. And they're the bad ones.

And it's a military operation because what has been allowed to come into our country -- when you see gang violence that you've read about like never before and all

of the things -- much of that is people that are here illegally. And they're rough and they're tough, but they're not
tough like our people. So we're getting them out.

I thought what we could do is maybe we'll start with Ken
on my left, and we'll go around the room and introduce
yourselves to the press. Lots of media. One thing, we
have lots of media. How are you? Treats me -- that's one
that treats me very nicely, one of the few. Hi. And we'll
just start around -- go around the room and then we'll talk
privately without the press, and we're going to figure out
how to bring many, many millions of jobs more back to the
United States, okay?

Ken, go ahead.

MR. FRAZIER: Thank you, Mr. President, it's good to be
here. Ken Frazier from Merck & Co., Inc.

MR. FIELDS: Thank you, Mr. President. Mark Fields, CEO of
Ford Motor Company.

MS. MORRISON: Thank you, Mr. President. Denise
Morrison from Campbell Soup Company.

THE PRESIDENT: Good soup.

MS. MORRISON: Thank you.

MR. HAYES: Thank you, Mr. President. Greg Hayes from
United Technologies, the parent company of Carrier.

THE PRESIDENT: Did you bring any more of those jobs back
from Carrier? (Laughter.)

But one thing he did -- you know, I told -- I said, you were given so much credit for that, and I heard, two days ago, that you're selling far more Carrier air conditioners than you thought, just as a patriotic move. People are buying Carrier because of what you did -- bringing the jobs back to Indiana.

MR. HAYES: That's exactly right. It's a great success.

THE PRESIDENT: Right? So, I said that. I thought that was going to happen. Good. Thank you.

MR. STYSLINGER: Thank you, Mr. President. Lee Styslinger with Altec, Inc.

MR. GORSKY: Thank you, Mr. President. Alex Gorsky with Johnson & Johnson.

MR. FARR: Thank you, Mr. President. David Farr with Emerson. St. Louis.

MR. OBERHELMAN: Doug Oberhelman, executive chairman of Caterpillar. We have plenty of D10s available for you.

THE PRESIDENT: I love those D10s. (Laughter.)

I even like the D12. Are they still doing the D12?

MR. OBERHELMAN: We're doing a D11, and we have some of those around as well.

THE PRESIDENT: Because the D12, I'm waiting for, you know. That's going to be bigger than anything ever in history, right? But there's nothing like what you do. The

Caterpillars are the best.

MR. OBERHELMAN: Thank you.

THE PRESIDENT: And when we raise the dollar, and we let other people manipulate their currencies, it's the one thing that stops you, Doug -- right?

MR. OBERHELMAN: Well, we'll take them on. Bring them on.

THE PRESIDENT: Right, technology. No, but we have to give you a level playing field.

MR. OBERHELMAN: We need a level playing field.

THE PRESIDENT: We have to let other countries give you a level playing field. So, what a great company. I love Caterpillar. I've been driving them for a long time.

MR. OBERHELMAN: Well, come out and see us, and we'll put you in one. (Laughter.)

THE PRESIDENT: Okay, good. I might do that soon. Go ahead.

MR. KAMSICKAS: Jim Kamsickas, Dana Incorporated. Thank you.

MR. LONGHI: Mario Longhi, with U.S. Steel, Mr. President. Thank you for the opportunity.

THE PRESIDENT: And you're going to be doing pipelines now. You know that, right? We put you heavy into the pipeline business because we approved, as you know, the

Keystone Pipeline and Dakota. But they have to buy --
meaning, steel, so I'll say U.S. Steel -- but steel made in this
country and pipelines made in this country.

MR. LONGHI: 100 percent, Mr. President. We'll be there.

THE PRESIDENT: So the pipe is coming from the U.S.

MR. LONGHI: By the way, when you come drive trucks,
come up to Minnesota and our mines. You're going to see
us running up there.

THE PRESIDENT: Good. I'll do it. I'll be out there.

MR. FETTIG: Mr. President, thank you. Jeff Fettig,
Whirlpool Corporation.

THE PRESIDENT: Yep, good.

MS. HEWSON: Thank you, Mr. President. Marillyn
Hewson, Lockheed Martin Corporation. I just want to
thank you for this opportunity that we've spent this morning in the working groups, and the opportunity to talk to
you today about generating jobs. We're very excited about
the fact that this is one of the first actions that you want to
take on. So thank you very much.

THE PRESIDENT: Good. Well, thank you, and thank you for
what we did. Lot 10, we call it. Lot 10 -- 90 planes. It was
90 planes out of 3,000, but it was not doing so well, and
now it's doing great. Right?

MS. HEWSON: That's right, Mr. President.

THE PRESIDENT: Okay, good.

MS. HEWSON: And we welcome you to Fort Worth to see those aircraft on the production line.

THE PRESIDENT: Good. Very good. Thank you, Marillyn.

MR. IMMELT: Mr. President, good to see you again. Jeff Immelt with GE.

THE PRESIDENT: Good. Hi, Jeff.

MR. IMMELT: Great to be here. Look forward to really working you on creating more manufacturing jobs.

THE PRESIDENT: Jeff actually watched me make a hole-in-one, can you believe that? Should you tell that story?

MR. IMMELT: We were trying to talk President Trump into doing "The Apprentice." That was my assignment when we owned NBC. President Trump goes up to a par 3 on his course, he looks to the three of us and says, "You realize of course I'm the richest golfer in the world." That's a comment, then gets a hole-in-one. (Laughter.)

THE PRESIDENT: Crazy.

MR. IMMELT: I have to say, you know, I've seen the magic before. (Laughter.)

THE PRESIDENT: It's so crazy that -- no, I actually said I was the best golfer of all the rich people. (Laughter.)

To be exact. And then I got a hole-in-one.

MR. IMMELT: That's what you said.

THE PRESIDENT: So, it was sort of cool. Thank you. Thank you very much.

MR. BROWN: Thank you, Mr. President. Bill Brown from Harris Corporation. And thank you for coming to our headquarter location in Melbourne, Florida twice. Thank you.

THE PRESIDENT: Absolutely. Thank you.

MR. WEEKS: Wendell Weeks, Corning Incorporated. Thank you.

MR. FERRIOLA: Thank you, Mr. President. John Ferriola, Nucor Corporation.

THE PRESIDENT: Great.

MR. ALTHOFF: Thank you, Mr. President. Don Althoff with Veresen, Inc.

MR. SUTTON: Good morning, Mr. President. Mark Sutton, chairman and CEO of International Paper.

THE PRESIDENT: Great. Bob Craft is a big fan of yours. You know, that right?

MR. LEIMBACH: Thank you, Mr. President. Keith Leimbach, CEO of LiveOps, representing the services industry in a manufacturing form.

THE PRESIDENT: Yes, I know.

MR. LEIMBACH: Let's remember to bring those services jobs back as well.

THE PRESIDENT: Good. We will.

MR. LIVERIS: Good morning, Mr. President. I'm Andrew Liveris, Dow Chemical. Thank you for the opportunity, and bringing the language of business back to the White House, and I'm here to make chemistry sexy again. (Laughter.)

THE PRESIDENT: And I want to thank you for your help. You've been great. Thank you, Andrew, very much. Nobody knows Ivanka. (Laughter.)

MR. THULIN: Good morning, Mr. President. Inge Thulin, 3M.

THE PRESIDENT: Thank you. Reed, thank you also. Thank you. Say it again, please.

MR. THULIN: Inge Thulin, 3M. Good morning.

THE PRESIDENT: Yes. Great company.

MR. DELL: Good morning, Mr. President. Great to be back. It's Michael Dell, with Dell Technologies.

THE PRESIDENT: Hi, Michael. Nice to see you.

MS. NOVAKOVIK: Good morning, Mr. President. Phebe Novakovic, General Dynamics.

THE PRESIDENT: Great.

MR. LUCIANO: Good morning, Mr. President. Juan Luciano, Archer Daniels Midland.

THE PRESIDENT: Great. Great companies.

Jared. So, Jared, maybe I'll let you take over for a little while, and we'll then -- we're going to then go through the room very, very carefully. We're going to find out how we bring more jobs back. And thank you to the press and the media. We really appreciate it, and we'll see you later. Thank you very much.

END
11:12 A.M. EST

> *"I want to thank Jared Kushner, who has been so involved in this, and all of my guys.*
> *We have a great team.*
> *We have a team of all-stars."*

Chapter 54

23 February 2017

2:40 P.M. EST

THE PRESIDENT: Thank you, everybody, very nice. Nice to see you. Well, I want to thank Dina and Ivanka and everybody for working so hard to set this up. It's been so important to them, and I want to make it clear today that my administration will focus on ending the absolutely horrific practice of human trafficking. And I am prepared to bring the full force and weight of our government to the federal and at the federal level, and the other highest levels, whatever we can do, in order to solve this horrific problem. It's getting worse and it's happening in the United States in addition to the rest of the world, but it's happening in the United States, which is terrible.

Human trafficking is a dire problem, both domestically and internationally, and is one that's made really a challenge. And it's really made possible to a large extent, more of a modern phenomenon, by what's taking place on the Internet, as you probably know. Solving the human trafficking epidemic, which is what it is, is a priority for my administration. We're going to help out a lot. "Solve" is a wonderful word, a beautiful word, but I can tell you, we're going to help a lot.

I'll direct the Department of Justice, the Department of

Homeland Security and other federal agencies that have a role in preventing human trafficking to take a hard look at the resources and personnel that they're currently devoting to this fight. Now, they are devoting a lot, but we're going to be devoting more.

Dedicated men and women across the federal government have focused on this for some time, as you know. A lot of you have been dealing with the federal government and it's been much more focused over the last four weeks -- I can tell you that. I cannot thank each of you enough, and the dedicated men and women who run my staff and your staffs in getting everybody together was terrific. I was so glad I was able to be here.

You start with really a tremendous amount of energy and blood, sweat and tears. Government can be helpful, but without you, nothing would happen. So, again, I want to thank everybody in this room. It's a very, very terrible problem. It's not talked about enough. People don't know enough about it. And we're going to talk about it, and we're going to bring it out into the open and hopefully we're going to do a great deal to help prevent some of the horrific -- really horrific -- crimes that are taking place. And I can see -- I really can say, in this country, people don't realize how bad it is in this country, but in this country and all over the world. So thank you all for being here. Thank you very much.

END
2:44 P.M. EST

Chapter 55

**REMARKS BY PRESIDENT TRUMP AT
THE CONSERVATIVE POLITICAL ACTION CONFERENCE
GAYLORD NATIONAL RESORT & CONVENTION CENTER**

24 February 2017

10:23 A.M. EST

THE PRESIDENT: Thank you, everybody. So great to be with you. Thank you. (Applause.)

Great to be back at CPAC. (Applause.)

The place I have really --

AUDIENCE MEMBER: We love you!

THE PRESIDENT: I love this place. Love you people. (Applause.)

So thank you. Thank you very much.

First of all, I want to thank Matt Schlapp, and his very, very incredible wife and boss, Mercedes, who have been fantastic friends and supporters, and so great. When I watch them on television defending me, nobody has a chance. So, I want to thank Matt and Mercedes.

And when Matt called and asked, I said, absolutely, I'll be there with you. I mean, the real reason I said it -- I didn't want him to go against me because that one you can't beat. So I said, absolutely. And it really is an honor to be here.

I wouldn't miss a chance to talk to my friends. These are my friends. (Applause.)

And we'll see you again next year and the year after that, and I'll be doing this with CPAC whenever I can, and I'll make sure that we're here a lot.

You know, if you remember, my first major speech -- sit down, everybody. Come on. (Applause.)

You know, the dishonest media, they'll say he didn't get a standing ovation. You know why? No, you know why? Because everybody stood and nobody sat, so they will say he never got a standing ovation, right? (Applause.)

They are the worst.

AUDIENCE: USA! USA! USA! (Applause.)

THE PRESIDENT: So -- sit down. (Laughter.)

Donald Trump did not get a standing ovation. They leave out the part, they never sat down. They leave that out. So I just want to thank -- but you know, my first major speech was at CPAC. And probably five or six years ago -- first major political speech. And you were there.

And it was -- I loved it. I love the people. I love the commotion. And then they did these polls where I went through the roof, and I wasn't even running, right? But it gave me an idea, and I got a little bit concerned when I saw what was happening in the country, and I said, let's go do it. So it was very exciting. I walked the stage on CPAC. I'll never forget it, really. I had very little notes, and even less preparation. So when you have practically no notes and no preparation, and then you leave and everybody was thrilled, I said, I think I like this business.

I would have come last year, but I was worried that I would be, at that time, too controversial. We wanted border security. We wanted very, very strong military. We wanted all of the things that we're going to get, and people consider that controversial. But you didn't consider it controversial. (Applause.)

So I've been with CPAC for a long time. All of these years, we've been together. And now you finally have a President. Finally. Took you a long time. Took you a long time. (Applause.)

And it's patriots like you that made it happen, believe me -- believe me. You did it because you love your country, because you want a better future for your children, and because you want to **Make America Great Again**. (Applause.)

The media didn't think we would win.

AUDIENCE MEMBER: They knew. (Laughter.)

THE PRESIDENT: The pundits -- you're right. They had an idea. The pundits didn't think we would win. The consultants that suck up all that money. Oh, they suck it up, they're so good. (Laughter.)

They're not good at politics, but they're really good at sucking up people's money. Especially my opponent's, because I kept them down to a minimum.

THE PRESIDENT: But the consultants didn't think we would win. But they all underestimated the power of the people -- you. And the people proved them totally wrong. Never -- and this is so true, and this is what's been happening -- never underestimate the people. Never. I don't think it will ever happen again.

And I want you all to know that we are fighting the fake news. It's fake -- phony, fake. (Applause.)

A few days ago, I called the fake news "the enemy of the people" -- and they are. They are the enemy of the people. Because they have no sources, they just make them up when there are none. I saw one story recently where they said nine people have confirmed. There are no nine people. I don't believe there was one or two people. Nine people. And I said, give me a break. Because I know the people. I know who they talked to. There were no nine people. But they say, nine people, and somebody reads it and they think, oh, nine people. They have nine sources. They make up sources.

They are very dishonest people. In fact, in covering my comments, the dishonest media did not explain that I called the fake news the enemy of the people -- the fake news. They dropped off the word "fake." And all of the sudden, the story became, the media is the enemy. They take the word "fake" out, and now I'm saying, oh, no, this is no good. But that's the way they are. So I'm not against the media. I'm not against the press. I don't mind bad stories if I deserve them. And I tell you, I love good stories, but we won't -- (laughter) -- I don't get too many of them. But I am only against the fake news media or press -- fake, fake. They have to leave that word. I'm against the people that make up stories and make up sources. They shouldn't be allowed to use sources unless they use somebody's name. Let their name be put out there. Let their name be put out. (Applause.)

A source says that Donald Trump is a horrible, horrible human being. Let them say it to my face. (Applause.)

Let there be no more sources.

And remember this -- and in not all in all cases. I mean, I had a story written yesterday about me in Reuters by a very honorable man. It was a very fair story. There are some great reporters around. They're talented, they're honest as the day is long. They're great. But there are some terrible, dishonest people, and they do a tremendous disservice to our country and to our people. A tremendous disservice. They are very dishonest people, and they shouldn't use sources. They should put the name of the person. You will see stories dry up like you've never seen before.

So you have no idea how bad it is, because if you are not part of the story -- and I put myself in your position sometimes, because many of you, you're not part of the story, and if you're not part of the story, then you sort of know. If you are part of the story, you know what they're saying is true or not. So when they make it up, and they make up something else, and you saw that before the election -- polls, polls. The polls. They come out with these polls, and everybody was so surprised. Actually, a couple of polls got it right. I must say, Los Angeles Times did a great job. Shocking, because -- you know. They did a great job. (Applause.)

And we had a couple of others that were right. But

generally speaking, I mean, I can tell you the network. Somebody said a poll came out. And I say, what network is it? And they'll say, a certain -- let's not even mention names right? Should we? Well, you have a lot of them. Look, the Clinton New[s] Network is one. (Applause.)

Totally. Take a look. Honestly. Take a look at their polls over the last two years. Now, you would think they would fire the pollster, right? After years and years of getting battered. But I don't -- I mean, who knows, maybe they're just bad at polling. Or maybe they're not legit. But it's one or the other. Look at how inaccurate -- look at CBS, look at ABC also. Look at NBC. Take a look at some of these polls. They're so bad, so inaccurate.

And what that does is it creates a false narrative. It creates like this narrative that's just like we're not going to win, and people say, "Oh, I love Trump, but you know I'm not feeling great today. He can't win. So I won't go and vote. I won't go and vote." It creates a whole false deal and we have to fight it folks. We have to fight it. They're very smart, they're very cunning, and they're very dishonest. So just to conclude -- I mean, it's a very sensitive topic, and they get upset when we expose their false stories. They say that we can't criticize their dishonest coverage because of the First Amendment. You know, they always bring up the First Amendment. (Laughter.)

And I love the First Amendment. Nobody loves it better than me. Nobody. (Applause.)

I mean, who uses it more than I do?

But the First Amendment gives all of us -- it gives it to me, it gives it to you, it gives all Americans -- the right to speak our minds freely. It gives you the right and me the right to criticize fake news, and criticize it strongly. (Applause.)

And many of these groups are part of the large media corporations that have their own agenda, and it's not your agenda, and it's not the country's agenda. It's their own agenda. They have a professional obligation as members of the press to report honestly. But as you saw throughout the entire campaign, and even now, the fake news doesn't tell the truth. Doesn't tell the truth.

So just in finishing, I say it doesn't represent the people. It never will represent the people. And we're going to do something about it, because we have to go out and we have to speak our minds, and we have to be honest. Our victory was a win like nobody has ever seen before. (Applause.)

And I'm here fighting for you, and I will continue to fight for you.

The victory and the win were something that really was dedicated to a country and people that believe in freedom, security, and the rule of law. (Applause.)

Our victory was a victory and a win for conservative values. (Applause.)

And our victory was a win for everyone who believes it's time to stand up for America, to stand up for the American worker, and to stand up for the American flag. (Applause.)

Yeah, there we should stand up. Come on. (Applause.)

There we should stand up. Okay. (Applause.)

And, by the way, we love our flag. By the way, you folks are in here, the place is packed -- there are lines that go back six blocks. And I tell you that because you won't read about it, okay? (Laughter.)

But there are lines that go back six blocks. There is such love in this country for everything we stand for. You saw that on Election Day. (Applause.)

And you're going to see it more and more. (Applause.)

So we're all part of this very historic MOVEMENT, a MOVEMENT the likes of which, actually, the world has never seen before. There's never been anything like this. There's been some MOVEMENTS, but there's never been anything like this. There's been some MOVEMENTS that petered out, like Bernie -- petered out. (Laughter.)

But it was a little rigged against him -- super delegate, super delegate. She had so many delegates before the thing even started. I actually said to my people, how does that happen? (Laughter.)

Not that I'm a fan of Bernie, but a lot of Bernie people voted for Trump. You know why? Because he's right on one issue: Trade. He was right about trade. Our country is being absolutely devastated with bad trade deals. So he was right about that, but we've got a lot of Bernie support. So actually, I like Bernie, okay? I like Bernie. (Applause.)

But I'm here today to tell you what this MOVEMENT means for the future of the Republican Party and for the future of America.

First, we need to define what this great, great unprecedented MOVEMENT is, and what it actually represents. The core conviction of our MOVEMENT is that we are a nation that put and will put its own citizens **First**. (Applause.)

For too long we've traded away our jobs to other countries -- so terrible. We've defended other nations' borders while leaving ours wide open; anybody can come in.

AUDIENCE MEMBER: A wall!

THE PRESIDENT: Oh, we're going to build the wall, don't worry about it. We're building the wall. We're building the wall. In fact, it's going to start soon, way ahead of schedule, way ahead of schedule. (Applause.)

Way, way, way ahead of schedule. It's going to start very soon. General Kelly, by the way, has done a fantastic job. Fantastic job he's done. (Applause.)

And remember, we are getting the bad ones out. These are bad dudes. We're getting the bad ones out, okay? We're getting the bad -- if you watch these people it's like, oh, gee, that's so sad. We're getting bad people out of this country, people that shouldn't be -- whether it's drugs or murder or other things. We're getting bad ones out. Those are the ones that go first, and I said it from day one. Basically all I've done is keep my **promise**. (Applause.)

We've spent trillions of dollars overseas while allowing our own infrastructure to fall into total disrepair and decay. In the Middle East, we've spent as of four weeks ago $6 trillion. Think of it. And, by the way, the Middle

East is in what -- I mean, it's not even close -- it's in much worse shape than it was 15 years ago. If our Presidents would have gone to the beach for 15 years, we would be in much better shape than we are right now, that I can tell you. (Applause.)

Yeah, a hell of a lot better. We could have rebuilt our country three times with that money.

This is the situation that I inherited. **I inherited a mess**, believe me. We also inherited a failed health care law that threatens our medical system with absolute and total catastrophe.

Now, I've been watching -- and nobody says it -- but Obamacare doesn't work, folks. I mean, I could say -- I could talk -- it doesn't work. And now people are starting to develop a little warm heart, but the people that you're watching, they're not you. They're largely -- many of them are the side that lost. You know, they lost the election. It's like, how many elections do we have to have? They lost the election. (Laughter.)

But I always say, Obamacare doesn't work. And these same people two years, and a year ago, were complaining about Obamacare. And the bottom line: We're changing it. We're going to make it much better. We're going to make it less expensive. We're going to make it much better. Obamacare covers very few people.

And remember, deduct from the number all of the people that had great health care that they loved, that was taken away from them; was taken away from them. (Applause.) Millions of people were very happy with their health care. They had their doctor, they had their plan. Remember the lie -- 28 times. "You can keep your doctor, you can keep your plan" -- over and over and over again you heard it.

So we're going to repeal and replace Obamacare. (Applause.)

And I tell Paul Ryan and all of the folks that we're working with very hard -- Dr. Tom Price, very talented guy -- but I tell them from a purely political standpoint, the single-best thing we can do is nothing. Let it implode completely -- it's already imploding. You see the carriers are all leaving. I mean, it's a disaster.

But two years don't do anything. The Democrats will come to us and beg for help. They'll beg, and it's their problem. But it's not the right thing to do for the American people. It's not the right thing to do. (Applause.)

We inherited a national debt that has doubled in eight years. Think of it -- $20 trillion. It's doubled. And we inherited a foreign policy marked by one disaster after another. We don't win anymore. When was the last time we won? Did we win a war? Do we win anything? Do we win anything? We're going to win. We're going to win big, folks. We're going to start winning **Again**, believe me. We're going to win. (Applause.)

AUDIENCE: USA! USA! USA!

THE PRESIDENT: But we're taking a firm, bold and decisive measure -- we have to -- to turn things around. The era of empty talk is over. It's over. (Applause.)

Now is the time for action. So let me tell you about the

actions that we're taking right now to deliver on our **promise** to the American people, and on my promise to **Make America Great Again**.

We've taken swift and strong action to secure the southern border of the United States and to begin the construction of great, great border wall. (Applause.)

And with the help of our great border police, with the help of ICE, with the help of General Kelly and all of the people that are so passionate about this -- our Border Patrol, I'll tell you what they do. They came and endorsed me, ICE came and endorsed me. They never endorsed a presidential candidate before. They might not even be allowed to. (Laughter.)

But they were disgusted with what they saw.
And we'll stop it. We'll stop the drugs from pouring into our nation and poisoning our youth. (Applause.)

Pouring in, pouring in. We get the drugs, they get the money. We get the problems; they get the cash. No good, no good. Going to stop.

By stopping the flow of illegal immigration, we will save countless tax dollars, and that's so important because the tax -- the dollars that we're losing are beyond anything that you can imagine. And the tax dollars that can be used to rebuild struggling American communities -- including our inner cities. (Applause.)

We are also going to save countless American lives. As we speak today, immigration officers are finding the gang members, the drug dealers and the criminal aliens, and throwing them the hell out of our country. (Applause.)

And we will not let them back in. They're not coming back in, folks. (Applause.)

If they do, they're going to have bigger problems than they ever dreamt of.

I'm also working with the Department of Justice to begin reducing violent crime. I mean, can you believe what's happening in Chicago, as an example? Two days ago, seven people were shot --

AUDIENCE MEMBER: It's Iraq!

THE PRESIDENT: -- and, I believe, killed. Seven people. Seven people. Chicago, a great American city. Seven people shot and killed.

We will support the incredible men and women of law enforcement. (Applause.)

Thank you. And thank them. I've also followed through on my **campaign promise** and withdrawn America from the Trans-Pacific Partnership. (Applause.)

So that we can protect our economic freedom. And we are going to make trade deals, but we're going to do one-on-one, one-on-one. And if they misbehave, we terminate the deal. And then they'll come back, and we'll make a better deal. (Applause.)

None of these big quagmire deals that are a disaster. Just take a look -- by the way, take a look at NAFTA, one of the worst deals ever made by any country having to do with economic development. It's economic-undevelopment as far as our country is concerned. We're preparing to repeal and replace the disaster known as Obamacare. (Applause.)

We're going to save Americans from this crisis, and give them the access to the quality healthcare they need and deserve. We have authorized the construction, one day, of the Keystone and Dakota Access pipelines. (Applause.)

And issued a new rule. This took place while I was getting ready to sign. I said, who makes the pipes for the pipeline? Well, sir, it comes from all over the world, isn't that wonderful? I said, nope, it comes from the United States or we're not building one. (Applause.)

American steel. If they want a pipeline in the United States, they're going to use pipe that's made in the United States, do we agree? (Applause.)

But can you imagine -- I told this story the other day -- can you imagine the gentleman -- never met him, don't even know the name of his company. I actually sort of know it, but I want to get it exactly correct. Big, big, powerful company. They spent hundreds of millions of dollars on the pipeline -- same thing with the Dakota, different place. They got their approvals, everything, in the case of Dakota, then all of a sudden they couldn't connect it because they had people protesting that never showed up before.

But with the Keystone -- so they spend hundreds of millions of dollars with bloodsucker consultants, you know, sucking the blood out of the company -- "don't worry, I use them all my life; okay, don't worry, we're going to get it approved, I'm connected, I'm a lobbyist, don't worry." Bottom line, Obama didn't sign it. Could be 42,000 jobs -- somewhere around there. A lot of jobs. Didn't sign it. But

can you imagine -- he gave up. A year ago it was dead.
Now he's doing nothing, calling his wife, "Hello, darling,
I'm a little bored, you know that pipeline?" That has killed
us, that has killed our company. Knock, knock. "Mr. so-
and-so, the Keystone pipeline, sir, out of nowhere, has just
been approved." (Applause.)

Now, can you imagine the expression? And you know the
sad part? The same bloodsucking consultants that hit him
for all the money and failed? They're now going to go back
to him and say, didn't we do a great job? We want more
money, right, because that's the way the system works. A
little bit off, but that's the way the system works.
We're preparing bold action to lift the restrictions on
American energy, including shale, oil, natural gas, and
beautiful clean coal, and we're going to put our miners
back to work. (Applause.)

Miners are going back to work. (Applause.)

Miners are going back to work, folks. Sorry to tell you that,
but they're going back to work.

We have begun a historic program to reduce the regulations that are crushing our economy -- crushing. And not
only our economy, crushing our jobs, because companies
can't hire. We're going to put the regulation industry out
of work and out of business. (Applause.)

And, by the way, I want regulation. I want to protect our
environment. I want regulations for safety. I want all of
the regulations that we need, and I want them to be so
strong and so tough. But we don't need 75 percent of the
repetitive, horrible regulations that hurt companies, hurt
jobs, make us non-competitive overseas with other compa-

nies from other countries. That, we don't need. But we're going to have regulations. It's going to be really strong and really good, and we're going to protect our environment, and we're going to protect the safety of our people and our workers. (Applause.)

Another major promise is tax reform. We are going to massively lower taxes on the middle class, reduce taxes on American business, and make our tax code more simple and much more fair for everyone, including the people and the business. (Applause.)

In anticipation of these and other changes, jobs are already starting to pour back into our country -- you see that. In fact, I think I did more than any other pre-President -- they say President-elect. President-elect is meeting with Ford, he's meeting with Chrysler, he's meeting with General Motors. I just wanted to save a little time. (Laughter.)

Because Ford and Fiat-Chrysler, General Motors, Sprint, Intel and so many others are now, because of the election result, making major investments in the United States, expanding production and hiring more workers. And they're going back to Michigan, and they're going back to Ohio, and they're going back to Pennsylvania, and they're going back to North Carolina, and to Florida. (Applause.)

It's time for all Americans to get off of welfare and get back to work. You're going to love it! You're going to love it. You are going to love it. (Applause.)

We're also putting in a massive budget request for our beloved military. (Applause.)
And we will be substantially upgrading all of our military -- all of our military. Offensive, defensive, everything. Bigger

and better and stronger than ever before. And hopefully, we'll never have to use it. But nobody is going to mess with us, folks. Nobody. (Applause.)

It will be one of the greatest military build-ups in American history. No one will dare to question -- as they have been, because we're very depleted, very, very depleted. Sequester. Sequester. Nobody will dare question our military might again. We believe in peace through strength, and that's what we will have. (Applause.)

As part of my pledge to restore safety for the American people, I have also directed the defense community to develop a plan to totally obliterate ISIS. (Applause.)

Working with our allies, we will eradicate this evil from the face of the Earth. (Applause.)

At the same time, we fully understand that national security begins with border security. Foreign terrorists will not be able to strike America if they cannot get into our country. (Applause.)

And by the way, take a look at what's happening in Europe, folks. Take a look at what's happening in Europe. I took a lot of heat on Sweden. (Laughter.)

And then a day later, I said, has anybody reported what's going on? And it turned out that they didn't -- not too many of them did. (Laughter.)

Take a look at what happened in Sweden. I love Sweden. Great country. Great people. I love Sweden. But they understand I'm right. The people over there understand I'm right. Take a look at what's happening in

Sweden. Take a look at what's happening in Germany. Take a look at what's happened in France. Take a look at Nice and Paris.

I have a friend -- he's a very, very substantial guy. He loves the City of Lights. He loves Paris. For years, every year, during the summer, he would go to Paris -- it was automatic -- with his wife and his family. I hadn't seen him in a while. And I said, Jim, let me ask you a question: How's Paris doing? "Paris? I don't go there anymore. Paris is no longer Paris." That was four years -- four, five years -- hasn't gone there. He wouldn't miss it for anything. Now he doesn't even think in terms of going there. Take a look at what's happening to our world, folks, and we have to be smart. We have to be smart. We can't let it happen to us. (Applause.)

So let me state this as clearly as I can: We are going to keep radical Islamic terrorists the hell out of our country. (Applause.)

We will not be deterred from this course, and in a matter of days, we will be taking brand new action to protect out people and keep **America safe**. You will see the action. (Applause.)

I will never, ever apologize for protecting the safety and security of the American people. I won't do it. (Applause.)

If it means I get bad press, if it means people speak badly of me, it's okay. It doesn't bother me. The security of our people is number one -- is number one. (Applause.)

Our administration is running with great efficiency, even though I still don't have my Cabinet approved. Nobody mentions that. Do you know I still have people out there waiting to be approved? And everyone knows they're going to be approved. It's just a delay, delay, delay. It's really sad. It's really sad. And these are great people. These are some great people. We still don't have our Cabinet. I assume we're setting records for that. That's the only thing good about it is we're setting records. I love setting records. (Applause.)

But I hate having a Cabinet meeting and I see all these empty seats. I said, Democrats, please, approve our Cabinet and get smart on health care too, if you don't mind. (Applause.)

But we're taking meetings every day with top leaders in business, in science, and industry. Yesterday, I had 29 of the biggest business leaders in the world in my office -- Caterpillar tractor, Campbell's Soup. We had everybody. We had everybody. I like Campbell's Soup. (Laughter and applause.)

We had everybody, and we came to a lot of very good conclusions, and a lot of those folks that are in that room are going to be building big, big massive new plants, and lots of jobs. And you know what? They're going to be building them in this country, not in some other country. (Applause.)

We're meeting with unions, meeting with law enforcement, and we're meeting with leaders from all around the world, where the White House doors used to be totally closed -- they were closed, folks. You don't realize that. They were closed. They're now wide open. And they're open for people doing business for our country and putting people to work. (Applause.)

And when they come into the White House, we're translating these meetings into action. One by one, we're checking off the **promises** we made to the people of the United States. One by one -- a lot of **promises**. And we will not stop until the job is done. We will reduce your taxes. We will cut your regulations. We will support our police. We will defend our flag. (Applause.)

We will rebuild our military. We will take care of our great, great veterans. We're taking care of our veterans. (Applause.)

We will fix our broken and embarrassing trade deals that are no good -- none of them. You wonder, where did the people come from that negotiated these deals? Where did they come from?

AUDIENCE MEMBER: Government.

THE PRESIDENT: Well, they came also from campaign contributions, I must be honest with you. They're not as stupid as you think. (Laughter.)

We will cut wasteful spending. We will promote our values. We will rebuild our inner cities. We will bring back our jobs and our **dreams**. So true. (Applause.)

So true. And, by the way, we will protect our Second Amendment. (Applause.)

You know, Wayne and Chris are here from the NRA, and they didn't have that on the list. It's lucky I thought about it. (Laughter.)

But we will indeed. And they're great people. And by the

way, they love our country. They love our country. The NRA has been a great supporter. They love our country. The forgotten men and women of America will be forgotten no longer. That is the heart of this new MOVEMENT and the future of the Republican Party. People came to vote, and these people -- the media -- they said, where are they coming from? What's going on here? These are hardworking, great, great Americans. These are unbelievable people who have not been treated fairly. Hillary called them "deplorable". They're not deplorable.

AUDIENCE: Booo -- lock her up! Lock her up! Lock her up!

THE PRESIDENT: Who would have thought that a word was going to play so badly. That's the problem in politics. One wrong word and it's over. She also said irredeemable, but we won't mention that.

The GOP will be, from now on, the party also of the American worker. (Applause.)

You know, we haven't been, as a group, given credit for this, but if you look at how much bigger our party has gotten during this cycle. During the early days when we had 17 people running -- the primaries -- millions and millions of people were joining. Now, I won't say it was because of me, but it was, okay. (Applause.)

And we have an amazing, strong, powerful party that truly does want to see **America be Great Again**, and it will see it. And it's going to see it a lot sooner than you think, believe me. A lot sooner than you think. (Applause.)
We will not answer to donors or lobbyists or special interests, but we will serve the citizens of the United States of America, believe me. Global cooperation -- dealing with

other countries, getting along with other countries -- is good. It's very important. But there is no such thing as a global anthem, a global currency, or a global flag. This is the United States of America that I'm representing. I'm not representing the globe. I'm representing your country. (Applause.)

AUDIENCE: USA! USA! USA!

THE PRESIDENT: There is one allegiance that unites us all, and that is to America. America -- it's the allegiance to America.

No matter our background, or income, or geography, we are all citizens of this blessed land. And no matter our color, or the blood, the color of the blood we bleed, it's the same red blood of great, great patriots. Remember. Great patriots. (Applause.)

We all salute, with pride, the same American Flag. And we are equal -- totally equal -- in the eyes of Almighty God. We're equal. (Applause.)

Thank you.

And I want to thank, by the way, the evangelical community, the Christian community. (Applause.)

Communities of faith -- rabbis and priests and pastors, ministers -- because the support for me was a record, as you know, not only in terms of numbers of people, but percentages of those numbers that voted for Trump. So I want to thank you folks. It was amazing -- an amazing outpouring, and I will not disappoint you.

As long as we have faith in each other, and trust in God, then there is no goal, at all, beyond our reach. There is no dream too large, no task too great. We are Americans, and the future belongs to us. The future belongs to all of you. (Applause.)

And America is coming about, and it's coming back, and it's roaring and you can hear it. It's going to be bigger and better. It is going to be. It is going to be. Remember. And it's roaring. It's going to be bigger, and better, and stronger than ever before. (Applause.)

I want to thank you. And Matt and Mercedes, I want to thank the two of you, and all of the supporters that I have. I see them. They're all over the place. You are really great people. I want to thank you.

And I want to say to you, God bless you, and God bless the United States of America. Thank you, folks. Thank you. (Applause.)

END
11:04 A.M. EST

> *"...I called the fake news the enemy of the people -- and they are."*

Chapter 56

24 February 2017

12:07 P.M. EST

THE PRESIDENT: Thank you all very much for being here. We have tremendous people standing behind me, and the biggest in the world in terms of manufacturing and business. Some of the people involved are Ken Fisher and Ken Frazier, Chairman and President, CEO of Merck. Alex Gorsky, Chairman, CEO of Johnson and Johnson. Marillyn Hewson -- and she has been very tough to deal with but that's okay. (Laughter.)

She's a very tough negotiator, President of Lockheed Martin. Gregory Hayes, Chairman and CEO, United Technology. Andrew Liveris, my friend Andrew, Chairman and CEO of Dow Chemical Company. Mario Longhi, the President, CEO, United States Steel Corporation. Juan Luciano, Chairman, President, CEO of Archer Daniels Midland Company. Denise Morrison, President of Campbell's Soup Company. Lee Styslinger III, Chairman and CEO of Altec, Inc. Mark Sutton, Chairman, CEO of International Paper. And Inge Thulin, Chairman, President of 3M Company. And we have made tremendous progress with these great business leaders -- amazing progress. They're getting together in groups and they're coming up with suggestions about their companies and how to bring jobs back to the United States. And I think it will be a fantastic day for the country.

And we met yesterday, and -- I met with these folks and some more. Excessive regulation is killing jobs, driving companies out of our country like never before. Although, I must say, I think we've stopped it to a large part, Marillyn, right?

MS. HEWSON: Right.

THE PRESIDENT: Reducing wages and raising prices. I've listened to American companies and American work- ers. I've been listening to them for a long time. I've been listening to them complain for a long time. But today, this executive order directs each agency to establish a regula- tory reform task force, which will ensure that every agency has a team of dedicated -- and a real team of dedicated people to research all regulations that are unnecessary, burdensome and harmful to the economy, and therefore harmful to the creation of jobs and business.

Each task force will make recommendations to repeal or simplify existing regulations. The regulatory burden is for the people behind me and for the great companies of this country, and for small companies -- an impossible situa- tion, we're going to solve it very quickly. They will also have to really report every once in a while to us so we can report on the progress, and so we can come up with some even better solutions.

This executive order is one of many ways we're going to get real results when it comes to removing job-killing regulations and unleashing economic opportunity. We've already issued an order which says that for every one new regulation, two old regulations must be eliminated. So that in itself is going to be tremendous, but what we're doing is much more than even that.

Every regulation should have to pass a simple test: Does it make life better or safer for American workers or consumers? If the answer is no, we will be getting rid of it and getting rid of it quickly. We will stop punishing companies for doing business in the United States. It's going to be absolutely just the opposite. They're going to be incentivized for doing business in the United States.

We're working very hard to roll back the regulatory burdens so that coal miners, factory workers, small-business owners, and so many others can grow their businesses and thrive. We cannot allow government to be an obstacle to government opportunity. We are going to bring back jobs and create more opportunities to prosper, maybe more than ever before in our country. We've made tremendous strides over the last short period of time. This is -- I guess we're four weeks into it. I think for four weeks I've done a good job, wouldn't you say? (Laughter.)

But again, I want to thank these great business leaders. Some of them are with us and the White House, and they've had tremendous success -- Reed and Jared and so many others -- in business. And they're helping us sort out what's going on, because really, for many years, even beyond -- long beyond Obama, President Obama -- I will say that it's been disastrous for business. This is going to be a place for business to do well and to thrive.

And so with the signing of this executive order, I would like to just congratulate everybody behind me. And, Andrew, I'd like to thank you for initially getting the group together.

MR. LIVERIS: Thank you. Thank you, Mr. President.

THE PRESIDENT: Really a fantastic job you've done.

MR. LIVERIS: Thank you.

(The Executive Order is signed.)

THE PRESIDENT: Should I give this pen to Andrew? Dow Chemical. (Laughter.)

I think maybe, right? (Applause.)

MR LIVERIS: Thank you.

THE PRESIDENT: That means a lot of jobs. Thank you, everybody. Thank you very much.

END
12:12 P.M. EST

Chapter 57

24 February 2017

PRESIDENT TRUMP: Well, thank you very much, everybody. It's a great honor to have President Kuczynski with us from Peru. Peru has been a fantastic neighbor. We've had great relationships -- better now than ever before. And I have known him for quite a while through reading about the work that he's done, and I believe he's here to get an award at Princeton. An award for what? Explain, please.

PRESIDENT KUCZYNSKI: For being an alumnus who did okay, I guess. (Laughter.)

PRESIDENT TRUMP: Yeah, did very okay. And your daughter goes to --

PRESIDENT KUCZYNSKI: Alex? Oh, my other daughter, Susie, goes to Princeton.

PRESIDENT TRUMP: Right. That's exactly right.

PRESIDENT KUCZYNSKI: She wants to study medicine.

PRESIDENT TRUMP: And I assume she's very proud of you getting the big award tomorrow, right?

PRESIDENT KUCZYNSKI: Right. And Alex went to Columbia.

PRESIDENT TRUMP: That's great. Good students, good children. So a very, very special man, and it's an honor to have him in Washington, at the White House. And we're going to talk some business. I understand they're going to be buying quite a bit of our military -- some of our military vehicles. And they are great vehicles. I just looked at it and we're approving it. And use them well. Use them well.

And if you'd like to say something, Mr. President, please.

PRESIDENT KUCZYNSKI: Well, I'm happy to be in Washington. I lived here for a while. I lived in New York. We greatly respect the U.S. We have excellent relations. And Latin America needs to grow more, and we're going to talk about how to do that. Maybe you have a few ideas.

PRESIDENT TRUMP: I guess I do. I guess I do. And we have a problem with Venezuela. They're doing very poorly. And so we'll be talking about a lot of different things. And thank you all for being here. Thank you.

END
3:08 P.M. EST

Chapter 58

25 February 2017

Transcript:

My fellow Americans,
As Black History Month 2017 comes to a close, I am very
grateful for the many wonderful opportunities to honor
African American heroes, faith leaders, entrepreneurs and
the many others who changed the course of our Nation.
We are blessed by the lives and examples of those who
have made this Nation a beacon of freedom, talent, and
unbreakable **American Spirit**.

This week, I had the privilege of visiting the National
Museum of African American History and Culture right
here in Washington, D.C. It's a new, beautiful Smithsonian
museum that serves as a shining example of African
Americans' incredible contributions to our culture, our
society, and our history. It also tells of the great struggle
for freedom and equality that prevailed against the sins of
slavery and the injustice of discrimination.

The work and love of the people who helped create such a
masterpiece is a testament to the legacy of so many leaders it honors. I left that museum confident that together,
America can overcome any challenge.

There's a great quote by Muhammad Ali in the museum – "I shook up the world," he said. And that is what he did.

So did leaders like Sojourner Truth, Frederick Douglass, Booker T. Washington, Martin Luther King[Jr.], and so many others. They *shook up the world* for the better because they inspired our nation to march toward justice and freedom for all.

Today, and every day, I pledge to continue that march so that every American – no matter his background, no matter her background – has the chance to climb that great ladder of success.

It was very special to accompany Dr. Ben Carson and his family for the first time seeing the Carson exhibit. I am proud that soon he will serve in my cabinet as the Secretary of Housing and Urban Development. HUD has a very, very powerful meaning far beyond housing. It is about transforming our communities. About bringing back hope. And Ben will do a fantastic job.

That's what I am committed to doing also. I want every African-American child, family, and worker to have access to great schools, safe communities, and good-paying jobs. I want every disadvantaged child in America to have a choice about where they go to school – so important. I also want to honor and promote the achievements of Historically Black Colleges and Universities throughout our Nation. They do a fantastic job. They are not given the credit that they deserve, and they are going to start getting that credit.

In order to help African Americans thrive, we are working very hard to make sure every child can grow up in a safe community – and have access to high-paying jobs.

We've lost a lot of our best jobs to other countries – and this has hurt the African American community very badly.

This week I met with manufacturing CEOs – we're going to be working to bring back those jobs, and I mean really good-paying jobs.

I will be talking more about these issues in my Joint Session Address to Congress and to all Americans next Tuesday evening. I hope you will be watching.

Thank you, God bless you and God bless America.

Chapter 59

26 February 2017

7:29 P.M. EST

THE PRESIDENT: Thank you very much, everybody. I want to just congratulate the First Lady on having done a really beautiful job. The room, they say, has never looked better, but who knows. I'm sure it's looked very good many times. So, Melania, congratulations. (Applause.)

I also want to congratulate and thank a truly great Vice President of the United States, and his wonderful wife, Karen. And wherever you are, Mike, stand up just for a second. Mike Pence. (Applause.)

So I can say that after four weeks -- they were a lot of fun -- but we've accomplished almost everything we've started out to accomplish. The borders are stricter, tighter. We're going a really good job. General Kelly has does a fantastic job militarily. As you know, we have a fantastic team. We have an A Team. And I'm getting some good reports. There are some big problems in the world -- you know that very well -- but we're very happy with the way things are working. And again, we've made a lot of **promises** over the last two years, and many of those **promises** already are kept. So we're very honored by that. And I. (Applause.)

Thank you, thank you.

I just want to salute and toast the governors -- the great governors of the United States. They have done an amazing job. Such an easy job you have. (Laughter.)

So easy. But you have done a fantastic job, and your families and wives and -- well, everybody is here. I mean, I've seen daughters come tonight. I've seen wives. I've seen -- all I know is, everybody is lovely, and we're going to have a wonderful evening.

And tomorrow, we're going to meet, and we're going to discuss things, like perhaps healthcare will come up. Perhaps. (Laughter.)

And I think we've made a lot of progress on that. And we're going to have a speech on Tuesday night, and we're going to be speaking very specifically about a very complicated subject. Everybody is different, every state is different, and different requirements, but I think we have something that's going to really be excellent.

And as most of you know, the Obamacare has had tremendous problems. I won't say in front of the Democrats; I'll just say it to the Republicans. (Laughter.)

It doesn't work. But we're going to have it fixed, and we're going to repeal and replace. And I think you're going to see something very, very special. And for all of you, and even tonight, because we have Tom Price with us -- if you see something or want to discuss it, we don't have to discuss all friendly stuff. We can discuss a little bit of the healthcare. We might as well start. But tomorrow morning, we're going to meet and have some pretty big sessions on healthcare and other things -- whatever is on your mind. So I hear this is a record number of Governors -- 46. And that's the highest number that have ever shown up for this evening. (Applause.)

So, with that, I would like to toast the great, great governors of the United States. Thank you.

(A toast is offered.)

Now, I know it's inappropriate, but I'd like to ask a friend of mine -- I've just destroyed his political career -- (laughter) -- from the other side, a man from Virginia -- I've known him a long time, and he's a very good guy -- Governor Terry McAuliffe to come up and also, perhaps, make a toast. Thank you. Terry, where are you? Come on up, Terry. (Applause.)

GOVERNOR MCAULIFFE: Well, good evening. Let me, first of all, on behalf of our nation's governors, I want to thank the President and the First Lady. We have found out this is the first big social dinner of the calendar, and I think they did that out of respect to our nation's governors. So if we give a great round of applause to the President and the First Lady. (Applause.)

Now, Mr. President, as you know, I am Chairman of the National Governors Association, so I'm not sure if the 46 -- the largest crowd ever -- is due to my chairmanship or your presidency. (Laughter.)

But tonight, in the spirit of bipartisanship, sir, we will both take credit for the greatest NGA meeting in the history of NGA meetings. (Applause.)

I also want to thank the Vice President of the United States and Mrs. Pence. On Friday, for the first time ever, they opened the Vice Presidential Mansion -- the Naval Observatory -- to host the governors for lunch. That had never been done before. So if we could give a great round of applause to the Vice President and Karen Pence. (Applause.)

And let me just say, tomorrow we're all going to meet, we're going to discuss the issues tomorrow, but the one thing we all agree on -- all of us governors and this administration, what every governor wants -- we want good jobs. We want a good economy. We want the world-class education system in our respective states. We want a healthcare delivery system that works, with great, quality healthcare, efficiently at a low cost. We want people to get on our roads and our rail, and be able to ride around efficiently, and then go see their kids play a ballgame. That's what we all want.

And, Mr. President, I thank you for having us here tonight. We have a common goal: We are the greatest nation in the globe. And I want to toast to you, Mr. President, and just say, we want to work with you to build on those ideals that have instilled and brought all of us governors together, that we can respectively grow our states and grow our nation to be truly the great **destiny** that we are. So I would like to offer a toast to the President of the United States of America.

(A toast is offered.)

END
7:35 P.M. EST

Chapter 60

REMARKS BY PRESIDENT TRUMP IN LISTENING SESSION WITH HEALTH INSURANCE COMPANY CEOS ROOSEVELT ROOM

27 February 2017

11:03 A.M. EST

THE PRESIDENT: You are the big ones. You are the biggest of the big, right? (Laughter.)

That's very impressive. Thank you for being here. We just had a great meeting with the governors on the horrible effects that Obamacare is having. We're going to change it and straighten it out, and make -- we have a plan that's going to be, I think, fantastic. It will be released fairly soon. We'll be talking about it tomorrow night during the speech. But I think it's going to be something special, and we'll talk it about right here. I think we'll get you on, and I think you're going to like what you hear.

Again, thank you for being here. I want to thank also Secretary Tom Price who's with us, and who's doing a phenomenal job on a very complex subject, the subject of healthcare. He's an advocate for the patients. Tom is all about the patients. That's what he wants. He wants to have a great healthcare system.

Obamacare has been a disaster, and it's only getting worse. Last year alone, Obamacare premiums increased by double digits. Since it has gone into effect, premiums are up by almost 100 percent in many areas. And I think that this year it's going to be really the year that I've always predicted -- '17 is going to be a catastrophic year for Obamacare, for payments. And you just take a look at what's happening in various states like Arizona -- I believe it was up 116 percent; it's going to be worse this year.

Obamacare forced providers to limit the plan options they offered to patients and caused them to drive prices way up. Now, a third of United States counties are down to one insurer, and the insurers are fleeing. You people know that better than anybody.

Since Obamacare went into effect, nearly half of the insurers are stopped and have stopped from participating in the Obamacare exchanges. It has gotten so bad that nearly 20 million Americans have chosen to pay the penalty, or received an exemption rather than buy insurance. That's something that nobody has ever heard of or thought could happen, and they're actually doing that rather than being forced to buy insurance.

We must work together to save Americans from Obamacare -- you people know that, and everyone knows that at this point -- to create more competition and to bring down the prices substantially. The chaos that Obamacare has created, and for which congressional Democrats -- and you see that -- are alone and responsible for requires swift action. I actually told the Republicans that if we did nothing, just do nothing for a two-year period, let Obamacare totally implode -- which it's doing right now anyway -- that would be, from a political standpoint, the best thing we could do is to let it implode, and then people will come begging -- the Democrats will come begging to do something to help them out of the jam.

Once we start doing it, we sort of inherit the problem, we take over the problem, it becomes ours. But it's the right thing to do for the American people. I think allowing this to go on -- this disaster to go on -- is a mistake. So I'm asking Secretary Price to work with you to stabilize the insurance markets and to ensure a smooth transition to the new plan. And the new plan will be a great plan for the patients, for the people, and hopefully for the companies. It's going to be a very competitive plan. And costs will come down, and I think the healthcare will go up very, very substantially. I think people are going to like it a lot.

We've taken the best of everything we can take. It's our hope that Democrats will stop the obstruction and resistance. And that's what they have -- in fact, they have a sign, "resist, resist." They want to resist everything, including Cabinet members. I have many Cabinet members that haven't been approved yet, people that are extraordinary -- all of whom are going to be approved, but they just take forever. It's called obstruct and resist. Hope I didn't give them a new phrase, because their real phrase is "resist." I think I just gave them another word. I shouldn't have done that. I'm good at branding. (Laughter.)

You're going to see them now come out, "obstruct and resist." All right, well, at least I can take credit for it. And they worked with us, and we are going to hopefully work with the Democrats, because ultimately we're all people that love this country and we want to do the right thing, including reforms like expanded healthcare savings accounts, state flexibility, and the ability to purchase across state lines. The state lines are so important for competition. Everybody has wanted to do it for years. What's not to do? So that's going to be very important.

I want to thank you all for being here. I want to know and I want you to know that it's an honor to do business with you. It's a great honor to have you in the White House. And we look forward to providing healthcare that is that is extraordinary -- better than any other country anywhere in the world. And we can do that. We have the talent, we have the capacity, and we have the people.

So we'll work on that together. And maybe before the press leaves, you can just introduce yourself and your company, and the public will get to see what you're about. And then if things aren't working out, I'm blaming you anyway. (Laughter.)

So we'll start with Brad.

MR. WILSON: Thank you, Mr. President. I appreciate the opportunity to be here. I'm Brad Wilson, President and CEO of Blue Cross and Blue Shield of North Carolina, and pleased to represent our 3.9 million customers here today.

THE PRESIDENT: That's great, Brad. Great job.

MR. BERTOLINI: Mark Bertolini, chairman and CEO of Aetna.

THE PRESIDENT: Aetna -- good one.

PARTICIPANT: And I also represent America's health insurance plans. We represent all health insurance plans in Washington, D.C., including the plan to cover Medicaid managed care.

THE PRESIDENT: Great.

MR. BROUSSARD: Bruce Broussard, CEO of Humana.

MR. GARRITY: Pat Garrity, I'm the CEO of Florida Blue, the Blue Cross Blue Shield plan in the state of Florida.

THE PRESIDENT: Great.

MR. HEMSLEY: I'm Steve Hemsley from UnitedHealth Group. We're a diversified health care company of about 230,000 employees. We serve about 120 million Americans. And we are contributing in terms of the jobs we've -- 35,000 in the last five years and 10,000 in the coming year. We're a mission-driven enterprise, help people live healthier lives, and make the system work for everyone.

THE PRESIDENT: Good, thank you very much.

MR. CORDANI: Mr. President, David Cordani from Cigna Corporation. We're a global health service company.

MR. SEROTA: Scott Serota, Blue Cross Blue Shield Association. We represent 108 million subscribers.

THE PRESIDENT: 108 million, that's a pretty big deal, right?

MR. SEROTA: Yes, it is.

THE PRESIDENT: Pretty big.

MR. SWEDISH: Good morning, Mr. President. I'm Joe Swedish with Anthem. We're in 14 states, representing 40 percent of the American public. We have 40 million members, and we've been involved in the individual (inaudible) for probably seven decades, and deeply embedded in the

Affordable Care Act situation that has evolved over the last three years. I don't want to miss the opportunity to thank you for the swift and decisive action that occurred most recently regarding some adjustments that have occurred in and around --

THE PRESIDENT: We had to step in.

MR. SWEDISH: Thank you very much.

THE PRESIDENT: It was going to be an implosion. We had to step in. Thank you for saying that.

MR. SWEDISH: Thank you, sir. Thank you.

MR. TYSON: I'm Bernard Tyson, Chairman and CEO of Kaiser Foundation Health Plan, better known as Kaiser Permanente. We cover 11.7 million Americans. We also are an integrated delivery system, so we both provide the coverage and the care. We have Permanente medical groups that contract exclusively with Kaiser Foundation Health Plan. And we're proud to care for 11.7 million people.

THE PRESIDENT: Thank you, Bernard.

MR. HILFERTY: Mr. President, I'm Dan Hilferty. I'm based in Philadelphia with Independence Blue Cross, Independence Health Group. We're in 32 states and the District of Columbia and a large Medicaid managed care population.

We're the only player on the exchange in the five-county Philadelphia area. And again, I'd like to echo Joe's point. We were thrilled with the initial steps to stabilize the market. We look forward to working with you, Vice

President Pence, Secretary Price in making sure that we have a sustainable program for years to come. So thank you.

THE PRESIDENT: Well, thank you very much. And the market, as you know, and we talk about stabilizing the market -- the market is disastrous. It's going to absolutely implode. That's why we're meeting today. And I think we're going to come up with something where not only will the market be great, but the people are going to be taken care of. So we will work that out I think quite easily, actually.

Thank you very much. Thank you, everybody.

END
11:12 A.M. EST

Chapter 61

27 February 2017

9:45 A.M. EST

THE PRESIDENT: Thank you very much. (Applause.)

That is pretty good, I'll tell you. Coming from governors, I can't really -- I can't even believe it. That's so impressive. And I very much appreciate you being here. And thank you to Vice President Pence. He has been so wonderful to work with. He's a real talent, a real guy. And he is central casting, do we agree? Central casting. He's been great. (Applause.)

Good morning, everybody, and welcome back to the White House. The First Lady and I were very, very happy last night to host you. We saw some real talent, military talent, musicians who were fantastic. And everybody enjoyed it. (Applause.)

I'm very proud to have so many former governors in my Cabinet. Vice President Pence, as you know, big governor from a very great state -- I state I like very much -- Indiana. Nikki Haley at the U.N. -- is Nikki here someplace? I think so -- yes. We have Rick Perry -- is going before. We're trying to get people approved, we can't get them out. But Rick is going to do a fantastic job. Sonny Purdue will be joining the Cabinet very soon. Terry

Branstad will be our ambassador to China. And an interesting story on Terry -- every time I spoke in Iowa, he'd say,
please don't say anything bad about China. (Laughter.)

I said, what do you mean? What do you mean? He said,
I like China and we do a lot of business with China. "And
really, just don't" -- and I said, "hmm." So when it came
down to picking an ambassador, I called him up, I said, you
like China. And I can tell you, China is very, very happy
with our choice. So we made everybody happy. (Applause.)

Right? These Governors -- thank you. And thank you,
Terry.

These Governors have been bold reformers, and their success shows why we need to make states the laboratories
of democracy once again. Many of you have shared past
frustrations with waiting for permission from the federal
government and agencies -- and I understand that, and I've
had many people tell me about it, and it's been catastrophic for some of your states. You know your citizens and you
know they want things done. But they don't get things
done and it's not your fault. Sometimes it's your fault,
but they understand that. But sometimes it's not your
fault. We're going to speed it up.

Because that's not how a partnership is supposed to
work. The government should not stand in your way in delivering needed reforms and services -- and it won't. We're
going to move very, very quickly, environmentally, with
Scott and so many others that are involved in the process
of regulation. We are going to be cutting -- we're going to
be doing the right thing. We're going to be protecting people environmentally and safety-wise, but we're going to be

moving it quickly, very quickly. (Applause.)

And speaking of that, I know many of you -- and I've spoken to some of you last night about it -- have many projects that are -- I mean, just literally tied up because of environmental concerns, and it's been in for years and years and years the project your state wants, great for employment -- everybody wants them -- and they couldn't get them out of environmental protection. And we will get them out. Now, that doesn't mean they're going to be approved, but they'll be rejected quickly one way or the other. They'll be either rejected quickly or they're going to get approved. I would say most will be approved, but you're going to know you're not going to wait nine years or eleven years -- some of the horror stories that I've heard.

Under my administration, we're going to have a true partnership of collaboration and cooperation. We will get to the answers and we will get them quickly, and the flexibility you need to implement the reforms that you are going to have in order to make decision-making proper and decision-making fast. So we're going to do both those things -- proper and fast.

One of the most important responsibilities for the federal government is the budget of the United States. My first budget will be submitted to the Congress next month. This budget will be a public safety and national security budget, very much based on those two with plenty of other things, but very strong. And it will include a historic increase in defense spending to rebuild the depleted military of the United States of America at a time we most need it. (Applause.)

And you'll be hearing about that tomorrow night in great

detail. This is a landmark event, a message to the world, in these dangerous times, of American strength, security and resolve. We must ensure that our courageous servicemen and women have the tools they need to deter war, and when called upon to fight in our name only do one thing: Win. We have to win. We have to start winning wars again.

I have to say, when I was young, in high school and college, everybody used to say "we haven't lost a war" -- we never lost a war -- you remember. Some of you were right there with me, and you remember we never lost a war. America never lost. And now we never win a war. We never win. And we don't fight to win. We don't fight to win. So we either got to win, or don't fight it at all. But where we are -- 17 years -- almost 17 years of fighting in the Middle East. I saw a chart the other day -- as of about a month ago, $6 trillion we've spent in the Middle East -- $6 trillion. And I want to tell you, that's just unacceptable. And we're nowhere. Actually, if you think about it, we're less than nowhere. The Middle East is far worse than it was 16, 17 years ago. There's not even a contest. So we've spent $6 trillion. We have a hornet's nest. It's a mess like you've never seen before. We're nowhere. So we're going to straighten it out.

This defense spending increase will be offset and paid for by finding greater savings and efficiencies across the federal government. We're going to do more with less. I got involved in an airplane contract, I got involved in some other contracts, and we cut the hell out of the prices. I mean, we saved a lot of money, tremendous amount of money, beyond anything that the generals that were involved -- they said they'd never seen anything like this before. On one plane, on a small order of one plane, I saved $725 million. And I would say I devoted about, if I added it up, all those calls, probably about an hour. So I think that might be my highest and best use. (Laughter.)

Because if we can do that, our budget will be -- might be my highest and best. (Applause.)

And there are many other places; it's all the same. And in one way, that's a good thing because we have an answer. And David is going to do a fantastic job at the VA. I see David is sitting there, shaking his head. Stand up, David. (Applause.)

So we can't get our people through Cabinet, but he went through -- was it 95 to nothing?

SECRETARY SHULKIN: A hundred to zero.

THE PRESIDENT: How the hell did you do that? (Laughter.)

Boy, oh boy. He must be good. You were the one. One hundred to zero, wow. Chose you -- hey, we can do it. But we do -- we have still quite a few Cabinet members, and they're just in limbo waiting and waiting. It's like obstruction. It's obstruction. But eventually we'll get them, and they'll put their people in, and we'll get those agencies, et cetera, to work.

We're going to do more with less and make the government lean and accountable to the people. We can do so much more with the money we spend. With $20 trillion in debt -- can you imagine that -- the government must learn to tighten its belt, something families all across the country have had to learn to do, unfortunately. But they've had to learn to do it, and they've done it well.

My budget increases spending, and the increase in all spending, for federal law enforcement also. And activities having to do with law enforcement will be substantially increased. And we will fight violent crime. If you look at what's happening in our cities, you look at what's happening in Chicago, what's going on in Chicago -- we will fight violent crime, and we will win. And we'll win that one fairly quickly. Once we give the local police, the local law enforcement the right to go in and fight it, and we back them monetarily and also otherwise, we're going to win that one. We're going to win it fairly quickly, I believe.

My budget also puts **America First** by keeping tax dollars in America to help veterans and first responders. So important. This budget follows through on my **promise** to focus on keeping Americans **safe**, keeping out terrorists, keeping out criminals, and putting violent offenders behind bars, or removing them from our country altogether. And I must say that we've been treated very well -- very, very well -- on the job that General Kelly has done at the border. It's tough, it's strong.

I was talking last night to Terry McAuliffe, and he said, you have to mention this -- because he met with -- where is Terry? He's around here someplace. Terry -- he met with General Kelly, and I think I can say you were impressed with General Kelly. And he said, you have to get the point out that they're removing the bad ones. And that's where our focus is -- it's the bad ones. We're getting some very, very bad players out of this country -- drug lords, gang members, heads of gangs, killers, murderers -- we're getting them out. That's what we're focused on.

The press isn't covering that, unfortunately, but it's something that is very important. We're getting the bad ones out. And that's always where I said I was going to start. I was going to start with these bad players. And they are bad. They are rough and tough, and we're getting them the hell out of our country, and we're bringing them to where they started out. Let their country do what they have to do with them.

So the budget, which is going to be a very big part of tomorrow night's speech, it's going to be I think a budget of great rationality. But it's going to have to do with military, safety, economic development, and things such as that. Great detail tomorrow night.

We're also going to do whatever we can to restore the authority of the states when that is the appropriate thing to do. We're going to give you back a lot of the powers that have been taken away from states and great people and great governors. And you can control it better than the federal government because you're right on top of it. You have something that's controllable. So I think that's going to be very important. You see that already taking effect.

We have to let the states compete and to see who has the best solutions. They know the best how to spend their dollars and how to take care of the people within each state. And the states are different, and people are different. So the governors are going to have a lot more decision-making ability than they have right now.

All states will benefit from our economic agenda. We will reduce taxes very, very substantially, and simplify the tax code. We're also going to make taxes between countries much more fair. We're one of the only countries in the world that people can sell their product into us and have no tax, no nothing, and they get rich. And yet if you want to do business with them, you'll have taxes, I've seen, as high as 100 percent. So they sell into us, no problem; we sell into them -- because we don't sell them because the tax is so high that they don't want us to sell into them.

So I know that's always been a point of contention, but to me it's just fair. It's just fair. It's reciprocal. It's fair. And so we're going to be doing a lot of work on that, and that's becoming a very, very important factor -- fairness. Because I believe in free trade. I want so much trade -- somebody said, oh, maybe he's a total nationalist -- which I am, in a true sense -- but I want trade. I want great trade between countries.

But the word "free" is very deceiving, because it's good for them, it's not good for us. I want fair trade. And if we're going to be taxed, they should be taxed at the same amount, the other countries. And one of two things is going to happen: We're going to make a lot of money or the other country is going to get rid of its tax. And that's good, too, because now the product, like Harley-Davidson -- I was talking to them -- the product will now flow into other countries where right now they can't do it.

So we're going to make it easier for states to invest in infrastructure, and I'm going to have a big statement tomorrow night on infrastructure. We spent $6 trillion in the Middle East, and we have potholes all over our highways and our roads. I have a friend who is in the trucking business. He said, my trucks are destroyed going from New York to Los Angeles. They're destroyed. He said, I'm not going to get the good trucks. He always prided himself on buying the best equipment. He said, the roads are so bad that, by the time we make the journey from New York to Los Angeles or back, he said the equipment is just beat to hell. I said,

when has it been like that before? He said, it's never --
he's been in the business for 40 years -- he said it's never
been like that. Forty years -- never been like that. So
we're going to take care of that.

Infrastructure -- we're going to start spending on infrastructure big. And it's not like we have a choice. It's not
like, oh, gee, let's hold it off. Our highways, our bridges
are unsafe. Our tunnels -- I mean, we have tunnels in New
York where the tiles are on the ceiling, and you see many
tiles missing. And you wonder, you know, you're driving at
40 miles an hour, 50 miles an hour through a tunnel. Take
a look at the Lincoln Tunnel and the Queens-Midtown
Tunnel, and you're driving, and you see all this loose material that's heavy. And it was made many years ago, so it's
heavy. Today, it's light. It used to be better. The problem
is, you got to hold it up. And I say to myself -- every time
I drive through, I say, I wonder how many people are hurt
or injured when they are driving at 40, 50 miles an hour
through a tunnel, and the tile falls off. And there are so
many missing tiles and such loose concrete. So we have to
fix our infrastructure. It's not like we have a choice. We
have no choice, and we're going to do it, and it also happens to mean jobs, which is a good thing.

We're going to repeal and replace Obamacare, and get
states the flexibility that they need to make the end result
really, really good for them. A very complicated issue. We
have Tom Price, just got confirmed -- sitting here. (Applause.)

Stand up, Tom. And I spent a lot of time with Governor
Walker and Governor Rick Scott the other day -- we were
talking about it. They're really very expert on the subject,
and I want to thank them. They spent a lot of time with

me. Governor Christie who's here someplace. Where's Chris? Governor Christie, thank you. And so we have a lot of talent and a lot of expertise here, I will tell you. And we have come up with a solution that's really, really, I think, very good.

Now, I have to tell you, it's an unbelievably complex subject. Nobody knew that healthcare could be so complicated. And statutorily and for budget purposes, as you know, we have to do healthcare before we do the tax cut. The tax cut is going to be major, it's going to be simple, and the whole tax plan is wonderful. But I can't do it until we do healthcare because we have to know what the healthcare is going to cost. And, statutorily, that's the way it is. So for those people that say, oh, gee, I wish we could do the tax first -- it just doesn't work that way. I would like to do that first. It's actually -- tax cutting has never been that easy, but it's a tiny, little ant compared to what we're talking about with Obamacare.

And you have to remember -- and I say this to Democrats in the room -- of which we have many -- Obamacare has failed. If you go to Minnesota, where they had a 66-percent increase, and the governor of Minnesota, who is with us today, said, Obamacare -- the Affordable Care Act -- is no longer affordable -- something to that effect. I think that might be it exactly. But the Affordable Care Act is no longer affordable. Obamacare has failed.

I say to the Republicans, if you really want to do politically something good, don't do anything. Sit back for a period of two years, because '17 is going to be a disaster -- a disaster -- for Obamacare if we don't do something. Let it be a disaster because we can blame that on the Dems that are in our room, and we can blame that on the Democrats and

President Obama. Let it implode, and then let it implode in '18 even worse. Don't do anything, and they will come begging for us to do something. But that's not the fair thing to do for the people. It's not the fair thing.

Politically, I think it would be a great solution, because as soon as we touch it, if we do the most minute thing -- just a tiny, little change -- what's going to happen? They're going to say, it's the Republicans' problem. That's the way it is. But we have to do what's right because Obamacare is a failed disaster.

And it's interesting, it's sort of like, when you see -- you see it with politicians, you see it with President Obama -- when you know he's getting out of office and the clock is ticking, and he's not going to be there, his approval rating goes way up, even though, you know, not that active in the last period of time. The approval rating goes up. That's not him; that's like almost everybody. I see it happening with Obamacare. People hate it, but now they see that the end is coming, and they're saying, oh, maybe we love it. There's nothing to love. It's a disaster, folks, okay? So you have to remember that.

And, very importantly, we are going to work to restore local control to our nation's education system. Betsy is here someplace, and she is going to be, I think, fantastic. (Applause.)

I think she's going to be fantastic. Stand up, Betsy. Betsy feels so strongly, and she has had such support from so many people. You know, you don't see that too much because you see the anti, you never see the positive. But I can tell you, I've had so many calls while she was going through that horrible process. That was a tough, tough, nasty process. And she hung in, she was as strong as you get. But so many people were calling Betsy, saying you will do such a fantastic job once you get it.

It's like sometimes I'd say, it's much tougher to get into Harvard than it is to stay there. Does that make sense? It's tougher to get into the Wharton School of Finance -- you can't get in. But if you get in, it's fine, you get through, right? I think you're going to do a fantastic job, and we're very proud of you. And you took a lot of heat, but you're going to do great. So she wants to bring decision-making powers back to parents, back to the families and back to the states, where they can really control education.

And just finally, I'm looking forward to working with you on these projects and so much more. We're going to do these projects and so many more. And I thank you all again for being here. It's going to be a really productive discussion -- so productive that I'm going to ask the press to start leaving because I wouldn't want them to see any great, productive session. (Laughter.)

But they'll be seeing it and hearing about it.
Again, thank you very much all for being at the White House. We'll do this many times. I want the opinions of the governors of the states of the United States. So I want to just thank you all for being here, and let's take some questions, okay? (Applause.)

Thank you.

END
10:05 A.M. EST

Chapter 62

27 February 2017

5:36 P.M. EST

THE VICE PRESIDENT: Well, thank you. Thank you to Secretary DeVos, the Secretary of Education. Secretary Betsy DeVos. I can't tell you how wonderful it is to be able to say that. You can give her another round of applause. She's going to be working closely with all of you.

To the Presidents of our Historically Black Colleges and Universities, representatives of the United Negro College Fund, the Thurgood Marshall College Fund, distinguished guests, welcome to the White House.

It is my great privilege to serve as Vice President of the United States with the 45th President of the United States, Donald Trump. And I know -- I know that you all just came from a brief meeting in the Oval Office. (Laughter.)

So I know you've already experienced the President's warm hospitality and heard his expressions of appreciation for your leadership and for your willingness to come together to discuss the important work that each of you, and the desire of this administration to continue to partner -- partner with you on behalf of education all across this country.

My note said that the President wanted me to send greetings to you, but he already did. (Laughter.)

Which happens to me a lot. The President is a very hospitable person. And when he hears that there are wonderful people like yourselves in the White House, you see what happens. And I'm so pleased that you had a chance to share a few minutes with him today.

Earlier this month, President Trump signed a proclamation marking Black History Month. In that proclamation, it read that, **"the history of African Americans exemplifies the resilience and the spirit that continue to make our Nation great**."

And those words are true and we celebrate them with you today.

Over the past month he visited the African American History Museum, and just last week he dedicated his weekly radio address to Black History Month. The President understands, as you saw firsthand today, the importance of recognizing the African American community's amazing contributions to the life of this nation.

And that's why I wanted to come over here today on the President's behalf. And the schools represented here really have made an indelible mark for generations on the life of this nation.

It's amazing to think about it, for more than 150 years, historically black colleges and universities have educated African American leaders, often when no other opportunity was available to them.

The first school -- Cheyney University, in Pennsylvania, founded in 1837, more than 20 years before the Civil War. It and the schools that followed have furnished the type of learning that the Reverend Dr. Martin Luther King, Jr., would describe over a century later as "Intelligence plus character -- the goal of true education."

The path has not been an easy one throughout the long 150-year history for your institutions. And your students, your faculty, your professors have stood firm through a transformational time in the life of the nation and been a part of that transformation in countless ways.

You've transformed lives through education. You've helped lead our country toward a more perfect union. And just know the President and I and all the members of our administration appreciate and admire the contribution of our historically black colleges and universities. Would you just give yourselves a round of applause? It is a history to be proud of. (Applause.)

Today, with over 100 historically black colleges and universities in 19 states, the District of Columbia, and the U.S. Virgin Islands, hundreds of thousands of African American students have turned to you for quality education, including, I'm told, more than 300,000 students as we speak today. (Applause.)

Even more inspiring than that, I am told that many of those students were the first in their family to go to college. My dad was in that category and went off to college and raised each one of us kids with that finger pointed in the middle of our chest. (Laughter.)

You know what I'm talking about? I just don't ever remember a day that Dad didn't look at me and say, I don't care what you else you do with your life, but you're going to college. (Laughter.)

And those first generation college students transform families and they transform a nation. And we celebrate them and their role on your campuses even through this day. And throughout the history of your institutions when those first-time students graduated, they departed, degree in hand, prepared and determined to add their own unique brush stroke to the beautiful American tapestry and the legacy of African Americans.

And so many have in some many countless ways. They've done just that. If you think about it, nearly one in four African Americans with a bachelor's degree graduated from your schools. (Applause.)

This includes leaders in every industry in this country and in every walk of life. Forty percent of African American members of Congress -- as a former member of Congress, I'm happy to report 40 percent of African American members of Congress graduated from a historically black college and university. (Applause.)

The indisputable conclusion is that your schools have played a major role, not only in the African American community, but in the life of nation, and the life of the nation's economy.

And we really gather today to reflect on that and to celebrate that. And those gathered here from across our administration look forward to a dialogue with each one of you about how we can continue to strengthen the role that historically black colleges and universities play in the lives of families across this country and in the life of this nation. America is unquestionably stronger because of the institutions that are represented here.

And this evening, President Trump and I just wanted to express our thanks. As the President said in his recent radio address, your schools "do a fantastic job." His words. (Laughter.)

And you deserve far more credit than you get, and know that beginning today, this administration is committed to making sure that our historically black colleges and universities get the credit and the attention they deserve. (Applause.)

Our administration at the President's direction is working to find new ways to expand your impact so that more students, especially in the underserved communities in this country, have the chance at a quality education. We want to partner with you. We want to partner with you to help train the students of today to face the challenges and to lead in America tomorrow.

This also requires us to help students at an even earlier age -- make no mistake about it. Secretary DeVos is dedicated to expanding opportunities through educational choice all across this country, ensuring that whether it's a public school, a public charter school, or even a private school -- that parents on an increasing basis will have the ability to choose where their young children go to school regardless of their income and area code. And we're going to work with each one of you to make that a reality.

We're also going to be working on economic development, not only increasing educational opportunities but doing all we can to revitalize communities across this country -- large and small -- and create opportunities for students that will be joining you on your campuses.

We're committed to this mission. As you've heard the President over the course of his campaign, and now you've seen him firsthand today, this President has a passion for equality of opportunity. He has a passion for expanding opportunities and the hopes and **dreams** of every American, including those in the African American community who are not yet experiencing the full range of benefits of the **American Dream**.

So get ready for a great and energetic partnership in the days ahead. As Frederick Douglass reminds us, education is the means -- or education means the lifting up of the soul of man into the glorious light of truth. Powerful words -- "uplifting of the soul of man into the glorious light of truth." That's what your institutions have been about for now a century and a half in America.

And so I came to say thank you on behalf of the President of the United States. Thank you for all you do. Beyond the profound words that I quoted before, when I look at the role of historically black colleges and universities, I can't help but think of even more ancient words that: If you train up a child in the way they should go, then after they're old, they'll not depart from it.

The contributions of historically black colleges and universities for a century and a half in our nation's history have trained up young men and women who have gone on to lead this nation and to lead us to a more prosperous and more perfect union. And our commitment to all of you and our hope and our prayer is that we're going to partner

with you that that will be even more true; and your contribution and your influence in America will only grow in the
years ahead.

Thank you very much. God bless you for your work. And
thank you for coming today. (Applause.)

END
5:47 P.M. EST

*"the history of African Americans
exemplifies the resilience and
the spirit that continue to
make our Nation great."*

Chapter 63

28 February 2017

10:14 A.M. EST

THE VICE PRESIDENT: Good morning. Thank you for joining us. On behalf of the President of the United States, it's
my great privilege to administer the oath of office to a man
who will become the 39th Secretary of Commerce for the
United States of America, Wilbur Ross. (Applause.)

Since this department was founded in 1903, the position
of Secretary of Commerce has been filled by many distinguished Americans, and Wilbur Ross' addition to those
rolls is fitting and appropriate given his extraordinary career and the integrity and the ability that he brings to lead
the Department of Commerce.

We are also joined today by his wife, Hilary, and you could
give her a round of applause. (Applause.)

We appreciate a commitment of public service is a commitment of families. And we are grateful to both of you for
your dedication to the United States today.

Also pleased to be joined by many friends and associates,
as well as the future Deputy Secretary of Commerce, Todd
Ricketts. So thank you all for being here today.

President Trump used to say on the campaign trail that he had a three-part agenda for the American economy: Jobs, jobs, and jobs. And with Wilbur Ross as our new Secretary of Commerce, the President and I are confident that the Department of Commerce is going to take its right and leading role in fostering the growth that will create good-paying jobs for every American.

And, Wilbur, you're well-suited for this task. You established yourself as a leading American businessman in a career that spans over 40 years -- incredible number of fields and industries. You understand the American economy because you've participated in so many different parts of it with such great success. From steel to textiles, from energy to manufacturing, you have first-hand experience with the building blocks of the American economy. You've also seen for yourself the struggles that American workers can face in difficult times. And your stewardship of companies -- one after another -- have time and again saved thousands of jobs and put those companies and firms in a position to survive and thrive in the years ahead. It is a credit to your ability and to your dedication to the American worker.

Now President Trump has called on you to serve your country as Secretary of Commerce. And given your decades of experience, your record of leadership, your integrity, and your commitment to protecting America's economic future, President Trump and I have full confidence that you will succeed. And when you succeed as Secretary of Commerce, you will help America succeed to a more prosperous future.

Now on behalf of President Trump, it's my great privilege to administer to you the oath of office.

(The Oath is administered.) (Applause.)

THE VICE PRESIDENT: Ladies and gentlemen, the Secretary of Commerce, Wilbur Ross. (Applause.)

SECRETARY ROSS: Thank you, Mr. Vice President. And thanks to all of you -- friends and supporters and people from the department -- for coming here today.

I'm very gratified at the confidence that the President and the Vice President have shown in me and in the department. And I promise I'll live up to every word that I just said.

I was also very gratified last night with the vote being 72 to 29 because that suggests that perhaps finally building America up again may become a bipartisan thing rather than contentious. (Applause.)

And I hope that **Spirit** will carry over as people deal with the results of the State of the Union message tonight.

So I thank you very much. Now let's get to work. (Laughter and applause.)

END
10:20 A.M. EST

Chapter 64

28 February 2017

2:11 P.M. EST

THE PRESIDENT: Thank you all very much. I appreciate you being here. We have a number of bills that we're signing and things that we're doing today. It's a busy day. And then I guess tonight will be a rather busy night. We look forward to it.

I want to thank Majority Leader Kevin McCarthy, who has been a tremendous friend to a lot of people. He's done an amazing job. And, Kevin, I want to thank you for being here. I very much appreciate it. You had so much to do with this.

I also want to thank everyone else who's with us today. In fact, I have some names, and I'll read some of them off, because not everybody knows everybody. But we have Leader McCarthy. Representative Barbara Comstock. Lamar Smith -- thank you, Lamar, very much. I appreciate it. Joni Ernst, who's been a terrific, terrific senator. A very talented woman, and a very good military person. A very good military person. And, Deb Fischer, thank you very much. Thanks. We also have Senator Barrasso and Senator Boozman. Joni, we said hello. Deb, we said hello. Heidi Heitkamp -- thank you, Heidi. Senator Jim Inhofe. Senator Pat Roberts. Senator Dan Sullivan. Representative Bob

Gibbs. Bill Shuster. And Representative Lamar Smith. We really appreciate you being here.

Of course, we have our new SBA Director, Linda McMahon, and Secretary DeVos. (Applause.)

So we have a lot of great talent.

Today I'm signing two bills that promote women entering and leading the STEM fields -- science, technology, engineering, and math. Currently, only 1 in every 4 women who gets a STEM degree is working in a STEM job, which is not fair and it's not even smart for the people that aren't taking advantage of it. It's unacceptable that we have so many American women who have these degrees but yet are not being employed in these fields. So I think that's going to change. That's going to change very rapidly.

Protecting women with STEM degrees, and all Americans with STEM degrees is very important, but it also means you have to crack down on offshoring, because the offshoring is a tremendous problem that displaces many of our best American workers and brains -- the brain power.

So I just want to thank you all for being here. Vice President Pence always felt very, very strongly about this issue and many others. And I appreciate -- Mike, I appreciate that very much.

And I'm going to sign this right now, and I want congratulate everybody in the room. And we have to sign it today. I know we have a lot of things coming on later on, but if we don't sign this one and the next one today, we have to start the process all over again, Joni, right? (Laughter.)

So that's why we're here.

Okay, thank you very much. (Applause.)

Q   Big speech tonight?

THE PRESIDENT: We look forward to it.

Okay, I think we all know what this is. Even though somebody took my notes, it makes no difference. (Laughter.)

AIDE: It's the second bill you just read.

THE PRESIDENT: It really makes no difference. But this is the second bill that was signed, and that's the H.R. 321, the INSPIRE Women Act. It ensures that the existing NASA programs recruit women to STEM-related jobs and aerospace careers. Great news. Really the way to go. Very heavy into the whole NASA situation. So women will be a big, big part of it.

H.R. 255, the Promoting Women in Entrepreneurship Act, enables the National Science Foundation to support women inventors -- which there are many -- researchers, and scientists in bringing their discoveries to the business world, championing science and entrepreneurship, and creating new ways to improve people's lives. So important.

We need policies that help support women in the workforce, and that's really very much going to be addressed by my administration over the years, and to get more and more of these bills coming out, and address the barriers faced by female and those in STEM fields. We want American women who graduate from college with STEM degrees to be able to get STEM jobs that can support their families and help these American women to live out the **American Dream**, which they are so qualified to live out.

So again, I want to thank you all for being here. Fantastic. This is so important. Thank you all for being here.

END
2:17 P.M. EST

Chapter 65

28 February 2017

2:23 P.M. EST

THE PRESIDENT: Well, thank you, everybody. We appreciate you being here. Thank you very much. First of all, I want to congratulate Scott Pruitt, who's here someplace. Where's Scott? (Applause.)

So important. We're going to free up our country, and it's going be done in a very environmental and positive environmental way, I will tell you that, but create millions of jobs. So many jobs are delayed for so many years, and it's unfair to everybody. So I want congratulate Scott.

I want to thank everyone for being here today. We have a great group of farmers, homebuilders, and county commissioners. They're all represented. They're standing alongside of me. I'd also like to thank Jim Inhofe, who's been so terrific in so many different ways, beyond even this. So I [to] want thank Jim and also the leadership in the Senate on the issue, a friend of mine -- a great friend of mine -- John Barrasso.

The EPA's so-called "Waters of the United States" rule is one of the worst examples of federal regulation, and it has truly run amok, and is one of the rules most strongly opposed by farmers, ranchers and agricultural workers all across our land. It's prohibiting them from being allowed to do what they're supposed to be doing. It's been a disaster.

The Clean Water Act says that the EPA can regulate "navigable waters" -- meaning waters that truly affect interstate commerce. But a few years ago, the EPA decided that "navigable waters" can mean nearly every puddle or every ditch on a farmer's land, or anyplace else that they decide -- right? It was a massive power grab. The EPA's regulators were putting people out of jobs by the hundreds of thousands, and regulations and permits started treating our wonderful small farmers and small businesses as if they were a major industrial polluter. They treated them horribly. Horribly.

If you want to build a new home, for example, you have to worry about getting hit with a huge fine if you fill in as much as a puddle -- just a puddle -- on your lot. I've seen it. In fact, when it was first shown to me, I said, no, you're kidding aren't you? But they weren't kidding.

In one case in a Wyoming, a rancher was fined $37,000 a day by the EPA for digging a small watering hole for his cattle. His land. These abuses were, and are, why such incredible opposition to this rule from the hundreds of organizations took place in all 50 states. It's a horrible, horrible rule. Has sort of a nice name, but everything else is bad. (Laughter.)

I've been hearing about it for years and years. I didn't know I'd necessarily be in this position to do something about it, but we've been hearing about it for years.

With today's executive order, I'm directing the EPA to take

action, paving the way for the elimination of this very destructive and horrible rule.

So I want to thank everybody for being here. And I will sign wherever I'm supposed to sign. There we are. Thank you very much. (Applause.)

END
2:27 P.M. EST

Chapter 66

28 February 2017

2:38 P.M. EST

THE PRESIDENT: So this is Historically Black Colleges and Universities executive order. Very important to all of us. This group has been fantastic, and many of which we were with yesterday and really developed something very special. So thank you. Thank you all for being here. Thank you, Mr. Vice President, also -- Mike, for being here.

This is a very important moment, and a moment that means a great deal to me. This month has been a wonderful opportunity to celebrate African-American history, and to begin working together to create a better future for African-Americans and universities and colleges, and everything that is African-American. Today, we're taking action to help make that future happen and that future better.

Historically Black Colleges and Universities are incredibly important institutions, woven into the fabric of our history just about like no other. Church is very important, right?

Colleges and universities. Mike is my defender. (Laughter.)

Education has the power to uplift. It has the power to transform. And, perhaps most important, education has the power to create greater equality and justice in our lives.

That's why today I'm thrilled to be signing an executive order to recognize the importance of Historically Black Colleges and Universities. Very important. They have played such an important role in achieving progress for African-Americans and in our nation's march for justice. HBCUs have been really pillars of the African-American community for more than 150 years -- amazing job -- and a grand and enduring symbol of America at its absolute best. And I congratulate you all.

With this executive order, we will make HBCUs a priority in the White House -- an absolute priority. (Applause.)

A lot of people are going to be angry that they're not a priority, but that's okay. (Laughter.)

And we will pledge our support to you, your mission, and to our shared mission of bringing education and opportunity to all of our people. And so I just want to congratulate -- these are very, very special people surrounding me. You've done an amazing job. It's not easy. Nothing is easy. But you've done an amazing job. And I just want to congratulate you all, and I want to thank you on behalf of our country.

And so I'm going to sign this. This is really fantastic. (Applause.)

END
2:41 P.M. ES

Chapter 67

28 February 2017

9:09 P.M. EST

THE PRESIDENT: Thank you very much. Mr. Speaker, Mr. Vice President, members of Congress, the First Lady of the United States. (Applause.)

And citizens of America:
Tonight, as we mark the conclusion of our celebration of Black History Month, we are reminded of our nation's path towards civil rights and the work that still remains to be done. (Applause.)

Recent threats targeting Jewish community centers and vandalism of Jewish cemeteries, as well as last week's shooting in Kansas City, remind us that while we may be a nation divided on policies, we are a country that stands united in condemning hate and evil in all of its very ugly forms. (Applause.)

Each American generation passes the torch of truth, liberty and justice in an unbroken chain all the way down to the present. That torch is now in our hands. And we will use it to light up the world. I am here tonight to deliver a message of unity and strength, and it is a message deeply delivered from my heart. **A new chapter...** (Applause.)

... of American Greatness is now beginning. A new nation-al **pride** is sweeping across our nation. And a new surge of optimism is placing impossible **dreams** firmly within our grasp.

What we are witnessing today is the renewal of the **American Spirit**. Our allies will find that America is once **Again** ready to lead. (Applause.)

All the nations of the world -- friend or foe -- will find that **America is Strong, America is Proud**, and **America is Free**. In nine years, the United States will celebrate the 250th anniversary of our founding -- 250 years since the day we declared our Independence. It will be one of the great milestones in the history of the world. But what will America look like as we reach our 250th year? What kind of country will we leave for our children?

I will not allow the mistakes of recent decades past to define the course of our future. For too long, we've watched our middle class shrink as we've exported our jobs and wealth to foreign countries. We've financed and built one global project after another, but ignored the fates of our children in the inner cities of Chicago, Baltimore, Detroit, and so many other places throughout our land.

We've defended the borders of other nations while leaving our own borders wide open for anyone to cross and for drugs to pour in at a now unprecedented rate. And we've spent trillions and trillions of dollars overseas, while our infrastructure at home has so badly crumbled.

Then, in 2016, the Earth shifted beneath our feet. The rebellion started as a quiet protest, spoken by families of all colors and creeds -- families who just wanted a fair shot for their children and a fair hearing for their concerns.

But then the quiet voices became a loud chorus as thousands of citizens now spoke out together, from cities small and large, all across our country.

Finally, the chorus became an earthquake, and the people turned out by the tens of millions, and they were all united by one very simple, but crucial demand: that **America** must put its own citizens **First**. Because only then can we truly **Make America Great Again**. (Applause.)

Dying industries will come roaring back to life. Heroic veterans will get the care they so desperately need. Our military will be given the resources its brave warriors so richly deserve. Crumbling infrastructure will be replaced with new roads, bridges, tunnels, airports and railways gleaming across our very, very beautiful land. Our terrible drug epidemic will slow down and, ultimately, stop. And our neglected inner cities will see a **rebirth** of hope, safety and opportunity. Above all else, we will keep our **promises** to the American people. (Applause.)

It's been a little over a month since my inauguration, and I want to take this moment to update the nation on the progress I've made in keeping those **promises**.

Since my election, Ford, Fiat-Chrysler, General Motors, Sprint, Softbank, Lockheed, Intel, Walmart and many others have announced that they will invest billions and billions of dollars in the United States, and will create tens of thousands of new American jobs. (Applause.)

The stock market has gained almost $3 trillion in value since the election on November 8th, a record. We've saved taxpayers hundreds of millions of dollars by bringing down the price of a fantastic -- and it is a fantastic -- new F-35 jet fighter, and we'll be saving billions more on contracts all across our government. We have placed a hiring freeze on non-military and non-essential federal workers.

We have begun to drain the swamp of government corruption by imposing a five-year ban on lobbying by executive branch officials and a lifetime ban -- (applause) -- thank you -- and a lifetime ban on becoming lobbyists for a foreign government.

We have undertaken a historic effort to massively reduce job-crushing regulations, creating a deregulation task force inside of every government agency. (Applause.)

And we're imposing a new rule which mandates that for every one new regulation, two old regulations must be eliminated. (Applause.)

We're going to stop the regulations that threaten the future and livelihood of our great coal miners. (Applause.)

We have cleared the way for the construction of the Keystone and Dakota Access Pipelines. (Applause.)

Thereby creating tens of thousands of jobs. And I've issued a new directive that new American pipelines be made with American steel. (Applause.)

We have withdrawn the United States from the job-killing Trans-Pacific Partnership. (Applause.)

And with the help of Prime Minister Justin Trudeau, we have formed a council with our neighbors in Canada to help ensure that women entrepreneurs have access to the networks, markets and capital they need to start a business and live out their financial **dreams**. (Applause.)

To protect our citizens, I have directed the Department of Justice to form a Task Force on Reducing Violent Crime. I have further ordered the Departments of Homeland Security and Justice, along with the Department of State and the Director of National Intelligence, to coordinate an aggressive strategy to dismantle the criminal cartels that have spread all across our nation. (Applause.)

We will stop the drugs from pouring into our country and poisoning our youth, and we will expand treatment for those who have become so badly addicted. (Applause.)

At the same time, my administration has answered the pleas of the American people for immigration enforcement and border security. (Applause.)

By finally enforcing our immigration laws, we will raise wages, help the unemployed, save billions and billions of dollars, and make our communities safer for everyone. (Applause.)

We want all Americans to succeed, but that can't happen in an environment of lawless chaos. We must restore integrity and the rule of law at our borders. (Applause.)

For that reason, we will soon begin the construction of a great, great wall along our southern border. (Applause.)

As we speak tonight, we are removing gang members, drug dealers, and criminals that threaten our communities and prey on our very innocent citizens. Bad ones are going out as I speak, and as I **promised** throughout the campaign. To any in Congress who do not believe we should enforce our laws, I would ask you this one question: What would you say to the American family that loses their jobs, their income, or their loved one because America refused to uphold its laws and defend its borders? (Applause.)

Our obligation is to serve, protect, and defend the citizens of the United States. We are also taking strong measures to protect our nation from radical Islamic terrorism. (Applause.)

According to data provided by the Department of Justice, the vast majority of individuals convicted of terrorism and terrorism-related offenses since 9/11 came here from outside of our country. We have seen the attacks at home -- from Boston to San Bernardino to the Pentagon, and, yes, even the World Trade Center.

We have seen the attacks in France, in Belgium, in Germany, and all over the world. It is not compassionate, but reckless to allow uncontrolled entry from places where proper vetting cannot occur. (Applause.)

Those given the high honor of admission to the United States should support this country and love its people and its values. We cannot allow a beachhead of terrorism to form inside America. We cannot allow our nation to become a sanctuary for extremists. (Applause.)

That is why my administration has been working on improved vetting procedures, and we will shortly take new steps to keep our nation **safe** and to keep out those out who will do us harm. (Applause.)

As promised, I directed the Department of Defense to develop a plan to demolish and destroy ISIS -- a network of lawless savages that have slaughtered Muslims and Christians, and men, and women, and children of all faiths and all beliefs. We will work with our allies, including our friends and allies in the Muslim world, to extinguish this vile enemy from our planet. (Applause.)

I have also imposed new sanctions on entities and individuals who support Iran's ballistic missile program, and reaffirmed our unbreakable alliance with the State of Israel. (Applause.)

Finally, I have kept my **promise** to appoint a justice to the United States Supreme Court, from my list of 20 judges, who will defend our Constitution. (Applause.)

I am greatly honored to have Maureen Scalia with us in the gallery tonight. (Applause.)

Thank you, Maureen. Her late, great husband, Antonin Scalia, will forever be a symbol of American justice. To fill his seat, we have chosen Judge Neil Gorsuch, a man of incredible skill and deep devotion to the law. He was confirmed unanimously by the Court of Appeals, and I am asking the Senate to swiftly approve his nomination. (Applause.)

Tonight, as I outline the next steps we must take as a country, we must honestly acknowledge the circumstances we inherited. Ninety-four million Americans are out of the labor force. Over 43 million people are now living in poverty, and over 43 million Americans are on food stamps. More than one in five people in their prime working years are not working. We have the worst financial recovery in 65 years. In the last eight years, the past administration has put on more new debt than nearly all of the other Presidents combined.

We've lost more than one-fourth of our manufacturing jobs since NAFTA was approved, and we've lost 60,000 factories since China joined the World Trade Organization in 2001. Our trade deficit in goods with the world last year was nearly $800 billion dollars. And overseas we have inherited a series of tragic foreign policy disasters.

Solving these and so many other pressing problems will require us to work past the differences of party. It will require us to tap into the **American Spirit** that has overcome every challenge throughout our long and storied history. But to accomplish our goals at home and abroad, we must restart the engine of the American economy -- making it easier for companies to do business in the United States, and much, much harder for companies to leave our country. (Applause.)

Right now, American companies are taxed at one of the highest rates anywhere in the world. My economic team is developing historic tax reform that will reduce the tax rate on our companies so they can compete and thrive anywhere and with anyone. (Applause.)

It will be a BIG, BIG CUT.

At the same time, we will provide massive tax relief for the middle class. We must create a level playing field for American companies and our workers. We have to do it. (Applause.)

Currently, when we ship products out of America, many

other countries make us pay very high tariffs and taxes. But when foreign companies ship their products into America, we charge them nothing, or almost nothing.

I just met with officials and workers from a great American company, Harley-Davidson. In fact, they proudly displayed five of their magnificent motorcycles, made in the USA, on the front lawn of the White House. (Laughter and applause.)

And they wanted me to ride one and I said, "No, thank you." (Laughter.)

At our meeting, I asked them, how are you doing, how is business? They said that it's good. I asked them further, how are you doing with other countries, mainly international sales? They told me -- without even complaining, because they have been so mistreated for so long that they've become used to it -- that it's very hard to do business with other countries because they tax our goods at such a high rate. They said that in the case of another country, they taxed their motorcycles at 100 percent. They weren't even asking for a change. But I am. (Applause.)

I believe strongly in free trade but it also has to be fair trade. It's been a long time since we had fair trade. The first Republican President, Abraham Lincoln, warned that the "abandonment of the protective policy by the American government... will produce want and ruin among our people." Lincoln was right -- and it's time we heeded his advice and his words. (Applause.)

I am not going to let America and its great companies and workers be taken advantage of us any longer. They have taken advantage of our country. No longer. (Applause.)

I am going to bring back millions of jobs. Protecting our workers also means reforming our system of legal immigration. (Applause.)

The current, outdated system depresses wages for our poorest workers, and puts great pressure on taxpayers. Nations around the world, like Canada, Australia and many others, have a merit-based immigration system. (Applause.)

It's a basic principle that those seeking to enter a country ought to be able to support themselves financially. Yet, in America, we do not enforce this rule, straining the very public resources that our poorest citizens rely upon. According to the National Academy of Sciences, our current immigration system costs American taxpayers many billions of dollars a year.

Switching away from this current system of lower-skilled immigration, and instead adopting a merit-based system, we will have so many more benefits. It will save countless dollars, raise workers' wages, and help struggling families -- including immigrant families -- enter the middle class. And they will do it quickly, and they will be very, very happy, indeed. (Applause.)

I believe that real and positive immigration reform is possible, as long as we focus on the following goals: To improve jobs and wages for Americans; to strengthen our nation's security; and to restore respect for our laws. If we are guided by the wellbeing of American citizens, then I believe Republicans and Democrats can work together to achieve an outcome that has eluded our country for decades. (Applause.)

Another Republican President, Dwight D. Eisenhower, initiated the last truly great national infrastructure program -- the building of the Interstate Highway System. The time has come for a new program of national rebuilding. (Applause.)

America has spent approximately $6 trillion in the Middle East -- all the while our infrastructure at home is crumbling. With this $6 trillion, we could have rebuilt our country twice, and maybe even three times if we had people who had the ability to negotiate. (Applause.)

To launch our national rebuilding, I will be asking Congress to approve legislation that produces a $1 trillion investment in infrastructure of the United States -- financed through both public and private capital -- creating millions of new jobs. (Applause.)

This effort will be guided by two core principles: **Buy American and Hire American**. (Applause.)

Tonight, I am also calling on this Congress to repeal and replace Obamacare -- (applause) -- with reforms that expand choice, increase access, lower costs, and, at the same time, provide better healthcare. (Applause.)

Mandating every American to buy government-approved health insurance was never the right solution for our country. (Applause.)

The way to make health insurance available to everyone is to lower the cost of health insurance, and that is what we are going do. (Applause.)

Obamacare premiums nationwide have increased by double and triple digits. As an example, Arizona went up 116 percent last year alone. Governor Matt Bevin of Kentucky just said Obamacare is failing in his state -- the state of Kentucky -- and it's unsustainable and collapsing.

One-third of counties have only one insurer, and they are losing them fast. They are losing them so fast. They are leaving, and many Americans have no choice at all. There's no choice left. Remember when you were told that you could keep your doctor and keep your plan? We now know that all of those promises have been totally broken. Obamacare is collapsing, and we must act decisively to protect all Americans. (Applause.)

Action is not a choice; it is a necessity. So I am calling on all Democrats and Republicans in Congress to work with us to save Americans from this imploding Obamacare disaster. (Applause.)

Here are the principles that should guide the Congress as we move to create a better healthcare system for all Americans:

First, we should ensure that Americans with pre-existing conditions have access to coverage, and that we have a stable transition for Americans currently enrolled in the healthcare exchanges. (Applause.)

Secondly, we should help Americans purchase their own coverage through the use of tax credits and expanded Health Savings Accounts -- but it must be the plan they want, not the plan forced on them by our government. (Applause.)

Thirdly, we should give our great state governors the

resources and flexibility they need with Medicaid to make sure no one is left out. (Applause.)

Fourth, we should implement legal reforms that protect patients and doctors from unnecessary costs that drive up the price of insurance, and work to bring down the artificially high price of drugs, and bring them down immediately. (Applause.)

And finally, the time has come to give Americans the freedom to purchase health insurance across state lines -- (applause) -- which will create a truly competitive national marketplace that will bring costs way down and provide far better care. So important.

Everything that is broken in our country can be fixed. Every problem can be solved. And every hurting family can find healing and hope.

Our citizens deserve this, and so much more -- so why not join forces and finally get the job done, and get it done right? (Applause.)

On this and so many other things, Democrats and Republicans should get together and unite for the good of our country and for the good of the American people. (Applause.)

My administration wants to work with members of both parties to make childcare accessible and affordable, to help ensure new parents that they have paid family leave -- (applause) -- to invest in women's health, and to promote clean air and clean water, and to rebuild our military and our infrastructure. (Applause.)

True love for our people requires us to find common ground, to advance the common good, and to cooperate on behalf of every American child who deserves a much brighter future.

An incredible young woman is with us this evening, who should serve as an inspiration to us all. Today is Rare Disease Day, and joining us in the gallery is a rare disease survivor, Megan Crowley. (Applause.)

Megan was diagnosed with Pompe disease, a rare and serious illness, when she was 15 months old. She was not expected to live past five. On receiving this news, Megan's dad, John, fought with everything he had to save the life of his precious child. He founded a company to look for a cure, and helped develop the drug that saved Megan's life. Today she is 20 years old and a sophomore at Notre Dame. (Applause.)

Megan's story is about the unbounded power of a father's love for a daughter. But our slow and burdensome ap- proval process at the Food and Drug Administration keeps too many advances, like the one that saved Megan's life, from reaching those in need. If we slash the restraints, not just at the FDA but across our government, then we will be blessed with far more miracles just like Megan. (Ap- plause.)

In fact, our children will grow up in a nation of miracles. But to achieve this future, we must enrich the mind and the souls of every American child. Education is the civil rights issue of our time. (Applause.)

I am calling upon members of both parties to pass an education bill that funds school choice for disadvantaged youth, including millions of African American and Latino children. (Applause.)

These families should be free to choose the public, private, charter, magnet, religious, or home school that is right for them. (Applause.)

Joining us tonight in the gallery is a remarkable woman, Denisha Merriweather. As a young girl, Denisha struggled in school and failed third grade twice. But then she was able to enroll in a private center for learning -- a great learning center -- with the help of a tax credit and a scholarship program.

Today, she is the first in her family to graduate, not just from high school, but from college. Later this year she will get her master's degree in social work. We want all children to be able to break the cycle of poverty just like Denisha. (Applause.)

But to break the cycle of poverty, we must also break the cycle of violence. The murder rate in 2015 experienced its largest single-year increase in nearly half a century. In Chicago, more than 4,000 people were shot last year alone, and the murder rate so far this year has been even higher. This is not acceptable in our society. (Applause.)

Every American child should be able to grow up in a **safe** community, to attend a great school, and to have access to a high-paying job. (Applause.)

But to create this future, we must work with, not against -- not against -- the men and women of law enforcement. (Applause.)

We must build bridges of cooperation and trust -- not drive the wedge of disunity and, really, it's what it is, division. It's pure, unadulterated division. We have to unify. Police and sheriffs are members of our community. They're friends and neighbors, they're mothers and fathers, sons and daughters -- and they leave behind loved ones every day who worry about whether or not they'll come home **safe** and sound. We must support the incredible men and women of law enforcement. (Applause.)

And we must support the victims of crime. I have ordered the Department of Homeland Security to create an office to serve American victims. The office is called VOICE -- Victims of Immigration Crime Engagement. We are providing a voice to those who have been ignored by our media and silenced by special interests. (Applause.)

Joining us in the audience tonight are four very brave Americans whose government failed them. Their names are Jamiel Shaw, Susan Oliver, Jenna Oliver, and Jessica Davis.

Jamiel's 17-year-old son was viciously murdered by an illegal immigrant gang member who had just been released from prison. Jamiel Shaw, Jr. was an incredible young man, with unlimited potential who was getting ready to go to college where he would have excelled as a great college quarterback. But he never got the chance. His father, who is in the audience tonight, has become a very good friend of mine. Jamiel, thank you. Thank you. (Applause.)

Also with us are Susan Oliver and Jessica Davis. Their husbands, Deputy Sheriff Danny Oliver and Detective Michael Davis, were slain in the line of duty in California. They were pillars of their community. These brave men were viciously gunned down by an illegal immigrant with a criminal record and two prior deportations. Should have never been in our country.

Sitting with Susan is her daughter, Jenna. Jenna, I want you to know that your father was a hero, and that tonight you have the love of an entire country supporting you and praying for you. (Applause.)

To Jamiel, Jenna, Susan and Jessica, I want you to know that we will never stop fighting for justice. Your loved ones will never, ever be forgotten. We will always honor their memory. (Applause.)

Finally, to keep **America Safe**, we must provide the men and women of the United States military with the tools they need to prevent war -- if they must -- they have to fight and they only have to win. (Applause.)

I am sending Congress a budget that rebuilds the military, eliminates the defense sequester -- (applause) -- and calls for one of the largest increases in national defense spending in American history. My budget will also increase funding for our veterans. Our veterans have delivered for this nation, and now we must deliver for them. (Applause.)

The challenges we face as a nation are great, but our people are even greater. And none are greater or braver than those who fight for America in uniform. (Applause.)

We are blessed to be joined tonight by Carryn Owens, the widow of a U.S. Navy Special Operator, Senior Chief William "Ryan" Owens. Ryan died as he lived: a warrior and a hero, battling against terrorism and securing our nation. (Applause.)

I just spoke to our great General Mattis, just now, who reconfirmed that -- and I quote -- "Ryan was a part of a highly successful raid that generated large amounts of vital intelligence that will lead to many more victories in the future against our enemies." Ryan's legacy is etched into eternity. Thank you. (Applause.)

And Ryan is looking down, right now -- you know that -- and he is very happy because I think he just broke a record. (Laughter and applause.)

For as the Bible teaches us, "There is no greater act of love than to lay down one's life for one's friends." Ryan laid down his life for his friends, for his country, and for our freedom. And we will never forget Ryan. (Applause.)

To those allies who wonder what kind of a friend America will be, look no further than the heroes who wear our uniform. Our foreign policy calls for a direct, robust and meaningful engagement with the world. It is American leadership based on vital security interests that we share with our allies all across the globe.

We strongly support NATO, an alliance forged through the bonds of two world wars that dethroned fascism, and a Cold War, and defeated communism. (Applause.)

But our partners must meet their financial obligations. And now, based on our very strong and frank discussions, they are beginning to do just that. In fact, I can tell you, the money is pouring in. Very nice. (Applause.)

We expect our partners -- whether in NATO, the Middle East, or in the Pacific -- to take a direct and meaningful role in both strategic and military operations, and pay their fair share of the cost. Have to do that.

We will respect historic institutions, but we will respect the foreign rights of all nations, and they have to respect our rights as a nation also. (Applause.)

Free nations are the best vehicle for expressing the will of the people, and America respects the right of all nations to chart their own path. My job is not to represent the world. My job is to represent the United States of America. (Applause.)

But we know that America is better off when there is less conflict, not more. We must learn from the mistakes of the past. We have seen the war and the destruction that have ravaged and raged throughout the world -- all across the world. The only long-term solution for these humanitarian disasters, in many cases, is to create the conditions where displaced persons can safely return home and begin the long, long process of rebuilding. (Applause.)

America is willing to find new friends, and to forge new partnerships, where shared interests align. We want harmony and stability, not war and conflict. We want peace, wherever peace can be found.

America is friends today with former enemies. Some of our closest allies, decades ago, fought on the opposite side of these terrible, terrible wars. This history should give us all faith in the possibilities for a better world. Hopefully, the 250th year for America will see a world that is more peaceful, more just, and more free.

On our 100th anniversary, in 1876, citizens from across our nation came to Philadelphia to celebrate America's centennial. At that celebration, the country's builders and artists and inventors showed off their wonderful creations. Alexander Graham Bell displayed his telephone for the first time. Remington unveiled the first typewriter. An early attempt was made at electric light. Thomas Edison showed an automatic telegraph and an electric pen. Imagine the wonders our country could know in America's 250th year. (Applause.)

Think of the marvels we can achieve if we simply set free the **dreams** of our people. Cures to the illnesses that have always plagued us are not too much to hope. American footprints on distant worlds are not too big a **dream**. Millions lifted from welfare to work is not too much to expect. And streets where mothers are **safe** from fear, schools where children learn in peace, and jobs where Americans prosper and grow are not too much to ask. (Applause.)

When we have all of this, we will have **Made America Greate**r than ever before -- for all Americans. This is our **vision**. This is our **mission**. But we can only get there together. We are one people, with one **destiny**. We all bleed the same blood. We all salute the same great American flag. And we all are made by the same God. (Applause.)

When we fulfil this vision, when we celebrate our 250 years of glorious freedom, we will look back on tonight as when this **new chapter** of **American Greatness** began. The time for small thinking is over.

The time for trivial fights is behind us. We just need the courage to share the **dreams** that fill our hearts, the bravery to express the hopes that stir our souls, and the confidence to turn those hopes and those **dreams** into action.

From now on, America will be empowered by our aspirations, not burdened by our fears; inspired by the future, not bound by the failures of the past; and guided by our vision, not blinded by our doubts.

I am asking all citizens to embrace this **renewal** of the **American Spirit**.

I am asking all members of Congress to join me in **Dreaming Big, and Bold**, and daring things for our country.

I am asking everyone watching tonight to seize this moment. Believe in yourselves, believe in your future, and believe, once more, in America.

Thank you, God bless you, and God bless the United States. (Applause.)

END
10:09 P.M. EST

"This effort will be guided by
two core principles:
buy American and hire American."

Chapter 68

02 March 2017

2:28 P.M. EST

THE PRESIDENT: Thank you. Thank you very much. What an honor. They just gave me this beautiful jacket. They said, here, Mr. President, please take this home. I said, let me wear it. (Laughter.)

And then they gave me the beautiful hat, and I said, you know, maybe I'll do that. We have a great "**Make America Great Again**" hat, but I said, this is a special day, we're wearing this. Right? (Applause.)

I have no idea how it looks, but I think it looks good. It's a great-looking hat -- just like this is a great-looking ship.

Thank you. I'm privileged to stand here today with the incredible men and women of the United States Navy. (Applause.)

American sailors are the best warfighting sailors anywhere in the world. And it's not even close. And, Susan, I am so glad you could be with us. I know how hard you work -- 17 visits. And she wanted things done right, I will tell you. They told me she wanted this one done right, in honor of both of her parents, who were great, great people. And we wanted to introduce this beautiful vessel to the American people. And I wanted to be here, I wanted to be with you. So, Susan, and to your family -- unbelievable job. Unbelievable. (Applause.)

The soon-to-be commissioned Gerald R. Ford USS -- what a place. It really feels like a place. You stand on that deck, and you feel like you're standing on a very big piece of land. But this is better than land. It will not only be a great symbol of American strength, but a great legacy for your father, and our former President, Gerald Ford.

President Ford was a Navy man. By the way, he was also a great athlete, for those of you that didn't know. He saw action in the South Pacific during World War II. He served this country with honor -- in the military, in Congress, and in the White House. The proud dignity of this ship is a fitting tribute to Gerald Ford, the man and the President.

Congratulations to all of the men and women who helped build it. This is American craftsmanship at its biggest, at its best, at its finest. American workers are the greatest anywhere in the world. This warship, and all who serve on it, should be a source of shared pride for our nation. We are joined toda[y] -- (applause) -- better believe it, right? Better believe it. (Applause.)

Better believe it. And, by the way, we're going to soon have more coming. We'll have more coming. (Applause.)

We are joined today by General Mattis, now Secretary Matti -- (applause) -- where is he? -- who will be charged with overseeing this great rebuilding of our military might. We will give the men and women of America's armed services the resources you need to keep us **safe**. We will have the finest equipment in the world

-- planes, ships and everything else. We are going to have, very soon, the finest equipment in the world. (Applause.)

We will give our military the tools you need to prevent war and, if required, to fight war and only do one thing -- you know what that is? Win! Win! (Applause.)

We're going to start winning **Again**.

Admiral John Richardson, Chief of Naval Operations, is with us today as well -- great gentleman. Admiral, we're going to ensure our Navy has the resources, personnel training and equipment -- the kind of equipment that you need. So, congratulations, Admiral. And a lot more is coming. (Applause.)

Let me congratulate Captain Richard McCormack, Commanding Officer of the Gerald R. Ford. This ship will make an extraordinary addition to the fleet like no other -- like no other. Anywhere in the world there's nothing like this. It represents the future of naval aviation.

I have no greater privilege than to serve as your Commander-in-Chief and the Commander-in-Chief of the men and women of the United States military. Great people. (Applause.)

Great, great people.

I salute you, and I salute our sailors. I will always support you and your mission. I will never, ever let you down. And I also have to recognize Mike Petters, President and CEO of Huntington Ingalls Industries along with Matt Mulherin, President of Newport News Shipbuilding. (Applause.)

They won't let you down either. (Applause.)

They're not going to let you down either. (Applause.)

To those who serve our nation in uniform and to those who build the instruments of our defense, I thank you on behalf of our nation.

AUDIENCE MEMBER: U-S-A!

THE PRESIDENT: (Laughter.)

I agree, I agree. (Laughter.)

Our carriers are the centerpiece of American military might overseas. We are standing today on 4.5 acres of combat power and sovereign U.S. territory, the likes of which there is nothing to compete. There is no competition to this ship. It is a monument to American might that will provide the strength necessary to ensure peace. This ship will carry 4,500 personnel and 70 aircraft, and will be a vital component of our defense. This carrier and the new ships in the Ford class will expand the ability of our nation to carry out vital missions on the oceans to project American power in distant lands. Hopefully, it's power we don't have to use, but if we do, they're in big, big trouble. (Applause.)

This great aircraft carrier provides essential capabilities to keep us safe from terrorism and take the fight to the enemy for many years in the future. The great Admiral Nimitz, who commanded the U.S. Pacific fleet through the Second World War, once said, "It is the function of the Navy to carry the war to the enemy so that we'll not be fought on U.S. soil." True. (Applause.)

And it was under Admiral Nimitz's command 75 years ago this June that the Navy did just that at the Battle of Midway. You've all known about the Battle of Midway, where the sailors of the U.S. Navy fought with the bravery that will be remembered throughout the ages. Storied bravery throughout the ages.

The backbone of the American fleet at Midway was three beautiful aircraft carriers: the Yorktown, the Enterprise and the Hornet. All three were built with American hands right here at the Newport News Shipyard. (Applause.)

At Midway, America was greatly outnumbered by, I mean, a lot -- (laughter) -- and its fleet badly damaged. But the heroic deeds changed the course of history. Many brave Americans died that day, and, through their sacrifice, they turned the tide of the Pacific War. It was a tough tide, it was a big tide, it was a vicious tide, and they turned it.

Countless other Americans in that war, some of them parents and grandparents to people in this room today, came home thanks to their very heroic deeds. The sailors at Midway are part of a long line of American heroes, an unbroken chain of patriots from each generation to the next, who rose to defend our flag and our freedom.

That legacy continues today as American warriors protect our people from the threat of terrorism. On Tuesday, in my address to a joint session of Congress, I asked Congress to eliminate the defense sequester and to support my request for a great rebuilding of the United States military and the United States Navy. (Applause.)

After years of endless budget cuts that have impaired our defenses, I am calling for one of the largest defense-spending increases in history. And by eliminating the sequester and the uncertainty it creates, we will make it easier for the Navy to plan for the future and thus to control costs and get the best deals for the taxpayer, which, of course, is very important, right? Got to get a good deal. If we don't make a good deal, we're not doing our job.

The same boat for less money. The same ship for less money. The same airplanes for less money. That's what we're doing. That's what we're doing. Means we're going to get more of them, and we can use them.

Our military requires sustained, stable funding to meet the growing needs placed on our defense. Right now, our aging frontline strike and strike-fighters -- the whole aircraft; many, many aircraft -- are often more likely to be downed for maintenance than they are to be up in the sky.

Our Navy is now the smallest it's been since, believe it or not, World War I. Don't worry, it's going to soon be the largest it's been. Don't worry. (Applause.)

Think of that. Think of that.

In these troubled times, our Navy is the smallest it's been since World War I. That's a long time ago. In fact, I just spoke with Navy and industry leaders and have discussed my plans to undertake a major expansion of our entire Navy fleet, including having the 12-carrier Navy we need. (Applause.)

We also need more aircraft, modernized capabilities, and greater force levels. Additionally, we must vastly improve our cyber capabilities. This great rebuilding effort will create many jobs in Virginia, and all across America, and it will also spur new technology and new innovation.

America has always been the country that boldly leads the world into the future, and my budget will ensure we do so and continue to do exactly that. American ships will sail the seas. American planes will soar the skies. American workers will build our fleets. (Applause.)

And America's military will ensure that even though the darkest nights and throughout, a bright and glowing sun will always shine on our nation and on our people. Our Navy is great. Our Navy is great. Our people are great. Great. (Applause.)

Our Republic will meet any challenge, defeat any danger, face any threat, and always seek true and lasting peace.

May God bless our military. May God bless our Navy. May God bless the wonderful Gerald Ford family. And may God continue to bless the United States of America. Thank you very much. (Applause.)

END
2:42 P.M. EST

Chapter 69

PRESBYTERIAN WEILL CORNELL MEDICAL CENTER
NEW YORK

02 March 2017

[The First Lady interacts with the staff and patients.]

THE FIRST LADY: So you do know what is today? Do you know what is today? It is *Read Across America Day*. So it's a reading day.

And I came here today to encourage everyone to read and to just think about the books and what you want to achieve in life. And just to extend your horizon and to think very very outside of the box.

So, I have brought some books today so, all the patients can, all the kids can read it.

It's Dr Seuss. It is one of my favorite authors. And this is one of my favorite books and I will read it today.

Do you know this book?

Do you know it – *Oh, The Places You'll Go!* Yes?

So, this is one from my library.

[FLOTUS reads *Oh, The Places You'll Go!*]

So, I encourage you to read a lot. And just to get educated. And, there are beautiful books and beautiful stories, in the ones that I brought.

And I hope you are all feeling well. I pray for you.

You are in my thoughts. And just get betters very fast. Okay.

And Happy Reading Day.

Nice to see you all. Thank you. Thank you.

[The First Lady, takes photographs with patients and parents.]

THE FIRST LADY: Stay well.

END

[NOTE: For more information, contact www.readacrossamerica.org]

Chapter 70

**REMARKS BY THE VICE PRESIDENT ON PRESIDENT TRUMP'S
VISION FOR THE FUTURE
BLAIN'S FARM AND FLEET DISTRIBUTION CENTER
JANESVILLE, WISCONSIN**

03 March 2017

12:35 P.M. CST

THE VICE PRESIDENT: Hello, Wisconsin!

AUDIENCE: Hello!

THE VICE PRESIDENT: Thank you so much. Thank you to my friend, Speaker Paul Ryan, for your wonderful introduction. It is great to be in Janesville, the home of the Speaker of the House of the United States of America. (Applause.)

Janesville has almost taken on an epic category in America because what works in Janesville will work for the American people. And I'm just delighted to be with all of you today. And I'm deeply humbled by the esteem expressed by my friend and your neighbor, Paul Ryan. And let me just assure you, people all across America are grateful to the people of Janesville for continuing to send Speaker Paul Ryan to Washington, D.C. So thank you for that. (Applause.)

I also understand that your mom, Betty, is here. Where is mom at? Can mom take a bow? Would you mind standing up? Paul Ryan's mom, everybody. This is a big deal. Turn around and wave at the media. (Applause.)

Wonderful to see you and thank you for being with us today.

The President and I are grateful for your son's principled leadership in the House of Representatives. It seems like just yesterday, 16 years ago, when I arrived in Washington, D.C. -- just a couple of years after Paul arrived there. We were both young and dashing congressmen. (Laughter.)

And one of us changed -- (laughter) -- and one of us looks exactly like he did the day you sent him.

But I'm deeply humbled to call your congressmen and our Speaker my friend. And I know for a fact that, Paul, your partnership with this administration is going to benefit the American people for generations to come, and we're grateful. (Applause.)

Would you mind just giving him one of those standing ovations that you gave out to a few of us? He sure does deserve it. (Applause.)

Also, it's really great to be back in Wisconsin. Thanks to all of you, your hard work, your support and your prayers, Wisconsin voted to make Donald Trump the 45th President of the United States of America, and he and I couldn't be more grateful. (Applause.)

It was quite a campaign. And it's already been quite an administration too, hasn't it? (Laughter.)

How many of you watched the President's address to the Congress on Tuesday night, show of hands. How about that? What you saw three nights ago is literally what I see every day -- the boundless optimism, the energy and unshakeable faith in the American people and the ability of the American people to **Make America Great Again**. That's what you saw, and that's what inspired the nation. (Applause.)

It's deeply humbling for me to serve as Vice President of the United States. I'm just a small-town guy from southern Indiana. My grandfather actually immigrated to this country, came over on a boat from Ireland, went through Ellis Island and drove a bus in Chicago for 40 years. I was actually named after my grandfather, Richard Michael Cawley. That's who Michael Richard Pence got his name from. I mean, I can't imagine what my grandfather is thinking about looking down from glory, except that he's very surprised about his grandson. (Laughter.)

But also that he was right. He was right about America. Because anybody can be anybody in "the land of the free and the home of the brave." And it's a joy to be with you today.

And it's a joy for me to serve as Vice President in this country because America has a President with broad shoulders and a big heart. And speaking of which, on behalf of the President of the United States, let me say thank you, Wisconsin, for your support for our new Commander-in-Chief and our new President, Donald Trump. (Applause.)

It was hardworking Americans like all of you who were some of our biggest supporters. Communities just like Janesville were really the wellspring of support for President Donald Trump in this campaign. And on his behalf, I want to thank you for that support, and thank you for being here today. It's a privilege to be joined by a couple other people I want to mention before I get to the body of my remarks.

I hope you can sense the caliber, the character, the experience, and the extraordinary confidence that our new
secretary of Health and Human Services brings to this
task. Dr. Tom Price, President Trump and I and people
across this country are grateful that you have stood up to
fill this important role in the life of our nation at such a
time as this. Would you thank him again? (Applause.)

And I'm also honored to be joined today by another great,
dedicated public servant. Senator Ron Johnson, thank you
for being here, thank you for your great leadership, and
congratulations. (Applause.)

Congratulations on the renewal of your six-year contract
here in Wisconsin. We couldn't be more pleased.
But I also want to thank all the business leaders who are
with us today, including and maybe most especially, our
host, Jane Blain Gilbertson, and the Blain's Farm and Fleet
team. What an awesome company. What an awesome
leader. What a great American success story. (Applause.)

Jane got together all these great people from here in
Janesville, and we did some listening today, didn't we? As
Paul said, we listened to the local farmers, and builders,
and job creators. I really enjoyed our discussion, and I appreciate the candid feedback that you shared with us that
we'll carry back to Washington, D.C.

But last but not least, let me just say thanks -- thanks to all
of you here who are part of this incredible Farm and Fleet
team. The employees and the families that came out today -- you are the backbone of our economy, of our country, of Janesville, and the President, the Speaker, and all

of us are grateful for your character, your work ethic, and all you do to make this a great place to live, and to work, and to raise a family. Give yourselves a round of applause, folks. (Applause.)

But I'm grateful to be here to talk about family business. The President and I are going to continue to work tirelessly on behalf of small businesses across this country because I grew up in a small-business family, in a small-business town. My dad was in the gas station business. I worked at a gas station as a gas station attendant -- had my name on my shirt, right. Little blue short-sleeve shirt, when I was only fourteen years of age, and used to -- for those of you that are a little bit younger, a gas station attendant -- (laughter) -- if you could imagine, if you pulled into a gas station and someone came running toward your car, and filled it up, and washed the windshield, and checked the tires, and didn't charge you any more money for it. That was where I grew up in a small business.

And as the world knows, the President grew up in a family business too. I mean, he and I both know the sacrifices that are required for a small family business in communities like where I grew up, Queens where he grew up and in -- and right here in Janesville -- long hours, hard work. And we both know the fundamental truth of our economy: When small business is strong, America is strong, and we're going fight every day for small business America. (Applause.)

President Trump and I want you to become stronger than ever, and I'll tell you what right now. President Donald Trump is the best friend Wisconsin businesses will ever have. (Applause.)

You might have gotten that impression Tuesday night, just a couple days ago. He actually talked about an employer up here. I don't know if you heard about Harley-Davidson -- (laughter) -- here in Wisconsin. The President actually hosted Harley-Davidson at the White House. It was an honor for me to join him. And you saw him talk about that in his speech to the Congress. And companies like Blain's Farm and Fleet are the engines of the economy, Harley-Davidson, and as President Trump said, whether it's going to be to kick start that engine or turn the key of that engine, we're going to restart the engine of the American economy and create jobs and prosperity and growth like never before. I **promise** you that. (Applause.)

In fact, exactly what he's doing -- it's, in fact, already happening. On day one, he went right to work on doing job-destroying policies and executive orders of the -- eight years. After years of delays, for instance, President Trump authorized the construction of the Keystone and Dako- ta pipelines, creating thousands of American jobs and strengthening our energy infrastructure. (Applause.)

He signed legislation, thanks to the Congress and Speaker Ryan and Senator Johnson, he signed legislation already to roll back reams of red tape and he's instructed every agency in Washington, D.C., to find two regulations to get rid of before they issue any new regulations on businesses and entrepreneurs in America. (Applause.)

He's taken decisive action to end illegal immigration once and for all to strengthen our borders and uphold the laws of the United States of America. (Applause.)

And businesses around America are already reacting and responding to President Trump's call to **Buy American and**

Hire American, and they're doing that with optimism and investment all across the country. Literally from coast to coast, and especially here in the Midwest, companies are announcing they're keeping jobs and creating new ones -- tens of thousands of jobs literally since Election Day. It's not just the stock market that's taken a positive leap forward, but companies like Ford Motor Company, just next door in Michigan, recently announced that they were not going to do a plant in Mexico and, instead, they were going to expand a plant in Michigan. And they called it a "vote of confidence" in President Donald Trump and his vision for America. And other businesses are joining them. (Applause.)

I've got to tell you, this administration has the biggest, boldest and best agenda this country has ever seen, and we're going to pass it with the support of Speaker Ryan and our great leadership in the House and in the Senate, from top to bottom. And let me make you a **promise**: The Obamacare nightmare is about to end. (Applause.)

Despite the best efforts of some activists and town hall meetings around the country, the truth of the matter is the American people know -- Obamacare has failed and Obamacare must go. (Applause.)

I heard it today. (Applause.)

I heard it today. I don't know if we're going to stop by Italian House later -- (laughter) --but I'm hungry. (Laughter.)

AUDIENCE MEMBER: Now we're not. (Laughter.)

THE VICE PRESIDENT: Paul said, "Now we're not." (Laughter.)

Can't announce that stuff in advance. (Laughter.)

But come on, Edmund, do you got, like, a to-go thing or something there? (Laughter.)

Would that be all right? Can I get Italian House to go? Would that be all right with everybody, man? (Applause.)

We were just hearing from Edmund a minute ago -- he's a great employer, a great American success story here in Janesville, but he talked about the weight that Obamacare has placed on his great family-owned business. And it's a weight that's been placed on businesses and employers all across this country, let alone the weight it's placed on American families.

I mean, literally, it literally is just a long list of broken promises, isn't it? I mean, remember all the promises about Obamacare? They told you the cost of health insurance would go down, right? Not true. They told us if you like your doctor, you could keep him. Not true. They told us if you like your health insurance plan, you could keep it. Not true. I mean, talk about your fake news. I mean, the truth is -- the truth is just virtually every promise of Obamacare has been broken.

Today, Americans are paying $3,000 a year more on average for their health insurance than when Obamacare was passed into law. And premiums are skyrocketing -- last year by more than 25 percent on average around the country, millions have lost their plans and lost their doctors. And not only that, Obamacare, as Edmund was describing, is a job-killer, and everybody knows it.

The last few years, it's been hard enough to get ahead and Obamacare has only made it much harder and, in many ways, if not impossible for many small businesses. The endless premium hikes, the reams of red tape eat up time and money that would be better spent growing your business and benefitting your workers. And every year the burden grows, so do the hard choices that you have to make. But not for long. I'm going to make you a **promise** -- you heard the President say it -- and give direction to the Congress. And it's just going to start happening in just a few days. We're going to repeal Obamacare once and for all, and eliminate all its mandates and taxes and intrusion into your personal lives and into the lives of your business. (Applause.)

And best of all -- best of all, the President directed the Congress right after that election today to -- at the same time that we repeal Obamacare, we're going to replace it with something that actually works and lowers the cost of health insurance for every American. (Applause.)

The President and I want every American to have access to quality, affordable health insurance. That's why we're going to pass a better law that lowers the cost of health insurance without growing the size of government. And we've got an incredible team working literally every single day around the clock to get that done. In Secretary Price, America has one of the leading experts on healthcare in the country -- I hope you picked up he's a medical doctor. (Laughter.)

All right? I mean, how many times in Washington -- this is only the third time in the history of the Department of Health and Human Services that a physician has led that Department.

The President and I are working with him, with Speaker Ryan and his outstanding team in the House of Representatives with Leader McConnell, Senator Johnson, with all of our leaders in Congress, and we're putting the finishing touches on our plan, even as this weekend rolls out. A better plan for a brighter future that's built on a foundation of individual freedom and personal responsibility will replace Obamacare. (Applause.)

The President talked about it the other night, but you know the outlines -- we're going to give Americans the freedom to buy health insurance that's best for you and end the era of government-mandated health insurance in this country. We're going to let you buy health insurance across state lines, the way you buy life insurance, the way you buy car insurance. That's how you bring down the cost of health insurance -- you create a national marketplace and then you get that little lizard and you get Flo on television -- (laughter) -- and let them start selling cheaper health insurance to every American. That's the American way. (Applause.)

We'll make also -- make sure, I **promise** you, that Americans struggling with pre-existing conditions have access to the coverage and the care that they need. And we'll give states the flexibility and the freedom and the resources they need to take care of our most vulnerable. You know, just the other day, I was talking to one of my favorite elected officials in America, Governor Scott Walker. (Applause.)

I mean, what is in the water here in Wisconsin? Governor Scott Walker is not only leading the association of fellow governors of his party across the country, but he's a recognized national leader and I'm honored to call him a friend. As a former governor myself, he and I both know that every state is unique. The challenges here in Wisconsin are different than they are down in Illinois, different than they are in the state of Indiana, Minnesota. And what Scott Walker is doing is he's pulled together governors from around the country, we met last weekend in Washington, D.C. And we're working on ensuring that when we repeal and replace Obamacare, that we're going to allow states to have the flexibility to craft state-based solutions that will work for the people of their individual states. What will work in Wisconsin is better designed by the people of Wisconsin for the needs of the most vulnerable in this state. And I'm grateful for his leadership. (Applause.)

And despite what the other side is saying, all the -- creating anxiety for Americans, the President said it last fall in Philadelphia, he said it again this week: We're going to have an orderly transition to a better healthcare system that finally puts the **American** people **First**.

So it's about healthcare right out of the gate. And our 45th President has said that's the number-one priority, and we're going right to work on it in just a matter of days. But President Trump's agenda doesn't stop there. I could keep you here the rest of the afternoon to tell you about all the things the President planned, but let me touch on a few.

I loved it when he was out campaigning in Wisconsin and I was a little bit myself. President Trump, you see, had a three-part agenda: Jobs, jobs and jobs. And this President is going to get this economy moving again by passing the biggest package of tax relief since the days of Ronald Reagan. (Applause.)

With the strong support of Speaker Ryan and Senator Ron Johnson, we're going to cut taxes across the board for working families, small businesses and family farms. We're also going to keep rolling back job-killing regulations, rein in unelected bureaucrats so they can't cripple the economy from the comfort of their taxpayer-funded metal desks in Washington, D.C.

We're going to end wasteful government spending and restore fiscal responsibility to our nation's capital. We're going to pass an infrastructure package so that America, once again, has the best roads, bridges, highways, airports that we've ever had in the history of this nation. (Applause.)

President Trump and I believe that roads mean jobs. And not just road jobs; when you have the right infrastructure, this builder who's become President knows the right investments and the right infrastructure is going to make for a more **Prosperous** Wisconsin and a more **Prosperous America**.

And, ladies and gentlemen, make no mistake about it: Thanks to President Trump, this economy is going to grow faster than ever before. But **Making America Great Again** also means **restoring safety** to our streets, keeping our country **secure**, and President Trump hasn't wasted any time on that either.

I'll tell you what, in my lifetime, I couldn't be more proud, because I've never seen at this level -- and they know it -- President Trump stands with the men and women who serve in law enforcement all across this country like no one I've ever met. (Applause.)

We're going to stand with those men and women who keep our communities **safe** every single day. And we're going to continue to take steps to make sure that people that are coming into this country don't represent a threat to our families or to our way of life.

President Trump is standing tall with our allies, standing up to our enemies. He's also working to rebuild our military. I'm the proud father of a United States Marine. (Applause.)

And truth of the matter, in recent years, we've seen budget cuts that have failed to provide our soldiers, sailors, airmen and Marines with the resources that they need to do their jobs. That's all about to change.

Under President Donald Trump, with the leadership of this Congress, we're going to rebuild our military. We're going to restore the arsenal of democracy. We're going to make sure our armed forces have the resources and training they need to protect our nation starting right now. (Applause.)

My friends, President Trump is keeping his **promises**, **promises** he made to the people of Wisconsin and **promises** he made to the American people. And that includes one of his most consequential **promises**. Out on the campaign trail, there was a vacancy on the Supreme Court of the United States. The President said that he would **promise** to name someone to the Supreme Court in the tradition of the late and great Justice Antonin Scalia. And I **promise** you, in Judge Neil Gorsuch, President Trump has kept his word to nominate a jurist who will uphold the God-given liberties enshrined in the Constitution of the United States of America. And we look forward to him being confirmed by the United States Senate. (Applause.)

Healthcare reform, tax reform, regulatory reform, taking steps to **Make America Secure**, ensuring that the highest court in the land upholds our highest ideals. That's what it looks like to **Make America Great Again**. And President Trump is fighting to make that happen every single day, every single moment. And we're going to continue fighting.

Now, we're hearing from plenty who want to stick with the status quo, whether it be on healthcare or other issues -- whether it's the media, the establishment, insiders and the rest, they have no problem standing in the way of change. But trust me, whatever challenges face us today, we're going stay in the **promise-keeping** business. And President Trump is going to deliver on this moment for the people of the United States of America.

And we're going to **Make America More Prosperous Again**.

We're going to have a better healthcare system that respects the doctor-patient relationship and harnesses the power of the private marketplace.

We're going to **Make America Safe Again**.

And with your help and with God's help, I **promise** you, Wisconsin, I **promise** you, Janesville, we're going to **Make America Great Again**.

Thank you very much. Thank you for coming out today. And just God bless you. God bless America. (Applause.)

END
12:58 P.M. CST

Chapter 71

REMARKS BY PRESIDENT TRUMP IN
PARENT-TEACHER CONFERENCE LISTENING SESSION
ST. ANDREW CATHOLIC SCHOOL
ORLANDO, FLORIDA

03 March 2017

1:51 P.M. EST

PRESIDENT TRUMP: Well, first of all, I want to thank you very much. Great job. Really a fantastic job. We just did a tour. I was given a couple of beautiful cards by the students -- really well done. And I appreciate it.

And Bishop Noonan, thank you so much. A very powerful man, and I -- the most powerful man, right? (Laughter.)

And I appreciate it very much for your uplifting prayer. I have to say that your support of schools like St. Andrews Catholic School has been incredible. Everybody talks about it. They talk about you. You understand how much the students benefit from full education, one that enriches both the mind and the soul, a combination -- and that's a good combination.

Latrina, I want to just thank you. The job you've done is incredible. Everyone -- we've been talking about you actually you have a big reputation in Florida. You do know that, right? (Laughter.)

For your talent and a lot of other things. But I see it -- and for your love of what you do. Because I could see as soon as I met you, the love that you have for what you do is really fantastic. So I want to thank you very much.

And Superintendent Fortier -- where is Superintendent?

Where is Superintendent?

You have been -- come here. You have been fantastic. And the job you're doing and willing to do is going to be -- I think with what's happening and with people like Marco and Rick Scott and the President and seeing this today -- I mean, it just -- it's going to get further and further because I know they're big fans.

So I'm grateful to have everybody here today. I'm also very pleased and -- where is Rick Scott? Right over here, Governor Scott and Senator Marco Rubio and, as you know, Secretary DeVos -- she was approved a couple of weeks ago. And she's the one that we all report to when it comes to education. And I know you're going to have a fantastic relationship with the Secretary, and that's going to be a lot of good things for your school and for the entire system.

St. Andrews Catholic School represents one of the many parochial schools dedicated to the education of some of our nation's most disadvantaged children. But they're becoming just the opposite very rapidly through education and with the help of the school choice programs.

This month, we commemorate the thousands of peaceful activists for justice who joined Martin Luther King [Jr.] on the march from Selma to Montgomery. And that day, Reverend King [Jr.] hoped that inferior education would become, as he said, "a thing of the past." And we're going to work very much for the future and what he predicted would be with the future. As I've often said in my address to Congress and just about anyplace else I can speak, education is the civil rights issue of our time. And it's why I've asked Congress to support a school-choice bill. And we've come a long way. I think we really -- we're right out there and we're ahead of -- we're ahead of schedule in so many ways when it comes to education. And, again, Betsy is going to lead that -- you're going to lead that charge, right?

SECRETARY DEVOS: You bet.

THE PRESIDENT: You're going to do a fantastic job. Denisha Merriweather is with us today and you were so wonderful the other night.

MS. MERRIWEATHER: Thank you.

THE PRESIDENT: That was quite a night. I will say that, Denisha. I was honored that Denisha joined Melania and myself as our guest to my address to Congress. Denisha is the first in her family to graduate high school and college, and is about to complete her master's degree in social work, right? (Applause.)

And Denisha, we want millions more to have the same chance to achieve the great success that you're achieving right now. And you think that can be done, I'll bet, right?

MS. MERRIWEATHER: Of course.

THE PRESIDENT: Look at that. (Laughter.)

Her eyes light up. And that's good news. So I want to thank all of the parents and teachers and students at St. Andrews and all of the graduates that are with us to-

day. It's a special place. It's also a special state.
Florida, to me, is a very, very special, special state. I mean,
I know those people back there -- they know why I like it
so much. We've had a lot of success in Florida and I love
it. It's my second home. I'm here all the time. We have
the *Southern White House* in Florida*. (Laughter.)

And we get a lot of work done -- believe me, there's no rest
at the *Southern White House* -- it's all work. And we love
this state. And we love this state, the way it's managed
between Marco and Rick and some of the others. They're
doing a great job and we appreciate it very much. And
thank you. And thank you very much. (Applause.)

END
1:56 P.M. EST

[*Note: Mar-a-Lago was built around 1924-7, by the heir-
ess Marjorie Merriweather Post. In 1973, the property was
donated to the government and then it became a National
Historic Landmark. Due to increasing costs, the property
was placed on the market.

In 1985, the property was purchased by Donald Trump. It
is part of the Trump Organization. The Mar-a-Lago Club is a
private members club, boasting a spa, golf course, sports,
recreation, ballrooms and hotel facilities. Donald Trump
has retained private accommodation there.

Since Donald Trump has taken office, he has referred to the
property as the *Winter White House* or the *Southern White
House*. For further information www.trump.com]

Chapter 72

President Trump's Weekly Address
The President's Weekly Address aired today on
Facebook Live and is now available to watch on
YouTube.

03 March 2017

Transcript:

My fellow Americans,
I'm joining you today from the deck of what will be our Nation's newest aircraft carrier, the soon-to-be commissioned Gerald R. Ford, and as you can see, I'm wearing a jacket and a hat that they just gave me. Not really used to it, but it feels awfully good – I'm very proud of it actually.

Our carriers are the centerpiece of American military might, projecting power and our totally unparalleled strength at sea.

This beautiful new warship represents the future of naval aviation, and she will serve as a cornerstone of our national defense for decades and decades to come.

A famous aviator once wrote that, to build a truly great ship, we shouldn't begin by gathering wood, cutting boards, or distributing work, but instead by awakening within the people a "desire for the vast and endless sea." So true.

In the same way, we must continue to **renew** the **American Spirit** in order to rebuild our country, and rebuild it we will.

On Tuesday, before a Joint Session [of] Congress, I laid out a vision – I hope you all watched – for how to accomplish that national rebuilding.

My **vision** includes the elimination of the defense sequester, which has imposed steep cuts on our military.

We must give our sailors, soldiers, airmen, marines, and coastguardsmen the tools, equipment, resources and training they need to get the job done, and get it done right - especially in these very dangerous times.

The active duty Army has been reduced by more than 85,000 men since 2009, and we have over 18,000 fewer active duty marines.

The Air Force, it's the smallest it has been since 1947, and their planes are, on average, nearly thirty years old, if you can believe that.

Our Navy's fleet is the smallest it has been since World War I, and that's a long time ago.

Frontline Navy and Marine strike fighter aircraft are more likely to be down for maintenance than to be in the sky.

We cannot afford to continue down this path. My budget will give America's armed forces the resources they need to achieve full and total military preparedness to meet any and all global challenges – and meet them, we will.

Investing in the military means investing in peace - because the best way to prevent war, as George Washington said, is to be prepared for it.

Most importantly, an investment in the military is an investment in the incredible men and women who serve our country in uniform. They are the best of us. They are the greatest force for peace and justice the world has ever known - and we will support them every single step of the way.

These are truly exciting times. Amazing opportunities are unfolding before us - to strengthen our military, to reboot our economy, and to bring back our jobs. If we all work together, and put our country **First**, then anything is possible.

Let us seize this moment and make the most of this incredible opportunity for **national renewa**l.

May God bless the men and women of our military, and may God bless the United States of America, the country we love.

> *"...we must continue to*
> *renew the American Spirit*
> *in order to*
> *rebuild our country,*
> *and rebuild it we will..."*

Chapter 73

07 March 2017

3:34 P.M. EST

THE PRESIDENT: Thank you, everybody, and Mike Pence is going to be here in a few minutes. We miss Mike when he's not around. (Laughter.)

So I want to thank the members of the House Deputy Whip team. It will be very important over the next number of months. We have a great team and we're going to have a lot of victories, a lot of wins, but we have a great team.

Together, we're going to do incredible things for the great citizens of our country. As I said during my Joint Address to Congress -- and I think you mostly liked that, right? (Laughter.)

PARTICIPANT: We loved that. (Laughter.)

PARTICIPANT: We liked it a lot. (Laughter.)

THE PRESIDENT: We're witnessing a **renewal** of the **American Spirit**, a surge of optimism and a new **national pride**, which is sweeping across the land. I see it -- there's such **Spirit**, whether it's for the business things we're doing or whatever. It's such **Spirit** that we haven't seen in the country in a long time. Jobs are pouring back here. You saw what happened with Exxon, where they just announced a massive job program. So we're going to have some fun.

Now, we have to remember, Obamacare is collapsing and it's in bad shape. And we're going to take action. There's going to be no slowing down. There's going to be no waiting and no more excuses by anybody. We're all now -- I can probably say I'm a politician. (Laughter.)

Okay? I am a politician.

But we're going to get it done, and you're the leaders that really will get it done for all of us and for the American people. Obamacare is in very bad shape. I believe that if we wait two years, it will totally implode. It's really pretty much imploding now, Steve, when you think. But it will implode and people will be, like, please help us, please help us, and that will be the Democrats asking for help. They already are asking for help in the true sense of the word, because it's a disaster. The insurance companies are fleeing. Some states are up over 100 percent in costs. The deductibles are through the roof -- you don't even get to use it.

So we're going to do something that's great, and I'm proud to support the replacement plan, released by the House of Representatives and encouraged by members of both parties. I think really that we're going to have something that's going to be much more understood and much more popular than people can even imagine. It follows the guidelines I laid out in my congressional address -- a plan that will lower costs, expand choices, increase competition, and ensure healthcare access for all Americans.

This will be a plan where you can choose your doctor. This will be a plan where you can choose your plan. (Laughter.)

And you know what the plan is -- this is the plan. And we're going to have a tremendous -- I think we're going to have a tremendous success. It's a complicated process, but actually it's very simple. It's called good healthcare. So I want to thank you folks for being with us today, ladies and gentlemen. And we will do something really, really important and really good for the American people. I think it's going to go very quickly. I hope it's going to go very quickly. And as you know, after that, we work on the tax cut. We're going to be planning a major tax cut. I know exactly what we're looking at -- most of us know exactly the plan. It's going to put our country in great shape and we're going to reduce taxes for companies and for people, and I can use the word again -- massively. It's going to be a big tax cut, the biggest since Reagan, maybe bigger than Reagan.

So I look forward -- I really look forward to working on that, but we can't really get to that, unfortunately, because of the way your system works. We can't get to that until we take care of healthcare. So we'll take care of the health-care. I appreciate your great support and let's get it done. Thank you. Thank you all. Fantastic. Thank you.

REPRESENTATIVE SCALISE: Well, Mr. President, thank you for having our Deputy Whip team to the White House. And thank you for your commitment on following through on what, to most Americans, is probably one of the most important **promises** that was made not only by you, but by all of us in getting this majority -- both in the House and Senate -- and the White House, and that is res-cuing the American people from the failures of

Obamacare.

We've heard the message for years. We've seen the dramatically skyrocketing costs. You're seeing double-digit increases every year in most part of the country in health premiums for families. Many families are seeing deductibles that rise about the $10,000 range, which means people don't have access to healthcare. People don't have the ability to choose their own doctor.

You talked about this the other night in just one of the best speeches I've heard from a President standing at that well in the House Chamber when you addressed the joint session and gave an inspirational speech to the country laying out the things that need to happen and that you're going to do to get this country back on track, and to create jobs, and to **secure** America.

But one of the things you talked about is how it's wrong that unelected bureaucrats in Washington have the ability to tell you what you can and can't buy for your family in healthcare, one of the most personal decisions families make.

This bill finally starts the process of not only repealing Obamacare, but also replacing it with reforms that put patients back in charge of their healthcare decisions, that lower costs for families. Let them actually choose the decisions between them and their doctor, which are so personal.

And so as we start this process, the people in this room, the chief deputy whips are the ones that are going to be working directly with members to ultimately pass this bill to your desk so that we can quickly provide that relief from

Obamacare to the people of the United States.

And I know we are honored to have our former House colleague and now our Vice President of the United States who has been involved in this fight from the beginning, as well, Vice President Mike Pence joining us, too.

Thank you, Mr. Vice President.

THE PRESIDENT: Well, thank you very much, Steve. And again, we're going to work quickly. It's a great bill. We're going to have -- I really believe we're going to have tremendous support. I'm already seeing the support -- not only in this room, I'm seeing it from everybody. And I'm seeing it from the public.

And they want Obamacare over.

I got elected to a certain extent -- I would say a pretty good little chunk -- based on the fact repeal and replace Obamacare. And many of you people are in the same boat. Very important. So let's get it done.

Thank you all very much for being here. Thank you. Okay, thank you.

END
3:41 P.M. EST

"Okay? I am a politician."

Chapter 74

09 March 2017

11:17 A.M. EST

THE PRESIDENT: Thank you, everybody, very much. Good morning and I greatly appreciate you being here. We have some real experts with us and we have some great bankers with us.

Today's discussion is crucial to my jobs agenda and to the American people. Community banks play a vital role in helping create jobs by providing approximately half of all loans to small businesses, and that's been dwindling because the community banks have been in big trouble.

Nearly half of all private-sector workers are employed by small businesses. We must ensure access to capital. Small businesses -- small businesses to grow. Community banks are the backbone of small business in America. We are going to preserve our community banks.

You probably know this -- I signed an executive order on regulation on February 3rd, I believe it was. And that's a big executive order, a very powerful executive order. It's taking a lot of the regulation away.

You'll be able to loan.

You'll be able to be **safe**.

But you'll be able to provide the jobs that we want and also create great businesses.

So it's an honor to have you with us today, and perhaps we could go around the room. And we'll start with Dorothy, and say who you are and who you represent.

Go ahead, Dorothy.

MS. SAVARESE: Thank you, Mr. President. I'm Dorothy Savarese. I'm from Cape Cod Five Mutual Company on Cape Cod, Massachusetts.

MS. ANDERSEN: And I'm Leslie Andersen, and I'm with the Bank of Bennington in Bennington, Nebraska.

MR. ZIMMERMAN: Tim Zimmerman, Standard Bank in the suburbs of Pittsburgh, Pennsylvania.

THE PRESIDENT: Great.

MS. ROMERO RAINEY: Rebeca Romero Rainey from Centinel Bank in beautiful Taos, New Mexico.

THE PRESIDENT: Very good.

MS. CUNDIFF: I'm Luanne Cundiff with First State Bank of St. Charles.

MR. HEITKAMP: I'm Scott Heitkamp, ValueBank Texas in Corpus Christi, Texas.

THE PRESIDENT: Good. Thanks, Scott.

MS. STEWART: Laura Steward from the other Washington -- Seattle. (Laughter.)

MR. SZYPERSKI: Jeff Szyperski from Chesapeake Bank from Kilmarnock, Virginia.

THE PRESIDENT: Good, thank you.

MR. BURGESS: And I'm Ken Burgess with FirstCapital Bank of Texas in Midland, Texas.

THE PRESIDENT: Good. Thank you.

Okay, thank you very much. Thank you.

END
11:20 A.M. EST

"Community banks are the backbone of small business in America."

Chapter 75

10 March 2017

Transcript:

My fellow Americans,
In March, we celebrate Women's History Month, honoring the countless contributions that women leaders, scientists, and entrepreneurs have made throughout American history.

We are a greater, stronger, and more just Nation today because of women like Clara Barton, Susan B. Anthony, Harriet Tubman, and so many others.

We honor them and we recommit ourselves to a better future for every woman in America today.

On my 50th day in office, I want to talk about an issue of paramount importance to families across our nation – healthcare.

Seven years ago this month, Obamacare was signed into law over the profound objections of American people. Our citizens were told they would have to pass Obamacare to find out what it was and how bad it was.

Now we know that the hundreds of pages were full of

broken promises.

Americans were promised that Obamacare would bring premiums down $2,500 for a typical family. Instead, they've gone up by more than $4,000.

Americans were promised that Obamacare would increase competition and provide them with more choices. Instead, the number of plans to choose from has plummeted – and I mean plummeted.

This year, Americans in nearly one-third of all counties have only one insurer to choose from on the exchanges – or, in effect, no real choice at all.

Americans were promised that if they liked their health insurance and their doctors, they could keep them. Instead, millions of Americans lost the insurance and lost the doctor that they liked and were thrust into a cold new reality of higher costs and less coverage.

Through seven long years of botched rollouts, soaring costs, cancelled plans, and bureaucratic mandates, Americans have called out for relief. And relief is what we are determined to give them.

I want every American to know that action on Obamacare is an urgent necessity.

The law is collapsing around us, and if we do not act to save Americans from this wreckage, it will take our healthcare system all the way down with it. If we do nothing, millions more innocent Americans will be hurt – and badly hurt.

That's why we must repeal and replace Obamacare.

House Republicans have put forward a plan that gets rid of this terrible law and replaces it with reforms that empower states and consumers.

You will have the choice and the freedom to make the decisions that are right for your family.

The House plan follows the guidelines I laid out in my recent address to Congress – expanding choice, lowering costs, and providing healthcare access for all.

This plan is part of a three-pronged reform process. In concert with the plan in front of Congress, I have directed Dr. Tom Price, our Secretary of Health and Human Services, to use his authority to reduce regulations that are driving up costs of care.

We are also working on reforms that lower the costs of care, like allowing Americans to purchase health insurance across state lines. You've heard me say that many, many times during the debates.

I encourage Democrats to work with us to improve the healthcare system for the American people. Also, we will be driving down the costs.

We will deliver relief to American workers, families, and small businesses, who right now are being crushed by Obamacare, by increasing freedom, choice, and opportunity for the American people.

Thank you very much.

Chapter 76

REMARKS BY PRESIDENT TRUMP IN
A HEALTHCARE DISCUSSION WITH
KEY HOUSE COMMITTEE CHAIRMEN
ROOSEVELT ROOM

10 March 2017

11:50 A.M. EST

THE PRESIDENT: Hello, everybody. I want to thank each of the House committee leaders for being with us today. Your devotion and leadership has been amazing, and I want to just applaud you and the diligent work of your committees to advance the Obamacare repeal-and-replacement legislation that we've been talking about for a long time, and that we've been running with and I ran with, and I can tell you. And that's what people want, they want repeal-and-replace. The bill passed just now through Ways and Means, and it will -- I think the committee just voted recently, right?

REPRESENTATIVE WALDEN: Yep.

THE PRESIDENT: Your other committee --

REPRESENTATIVE WALDEN: Energy.

THE PRESIDENT: Energy and Commerce. And it was a very good vote, and congratulations. That was a good job. Amazing. We must act now to save Americans from the imploding Obamacare disaster. Premiums have sky-rocketed by double-digits and triple-digits in some cases. As an example, Arizona -- which I talk about all the time -- 116 percent increase and it's going up a lot higher. '17 would be a disaster for Obamacare. That's the year it was meant to explode, because Obama won't be here. That was when it was supposed to be -- it will get even worse. As bad as it is now, it'll get even worse.

Choices are disappearing as one insurer drops out after another. Today, one-third of all counties now have only one insurer on the Obamacare exchanges, and the exchanges themselves are a disaster. The House repeal-and-replace plan ends the Obamacare tax hikes, cutting taxes by hundreds of billions of dollars. It eliminates the Obamacare mandate that forces Americans to buy government-approved plans. We all know that one.

It provides states with flexibility over how Medicaid dollars are spent, giving power from Washington and back to local government, which we all want to see. We're going to do a much better job. And the plan empowers individual Americans to buy the health insurance that is right for them, not the plan forced on them by government. You all remember, you can keep your doctor, you can keep your plan. I know, Greg, you've never heard that, right? But it was said many, many times, and it turned out to be not true.

This is the time we're going to get it done. We're working together, we have some great results, we have tremendous **Spirit**, and I think it's something that is just going to happen very shortly.

So thank you all very much, and we're going to get to work.

END
11:52 A.M. EST

Chapter 77

10 March 2017

12:45 P.M. EST

THE VICE PRESIDENT: Thank you so much. And buenas tardes a todos. It's wonderful to be with you all. You know, the last time I addressed the Latino Coalition I promised myself I wouldn't come back until I learned some Spanish. (Laughter.)

That was six years ago, and as you can tell, I'm a slow learner.

All kidding aside, would you join me in just thanking your great Chairman, Hector Barreto, for that wonderful speech and the overly gracious introduction? (Applause.)

Hector, thank you for your continued leadership of the Latino Coalition, as well as your years in public service. His record as head of the Small Business Administration was one of distinction. And I know our current Administrator of the Small Business Administration would strongly agree. I know Linda McMahon is with us today. Would you give her another big round of applause? (Applause.)

Linda, could you stand and take a bow? We couldn't be more excited, the President and I, about our new leader of the SBA. (Applause.)

You can give her a standing ovation if you want. I don't want to hold back on that. You can get on your feet. (Applause.)

Linda McMahon, everybody. (Applause.)

You know, our nation is really fortunate.

I just love that Reagan line -- didn't you like that? I love it when I come across a new Reagan line. The difference between a small business and a big business is big government. Get government out of the way. And it's just wonderful to have someone of Linda's caliber and experience, someone who built an incredible career -- incredible career and an incredible business as a small family business into an international business, being able to lead the SBA. So thank you, thank you so much, Linda, for stepping up to serve the country.

It is a great privilege, great privilege to be back to the Latino Coalition once again. The last time I was here I was a congressman from the great state of Indiana. And today, I am deeply humbled to stand before you today as Vice President of the United States of America. (Applause.)

The reason I'm in this position is because of the confidence of my friend, the 45th President of the United States of America, and because of the support of people like you all across this country.

And I want to tell you that I bring greetings from the President. Just before I left the Oval Office I told him I was headed your way, and he was pleased to hear about it. And I told him I was headed to a conference entitled: **"Make Small Business Great Again Policy Summit**," and he was very pleased. (Applause.)

I think the President wants you to know that our administration, simply put -- and Linda will back me up on this -- the Trump administration will be the best friend American small businesses will ever have. (Applause.)

The President and I know what our whole team knows, is that small businesses are the engines of the American economy. As President Trump said in his joint address to Congress last week -- did everybody see that speech? He said we're going to restart the engine to create jobs and prosperity and growth in America like never before. And it's already begun.

You know, I grew up in a small business family in a small town in southern Indiana. I went to work at one of my dad's gas stations when I was only 14-years of age. Had a dark blue shirt with a stripe on it, had my name on it. I was really proud of myself. Now, for those of you under the age of 30, if you're wondering what a gas station attendant was -- (laughter) -- just imagine if when you pulled into a gas station, some young person ran out with a name on their shirt, pumped your gas, cleaned your windshield, checked your tires, and didn't charge you any more money for it. It was a great job, a great experience.

But I grew up in a family business so I know the sacrifices all of you make. And as the world knows, President Trump also grew up in a family business as well. It was a little bit bigger than my dad's. By the end of the day, it's the same principle.

I was just in a meeting yesterday with the President in the Cabinet Room, and we were talking about infrastructure with leaders. And an old friend of his said that he and the President had grown up the same way. He said, come Saturday mornings, even when we were very young, the time that we spent with our dad was we were out on a job site. And that's what it is to be in a small business family. I told him afterwards, I said, you know, for me, it was headed to the plant or headed to the gas station with my dad. And I know the small businesses that are gathered here know where of I speak. And I just want to assure you that President Trump and I both know the sacrifices that are required to make a small business work. And most importantly, we know this: When small business is strong the American economy is strong. And we're going to fight every day to make that a reality. (Applause.)

Now, the Latino Coalition knows this truth -- this statement better than most. Businesses represented in this room have made an incredible impact not just in the lives of your employees, but in your communities, and frankly, in the nation as a whole. The fact is that Hispanics are driving entrepreneurship and economic growth like never before -- just like Hector said. The number of Latino-owned businesses grew by more than 50 percent over the past decade -- leaps and bounds over every other American demographic. (Applause.)

And Hispanic firms have also been hiring at a record pace. This was clear just yesterday -- I don't know if you all saw that news. It's just amazing. We had the most jobs created in a single month in over three years -- the February reports 298,000 jobs. (Applause.)

And Hispanic businesses were a part of that success.

It's incredible to think that today Hispanics own an amazing 4 million American companies, and their combined annual revenue is over $650 billion. It might be a small business, but that's big business where I come from. And Latino-owned small businesses continue to be the fastest growing sector of the entire economy.

Now, let me pause for just a second here, if I can -- it is Women's History Month. Could we give a round of applause to all the Latina small business owners who are with us today who are charting a great, great force of success in the American economy? (Applause.)

Incredible leadership demonstrated, and it's great to see your peers all honor you. I know the President honors you as well in this important month of celebration.

Before I move on, let me just ask -- could I ask all of those who've worn the uniform in the United States of America to rise -- the men and women who have served their country in uniform. (Applause.)

The President and I just never want to fail to acknowledge the contributions of every American through our armed forces. It's amazing that the contribution of the Hispanic community in America continues to this day -- over 250,000 Hispanics are serving in the Army, the Navy, the Air Force, the Marines, the Coast Guard, and the Reserves at this very moment.

I know we asked them to stand, but will the rest of you mind standing to demonstrate just how proud we are of those who serve in the armed forces in the United States and those who have served in the defense of this nation? (Applause.)

Thank you for your service. And thank you for honoring all of them.

You know, you can't look at these numbers that we're all talking about and not be impressed. You get right down to it, the Hispanic community is one of the most dynamic communities in the entire country. Your success is America's success, and President Trump and I both know it. The President has held at least a dozen key meetings with the Latino community, especially small business owners, in the build-up of the November 8th election. He did this because he recognizes just how crucial you are to the American economy. And as a businessman himself, he knows what it takes to be successful in a tough and a competitive environment.

He **promised** in those meetings, and I reiterate today, to give you the help you need to become even more successful in the years ahead. All my friends -- I like to say, if you haven't noticed, that the White House these days, we're in the **promise-keeping** business again in Washington, D.C. (Applause.)

It's been incredibly exciting since literally -- I'd like to say day one, but it was actually night one. We came in from that parade, and the President sat down at his desk and went right to work and hadn't slowed down for a minute since. Literally, from that very first day, President Trump went right to work, undoing job-destroying policies and executive orders over the last eight years. After years of delay, for instance, the President signed his executive order to authorize the construction of the Keystone and Dakota pipelines that will create tens of thousands of jobs and support our energy infrastructure. (Applause.)

He's already signed several bills that Congress has provided, rolling back reams of red tape in Washington, D.C. And he signed an executive order instructing every agency in our nation's capital to find two regulations to get rid of before they issue any new regulations on Americans and American businesses. (Applause.)

So it is an especially big deal for small business. And, folks, we're just getting started, I can promise you that. By now, all of you know that President Trump and our administration has the boldest and best agenda America has seen for a very long time. And what I can tell you now is that on the very top of that list, I can **promise** you, the Obamacare nightmare is about to come to an end. (Applause.)

Now, I don't have to tell small business owners gathered here today about why this failed law has got to go. In the last few years it's been hard enough for hardworking Americans in small businesses to get ahead, and frankly, Obamacare has only made it more difficult to grow a business and make ends meet. Millions of Americans have felt Obamacare's disappointments firsthand. Today the average American is paying $3,000 more a year for health insurance. And the premiums just last year alone, the average premiums across the country spiked by more than 25 percent.

I mean, I remember -- I was in the Congress at the time when we fought against this government takeover of health care that came to be known as Obamacare. And I remember they told us that it was all about lowering the cost of health insurance. But think about that. The premiums have gone up -- like I got to tell you all anything -- the premiums have gone up 100 percent in some jurisdictions since this bill was signed into law. And last year alone, that average of 25 percent increase has really worked hardships on Americans.

In one-third of our nations' counties, consumers have only one insurance company to choose from, which essentially means they have no choice at all. And American businesses have been struggling, too. I'm sure everyone in this room can attest to the fact that Obamacare has hit you with more regulations, more mandates, higher costs, higher taxes.

The fact is Obamacare has placed a crushing burden on job creators, just like all of you in this room today. It's resulted in lost jobs, slower growth in an economy that until very recently seemed to be stuck in up to the axle.

Now, I hear the same thing everywhere I go: Small businesses tell me that Obamacare places a weight on them that grows each and every year. They're facing hard choices -- choices businesses shouldn't have to make. They felt for the longest time that there's nothing they can do about it. And then along came President Donald Trump. And now the American people know there is something we can do, and President Trump is determined to work with this Congress and we will repeal and replace Obamacare at last with something that actually works. (Applause.)

See, literally, the day after the election -- and it's kind of funny -- people say, did you go right to work after Election Night? And I don't remember a night. I remember the President was able to give that victory speech about 4:00 in the morning, we got about two hours' sleep, he said, I'll see you in the office at 8:30 a.m. And we were there. One of the first decisions the President made was that the number-one priority in the Congress when they would convene is to repeal and replace Obamacare and do it at the same time.

And we worked with leaders in the Congress in the intervening months to go to work on that. We've made incredible progress. Now, this week, the House released its repeal and replace bill to begin that process, and as the legislative process begins, the President and I are proud to lead the charge. Our plan to repeal and replace Obamacare, in a word, is going to keep the promises that we all made with the American people from the Republican majorities in the House and the Senate and all of this administration and this campaign. We're going to repeal Obamacare's individual mandates and employer mandates. We're actually going to get rid of over $500 billion in tax increases when Obamacare goes away. (Applause.)

We're going to roll back reams of regulations that are strangling businesses and our economy. And we're going to expand the use of health savings account and create a new, refundable tax credit that will help low- and middle-income consumers the most. We're going to make sure that Americans with preexisting conditions still have access to the coverage and the care that they need. And we're even going to let you parents out there keep your kids on your plan until they're 26-years of age.

And last but not least, we're going to give states the freedom and flexibility that they have longed for, for so long, to design their Medicaid program in you state to best meet the needs of our most vulnerable population. State resources, state flexibility will bring about the kind of health care to the underprivileged that we have long sought and deserve. (Applause.)

Our plan to repeal and replace Obamacare will do what Obamacare can't, and that is actually give the American people access to affordable, high-quality health insurance. And that's what President Trump promised, and that's what our plan will deliver.

Now, let me say, despite some of the fear-mongering that you've seen among some activists on the left, we're going to have an orderly transition to a better health care system. And we're working with the Congress right now to ensure that as we move into a system that's based on free market principles and state-based flexibility, that that system will work and be unfolding in an orderly way for your enterprises in a predictable way.

But passing the legislation that's moving through the Congress now is just the first component of a larger strategy to repeal and replace Obamacare. Rest assured this bill in the Congress is a beginning. Our administration is also working right now with the new Secretary of Health and Human Services, Dr. Tom Price, and taking every available action to give Americans increased choices and the lower cost that they deserve in purchasing health insurance. The name of the game is deregulation.

And last but not least, we're going to work with the Congress and work with HHS to make the best health care system in the world even better -- with legal reforms, small business reforms, and ultimately, at the centerpiece of the President's **vision**, we're going to enact policies administratively and through legislation that will give Americans the freedom to purchase health insurance across state lines -- just the way you buy life insurance, just the way you buy car insurance. (Applause.)

The creation of a national marketplace is the center of the President's vision. And we're working now through administrative policy and through the legislative process that will go forward to this spring to accomplish that.

In fine print, I like to say what we need to do is get that little lizard on television, or get Flo out there selling health insurance. (Laughter.)

Am I right about that? (Applause.)

It's just the whole idea that you all know in a competitive marketplace -- you all are successful in business -- the way you lower costs is not by growing government; it's by increasing competition, allowing Americans to participate in association health plans, allowing Americans to purchase health insurance nationwide.

The President's vision for health care I truly do believe is -- it represents the best of this country. It's unleashing the full power of the marketplace. And with your help and with your support, we're well on our way to a better health care future for every American. (Applause.)

It will benefit everybody in this room. It will benefit the country as a whole.

But so will the rest of our agenda, for that matter. So let me talk on that before I take my leave and head back to Capitol Hill to talk to a few members of Congress. We're going to get this economy moving again after we repeal and replace Obamacare. We're going to cut taxes across the board for working families, small businesses and family farms. (Applause.)

I **promise** you we're going to keep rolling back red tape, slashing all the job-killing regulations. We're going to rein in unelected bureaucrats so they can't cripple the economy from the comfort of their taxpayer-funded metal desk. (Applause.)

We're going to keep rolling back -- we're going to roll back Dodd-Frank so small businesses like yours have access to capital, access to the best financial system in the world. You got to be able to borrow to grow in small business America. (Applause.)

And we're going to pass an infrastructure package so that Americans have the best roads, the best bridges, the best highways and airports, and the best future that we could ever imagine.

And we're going to stand up for real education reform. The President is absolutely committed to ensuring that every American parent have the freedom to send their children to the school of their choice -- public, private, parochial, charter, or home -- regardless of income or area code. (Applause.)

I know how much that last issue particularly means to the Hispanic community. And rest assured, with the leadership of our new Secretary of Education, Betsy DeVos, we're going to work with members of Congress to make historic strides so that every child in America has access to a world-class education.

We're going to do all this and more, so that everyone can climb the ladder of opportunity in the days ahead. And when the President said we're going to **Make America Great Again**, he meant it. And President Trump is a man of his word.

But America's greatness isn't simply about policy. Ultimately the strength of this country comes from our people. And as I close, let me say I count one of the greatest blessings of my life is just simply to be an American. (Applause.)

All of us, with very few exceptions, are descended from those who came here to this country, came here looking for a brighter future. Some were brought here involuntarily. Our Native American brothers and sisters were here when we arrived. But America, from our nation's founding, emerged as a land of opportunity in a merit-based society. And the truth of the matter is that it's precisely that vision of America, that merit-based society, that all of you personify. And it's been a truth, literally, a truth since our nation's birth. And as we've strived every day to a more perfect union, we continue to live out that aspiration and that vision.

In his joint address to the Congress just last week, the President made a couple more **promises**. He **promised** to serve, protect, and defend the citizens of the United States; to strengthen our nation's security and, in his words, to respect -- to restore and respect, rather, the laws of this country. Now, that includes the important work that's before us today -- securing our borders, upholding our laws. And make no mistake about it, as we do that, the President has placed a priority -- as we move through these issues, the top priority, in his words, is removing gang members, drug dealers and criminals that threated our communities and prey on our citizens. And that will be this administration's focus for every community. (Applause.)

The President and I believe that a system based on the rule of law will benefit every American, including our Hispanic Americans. Every community from coast to coast will benefit from upholding our laws and expanding our economy. As President Trump said to Congress, and I quote -- "Real and positive immigration reform is possible." And I can assure everyone here that as that debate goes forward, we will, as the President **promised**, show great heart every step of the way. (Applause.)

Now, for my part, I take all this very personally. You see, as I said last time I was here at this Coalition meeting, I'm actually the grandson of an immigrant. So is the President. The story in my family was that nearly a century ago, my great-grandmother walked my grandfather out of that two-room house they lived in, in northwestern Ireland, walked up the hill across from their home where I've stood, and looked out at the Ox Mountains, and looked to the west. And she told him she was going to get him a one-way ticket to America because, she said, there's a future there for you.

Richard Michael Cawley actually stepped ashore on Ellis Island as a young man on April 11, 1923. And that's how Michael Richard Pence grew up to be Vice President of the United States of America. (Applause.)

That young man made his way to Chicago. He drove a bus for 40 years, and he was the proudest man I ever knew, and the best man I ever knew.

On Inauguration Day, I'll be honest with you, I had him on my heart and on my mind. And as I sat on that stage, as I raised my right hand, I actually couldn't imagine what that Irishman was thinking, looking down from glory. Except two thoughts. I'm sure he was very surprised. (Laughter.)

Because he knew me well. The other thing I have to think he had to conclude is that he was right, his mother was right -- was right about America. It is the land of opportunity. It's the place where **dreams** come true.

It's what each of you proves each and every single day. If you work hard, play by the rules, look after your family, you look after your neighbors, and you keep working hard, anybody can be anybody in America. And I just **promise** you, this grandson of that immigrant, and the grandson of an immigrant that I work for, I'm going to work with each and every one of you to keep the **American Dream** alive and to renew it and make it greater than it's ever been before. (Applause.)

And really what I've laid out today is President Trump's vision and his plan to **Make America Great Again** and really **renew** the **American Dream**. We have our work cut out for us, and I'm confident that with your help and with God's help, and with President Donald Trump in the White House, America's best days are yet to come. Let's get to work.

Thanks, everybody. (Applause.)

God bless you, and God bless the United States. (Applause.)

END

CHAPTER 78

REMARKS BY THE VICE PRESIDENT IN LOUISVILLE, KY
ON OBAMACARE
HARSHAW TRANE
LOUISVILLE, KENTUCKY

12 March 2017

11:20 A.M. EST

THE VICE PRESIDENT: Hello, Kentucky!

AUDIENCE MEMBERS: Hello!

THE VICE PRESIDENT: Thank you, Governor, for that great introduction. And, ladies and gentleman, how about that Governor Matt Bevin? Everybody, isn't he something. (Applause.)

Kentucky, I truly do believe -- I like to say to people I was for Matt Bevin before it was cool. (Laughter.)

Kentucky really is blessed to have such a principled leader who's doing such great things for the state, restoring fiscal responsibility, rolling back red tape, and today, because of Governor Matt Bevin, Kentucky is now a right-to-work state. Kentucky is open for business. (Applause.)

Governor, the President and I are proud to partner with you to Make Kentucky Great Again, as we **Make America Great Again.** (Applause.)

I get along great with people from Kentucky, except in

March. (Laughter.)

It's gets a little testy some evenings.

But the same goes with all my strong feeling about your governor goes for other dedicated public servants who are here. State Senator Ralph Alvarado just joined us for a great discussion. And two great congressmen who I served with in Washington, D.C. Congressman Andy Barr and Congressman Brett Guthrie, would you all just take -- stand up and let these people show how much they appreciate your conservative stand in Washington, D.C. (Applause.)

Thank you both.

And I got to tell you it's great to be in the home state of the Senate Majority Leader, Mitch McConnell. He's a true friend to me, to our President, and to the people of America. (Applause.)

Great to have the privilege to be back in the Bluegrass State. Last fall, thanks to all of you here in Kentucky, to your hard work, your support, and your prayers, Kentucky voted to make Donald Trump the 45th President of the United States of America in a decisive vote. (Applause.)

And it was quite a campaign, wasn't it? And it's been quite an administration, too. I got to tell you on a very personal level, it's the greatest honor of my life to serve as Vice President to President Donald Trump. And I want to thank you all for the privilege. (Applause.)

The President is a man of boundless energy, optimism. I like to say he's got broad shoulders and a big heart.

And speaking of which, the President asked me late yesterday when we were leaving the White House in the evening to just say thanks to everyone gathered here today. Hardworking Americans like all of you were some of our biggest supporters. And on behalf of President Trump, thank you. Thank you for your support, and thank you for being here today. We're truly grateful. (Applause.)

And to all the business owners who are with us here today, I enjoyed our discussion earlier. The Governor and I had a brisk discussion about the challenges that -- changes in healthcare in this country since 2010 have presented to business. I appreciate your candid feedback about what our administration can do to help your businesses succeed and grow. And I have to tell you one other person I want to mention before I thank our host, it is always good to have Papa John in the house. John Schnatter and his wonderful wife are with us today. The Midwest is proud that you call Kentucky and America home. (Applause.)

John, thank you. There he is.

But last but not least, on behalf of the President, let me thank Harshaw Trane for their hospitality. While Frank Harshaw couldn't be here today, not only do I appreciate the warm welcome of his team -- Richard and Tom and Lou -- we just so admire Frank building an extraordinary business, someone who grew up in foster care. Frank and his story are the story of the **American Dream**. And would you join me in thanking them for allowing this great business to be our backdrop. (Applause.)

And all of those who run businesses, own businesses, or work in small business, let me make you a **promise**: The President wants you to know that our administration will be the best friend America's small businesses will ever have. (Applause.)

And the President and I know that small businesses are the engines of the American economy. As President Trump said in his joint address to Congress just last week, we're going to "restart the engine" to create jobs and prosperity and growth in America like never before.

You know, I grew up in a small business family, just a little bit north of here in Columbus, Indiana. I went to work at my father's gas station when I was only 14 years of age. I was actually what was called a gas station attendant. If you're under the age of 30, I'll explain to you after the program exactly what that was.

But as the world also knows, the President grew up in a family business, too. We both know the sacrifices that are required to make a business work. And more importantly, we know that when small business is strong, America is strong. And this President is going to fight every day to make that a reality. (Applause.)

President Trump wants to help you become stronger than ever before. He made a **promise** to you and to the American people -- and as I like to say, this White House is in the **promise-keeping** business.

Just look at what we've done over the past month-and-a-half. On day one, President Trump went straight to work rolling back reams of red tape. He actually instructed every agency in the federal government to find two regulations to get rid of before issuing any new regulations on job creators in America. (Applause.)

The President has taken decisive action to protect American jobs and American workers by taking measures to secure our border, to build a wall, and end illegal immigration once and for all. (Applause.)

The President authorized the Keystone and Dakota pipelines at last creating thousands of American jobs and building on America's energy infrastructure. (Applause.)

Businesses -- and if you haven't noticed already, businesses have been already reacting to President Trump's **vision**, his **"Buy American, Hire American" vision** with optimism and investment around the country.

From coast to coast, literally since Election Day, companies have been announcing that they're keeping jobs here. They're creating new ones. Last month alone, the economy added an amazing 235,000 jobs in the month of February. This economy is coming back and coming back strong. (Applause.)

And most importantly of all, the top priority the President gave us: to work with members of Congress and make sure that the Obamacare nightmare is about to end. (Applause.)

I'll tell you, it's amazing to think about -- virtually every promise of Obamacare has been broken. We all remember the promises that they made back in 2010 when this was signed into law. They told us the cost of health insurance would go down -- not true. They told us that if you liked your doctors, you could keep 'em -- not true. They told us that if you liked your health plan, you could keep it -- not true.

Here are the heartbreaking facts. Today, Americans are paying $3,000 more a year on average for health insurance than the day Obamacare was signed into law. Last year alone, premiums spiked by 25 percent, and millions of Americans have lost their health insurance plans and lost their doctors.

And in one-third of the nation's counties, Americans only have one insurance company to choose from, which essentially means they have no choice at all. The truth is the American people are struggling under Obamacare every day, and so are small businesses like those so well represented here.

You all know exactly what I'm talking about. The truth is Kentucky is a textbook example of Obamacare's failures. Here in the Bluegrass State, premiums skyrocketed by an average of 24 percent last year, with some plans spiking by 47 percent.

Nearly half of the state only has one health insurer to choose from. And next year, Humana, headquartered right here in Louisville, is pulling out of Kentucky's Obamacare exchange.

Today, one-third of the state is on Medicaid -- and as your Governor has said over and over again, it's unsustainable. And Medicaid here in Kentucky is threatening to bankrupt this state.

Folks, this just can't continue, and I **promise** you it won't. (Applause.)

Since the day that Kentucky helped send President Trump to the White House, his top priority has been to repeal and replace Obamacare with something that actually works. And we've already made incredible progress.

The House released its repeal-and-replace bill on Monday, and it already passed with unanimous support from two committees, one of which Congressman Guthrie sits on. And, Congressman, I just want to thank you for your strong support to repeal and replace Obamacare. (Applause.)

Now I know that not every politician in Kentucky supports our plan to repeal and replace Obamacare. I know your former Governor Steve Beshear has been defending Obamacare all over America. And he might even have something to say about my visit here today, and I welcome the debate. I really do.

Steve Beshear is actually a friend of mine. We worked together while I was Governor of Indiana to promote jobs and growth all across Kentuckiana. And I'm awful proud of those Ohio River bridges, aren't you? (Applause.)

The great story about collaboration between our two states, the Abraham Lincoln Bridge and the Lewis and Clark Bridge I believe are going to support economic growth across this region for generations. But your former Governor is wrong about Obamacare. (Applause.)

Obamacare has failed the people of Kentucky. It's failed the people of America, and Obamacare must go. (Applause.)

Now, the plan the President outlined in his joint address to the Congress is the plan we're working on. We're going to repeal and replace Obamacare once and for all, and we're going to replace it with health-care reform that will improve the lives of every American and strengthen our economy.

The truth is ordering every American to buy health insurance, whether they wanted it or not, was never the right solution for health care in this country. So we're going to start -- we're going to repeal the mandates and taxes and penalties of Obamacare. (Applause.)

We're going to end Obamacare's individual and employer mandates. We're actually going to get rid of more than $500 billion in Obamacare's tax increases. (Applause.)

And we're going to give Americans more choices. We'll expand health savings accounts. We'll give Americans a tax credit that will help people buy plans that they need at a price that they can afford.

We'll make sure that Americans with pre-existing conditions still have access to the coverage and the care that they need. And to all the parents here, we'll make sure you can keep your kids on your plan until they're 26 years of age.

And most significantly in my view, we'll give states like Kentucky the freedom and flexibility with Medicaid to meet the needs of your most vulnerable in the way that works here in Kentucky. (Applause.)

The bill moving through the Congress today is going to give Governor Bevin and, frankly, states all across the country the chance to reform Medicaid so it will better serve the underprivileged in your state, with better coverage, better health, and better outcomes just like the Governor said --

uniquely designed for the people of Kentucky -- a little like we did in the Hoosier State not too long ago.

I'll never forget being here for Governor Bevin's inaugural address. Anybody else remember that sunny day? (Applause.)

As I was sitting and listening on, I remember hearing the Governor say that announced his intention to reform Medicaid using some of the same conservative principles that we used in Indiana.

He said then, that he was inspired by Indiana's reforms, but he was pretty sure Kentucky could do better than Indiana. And I'd like to see him try. (Laughter.)

In fact, President Trump truly does believe that giving states like Kentucky, like Indiana, like every state in the union, the resources and flexibility to improve their health-care programs and Medicaid is the American way to meet the needs of our most vulnerable, and we're going to make it happen. (Applause.)

This competition between the states will give the American people better health-care choices.

And under President Trump's leadership, we're actually also going to finally allow Americans to purchase health insurance across state lines -- the way you buy life insurance, the way you buy car insurance. (Applause.)

President Trump and I both know the way to lower the cost of health insurance is to create a national marketplace and give Americans more choices to buy the insurance they want, not the insurance that the government mandates them to have.

But, folks, let me be clear, this is going to be a battle in Washington, D.C. And for us to seize this opportunity to repeal and replace Obamacare once and for all, we need every Republican in Congress -- and we're counting on Kentucky. President Trump and I know -- at the end of the day, after a good and vigorous debate -- we know Kentucky will be there. And we will repeal and replace Obamacare -- once and for all. (Applause.)

And let me say one more thing, despite some of the fear-mongering by those on the liberal left, I want to assure the people of Kentucky who might be looking on this morning: We're going to work with the Congress and work with our agency at Health and Human Services, and we're going to have an orderly transition to a better health-care system that makes affordable, high-quality health insurance available for every American. (Applause.)

In a word, we're going to make the best health-care system in the world even better. Now, while I came here to talk about Obamacare, it's really just the start of what our administration is doing to **Make America Great Again**.

And let me give you a quick preview of that before I head back on that airplane. First off, after we get this done, we're going to cut taxes across the board for working families, small businesses, and family farms. (Applause.)

We're going to keep slashing through red tape and rein in unelected bureaucrats so they can't cripple the economy from the comfort of their metal taxpayer-funded desks in Washington, D.C. (Applause.)

We're going to do a little bit more like we did with those bridges, we're going to rebuild America so we have the best roads and bridges and highways and airports that America has ever had. (Applause.)

But **Making America Great Again** doesn't stop just there. This President has no higher priority I **promise** you than the **safety** and **security** of the American people, and he's working every single day to protect our nation and our way of life.

This is a President I can tell you appreciates the men and women of our law enforcement community, and he is standing every day with those who serve and protect our country in law enforcement. (Applause.)

President Trump, as I mentioned, is also taking steps to strengthen our borders, to enforce our laws, and as the President said, we're working through Immigrations and Customs Enforcement in close concert with law enforcement in every community, and we're taking in his words the "gang members, the drug dealers, and the criminals that threaten our communities and prey on our citizens" off the streets of Kentucky and off the streets of our country. (Applause.)

Now, while we talk about those that serve in uniform, as the proud father of a United States Marine, let me tell you how grateful I am that in President Donald Trump we have a Commander-in-Chief who will rebuild our military, restore the arsenal of democracy, and give our soldiers, sailors, airmen, Marines, and Coast Guard the resources and training they need to accomplish their mission and protect our nation. (Applause.)

And by nominating Judge Neil Gorsuch to the Supreme Court of the United States, President Trump **kept his word** to appoint a Justice to the Supreme Court who will keep faith with the Constitution, and he'll be a justice who will uphold the God-given liberties that are enshrined in our Bill of Rights. (Applause.)

My friends, let me tell you, President Trump is a man of his word, and he's a man of action. And I believe he will **Make America Great Again**. I think we've come to a pivotal moment in our nation's history. I truly do.

In this moment, we need every freedom-loving American to join with us in this effort to **Make America Great Again**. We need all of you to stand up, to speak out, to let your voice be heard. There's no time like the present.

We need you to tell the world that we can do better. We can do better on healthcare. We can do better with a growing economy. We can stand tall and strong in a world again. We can restore this country, put it back to a path to a brighter future.

And I know we're going to do this. I truly do.

One of my favorite verses in the Old Book is from the Book of Jeremiah. It's hung over the mantle of our home since before I was actually first elected to office now more than 16 years ago. Now it hangs over the mantle in the Vice President's Residence in Washington, D.C.

It reads: "For I know the plans I have for you, plans to prosper you, and not to harm you, plans to give you a hope, and a future."

In November, the people of Kentucky voted to give America a President with the strength, and the courage, and the **vision**, to **Make America Safe Again**.

You voted to give us a new leader who I believe will **Make America Prosperous Again** and give us a fresh start on healthcare and economic growth.

And so I truly do believe with all my heart, that with your continued faith and support, and with God's help, together we will **Make America Great Again**.

Thank you very much for being here on this Saturday. God bless you and God bless the United States of America. (Applause.)

END
11:41 A.M. EST

Chapter 79

13 March 2017

THE PRESIDENT: Today we're beginning the process of a long-overdue reorganization of our federal departments and agencies.

We've assembled one of the greatest Cabinets in history, and I believe that so strongly. And we want to empower them to make their agencies as lean and effective as possible, and they know how to do it.

Today there is duplication and redundancy everywhere. Billions and billions of dollars are being wasted on activities that are not delivering results for hardworking American taxpayers, and not even coming close.

This order requires a thorough examination of every executive department and agency to see where money is being wasted, how services can be improved, and whether programs are truly serving American citizens.

The Director of Office of Management and Budget will oversee the evaluation working with experts inside and outside of the federal government, as well as seeking input from the American people themselves.

Based on this input, we will develop a detailed plan to make the federal government work better -- reorganizing, consolidating, and eliminating where necessary: In other words, making the federal government more efficient and very, very cost productive.

So we're going to do something I think very, very special -- they never have been done to the extent that we're going to be able to do it. And you're already seeing results.

We will then work with Congress to implement these recommendations on behalf of the American people.

So with that, I want to thank everybody very much, and I want to wish the Cabinet good luck. I think we have some of the finest people ever assembled for a Cabinet. We're going to do a great job for the American people.

Thank you very much.

END

Chapter 80

13 March 2017

11:27 A.M. EDT

THE PRESIDENT: Thank you all for being here today. It's a great honor for you to share your personal stories of struggle under the enormous strain imposed on you by the very, very failed and failing Obamacare law. Secretary Price and I, along with my entire administration, and a lot of people in the Senate and a lot of people in the House are committed to repealing and replacing this disastrous law with a healthcare plan that lowers cost, expands choice, and ensures access for everyone.

You represent the millions of Americans who have seen their Obamacare premiums increase by double digits and even triple digits. In Arizona, the rates were over 116 percent last year -- 116 percent increase. And the deductibles are so high you don't even get to use it.

Many Americans lost their plans and doctors altogether, and one-third of the counties -- think of it, one-third only have one insurer left. The insurance companies are fleeing. They're gone; so many gone. The House bill to repeal and replace Obamacare will provide you and your fellow citizens with more choices -- far more choices at lower cost. Americans should pick the plan they want. Now they'll be able to pick the plan they want, they'll be able to pick the doctor they want. They'll be able to do a lot of things that the other plan was supposed to give and it never gave. You don't pick your doctor, you don't pick your plan -- you remember that one.

We're not going to have one-size-fits-all. Instead, we're going to be working to unleash the power of the private marketplace to let insurers come in and compete for your business. And you'll see rates go down, down, down, and you'll see plans go up, up, up. You'll have a lot of choices. You'll have plans that nobody is even thinking of to-day. They will have plans that today nobody has even thought about, because the market is going to enforce that, with millions and millions of people wanting health-care. More competition and less regulation will finally bring down the cost of care, and I think it will bring it down very significantly. Unfortunately, it takes a while to get there, because you have to let that marketplace kick in, and it's going to take a little while to get there. Once it does, it's going to be a thing of beauty. I wish it didn't take a year or two years, but that's what's going to happen, and that's the way it works. But we're willing to go through that process.

Working together, we'll get the job done. And I have to say this just in closing, and then I want to hear some of your stories, and we'll let the press stay for your stories if you like. But the press is making Obamacare look so good all of a sudden. I'm watching the news -- looks so good. They're showing these reports about "this one gets so much and this one gets so much."

First of all, it covers very few people. And it's implod-ing. And '17 will be the worst year. And I said it once, I'll say it again -- because Obama is gone -- things are going to be very bad this year for the people with Obamacare. They're going to have tremendous increases.

And the Republicans, frankly, are putting themselves in a very bad position -- and I tell this to Tom Price all the time -- by repealing Obamacare -- because people aren't going to see the truly devastating effects of Obamacare. They're not going to see the devastation in '17 and '18 and '19. It'll be gone by then, whether we do it or not. It'll be imploded off the map.

So the press is making it look so wonderful so that if we end it, everyone is going to say, "Oh, remember how great Obamacare used to be, remember how wonderful it used to be, it was so great." It's a little bit like President Obama. When he left, people liked him. When he was here, people didn't like him so much. That's the way life goes. That's human nature.

The fact is, Obamacare is a disaster. And I say this to the Republicans all the time: By repealing it, by getting rid of it, by ending it, everyone is going to say, "Oh, it used to be so great." But it wasn't great. And I tell Tom Price and I tell Paul Ryan, I tell everyone of them -- I say, the best thing you can do politically is wait a year, because it's going to blow itself off the map. But that's the wrong thing to do for the country, it's the wrong thing to do for our citizens.

So with that, I'd like to introduce some of the folks and you could say a few words about your experience with Obamacare. And perhaps the press will even report it. (Laughter.)

Would you like to start?

MS. COUEY: Yeah, thank you for this opportunity, Mr. President.

THE PRESIDENT: Thank you. Thank you.

MS. COUEY: Our rates are three times what they were before Obamacare started. We have one provider in our county. We have very little options for what we can and cannot do. We're a small-business owner; we're actually not a brick-and-mortar, we are cattle ranchers. We can't afford our equipment if we're paying these rates year after year after year.

Our food source is in jeopardy because of this healthcare law. It's my basic --

THE PRESIDENT: I know. Sorry. Don't worry. Don't worry. This is what's happening. It's gone up three times, and then you have to pay -- if you don't want to use it, you have to pay. That's the all-time beauty. If you don't want to use it, you have to pay. And, Tom, you have to pay big league, right? Some people say, well, if I use it, I use it, I'm paying too much. If I don't use it, I have to pay a penalty. And do you have to pay penalties? Do you ever do that, or you have to --

MS. COUEY: We haven't as of yet, but we were uninsured in December. They dropped us for the fourth time, after we paid over $50,000 last year for healthcare expenses.

THE PRESIDENT: And it's gone up triple.

MS. COUEY: Yes.

THE PRESIDENT: And before Obamacare, you actually had

good healthcare.

MS. COUEY: We did. We had a fantastic plan.

THE PRESIDENT: A lot of people -- nobody ever takes that into account. I'm not saying the system before was good, because it wasn't, but millions of people had great healthcare that they loved.

Now, when you start deducting those millions of people from the so-called people that are happy, you have a very small number of people that are happy. That, I can tell you.

How about you?

PARTICIPANT: Well, we're kind of the same story as Carrie. In 2009, I left a full-time job to be a stay-at-home mom to two kids. For our family, it was never an option to get government assistance; we just don't believe our neighbors should work harder so that we don't have to. So my husband said, if you can pay for our insurance -- which at the time was $650 a month for private health insurance for a family of four -- then that was fine.

From 2009 to 2015, that private insurance went up by 102 percent. Finally, his employer told us in 2015, when it went up the final time an additional 34 percent, that they couldn't carry our family anymore, so I had to enter back into the workforce but I couldn't find a job that offered health insurance. So we entered under Obamacare, and we believed the sales pitch that, "If you like your doctor you can keep your doctor."

So even though we were going to have to pay $1,300 a

month for Obamacare, we thought we'd still be okay with our doctors. We were on it for five months. Our pediatrician for our children wouldn't take it, my doctor wouldn't take it, so we paid them $8,000 in five months and were never able to use it.

And I think what makes our family story unique is, we're by no means wealthy. In 2014, when we entered the exchange, we made $53,000 as a family, my husband and I together -- that was our gross income. And then in 2015, we made together -- since I had gone back to work -- $74,000. But when you look at paying $10,000 in health premiums and insurance -- and health costs --

THE PRESIDENT: So it's been a rough go.

PARTICIPANT: It has, it's been hard.

THE PRESIDENT: How have you found Obamacare?

PARTICIPANT: We'll be so happy to see it gone. I mean, it's almost put our family in financial ruin, and I think that's the story for a lot of people.

THE PRESIDENT: It's put businesses in financial ruin.

PARTICIPANT: That's right.

THE PRESIDENT: It's one of the biggest costs -- it has been disastrous for businesses.

Go ahead, sir.

MR. SEIFE: Yes, first of all, Mr. President, thank you for having us here.

THE PRESIDENT: Thank you.

MR. SEIFE: I think it's a great opportunity to talk to the American people, people like ourselves that have struggled with the healthcare law.

I myself am from Miami. I haven't had very much time to prepare, but the President of the United States calls and I'm here. (Laughter.)

So it just so happened I had -- every single year for the past couple of years I've had a different insurance every single year. Before, I had an individual plan, my wife and I -- my wife is an attorney, I'm a computer programmer; I'm a small business, my wife is a small business. And I just don't understand what happened. I have a daughter with a disability. We've changed our plan every year.

THE PRESIDENT: So your insurance was good before Obamacare.

MR. SEIFE: Oh, absolutely. I never had --

THE PRESIDENT: Many people are like that. Many, many plans were great before Obamacare. They were so happy. And that doesn't justify the system before Obamacare, but people are miserable now, and it's putting people out of business and it's putting them in the poorhouse. Go ahead.

MR. SEIFE: It's just that we had to -- they cancelled our plans, and I couldn't understand why they cancelled our plans. So we had no other choice. I remember the President of the United States say that individual plans will not be covered, you need to have an employer-based plan. I do not work for the government, I do not work for a large employer.

THE PRESIDENT: Very unfair.

MR. SEIFE: We are ground zero. My case is ground zero for the healthcare law.

THE PRESIDENT: And you represent a lot of people in the same situation.

MR. SEIFE: Absolutely.

THE PRESIDENT: It's very unfair.

MR. SEIFE: Like my friend here, she's in the same situation. And I think it's very, very unfair. And I think that the real scenario was that this law was supposed to implode, like you were saying. And my parents are from -- came from communist Cuba, they know what socialism is all about. So I know what socialism is, and that's pretty much what -- this whole system was meant to have one single provider.

THE PRESIDENT: Well, it turns out it's so expensive it's almost not socialism when you think about it. (Laughter.)

You have to pay so much.

What do you think? Go ahead.

MS. SERTICH: I'm from Arizona, and I can tell you that the 116-percent increase is real, it's not a myth. I lost my plan three times during the Obamacare era. After losing it this year I decided to opt out. So right now I do not have traditional healthcare.

And I went from a $365-a-month premium last year to a $809-premium this year.

THE PRESIDENT: And a higher deductible.

MS. SERTICH: The deductible was going to be $6,800, no copays. So if I went to the doctor, I would be paying out of my pocket, and it just didn't seem like a good use of my money. I thought I would be a better steward of that $17,000 at the end of the year should I have reached my deductible, and just decided to opt out. I went into a faith-based share program, and I'm doing that.

One of the reasons I felt like I can do this -- totally taking a leap of faith -- is because I think -- I know you're going to get this taken care of. So I thought it's only going to be for a year. I will be on this program, I will opt out of traditional healthcare, or health insurance. And I think you're going to get it done.

THE PRESIDENT: You have a lot of people in Arizona paying a big penalty?

MS. SERTICH: Yes.

THE PRESIDENT: You're paying the penalty?

MS. SERTICH: Well, and my husband also owns his own business and can't afford to offer insurance to employ-ees. And his employees who are also in the independent market, it's just getting too much. And I've had individual insurance for 25 years, since I started my business. So I've always been in that individual market, I've always done what was right. I took responsibility for myself, made sure I was covered for healthcare because I'm a businessperson, I don't want any huge healthcare expenses to affect the money that could be going to my business now having to go to a health expense.

So I was in my mid-20s when I said, you know what, I've got to get -- we've got to get square with this, I have to have independent insurance. So, I have.

THE PRESIDENT: Well, thank you very much. The people of Arizona have been hit very, very hard. At least 116 percent. Here's the bad news: It's going to go up more this year. Now, if we repeal it, nobody is going to know that, and the press is going to say how wonderful it was, and, gee, we miss Obamacare. That's the problem. It's the biggest problem I have, Tom. We're going to do them a big favor, but it's not the right way.

Go ahead.

MR. BROWN: Mr. President, thank you.

THE PRESIDENT: Thank you very much, Louis.

MR. BROWN: My name is Louis Brown. I work for the Christ Medicus Foundation. I'm an attorney by trade. In 2009, when the Affordable Care Act was going through Congress -- what became the Affordable Care Act -- I was working for the Democratic National Committee at the time. I resigned my position because I could tell that the Democratic bill that was going through Congress wanted to publicly fund abortion, and that's not something that I could go along with. So I resigned my position, later worked for Congressman Dan Lungren in Congress, and went on to eventually work for the Christ Medicus Foundation. And we're focused on building a culture of life, protecting religious liberty in healthcare, protecting the right of conscience, prohibiting the public funding of abortion, and also prohibiting non-discrimination against pro-life medical providers.

Especially as an African American, I'm a graduate of Howard University School of Law.

THE PRESIDENT: Good school.

MR. BROWN: Yeah. Thank you, Mr. President. And I know from Saint John Paul II -- he said that all of our human and civil rights that we believe in as Americans, that we share as Americans -- the right to healthcare, the right to medical care, to housing, to all of these different things -- are illusory if the right to life isn't defended with maximum determination.

Seventeen million African Americans, it's shown, that probably have been aborted since Roe v. Wade. And I supported you in the presidential election, gave several speeches in Michigan telling folks to vote pro-life in the general election, and I'm really happy that you're here to continue the bipartisan belief that there should be no taxpayer-funding of abortion, and also really to support your effort to show that the patient, the human person, should be at the center of our American healthcare system, not the government. The government has its place, but the patient should be the center. So I'm happy to support you, Mr. President.

THE PRESIDENT: Thank you. That's so nice. Thank you, I appreciate it. Great job.

Yes, go ahead.

DR. SETHI: Mr. President, thank you so much for inviting me. My name is Dr. Manny, and I run a nonprofit called Healthy Tennessee, and across Tennessee I'm a trauma surgeon. But what we do is --

THE PRESIDENT: I'll be in Tennessee on Wednesday.

DR. MANNY: We look forward to hosting you, sir.

THE PRESIDENT: I'll see you there.

DR. MANNY: Yes, sir. We do these large community events in rural Appalachia, across Tennessee, where we host these health fairs taking care of patients. So it's really a grassroots effort -- something that you understand better than anybody -- where people come out just to help people. Doctors, nurses on the ground, helping folks with preventative medicine, educating folks. That's what we do. But the one thing I've been seeing across Tennessee is that folks really can't afford these rising premiums. So what they're doing is, effectively, they're paying the tax penalty because it's cheaper and it works out better than paying for the insurance. And so that's been a big problem that we're seeing across the state. So thank you so much for what you're doing to tackle this problem.

THE PRESIDENT: So you've seen a big problem, and the way out of the problem is to do a plan much more like the plan we're going to get done.

DR. MANNY: Yes, sir.

THE PRESIDENT: We'll get that out -- without penalties

too, by the way. People don't mention all of the facts. You know, the other thing about what we're talking about -- we really have a three-phase plan. They only want to talk about the first phase. The first phase is just the most basic of phases, and then you have phase two, which is largely done by our Secretary, and then you have phase three, which is a lot of the bells and whistles. But they don't want to talk about the bells and whistles. So they're really comparing things to something that won't be there for long.

And the reason we have to do it that way is because of Congress. I'd love to do it all in one package, but if you did it that way, it can't get done. So we're going to get something done that's going to be terrific.

I appreciate it. Thank you, doctor, very much.

Yes, sir. Go ahead.

MR. BROWN: Thank you, Mr. President. I'd like to thank you for the opportunity to be here today. I, too, am from Tennessee, and I, too, am in the farming industry.

THE PRESIDENT: Good.

MR. BROWN: And the effect that I've had through Obamacare is my wife's and my daughter's insurance is supplied through her work, I buy my own. And I've seen the increases, since Obamacare, to the tune of about $5,000 a year, just for me. And I have considered taking the option of the penalty because -- my problem with the penalty is, though, if I opt out of the program, and buy a private plan -- just a catastrophic plan because I'm a very healthy man -- if I take that option, not only is my income penalized, but my wife's income as well, because she makes a considerable more amount of money than I do, but she has insurance. So I don't think that's fair.

And I don't think -- the rate increase is just astronomical, and I'm in the county that only has one option -- BlueCross BlueShield of Tennessee --and I've got about $540-a-month premium for the $7,000 out-of-pocket deductible before I see any help at all. And I even got to pay a high premium for a plan that I don't need or don't want --

THE PRESIDENT: Will you be able to continue, in the years to come, if you have to keep going like this?

MR. BROWN: They're dropping out every day -- the suppliers in other counties. There's 35 counties in Tennessee that has no options at all right now. I don't know what those folks do.

THE PRESIDENT: You know what that means? That means somebody is going to make a lot of money. You know that. They're going to make a lot of money. (Laughter.)

Somebody is going to -- well, a few. You're not going to make it. They're going to make it. There are people very happy about this situation.

MR. BROWN: Thank you for the opportunity to be here.

THE PRESIDENT: Well, I appreciate. Thank you, Joel.

Doctor?

DR. ARMSTRONG: Yes, sir. Well, I'm a physician in Texas, and thank you for allowing me to be here today. And I'll tell you, what I've seen is that a lot of patients really are not adequately covered by Obamacare. It was supposed to cover people who had -- like everyone has said here -- with the rising premiums and the rising deductibles. I take care of patients in the hospital, and the patients are shocked to get a $20,000 bill, and to find that they're responsible for $6,000 of that because their deductible is so high. And that's just the situation that cannot continue.

Medicaid expansion under Obamacare really doesn't cover folks either, because many physicians are not even taking Medicare. They're not accepting it any longer in the outpatient setting. And so folks who have chronic medical illnesses, like cancer -- I mean, my wife is a breast cancer survivor, and most of her treatment was actually as an outpatient. It was very expensive outpatient care. Most physicians don't even accept Medicaid, so those patients are still uncovered.

And so the Medicaid expansion really hasn't covered them. The folks who have Obamacare insurance really are inadequately covered as well because they're still paying extremely high premiums and then having to pay extremely high deductibles. And so it's really --

THE PRESIDENT: And do they even reach it with the high deductibles? They don't even reach it for the most part.

DR. ARMSTRONG: You know, oftentimes they do not, unless they have some sort of serious medical problem, and they're in the hospital, and it's very expensive -- they don't even reach their deductible oftentimes. And so it's unfortunate. So I really appreciate it.

I actually read the bill that's been produced that's coming

out of the House now, and I really like a lot of the changes in it. I think that this is going to correct a lot of the issues that Obamacare has had. So I really appreciate what you all are doing.

THE PRESIDENT: Well, I appreciate it, doctor. Thank you. Say hello to your wife.

DR. ARMSTRONG: Yes, sir. I will. Thank you.

THE PRESIDENT: Very nice. Thank you.

Gina.

MS. SELL: Hi, Mr. President, I'm Gina. I'm from Wisconsin. I'm a nurse, I'm a mom, and I am part of that huge group of middle-class families that were impacted by the ACA.

Before ACA, we had insurance that was eventually cancelled, and I had written a letter to our senator just asking him, what do I do? Do I quit my job completely so that we can obtain a subsidy -- a job that I love, as a nurse in a hospital that I love? Or do I uproot my family and try to find a job with benefits that doesn't even cover the medical --

THE PRESIDENT: So the healthcare is -- the Obamacare forced you to actually -- in a sense, forces you, economically and almost potentially, to get another job.

MS. SELL: Right.

THE PRESIDENT: Even though you like your job.

MS. SELL: Right. So I did end up getting a full-time position at the hospital that I worked at. But that came with a price because I was working three days a week, and spending time with my small children, who are my number-one priority. And after the ACA, I was forced -- because we could not afford a premium of $1,200 per month and a deductible that didn't cover anything -- to find a job with benefits.

THE PRESIDENT: Meaning the deductible was so high that, essentially, unless you had a really big problem, you wouldn't even be able to use it.

The deductible was so high that essentially unless you had a really big problem, you wouldn't even be able to use it.

MS. SELL: Correct, yes. And we're still in that boat. I mean, right now our deductible is $6,500. And so if I have a child who's extremely sick, it's going to cost me hundreds of dollars. Just last week, my daughter had a fever, and I sent her to school for three days straight because I had to work to afford our assurance, and I couldn't afford to bring her to the doctor. So it has been devastating for our family.

THE PRESIDENT: It's really not having insurance at all. A lot of Obamacare, you don't really have insurance because the deductibles are so high that you really don't have insurance, if you think about it.

All right. Thank you very much. Good luck.

MS. SELL: Thank you.

THE PRESIDENT: Yes, sir.

MR. KNOX: Mr. President, thank you very much for hosting us. This is great. I have to start with something. As I was leaving the house, my 11-year-old ran up to me and said, "Dad, I'd like to have you give this to Mr. President for me." (Laughter.)

THE PRESIDENT: What do you have there? I wished I looked that good. (Laughter.)

MR. KNOX: "Dear President Trump, it is a great honor to be able to write to the President of the USA. I think you are a great President and a great man. Also, don't worry, the picture of you on the front of this looks nothing like you." (Laughter.)

THE PRESIDENT: (Laughter.)

That's very nice. Thank you. Thank you. I wish I looked that good.

MR. KNOX: So I had the privilege of meeting with Secretary Price and Vice President Pence in Cincinnati about a week and a half ago at a roundtable, and I'll share with you what I shared with them. I started with a quote from the great President, Ronald Reagan, who said, "The most terrifying words in the English language are we're from the government and we're here to help.'" (Laughter.)

Kind of my feeling on healthcare.

Frankly, I think that the system was broken before the last administration got their hands on it. I started my company 21 years ago, and I had a vision of wanting to provide 100 percent full family healthcare for as long as I had a company, because I really felt in my heart that it was the right thing to do. I was one of the last holdouts. But, sadly, after about 15 years, I really had a choice of either having a company or being able to provide my employees that level of healthcare. And that's sad. I tell my wife all the time -- you can have anything you want, we just can't everything we want. We have the best healthcare system in the world -- we do -- but it needs to be fixed -- whether it's small business owners, like myself -- I'm a manufacturer, I'm on several boards in the Midwest in manufacturing.

What we'd like to see is not a government-operated market, but a free market. I sell (inaudible) equipment for a living. We have a trade show every year, and there's hundreds and hundreds of people selling competitive products. If we had a healthcare show in my town, there would be three or four people under that roof. And as a businessman yourself, you know what that does to driving down costs or the lack thereof. So we would like to see more of a free-market solution, going back to what made this country great -- entrepreneurialism instead of empowerments; work ethics instead of welfare. And that's what we'd like to ask you for. And I'd like to say thank you very much.

THE PRESIDENT: As you know, that's what we're doing largely, but we also have to take care of people that can't afford to be in a position like you are. So we're going to do that. Largely, I think beyond everything, if you look at what's going to happen -- the competitive bidding -- every element of what we're doing is competitive bidding, but we have to take care of people who need the help. And there are a lot of people like that.

MR. KNOX: There's always been a safety net in the United States, and there should be. And, unfortunately, when I see 50,000 -- or 50 million Americans taking assistance

in -- you know, they're market food stamps. That's like
-- for the people who really can't provide for themselves,
you know, we're all charitable people who are Americans, we're the most generous nation on the face of the
Earth. So I totally believe in safety nets for those who need
them, not free handouts for (inaudible).

THE PRESIDENT: We're going to help a lot of people, but
we are going to be very much free market people. They
can afford -- and they'll be off the cost.

Go ahead, Stan.

MR. SUMMERS: I'm Mr. Stan Summers from Box Elder
County, northern Utah. I think I'm probably the only
other elected official here besides you guys. It's been an
interesting ride to watch the healthcare system in the last
26 years. When my son was born, he was three and a
half months premature, 26 years ago. And we had really
good insurance. We basically didn't have to pay anything
out of pocket besides what we were doing from where I
worked. As time went on, you could kind of tell the healthcare system has been a little bit broke, and then all of a
sudden the ACA -- and I'm not going to call it the other
word -- I call it the last President's healthcare program. I
don't want to say that name.

So anyway --

THE PRESIDENT: Other than that, you like him a lot,
right? (Laughter.)

MR. SUMMERS: Yeah, exactly. (Laughter.)

It's gotten to the point where I own a couple of businesses too and do the things that I have to do. I actually ran for government so I could have insurance -- and won. But now I'm looking at these people, saying, how can I provide insurance for them without raising taxes and doing these things that are happening -- because everything has gone up. Utah didn't expand Medicaid -- we weren't a part of that -- and we can see why now, because of the things that are happening throughout the nation with states and companies and everybody else going bankrupt.

So it got to the point where I ended up -- not only with my businesses -- I have to drive a school bus to keep my wife at home with my kid that was ill. So now I own three businesses, I drive a school bus, and I'm an elected official, to be able to continue to do the things that I need to do with healthcare. The last three -- well, the last three years --

THE PRESIDENT: So it's gone through the roof.

MR. SUMMERS: Oh, I got a $6,000 deductible -- HSA -- but I will meet that again in three months. So I'm at -- I think my wife said morning, at 4,800 or 4,900 bucks already this year in March to be able to meet my out-of-pocket. And so by the time April comes, I would have met that to be able to continue to do. And if there was one thing I probably could ask you about -- and my boy has got a rare disease, and I appreciate you talking about the rare [disease] community in your speeches -- is that if somebody has cancer or somebody has a rare disease or continues to have problems, why do we have to do a deductible every year?

So I'm sitting there at Christmas going, okay, my deductible has been met for six or eight months, and I'm going to turn around and have to do it again for the same disease, for the same symptoms, for the same everything.

THE PRESIDENT: That's interesting. Tom, could you answer that? That would be interesting.

SECRETARY PRICE: It's all about the risk and spreading the risk with insurance over a period of time. But it is a challenge for individuals with chronic disease, there's no doubt about it.

MR. SUMMERS: And I appreciate you even thinking about it and talking about grassroots, and when you're talking about all the people that we support with the farmers and ranchers, and the small-business people, and the people that are in manufacturing, our county is one of the largest manufacturing counties in the nation per capita. And Nucor would love to tell you thanks -- Nucor Steel would love to tell you thanks for everything you've been doing.

THE PRESIDENT: Nucor has been very good. It's going to get better, too.

MR. SUMMERS: And we've got a ton of those. The space program -- we used to make the shuttle boosters out of ATK Thiokal. And we'd love to have the space program. I got a really good friend.

THE PRESIDENT: Those days are gone, but they're coming back.

MR. SUMMERS: I've got a friend that's going to go up in the next little bit, Lieutenant Commander Scott Maker Tingle, who is headed up on a spaceship from Russia. But he would love to come back to the United States and be able to go up through the United States. So all those jobs I know will come back with you.

THE PRESIDENT: Well, Gary Cohn, who is sitting right next to you, he's a big believer in what you're saying -- right, Gary?

MR. SUMMERS: If there's anything we can do to help you, the counties are behind you. We can find you low-hanging fruit to be able to pick off that tree to help with jobs. Just let us know where we can help.

THE PRESIDENT: Good. Thank you, Stan.

MR. SUMMERS: Thank you for your time.

THE PRESIDENT: Would you have anything to say, Tom, generally speaking?

SECRETARY PRICE: Well, let me start, Mr. President -- really powerful about the consequences of the current law, and you hear people's lives that have been affected in remarkably adverse ways that sometimes you don't think about as it relates to healthcare -- whether it's businesses that haven't been able to survive, or individuals who need to take three, four, five jobs; moms that can't be with their kids when they want. This is about real people. It's about real patients.

And so working with you and your leadership, we are really excited about the opportunity to put in place a patient-centered system where patients and families and doctors are making decisions, and not Washington, D.C.

THE PRESIDENT: What about the concept that -- and everybody knows it's happening -- that Obamacare is imploding, that if we don't do anything, it's not even going to be around in another year? The insurance companies are fleeing. But now it seems to be getting this wonderful press like it's a wonderful thing, and it's a horrible thing actually, and getting worse. And '17 will be, by far, the worst year so far.

SECRETARY PRICE: Yes.

THE PRESIDENT: Because a lot of things were put into '17. But '17 is going to be worse, and I assume '18 will be worse even than '17. So it's essentially gone. How do you respond to that? Because I've been telling you, "Why don't we wait? Just let it implode, and let's not take the blame." I've been telling you that as an option. It's not an option I like, frankly, but it's certainly an option. How do you respond to that?

SECRETARY PRICE: I think '18 can be better if we implement the law and we utilize the regulatory process to make some --

THE PRESIDENT: Well, I'm not saying that. I'm saying, if we don't implement the law, what happens with Obamacare? What's going on with Obamacare?

SECRETARY PRICE: What you'll see is a magnification of all these stories around this table: more businesses being harmed, more individuals not having the kind of income that they -- disposable income that they would use, more moms and dads not able to care for their kids in the way that they believe to be most appropriate, more people getting insurance but no care. This is about real people's lives, and that's why it's so important.

THE PRESIDENT: Getting insurance but not being able to use it because the deductibles are so high.

SECRETARY PRICE: That's exactly right.

THE PRESIDENT: And you hear these stories where they're paying a fortune for insurance, and then you hear how high their deductible is. And unless they have a tragedy in their family, they're never going to be able to use it.

SECRETARY PRICE: Yes, this fellow has to -- $13,000 before the insurance kicks in. That's what he has to pay -- $13,000.

MR. SEIFE: That's like not having insurance.

SECRETARY PRICE: That's like not having insurance.

THE PRESIDENT: Well, keep working it.

MS. SERTICH: They're catastrophic plans now.

SECRETARY PRICE: Exactly.

THE PRESIDENT: He's been working very hard, and he's doing a great job.

Mr. Vice President, do you have anything to say?

THE VICE PRESIDENT: Mr. President, I think what unequivocally these great Americans see in high relief is you're someone who puts people over politics. And I just want to thank all of them for coming, and in front of the national media, talking about the real world and impacts of Obamacare. You've said it consistently over the last two years that Obamacare has failed. But these people are emblematic of the Americans that Obamacare has failed. And I just am so grateful for their time, but so grateful for your compassionate leadership in driving the Congress and driving our nation toward better healthcare outcomes for them and better solutions built on those American principles of more consumer choices, more free market, but also, as you said, the caring for the most vulnerable by allowing our states to innovate and medicate in ways that will create even better healthcare coverage than they have today.

THE PRESIDENT: Thank you, Mike. Thank you, everybody. Thank you very much.

Q   Mr. President, do you have any message for those who are concerned about losing their insurance, whether it be Medicaid or higher costs (inaudible)?

THE PRESIDENT: It will get better. If we're allowed to do what we want to do, it will get better -- much better. Hopefully it will get very good.

Q   So will it take long?

THE PRESIDENT: It takes a period of time. Thank you, press.

END
12:00 P.M. EDT

Chapter 81

REMARKS BY PRESIDENT TRUMP IN
FIRST CABINET MEETING
CABINET ROOM

13 March 2017

3:07 P.M. EDT

THE PRESIDENT: Hello, everybody. I'm proud to welcome everyone to our first official Cabinet meeting.

I want to begin by updating the public on the severe weather situation. I've been receiving the latest information on the blizzard forecast, and I think we're in very good shape. We're prepared -- everybody in government is fully prepared and ready.   And the entire Northeast, it seems, is under a very severe winter storm warning. So let's hope it's not going to be as bad as some people are predicting. Usually it isn't.

Chancellor Merkel and I have just spoken, and she's going to be postponing the trip until Friday. She'll be coming on Friday, and we look forward to that. It will be a very good visit.

I've spoken with my Homeland Security Advisor. He's spoken with the acting FEMA Administrator, instructed him to make certain that the federal government is ready to provide assistance to the states that need federal help. FEMA and the federal government are ready to assist. They are literally waiting by the phones and ready to go.

Everyone should listen to their state and local officials who will be providing regular storm updates. We take that advice very seriously.

This Cabinet is here to serve and protect the American people, and that's what we're doing -- even more so than anybody would understand. The folks in this room have done an amazing job, whether it's security or anything else. I want to thank General Mattis, who is now Secretary Mattis. I want to thank General Kelly, who is now Secretary Kelly. They've done outstanding work. You see what's happening. All you have to do is just watch. Big difference.

Unfortunately, not all of our Cabinet members could join us. We have four empty seats -- which is a terrible thing -- because the Senate Democrats are continuing to obstruct the confirmation of our nominees for the Department of Labor, the Department of Agriculture, the Director of National Intelligence, and the United States Trade Representative, somebody I want very badly. We're in the midst of getting going, Wilbur, and they won't approve somebody who is highly qualified, and everybody understands that. The main victim of this very partisan obstruction is the American public.

Yet in spite of all of this, we've assembled a great team and already made historic progress in delivering results. We're rolling back job-crushing regulations at a faster clip than ever before by far; and we're seeing companies like Exxon, Walmart, Intel, Ford, Fiat Chrysler, and so many others announcing that they will keep and create tens of thousands of jobs in the United States. Many, many companies are not moving now, which normally they would have been out of here a long time ago. They're not moving because they understand there are going to be consequences. If they move, that's fine, but there will be consequences. It's not going to be so easy. They're not going to fire our people and move and think they're going to ship their jobs back here and we won't be doing anything about it.

The first two job reports that have come out since my Inauguration, we've already added nearly half a million new jobs. Right after this meeting, we'll be signing a new executive order to begin the process of reorganizing the executive branch to make it less wasteful and more productive. We're also working closely with the House and Senate Republicans to repeal and replace Obamacare.

Obamacare, all of a sudden, the last couple of weeks is getting a false rep that maybe it's okay. It's not okay; it's a disaster -- and people understand that. It's failed and it's imploding. And if we let it go for another year, it will totally implode. In fact, I've told the Republicans, why don't you just let it go for another year, that way everybody will really understand how bad it is. But it would be the wrong thing for us to do and for the American people.

The House plan will expand choice, lower cost, and ensure healthcare access for all. We're negotiating with everybody. It's a big, fat, beautiful negotiation, and hopefully we'll come up with something that's going to be really terrific.

I want to thank Paul Ryan and everybody -- Mitch, everybody, they're all working around the clock. And I think ultimately the big beneficiary will be the American people. We'll end up with a really great healthcare plan. We're also going to send Congress a budget request that will include one of the largest increases to defense spending in our history. And General/Secretary Mattis is extremely upset about that. (Laughter.)

And it will be fully paid for, okay? Fully paid for. And I saved a lot of money on those jets, didn't I? Did I do a good job? More than $725 million on them. He's very happy with me. (Laughter.)

In the first full month of my administration following the issuance of my executive orders, illegal immigration on our southern border fell by an unprecedented 40 percent. I want to congratulate General Kelly.

At the same time, I've issued a presidential memorandum directing the Department of State and the Department of Homeland Security to undertake immediate steps to enhance our vetting process. So we're further enhancing our vetting process. We want people in our country who love our country and have the potential to love our country and our people. That's who we want. My administration will work every day to serve and protect our great citizens, and we will not rest until the job is done.

So this is our first Cabinet meeting. I hope this is going to be a historic Cabinet meeting -- historic in the sense that we're going to do a fantastic job for the American people, for our country, and for the future of our country.

So thank you all very much. We'll see you later. Thank you.

END
3:14 P.M. EDT

Chapter 82

REMARKS BY THE VICE PRESIDENT AND
CMS ADMINISTRATOR VERMA AT A SWEARING-IN CEREMONY
VICE PRESIDENT'S CEREMONIAL OFFICE

14 March 2017

3:49 P.M. EDT

THE VICE PRESIDENT: Good afternoon. On behalf of the President of the United States, it is my great privilege to administer the oath of office to Seema Verma, who will become the 15th Administrator of the Centers for Medicare & Medicaid Services. You can applaud that if you want. I can tell you'd like to. (Applause.)

I'm very pleased today to be joined, despite the inclement weather, by her wonderful family, including her husband, Sanjay; her daughter, Maya; her son, Sean. And we're also pleased that her mother, Denash (ph), and her sister, Dia (ph) are here. Join me in welcoming Seema Verma's entire family. (Applause.)

My friends, we've come to a critical moment in the life of our nation -- seven years ago, this month, the failed law known as Obamacare was signed into law.

And it's proved to be a disaster. Its damage to our economy and our people literally grows with every passing year. We've all seen the headlines -- rising premiums, plummeting choices.

Obamacare is collapsing, and the American people know

it. The fact is that Obamacare has failed and Obamacare must go.

President Trump has made clear he's **promised** to repeal and replace Obamacare once and for all with a better health care system, one that will benefit the health and well-being of the American people for generations to come.

And, my friends, we're already in the process of keeping that **promise**. At this very moment, our administration is pursuing a multistep strategy to repeal Obamacare and replace it with something that actually works.

Step one, we're working with the Congress to pass the American Health Care Act, which begins the process of repealing and replacing Obamacare by ending its taxes and penalties, expanding the use of health savings accounts -- and just to name a few of the important reforms that are in it.

At the same time, our Secretary of Health and Human Services, Dr. Tom Price, is already taking steps to get government out of the way to lower prices and increase choices for Americans. And we're working with Congress to pass legislation later this year that will create a dynamic national health insurance marketplace that will make affordable, high-quality health insurance accessible for every American. Allowing Americans to buy health insurance across state lines is an idea whose time has come.

At each step of this process, one of President Trump's most important objectives, though, has been to give the freedom and flexibility to states across the country to design health care programs, especially Medicaid, to the unique needs of their most vulnerable citizens.

And that's where Seema Verma comes in. President Trump has chosen, frankly, one of the leading experts in America on state-based health care solutions to lead this important agency. Seema's extraordinary record stretches back for over 20 years. After graduating from Johns Hopkins University with a master's degree in public health, she went to work in the great state of Indiana for the Health & Hospital Corporation of Marion County.

She also worked for the Association of State and Territorial Health Officials before founding her own health care company in 2001. And that's where she has really made her mark across the country.

In my home state of Indiana, she helped design the much-heralded Healthy Indiana Plan 2.0 in 2015. Today, Indiana's program is leading the nation with its emphasis on personal responsibility and effective care for people who need it most.

And beyond Indiana, she's helped states like Iowa, Ohio, Kentucky, and Michigan seek to update their programs to better reflect the unique needs of those states.

Seema, President Trump has now asked you to bring your expertise to Washington, D.C. As Administrator of the Centers for Medicare & Medicaid Services, we're confident that you'll help restore health care decision-making to the states, and in the process, help make the best health care system in the world even better. And frankly, as a fellow Hoosier, I couldn't be more proud. Given your strong record of leadership, experience, and compassion, I can say with full confidence, along with the President, that we know you will rise to the challenge to help **Make American Health Care Great Again**.

And so, on behalf of President Trump, it's my great privilege to administer to you the oath of office.

(The Oath is administered.) (Applause.)

Ladies and gentlemen, it's my privilege to introduce the Administrator of the Centers for Medicare & Medicaid Services, Seema Verma. (Applause.)

ADMINISTRATOR VERMA: Thank you. First of all, I want to thank my family for being here tonight -- or today. Their flight was cancelled last night, and they drove through a snowstorm just to be here with me. So I'm very, very grateful. (Applause.)

I am humbled and honored to be here today and to have the opportunity to serve as the CMS Administrator. I'm grateful and appreciative of President Trump not only for asking me to be the Administrator but for putting together an incredibly talented group of individuals that he's brought from the private sector into government service. People like Dr. Tom Price. And I am proud to be a part of this team.

And thank you to my good friend, Vice President Pence, for believing in me and for all of your support these past years. Your leadership in Indiana is paving the way for all states, and the future of health care in America. So, thank you.

And thanks to all of you that have been involved in my confirmation process. Many of you have gone above and beyond to help me navigate the process, and I am so grateful for your support.

Today, our health care stands at a crossroads and we have no choice but to fix our health care system.

Under President Trump's leadership and **vision,** we finally have an incredible opportunity to move our health care system into one that puts Americans in charge of their health care and will ensure that all Americans have access to quality health care that they can afford.

I am honored to be a part of this critical effort. We have so much work to get done, and I can't wait to begin.

Thank you very much. (Applause.)

END
3:58 P.M. EDT

Chapter 83

15 March 2017

2:37 P.M. EDT

THE PRESIDENT: Thank you very much. It is truly great to be back here in Michigan -- great. (Applause.)

And it's also wonderful to be here with the leaders, workers, engineers and suppliers of Ford, and Fiat-Chrysler, and General Motors, and many others. We have so many leaders that we just met, all of the leaders of the major car companies and really the automobile business. It's a great business, it's a wonderful business, but it's been pretty much hurt here. But it's not going to be hurt for long, that I can tell you. (Applause.)

That I can tell you.

I'm sure you've all heard the big news that we're going to work on the CAFE standards, so you can make cars in America again. (Applause.)

We're going to help the companies, and they're going to help you.

There is no more beautiful sight than an American-made car. No more beautiful sight. (Applause.)

I love this state; I love the people of this state. And you did me a big favor, because you gave me a victory, and that victory hasn't been won by a Republican in a long time -- long time. (Applause.)

And you're going to be very happy, believe me. You're going to be very, very happy.

During the campaign, I came to Michigan again and again, and I made this **promise**, that I am going to fight for your jobs and fight very, very hard. (Applause.)

I'm going to fight for Michigan workers. I'm going to fight to keep the automobile production in the United States of America, not outside -- in the United States. (Applause.)

And, by the way, for those that have any doubts, many other industries do. That's okay, right?

So we're here not simply to honor the past, but to devote ourselves to a new future of American automotive leadership. We want to be the car capital of the world **Again**. We will be. And it won't be long, believe me. (Applause.)

And, by the way, we're going to have a very big announcement next week having to do with your industry. Very, very big. Very important. Everybody is saying, "what is it?" Let's keep them guessing back there. (Laughter.)

You've heard me say the words, and I'll repeat them, right now: **Buy American and Hire American**. (Applause.)

It's not just a motto, it's a **pledge**. It's a **pledge** to the working people of this country. The era of economic surrender for the United States is over -- it's over. And you see what's already been happening: plants are coming back; other plants that were expected to be built in other countries are not being built. I just want to tell the leaders they made some very wise decisions. Very wise. Very wise. (Applause.)

Some plants that were announced, they're not going to be built. They're smart.

We're going to stand up to foreign cheating. We're going to crack down on currency manipulation. And, yes, we're going to use the full economic powers of our country to protect our workers and to protect our jobs.

Let me also say how important it is for me that we have every segment of this great American industry represented in our audience today. We have everybody. To succeed as a country, we have to work together. We have to fight, side-by-side, to protect our industry and to stop the jobs from leaving our country. It's not going to happen anymore, folks. We've gone through it for many, many years, decades. It's not going to happen anymore. And if it is, there's consequences to pay for the companies that desert us and fire our employees. There are consequences. (Applause.)

Already, we're seeing jobs coming back. Since my election, Ford has announced 700 new jobs coming back to their plant in Flat Rock, Michigan. (Applause.)

Fiat-Chrysler has announced that they will create 2,000 new jobs in Michigan and Ohio. (Applause.)

And just today -- breaking news -- General Motors announced that they're adding or keeping 900 jobs right here in Michigan, and that's going to be over the next 12 months. And that's just the beginning, folks. In fact, I told them, that's peanuts -- that's peanuts. (Applause.)

We're going to have a lot more. They're going to be building new plants, expanding their plants.

My administration will work tirelessly to eliminate the industry-killing regulations, to lower the job-crushing taxes, and to ensure a level playing field for all American companies and workers.

Before NAFTA went into effect -- by the way, NAFTA, a total disaster -- there were 280,000 autoworkers in Michigan. Today, that number is roughly 165,000 -- and would have been heading down big league if I didn't get elected, I will tell you that right now. That I can tell you. (Applause.)

Plenty of things were stopped in their tracks. They were stopped in their tracks. A lot of bad things were going to happen. A lot of places were going to get built that aren't going to get built right now in other locations.

The number of auto plants in the state has been cut by a third. Motor City once set the standard of living for the nation. Now it has suffered under decades of failed economic decisions that have stripped our country of its jobs and of its wealth.

The Trans-Pacific Partnership -- another disaster -- threatened states like Michigan, Wisconsin, Ohio, Pennsylvania, and so many others with the loss of countless more jobs. That is why I'm proud to say I followed through on my **promise** -- and, by the way, many other **promis-**

es. You've seen what's happened. Many. (Applause.)

And immediately withdrew the United States from the TPP. I kept my word. The assault on the American auto industry, believe me, is over. It's over. (Applause.)

Not going to happen anymore.

We are setting up a task force in every federal agency to identify and remove any regulation that undermines American auto production and any other kind of production, including the production of high-end, low-end, big, small, every form of automobile and truck.

During my first week in office, I brought American auto companies to the White House. Mary Barra is here. Mark Fields is here. Sergio is here, and others. And none of them ever got to see the Oval Office before, because nobody took them into the Oval Office -- our Presidents. They employ tens of thousands of people, but I brought them into the Oval Office because they're going to be expanding their companies. (Applause.)

But they all told me the same thing. They explained that the previous administration promised you a so-called "mid-term review" of the federal fuel efficiency standards. It was necessary because the standards were set far into the future -- way, way into the future. If the standards threatened auto jobs, then common-sense changes could have and should have been made.

Just days before my inauguration, the previous administration cut short the **promised** mid-term review in an 11th-hour executive action. Today, I am announcing that we are going to cancel that executive action. (Applause.)

We are going to restore the originally scheduled mid-term review, and we are going to ensure that any regulations we have protect and defend your jobs, your factories. We're going to be fair. We're going to be fair.

This is an issue of deep importance to me. For decades, I have raised the alarm over unfair foreign trade practices that have robbed communities of their wealth and robbed our people of their ability to provide for their families. They've stolen our jobs, they've stolen our companies, and our politicians sat back and watched, hopeless. Not anymore.

As a private citizen, I looked, really with sadness, as massive shipments of foreign cars have been dumped onto our shores while those same countries have shut their borders to our cars. We take them -- "Come on in, folks. Come on in. No tax. Don't worry about it." We make cars; they don't take us. Not anymore. (Applause.)

Since NAFTA was approved, we've lost nearly one-third of our manufacturing jobs in the United States. Since China entered the World Trade Organization, we've lost 60,000 factories. Hard to believe. Our trade deficit last year reached nearly $800 billion. Who's making these deals? I can take anybody in the audience -- you'll do better, believe me. (Laughter.)

These statistics really should have shaken up Washington to do action, but nothing happened. But something did happen -- happened on November 8th. Believe me, it happened. It happened for you. (Applause.)

But the politicians made excuses. They have said these chronic trade deficits have helped us to win friends abroad. I don't want friends abroad if that's what it's going to take. We don't need friends abroad for that. Do you ever see that, where they said, "No, no, it's good for us because people like us abroad"? They don't like us -- they think we're stupid people. (Laughter.)

But no friendship is strengthened through economic abuse -- because we have been abused. And no country can long lead the free world if it does not protect its industries and care for its people and protect its borders. (Applause.)

America will be respected **Again**, and you, as workers, will be respected **Again**. Believe me, you will be respected **Again**. Soon. Now. I think it's already happened.

Our great Presidents, from Washington to Jefferson to Jackson to Lincoln, all understood that a great nation must protect its manufacturing, must protect itself from the outside. Today, I will be visiting the home of Andrew Jackson on the 250th anniversary of his birth. And they say my election was most similar to his -- 1828. That's a long time ago. Usually they go back like to this one, or that one, 12 years ago, 16. I mean, 1828, that's a long way. That's a long time ago.

In supporting tariffs, Jackson said, "I look at the tariff with an eye to the proper distribution of labor, and to revenue, and with a view to discharge our national debt." We owe $20 trillion -- $20 trillion with our policies. America cannot be a wealthy country if special interests game the system to profit from the exodus of our companies and from the exodus of our jobs.

We must embrace a new economic model. Let's call it **"The American Model."** (Applause.)

Under this system, we will reduce burdens on our companies and on our businesses. But, in exchange, companies must **hire and grow in America**. They have to hire and grow in our country. That is how we will succeed and grow together -- American workers and American industry side-by-side. Nobody can beat us, folks. Nobody can beat us. (Applause.)

Because whether we are rich or poor, young or old, black or brown or white, we all bleed the same red blood of patriots. (Applause.)

Great Americans of all backgrounds built the Arsenal of Democracy -- including the legendary Rosie the Riveter, who worked here at Willow Run. You know that. (Applause.)

Seventy-five years ago, during the Second World War, thousands of American workers filled this very building to build the great new airplanes -- the B-24 Liberator. At peak production -- listen to this -- it's not the country that we've been watching over the last 20 years -- they were building one B-24 every single hour. (Applause.)

We don't hear that. We don't hear that anymore, do we? We'll be back. We'll be back soon. Most amazing people.

And while that's incredible, it's a tribute really to the teamwork, determination, and patriotism that lives on today in each and every one of you. Great people. You're great people.

Now, these hundreds of acres that defended our democracy are going to help build the cars and cities of the future. (Applause.)

So I ask you -- that's fine because you're right -- (laughter) -- so I ask you today to join me in daring to believe that this facility, this city, and this nation will once again shine with industrial might. (Applause.)

I am asking you to place your faith in the American worker and these great American companies. (Applause.)

I'm also asking you to respect and place your faith in companies from foreign lands that come here to build their product. We love them too, right? We love them too. (Applause.)

I'm asking all of the companies here today to join us in this **new Industrial Revolution**.

Let us put American Workers, American Families, and **American Dreams First** once **Again**.

May God bless the American worker.
May God bless the Motor City.
And may God bless the United States of America.

Thank you. (Applause.)

Thank you. Thank you, everybody.

END
2:54 P.M. EDT

Chapter 84

15 March 2017

4:44 P.M. CDT

THE PRESIDENT: Thank you very much. (Applause.)

Wow, what a nice visit this was. Inspirational visit, I have to tell you. I'm a fan. I'm a big fan.

I want to thank Howard Kettell, Francis Spradley of the Andrew Jackson Foundation, and all of the foundation's incredible employees and supporters for preserving this great landmark, which is what it is -- it's a landmark of our national heritage.

And a special thank you to Governor Bill Haslam and his in-credible wife, who -- we just rode over together -- and Sen-ators Lamar Alexander and Bob Corker, two great friends of mine, been a big, big help. Both incredible guys.

In my address to Congress, I looked forward nine years, to the 250th anniversary of American Independence.

Today, I call attention to another anniversary: the 250th birthday of the very great Andrew Jackson. (Applause.)

And he loved Tennessee, and so do I -- to tell you that. (Applause.)

On this day in 1767, Andrew Jackson was born on the backwoods soil of the Carolinas. From poverty and obscurity, Jackson rose to glory and greatness -- first as a military leader, and then as the seventh President of the United States.

He did it with courage, with grit, and with patriotic heart. And by the way, he was one of our great Presidents. (Applause.)

Jackson was the son of the frontier. His father died before he was born. His brother died fighting the British in the American Revolution. And his mother caught a fatal illness while tending to the wounded troops. At the age of 14, Andrew Jackson was an orphan, and look what he was able to do. Look what he was able to build.

It was during the Revolution that Jackson first confronted and defied an arrogant elite. Does that sound familiar to you? (Laughter.)

I wonder why they keep talking about Trump and Jackson, Jackson and Trump. Oh, I know the feeling, Andrew. (Laughter.)

Captured by the Redcoats and ordered to shine the boots of a British officer, Jackson simply refused. The officer took his saber and slashed at Jackson, leaving gashes in his head and hand that remained permanent scars for the rest of his life. These were the first and far from the last blows that Andrew Jackson took for his country that he loved so much.

From that day on, Andrew Jackson rejected authority that looked down on the common people. First as a boy, when he bravely served the Revolutionary cause. Next, as the heroic victor at New Orleans where his ragtag -- and it was ragtag -- militia, but they were tough. And they drove the British Imperial forces from America in a triumphant end to the War of 1812. He was a real general, that one.

And, finally, as President -- when he reclaimed the people's government from an emerging aristocracy. Jackson's victory shook the establishment like an earthquake. Henry Clay, Secretary of State for the defeated President John Quincy Adams, called Jackson's victory "mortifying and sickening". Oh, boy, does this sound familiar. (Laughter.)

Have we heard this? (Laughter.)

This is terrible. He said there had been "no greater calamity" in the nation's history.

The political class in Washington had good reason to fear Jackson's great triumph. "The rich and powerful," Jackson said, "too often bend the acts of government to their selfish purposes." Jackson warned they had turned government into an "engine for the support of the few at the expense of the many."

Andrew Jackson was the People's President, and his election came at a time when the vote was finally being extended to those who did not own property.

To clean out the bureaucracy, Jackson removed 10 percent of the federal workforce.

He launched a campaign to sweep out government corruption. Totally. He didn't want government corruption.

He expanded benefits for veterans. He battled the central-ized financial power that brought influence at our citizens' expense.

He imposed tariffs on foreign countries to protect Ameri-can workers. That sounds very familiar. Wait till you see what's going to be happening pretty soon, folks. (Laugh-ter.)

It's time. It's time.

Andrew Jackson was called many names, accused of many things, and by fighting for change, earned many, many ene-mies.

Today the portrait of this orphan son who rose to the presidency hangs proudly in the Oval Office, opposite the portrait of another great American, Thomas Jefferson. I brought the Andrew Jackson portrait there. (Applause.)

Right behind me, right -- boom, over my left shoulder. Now I'm honored to sit between those two portraits and to use this high office to serve, defend, and protect the citizens of the United States. It is my great honor. I will tell you that.

From that desk I can see out the wonderful, beautiful, large great window to an even greater magnolia tree, standing strong and tall across the White House lawn. That tree was planted there many years ago, when it was just a sprout carried from these very grounds. Came right from here. (Applause.)

Beautiful tree.

That spout was nourished, it took root, and on this, his 250th birthday, Andrew Jackson's magnolia is a sight to behold. I looked at it actually this morning. Really beautiful. (Applause.)

But the growth of that beautiful tree is nothing compared to growth of our beautiful nation. That growth has been made possible because more and more of our people have been given their dignity as equals under law and equals in the eyes of God.

Andrew Jackson as a military hero and genius and a beloved President. But he was also a flawed and imperfect man, a product of his time. It is the duty of each generation to carry on the fight for justice.

My administration will work night and day to ensure that the sacred rights which God has bestowed on His children are protected for each and every one of you, for each and every American. (Applause.)

We must all remember Jackson's words: that in "the planter, the farmer, the mechanic, and the laborer," we will find muscle and bone of our country. So true. So true.

Now, we must work in our time to expand -- and we have to do that because we have no choice.

We're going to **Make America Great Again**, folks.

We're going to **Make America Great Again** ... (Applause.)

... to expand the blessings of America to every citizen in

our land. And when we do, watch us grow. Watch what's happening. You see it happening already. You see it with our great military. You see it with our great markets. You see it with our incredible business people.

You see it with the level of enthusiasm that they haven't seen in many years. People are **Proud Again** of our country. And you're going to get **prouder** and **prouder** and **prouder**, I can **promise** you that. (Applause.)

And watch us grow. We will truly be one nation, with deep roots, a strong core, and a very new springtime of **American Greatness** yet to come.

Andrew Jackson, we thank you for your service. We honor you for your memory. We build on your legacy. And we thank God for the United States of America.

Thank you very much, everybody. (Applause.)

END
4:54 P.M. CDT

*"I wonder why they
keep talking about
Trump and Jackson,
Jackson and Trump.
Oh, I know the feeling, Andrew."*

Chapter 85

REMARKS BY THE PRESIDENT AT
MAKE AMERICA GREAT AGAIN RALLY
NASHVILLE MUNICIPAL AUDITORIUM
NASHVILLE, TENNESSEE

15 March 2017

7:06 P.M. CDT

THE PRESIDENT: Thank you very much, everybody. Thank you. (Applause.)

So we're just going to let the other folks come in, fill it up. This is some crowd. You have to see what's outside, you wouldn't even believe it. (Applause.)

Unbelievable.

So I'm thrilled to be here in Nashville, Tennessee, the home -- (applause) -- of country music, Southern hospitality, and the great President Andrew Jackson. (Applause.)

I just came from a tour of Andrew Jackson's home to mark the 250th anniversary of his birth. Jackson's life was devoted to one very crucial principle -- he understood that real leadership means putting **America First**. (Applause.)

Before becoming President, Andrew Jackson served your state from the House of Representatives and in the United States Senate, and he also served as commander of the Tennessee militia. Tough cookie. Tough cookie. (Applause.)

So let's begin tonight by thanking all of the incredible men and women of the United States military and all of our wonderful veterans. The veterans. (Applause.)

AUDIENCE: USA! USA! USA!

THE PRESIDENT: Amazing. There's no place I'd rather be than with all of you here tonight, with the wonderful, hard-working citizens of our country. (Applause.)

I would much rather spend time with you than any of the pundits, consultants, or special interests, certainly -- or reporters from Washington, D.C. (Applause.)

It's patriotic Americans like you who make this country run, and run well. You pay your taxes, follow our laws, support your communities, raise your children, love your country, and send your bravest to fight in our wars. (Applause.)

All you want is a government that shows you the same loyalty in return. It's time that Washington heard your voice -- and believe me, on November 8th, they heard your voice. (Applause.)

The forgotten men and women of our country will never be forgotten **Again**, believe me. (Applause.)

I want to thank so many of your state leaders -- State Party Chairman Scott Golden; Congressman Scott DesJarlais; Congresswoman Marsha Blackburn; Congresswoman Diane Black; Congressman Jimmy Duncan -- right from the beginning. (Applause.)

Governor Bill Haslam. (Applause.)

A great friend of mine, Senator Bob Corker. (Applause.)

An incredible guy, respected by all -- Senator Lamar Alexander. (Applause.)

And so many more. Thank you all for being here. We're going to be working closely together to deliver for you, the citizens of Tennessee, like you've never been delivered for before. Thank you. Thank you. (Applause.)

Thank you. We're going to reduce your taxes -- big league. Big. (Applause.)

Big. I want to start that process so quickly. Got to get the healthcare done. We got to start the tax reductions. (Applause.)

We are going to enforce our trade rules and bring back our jobs, which are scattered all over the world. They're coming back to our country. (Applause.)

We're going to support the amazing -- absolutely amazing men and women of law enforcement. (Applause.)

Protect your freedoms, and defend the Second Amendment. (Applause.)

And we are going to restore respect for our country and for its great and very beautiful flag. (Applause.)

It's been a little over 50 days since my inauguration, and we've been putting our **America First** agenda very much into action. You see what's happening. We're keeping our promises. In fact, they have signs -- "He's Kept His Promise." They're all over the place. I have. (Applause.)

We have done far more -- I think maybe more than anybody's done in this office in 50 days, that I could tell you. (Applause.)

And we have just gotten started. Wait until you see what's coming, folks. We've appointed a Supreme Court justice to replace the late, great Antonin Scalia. His name is Judge Neil Gorsuch. (Applause.)

He will uphold and defend the Constitution of the United States. We are proposing a budget that will shrink the bloated federal bureaucracy -- and I mean bloated -- while protecting our national security. You see what we're doing with our military -- bigger, better, stronger than ever before. You see what's happening. (Applause.)

And you're already seeing the results. Our budget calls for one of the single largest increases in defense spending history in this country. (Applause.)

We believe -- especially the people in Tennessee, I know you people so well -- (applause) -- in peace through strength. That's what we're going to have. And we are taking steps to make sure that our allies pay their fair share. They have to pay. (Applause.)

We've begun a dramatic effort to eliminate job-killing federal regulations like nobody has ever seen before -- slash, slash. We're going to protect the environment, we're going to protect people's safeties, but, let me tell you, the regulation business has become a terrible business, and we're going to bring it down to where it should be. (Applause.)

AUDIENCE: USA! USA! USA!

THE PRESIDENT: Okay, let's go. One person -- and they'll be the story tomorrow -- did you hear there was a protestor? (Applause.)

We're going to put our miners back to work. We're going to put our auto industry back to work. Already because of this new business climate, we are creating jobs that are starting to pour back into our country like we haven't seen in many, many decades. (Applause.)

In the first two job reports since I took the oath of office, we've already added nearly half a million new jobs, and believe me, it's just beginning. (Applause.)

I've already authorized the construction of the long-stalled and delayed Keystone and Dakota Access pipelines. (Applause.)

A lot of jobs.

I've also directed that new pipelines must be constructed with American steel. (Applause.)

They want to build them here, they use our steel. We believe in two simple rules: **Buy American and Hire American**. (Applause.)

On trade, I've kept my promise to the American people, and withdrawn from the Trans-Pacific Partnership disaster. (Applause.)

Tennessee has lost one third of its manufacturing jobs since the institution of NAFTA, one of the worst trade deals ever in history. Our nation has lost over 60,000 factories since China joined the World Trade Organization

-- 60,000. Think of that. More than that.

We're not going to let it happen anymore. From now on, we are going to defend the American worker and our great American companies. (Applause.)

And if America does what it says, and if your President does what I've been telling you, there is nobody anywhere in the world that can even come close to us, folks. Not even close. (Applause.)

If a company wants to leave America, fire their workers, and then ship their new products back into our country, there will be consequences. (Applause.)

That's what we have borders for. And by the way, aren't our borders getting extremely strong? (Applause.)

Very strong.

AUDIENCE: USA! USA! USA!

THE PRESIDENT: Don't even think about it. We will build the wall. Don't even think about it. (Applause.)

In fact, as you probably read, we went out to bid. We had hundreds of bidders. Everybody wants to build our wall. (Applause.)

Usually, that means we're going to get a good price. We're going to get a good price, believe me. (Applause.)

We're going to build the wall.

Some of the fake news said, I don't think Donald Trump

wants to build the wall. Can you imagine if I said we're not going to build a wall?

Fake news. Fake, fake news. Fake news, folks.

A lot of fake.

No, the wall is way ahead of schedule in terms of where we are. It's under design, and you're going to see some very good things happening. But the border by itself right now is doing very well. It's becoming very strong. General Kelly has done a great job -- General Kelly.

My administration is also following through on our **promise** to secure, protect, and defend that border within our United States. Our southern border will be protected always. It will have the wall. Drugs will stop pouring in and poisoning our youth, and that will happen very, very soon. You're already seeing what's going on. The drugs are pouring into our country, folks. They are poisoning our youth and plenty of others, and we're going to stop it. We're not going to playing games. Not going to be playing games. (Applause.)

Following my executive action -- and don't forget, we've only been here for like -- what? -- 50 days -- we've already experienced an unprecedented 40-percent reduction in illegal immigration on our Southern border; 61 percent since Inauguration Day -- 61 percent. Think about it. And now people are saying, we're not going to go there anymore because we can't get in. So it's going to get better and better. We got to stop those drugs, though. We got to stop those drugs.

During the campaign, as I traveled all across this country, I met with many American families whose loved ones were viciously and violently killed by illegal immigrants because our government refused to enforce our already existing laws. These American victims were ignored by the media. They were ignored by Washington. But they were not ignored by me, and they're not ignored by you, and they never will be ignored certainly any longer. Not going to happen. (Applause.)

As we speak, we are finding the drug dealers, the robbers, thieves, gang members, killers and criminals preying on our citizens. One by one -- you're reading about it, right? They're being thrown out of our country. They're being thrown into prisons. And we will not let them back in. (Applause.)

We're also working, night and day, to keep our nation **safe** from terrorism. (Applause.)

We have seen the devastation from 9/11 to Boston to San Bernardino -- hundreds upon hundreds of people from outside our country have been convicted of terrorism-related offenses in the United States courts. Right now we have investigations going on all over -- hundreds of refugees are under federal investigation for terrorism and related reasons. We have entire regions of the world destabilized by terrorism and ISIS. For this reason, I issued an executive order to temporarily suspend immigration from places where it cannot safely occur. (Applause.)

But let me give you the bad news. We don't like bad news, right? I don't want to hear -- and I'll turn it into good. But let me give you the bad, the sad news. Moments ago, I learned that a district judge in Hawaii -- part of the much overturned 9th Circuit Court -- and I have to be nice;

otherwise I'll get criticized for speaking poorly about our courts. I'll be criticized by these people, among the most dishonest people in the world -- I will be criticized -- I'll be criticized by them for speaking harshly about our courts. I would never want to do that. A judge has just blocked our executive order on travel and refugees coming into our country from certain countries.

AUDIENCE: Booo --

THE PRESIDENT: The order he blocked was a watered-version of the first order that was also blocked by another judge and should have never been blocked to start with. This new order was tailored to the dictates of the 9th Circuit's -- in my opinion -- flawed ruling. This is, the opinion of many, an unprecedented judicial overreach. The law and the Constitution give the President the power to suspend immigration when he deems -- or she -- or she. Fortunately, it will not be Hillary she. (Applause.) When he or she deems it to be in the national interest of our country.

So we have a lot of lawyers here. We also have a lot of smart people here. Let me read to you directly from the federal statute, 212F, of the immigration -- and you know what I'm talking about, right? Can I read this to you? Listen to this. Now, we're all smart people. We're all good students -- some are bad students, but even if you're a bad student this is a real easy one, let me tell you. Ready? So here's the statute -- which they don't even want to quote when they overrule it. And it was put here for the security of our country. And this goes beyond me, because there will be other Presidents, and we need this. And sometimes we need it very badly for **security -- security** of our country.

It says -- now, listen how easy this is. "Whenever the President finds that the entry of any aliens or any class of aliens would be detrimental to the interests of the United States, he may, by proclamation, and for such period as he -- see, it wasn't politically correct, because it should say he or she. You know, today they'd say that. Actually, that's the only mistake they made. "as he shall deem necessary, suspending entry of all aliens, or any class of aliens, as immigrants or non-immigrants, or pose on the entry of aliens any restrictions he may deems to be appropriate." In other words, if he thinks there's danger out there, he or she -- whoever is President -- can say, I'm sorry, folks, not now, please. We've got enough problems. (Applause.)

We're talking about the **safety** of our nation, the **safety** and **security** of our people. (Applause.)

Now, I know you people aren't skeptical people because nobody would be that way in Tennessee. Right? Nobody -- not Tennessee. You don't think this was done by a judge for political reasons, do you? No.

AUDIENCE: Booo --

THE PRESIDENT: This ruling makes us look weak -- which, by the way, we no longer are, believe me. (Applause.)

Just look at our borders. We're going to fight this terrible ruling. We're going to take our case as far as it needs to go, including all the way up to the Supreme Court. (Applause.)

We're going to win. We're going to keep our citizens **safe**. And regardless, we're going to keep our citizens **safe**, believe me. (Applause.)

Even liberal Democratic lawyer, Alan Dershowitz ---- good lawyer -- just said that we would win this case before the Supreme Court of the United States. (Applause.)

Remember this, I wasn't thrilled, but the lawyers all said, let's tailor it. This is a watered--down version of the first one. This is a watered--down version. And let me tell you something, I think we ought to go back to the first one and go all the way, which is what I wanted to do in the first one. (Applause.)

The danger is clear, the law is clear, the need for my executive order is clear. I was elected to change our broken and dangerous system and thinking in government that has weakened and endangered our country and left our people defenseless. (Applause.)

And I will not stop fighting for the **safety** of you and your families, believe me. Not today, not ever. We're going to win it. We're going to win it. (Applause.)

We're going to apply common sense. We're going to apply intelligence. And we're never quitting, and we're never going away, and we're never, ever giving up. The best way to keep foreign terrorists -- or, as some people would say in certain instances, radical Islamic terrorists -- from attacking our country is to stop them from entering our country in the first place. (Applause.)

We'll take it, but these are the problems we have. People are screaming, break up the 9th Circuit. And I'll tell you what, that 9th Circuit -- you have to see. Take a look at how many times they have been overturned with their terrible decisions. Take a look. And this is what we have to live with.

Finally, I want to get to taxes. I want to cut the hell out of taxes, but -- (applause) -- but before I can do that -- I would have loved to have put it first, I'll be honest -- there is one more very important thing that we have to do, and we are going to repeal and replace horrible, disastrous Obamacare. (Applause.)

If we leave Obamacare in place, millions and millions of people will be forced off their plans, and your senators just told me that in your state you're down to practically no insurers. You're going to have nobody. You're going to have nobody. And this is true all over. The insurers are fleeing. The insurers are fleeing. It's a catastrophic situation, and there's nothing to compare anything to because Obamacare won't be around for a year or two. It's gone. So it's not like, oh, gee, they have this. Obamacare is gone.

Premiums will continue to soar double digits and even triple digits in many cases. It will drain our budget and destroy our jobs. Remember all of the broken promises? You can keep your doctor, you can keep your plan. Remember the wise guy -- remember the wise guy that essentially said the American people -- the so--called architect -- the American people are stupid because they approved it? We're going to show them.

Those in Congress who made these promises have no credibility whatsoever on healthcare. (Applause.)

And remember this -- remember this: If we took, because there's such divisiveness -- and I'm not just talking now, with me. There was with Obama. There was with Bush. The level of hatred and divisiveness with the politicians. I remember years ago, I'd go to Washington -- I was always very politically active -- and Republicans and Democrats, they'd fight during the day and they go to dinner at night. Today, there's a level that nobody has seen before. Just remember this: If we submitted the Democrats' plan, drawn everything perfect for the Democrats, we wouldn't get one vote from the Democrats. That's the way it is. That's how much divisiveness and other things there are. So it's a problem. But we're going to get it by.

So, I've met with so many victims of Obamacare ---- the people who have been so horribly hurt by this horrible legislation. At the very core of Obamacare was a fatal flaw -- the government forcing people to buy a government--approved product. There are very few people -- very few people.

AUDIENCE MEMBER: Booo --

THE PRESIDENT: By the way -- watch what happens. Now you just booed Obamacare. They will say, Trump got booed when he mentioned -- they're bad people, folks. They're bad people.

AUDIENCE: Booo --

THE PRESIDENT: Tonight, I'll go home, I'll turn on, I'll say -- listen, I'll turn on that television. My wife will say, darling, it's too bad you got booed. I said, I didn't get booed. This was a -- I said, no, no, they were booing Obamacare. Watch, a couple of them will actually do it, almost guaranteed.

But when we call them out, it makes it harder for them to do it. So we'll see. It's the fake, fake media. We want Americans to be able to purchase the health insurance plans they want, not the plans forced on them by our government. (Applause.)

The House has put forward a plan to repeal and replace Obamacare based on the principles I outlined in my joint address, but let me tell you, we're going to arbitrate, we're going to all get together and we're going to get something done. Remember this -- if we didn't do it the way we're doing it, we need 60 votes so we have to get the Democrats involved. They won't vote, no matter what we do, they're not going to vote. So we're doing it a different way, a complex way. It's fine. The end result is when you have phase one, phase two, phase three -- it's going to be great. It's going to be great.

And then, we get on to tax reductions, which I like. (Applause.)

The House legislation does so much for you. It gives the states Medicaid flexibility. And some of the states will take over their healthcare. Governor Rick Scott in Florida said, just send me the money -- they run a great plan. We have states that are doing great. It gives great flexibility. Thank you, folks. Thank you. (Applause.)

It repeals hundreds of billions of dollars in Obamacare taxes. It provides tax credits to purchase the care that is rightfully theirs. The bill that I will ultimately sign -- and that will be a bill where everybody is going to get into the room and we're going to get it done -- we'll get rid of Obamacare and make healthcare better for you and for your family. (Applause.)

And once this is done, and a step further, we are going to try and put it in phase three -- I'm going to work on bringing down the cost of medicine by having a fair and competitive bidding process. (Applause.)

We welcome this healthcare debate and its negotiation, and we're going to carry it out, and have been carrying it out, in the full light of day -- unlike the way Obamacare was passed. Remember, folks, if we don't do anything, Obamacare is gone. It's not like, oh, gee, it's going to be wonderful in three-years. It's gone. It's gone. It's gone. Not working. It's gone. What we cannot do is to be intimidated by the dishonest attacks from Democratic leaders in Congress who broke the system in the first place and who don't believe you should be able to make your own healthcare decisions. (Applause.)

I am very confident that if we empower the American people we will accomplish incredible things for our country -- not just on healthcare, but all across our government. We will unlock new frontiers in science and in medicine. We will give our children the right to attend the school of their choice, one where they will be taught to love this country and its values. (Applause.)

We will create millions and millions of new jobs by lowering taxes on our businesses, and very importantly for our workers, we're going to lower taxes. (Applause.)

And we will fight for the right of every American child to grow up in a **safe** neighborhood, attend a great school, and to graduate with access to a high-paying job that they love doing. (Applause.)

No matter our background, no matter our income, no matter our geography, we all share the same home. We all salute the same flag. And we all are made by the same God. (Applause.)

AUDIENCE: USA! USA! USA!

THE PRESIDENT: It's time to embrace our glorious **American destiny**. Anything we can **dream** for our country we can achieve for our country. All we have to do is tap into that **American Pride** that is swelling our hearts and stirring our souls. And we found that out very recently in our last election -- a lot of **pride**. (Applause.)

We are all Americans, and the future truly belongs to us.

The future belongs to all of you.
This is your moment.
This is your time.
This is the hour when history is made.

All we have to do is put our own citizens **First**, and together we will **Make America Strong Again**. (Applause.)

We will **Make America Wealthy Again**.
We will **Make America Proud Again**.
We will **Make America Safe Again**.
And we will **Make America Great Again**.
(Applause.)

Thank you. God bless you. Thank you. (Applause.)
God bless you, everybody. (Applause.)

END
7:43 P.M. CDT

Other Titles

Michael Jackson: Innocent
David Bowie: Love from Brixton

Sources

The White house
The State Department (United States)
Department of Defense (United States) Website
Youtube
The internet
ABC2news
Screengrabs - various Government + internet